Of Beggars and Buddhas

New Perspectives in Southeast Asian Studies

Series Editors

Alfred W. McCoy

Thongchai Winichakul

Ian Baird

Katherine A. Bowie

Anne Ruth Hansen

Associate Editors

Warwick H. Anderson

Ian Coxhead

Michael Cullinane

Paul D. Hutchcroft

Kris Olds

Of Beggars and Buddhas

The Politics of Humor
in the *Vessantara Jataka*
in Thailand

Katherine A. Bowie

The University of Wisconsin Press

Publication of this book has been possible, in part, through support from the Center for Southeast Asian Studies and the Anonymous Fund of the College of Letters and Science at the University of Wisconsin–Madison.

The University of Wisconsin Press
728 State Street, Suite 443
Madison, Wisconsin 53706
uwpress.wisc.edu

Gray's Inn House, 127 Clerkenwell Road
London EC1R 5DB, United Kingdom
eurospanbookstore.com

Copyright © 2017
The Board of Regents of the University of Wisconsin System
All rights reserved. Except in the case of brief quotations embedded in critical articles and reviews, no part of this publication may be reproduced, stored in a retrieval system, transmitted in any format or by any means—digital, electronic, mechanical, photocopying, recording, or otherwise—or conveyed via the Internet or a website without written permission of the University of Wisconsin Press. Rights inquiries should be directed to rights@uwpress.wisc.edu.

Printed in the United States of America

This book may be available in a digital edition.

Library of Congress Cataloging-in-Publication Data

Names: Bowie, Katherine Ann, 1950– author.
Title: Of beggars and Buddhas: the politics of humor in the Vessantara Jataka in Thailand / Katherine A. Bowie.
Other titles: New perspectives in Southeast Asian studies.
Description: Madison, Wisconsin: The University of Wisconsin Press, [2017]
  | Series: New perspectives in Southeast Asian studies
  | Includes bibliographical references and index.
Identifiers: LCCN 2016017724 | ISBN 9780299309503 (cloth: alk. paper)
Subjects: LCSH: Tipitaka. Suttapitaka. Khuddakanikāya. Jātaka. Vessantarajātaka.
  | Jataka stories, Thai—Political aspects. | Buddhist stories, Thai—Political aspects.
  | Jataka stories, Thai—Humor. | Buddhist stories, Thai—Humor.
  | Buddhism and politics—Thailand—History.
  | Buddhism and state—Thailand—History. | Buddhist giving.
Classification: LCC BQ1470.V487 B69 2017 | DDC 294.3/82325—dc23
LC record available at https://lccn.loc.gov/2016017724

ISBN 9780299309541 (pbk.: alk. paper)

To my parents,

E. J. Walter Bowie and **Gertrud S. Bowie** (née Ulrich),

who saw us through many a crisis

with laughter and love.

Contents

List of Illustrations	ix
Acknowledgments	xi
Note on Transliteration	xv
Introduction: Of Monarchs, Monks, and Peasant Masses	3

Part I: Diversity in Humor

1	Central Thailand: Humor Defeated	39
2	Northeastern Thailand: Humor Diverted	81
3	Northern Thailand: Humor Delighted	123

Part II: The Politics of Diversity

4	Jujaka as Trickster: The Peasant Imaginaire	169
5	Jujaka as Threat: Consolidating Control	208
6	Jujaka as Deity: Rebirths under Global Capitalism	243

Conclusion: The Journey's End	267
Notes	275
Bibliography	309
Index	345

Illustrations

Figures

1	Scene from Kumarn chapter: Vessantara gives his children to Jujaka	4
2	Memorial shrine to Luang Poh Bunthong	9
3	Jujaka's funeral procession	26
4	Jataka performance in honor of the birthdays of the Thai king and queen	41
5	Junk replica at Wat Yannawa, Bangkok	53
6	Jujaka chapter: bawdy village scene	60
7	Escorting the royal family to the village temple	82
8	Bawdy scroll scene from Jujaka chapter	104
9	Phiitaakhon ghosts at Dansai Folk Museum	113
10	A northern village performance	124
11	The maze	132
12	Jujaka in the palace	150
13	Jujaka in tree surrounded by Jetabutr's dogs	170
14	Villagers being taken as war captives	190
15	Jujaka surrounded at court	209
16	Statue of Khruubaa Srivichai	228
17	Jujaka statues	244
18	Coyote dancers at Jujaka house	249
19	"Grandfather" Jujaka at parade	257
20	Temple mural of Nakornkan chapter	268

Table

1	A regional comparison of the *Vessantara Jataka*	166

Acknowledgments

As I reflect back on how this book came to be, I have both warm and sad memories. I hear the sounds of laughter echoing through the decades back to my childhood. My father had a great laugh. He was known among his friends and family for his amazing recall of limericks and other poems. In high school he humored me by allowing me to record him laughing to begin a class presentation I made on Hilaire Belloc, helping to prove the point that laughter is infectious. More importantly he showed how a sense of humor can help in coping with life's unexpected turns. After a tragic ski accident left him partially paralyzed, his first words to me were "Do you know anyone who would like to buy a pair of skis?"

I would like to thank Frank Reynolds, who taught the first class on Buddhism I took as an undergraduate and mentored me throughout my career, also always with a laugh at the ready. His decision to spend a sabbatical at Stanford University that year shaped my life's trajectory, including my decision to attend the University of Chicago for graduate school. Kesa Noda, my fellow classmate in Frank Reynolds's class, decided to write her term paper on the jatakas; her fascination with them clearly lingers in this book. I also would like to remember Surasinghsamruam Shimbhanao, who took me to see Bruce Gaston's performance of Chuchok in Chiang Mai in 1977 and who loved northern Thai literature. I am also so grateful that I met Luang Poh Bunthong. At the time I interviewed him, he was already undergoing kidney dialysis but still found the strength to share some laughs with me. He was indeed one of those rare storytellers whose tapes, even after his death in 2007, can still bring laughter to his audiences.

I owe a particularly profound debt to Narong and Kongchan Mahakhom, who took me into their northern home forty years ago. They, together with their children, grandchildren, relatives, friends, and acquaintances, have provided me with friendships and networks that underlie this book. Their son and daughter-in-law, Amornwat (Aod) and Phunnaphat (Ning) Watcharawichaisri, now adults with their own children, have been wonderful, not only humoring my latest fascinations but sharing in the research. Some of my best memories have been sitting with Kongchan, helping her prepare my favorite northern dish, *saa phak muang* (mango leaf salad), and gossiping about village goings-on.

In Narong, I could not have found a better teacher and debate partner. Having received his early education at Lamphun's prestigious Rongrian Methi Wuthikon at Wat Phrathat Haripunchai and later at Chiang Mai's Teachers College, Narong kept abreast of local events and was never-endingly opinionated. After Narong retired from his position as principal of a village school, he spent many, many hours driving me to interviews and helping me to translate texts. Narong accompanied me to my first interview with a *tujok* (the monk who performs the comedic Jujaka chapter of the *Vessantara Jataka*) in 2004. When a close relative died a few years later, Narong decided to invite a monk to perform a chapter from the *Vessantara Jataka* at her funeral, both because of the northern tradition of performing chapters from this jataka at funerals and because he knew of my interest (the Matsi chapter was chosen for that funeral because a monk at the village temple was known for his performance of this chapter). His oldest brother, Ai Naan Saengmuang Ryansin, I learned in the course of working on this book, had himself been a tujok who, upon disrobing, went on to form a well-known *likay* troupe. Conversations with Lung Naan, now in his nineties, are always fun.

Narong's death in November 2014 not only affected his immediate family but left a huge hole in my life as well. I take some consolation in knowing that I was able to host a tujok performance at his funeral. Although the practice of tujok performing at funerals was once widespread, as will become clear in this book, the custom has been fading away in recent decades. The monk invited to perform as the tujok at Narong's funeral apologized profusely if anyone in the audience was upset by hearing him telling jokes. The performance turned out to be such a success that not only did Narong's family enjoy it but a member of the audience decided to invite a tujok to perform at a funeral being organized in another village. Given Narong's love of northern cultural traditions, I think this performance would have had him chuckling with approval. He would have enjoyed the irony of knowing that his funeral was reinfusing life into a dying northern custom. I can only hope he was there in spirit. His spirit certainly infuses this book.

So many monks and villagers in Thailand generously humored my questions, but I would particularly like to thank Phrakhruu Athong Visutikhul (Wat Nongtong, Hang Dong), Phrakhruu Winaithorn Dr. Manop Paalaphan (Wat Pho, Bangkok), Phrathammakittimethee (Wat Samphanthawongsaram, Bangkok), Phra Racha Thammawaathii (Wat Prayoon, Bangkok), Phra Racha Vijitphatiphaan (Chaokhun Phiphit, Wat Suthat, Bangkok), Phrakhruu

Winaitharam Thanom (Kukai, Wat Mongkol Kowithaaram, Ubon), and Phrakhruu Prachotipacharothai (Uthai Chutmanuto, Wat Pothiyen, A. Hoomkao, Petchabun). I would also like to thank former monks Khun Somchai Kuakoon (Ministry of Culture, Bangkok) and Ajarn Manee Phayomyong. In Sanpatong district, I would like to thank Narong's brother, Lung Naan Saengmuang Ryansin, and Thanom Sutthana for their help.

I am ever grateful to Narintip (Piak) Viriyabanditkul and Wimonked (Mint) Suwapattunakorn, who have never complained no matter how late I arrive at their home in Bangkok. For their help with various aspects of the research, I would like to thank my students and the networks of Prakirati (Biek) Satasut, Sujittra (Nion) Chanthakawanich, Boonlert Visetpricha, Chaiyaporn (Bass) Singdee, Wiriyaporn (Yim) Ekphon, Anthony Irwin, Kangwan (Jojoe) Fongkaew, Stephanie Du Chatellier, and Neeranooch (June) Malangpoo. I would also like to thank Sulak Sivaraksa, Sanitsuda Ekachai, Pracha Hutasingh, Aroonrut Wichienkheeo, Ratanaporn Settakul, Renoo Atthamaek, Paritta Chalermpow Koanantakool, Siraporn Nathalang, Suchitra Chongstitvatana, Arthid Sheravanichkul, Yukti Mukdawijitra, Kusra Mukdawijitra, Nalinee Tantuvanit, Jirapha Worasiangsuk, and Patcharin Lapanun. For his help driving me to interviews in the northeast, I would like to thank Jarin Boonmathya. I must also make a special mention of Davisakd Puaksom and his student, Krijakorn (Ice) Kokpuak, who not only drove me around Uttaradit, Phitsanulok, and Sukhothai but drove all the way back to Uttaradit when I realized I had, in exhaustion, left my notebook at a villager's home. I also thank all the myriad taxi drivers who indulged my weird obsessions with this jataka while we were stuck in Bangkok traffic.

Stateside I am grateful for the many conversations about Bun Pha Wet with Leedom Lefferts and Sandra Cate; indeed, Leedom accompanied me to the northeastern village recitation I describe in this book and kindly made his tape of the performance available to me. For conversations and e-mails providing insights into comparative jataka performances throughout mainland Southeast Asia and beyond, I also thank Forest McGill, Bonnie Brereton, John Hartmann, Alan Potkin, Catherine Raymond, Santikaro, F. K. Lehman, Tharaphi Than, Erik Davis, Nicola Tannenbaum, Juliane Schober, Ingrid Jordt, Alicia Turner, Pat Pranke, Ashley Thompson, Satoru Kobayashi, John Holt, Jonas Bens, Ken George, Kirin Narayan, Rob Brightman, and Maria Lepowsky. I thank UW librarians Larry Ashmun and Thomas Durkin for their help in tracking down library resources. I thank Steven Collins, Kelly Meister, Barbara Gaerlan, and Michael Herzfeld for providing opportunities to present aspects of this research at the University of Chicago, UCLA, and Harvard University, respectively.

The influence of Stanley Tambiah, my advisor as a beginning graduate student in anthropology at the University of Chicago, together with Frank Reynolds, Ralph Nicholas and Theda Skocpol, also runs through this book.

For reading and commenting on the original much, much longer draft of this book, I must express my gratitude to Anne Hansen, Alfred McCoy, Steven Collins, Frank Reynolds, Stephen Berkwitz, Justin McDaniel, Patrick Jory, Hugh Wilson, and Mike Cullinane, as well as students in my Spring 2016 Southeast Asia class and the press's anonymous reviewers. They helped me persevere while honing the book into its current shape. For their help seeing this book through the publication process, I would like to thank Hiram Woodward, Sheila McMahon, Judith Robey, Matthew Cosby, Sarah Hope Kapp, Jan Opdyke, Scott Smiley, and particularly Gwen Walker, who has a sense of humor of her own. I thank the Institute for Research in the Humanities and the Graduate School of the University of Wisconsin–Madison for providing me with funding at various stages to help research this book.

Moving closer to my Madison home, I would like to thank my parents, E. J. Walter and Gertrud S. Bowie, for their remarkable patience. My mother in particular helped with translating French and German texts, overcoming her frustrations with macular degeneration with her own love of reading. Other friends provided important breaks from academics, but I would particularly like to thank Susan Nelson for her help with the book's illustrations. I would also like to express my profound appreciation to my sons. James accompanied me on a portion of my travels in Thailand and has also helped with the illustrations. Even though Matthew does not think historical anthropology is a science, his support for my research has been unwavering. Neither complained when I ignored them to work on this book when they came home for winter breaks.

So many people have helped me in my journey in search of Jujaka. I can only hope that whatever mistakes in interpreting the *Vessantara Jataka* that I have made in this book serve to catalyze further research in a story that has had so many tellings through the centuries.

Note on Transliteration

Translation and transliteration always pose challenges. Because I am focusing on the Thai recensions, I will not use the Pali diacritics in my transliterations. The *Vessantara Jataka* is known in many languages, each leading to different transliterations. Throughout Thailand the *Vessantara Jataka* is often called the "Great Life," which could be transliterated as *Mahaachaat*, but it is more commonly found in English as *Mahachat*, so I will use this form. The Thai pronunciation of Vessantara is transliterated variously as Wessantara, Wetsandorn, and Pha Wet. The Thai transliteration of the character Jujaka is typically Chuchok or Choo Chok. I have chosen to use Vessantara and Jujaka throughout this book, since much of the current literature in English draws on these names. I have transliterated the Thai names of the other characters as follows (see Collins 2016, 26, for a more complete chart):

Pali	Transliteration	Character
Sañjaya	Sonchai	Vessantara's father
Phusatī	Phusadi	Vessantara's mother
Maddī	Matsi	Vessantara's wife
Kaṇhājinā	Kanhaa	Vessantara's daughter
Jāli	Chalii	Vessantara's son
Amittatāpanā	Amitataa	Jujaka's wife
the Cetan	Jetabutr	The forest hunter
Accuta	Ajuta	The forest hermit

The jataka is divided into thirteen chapters. There are some differences in the individual chapter names across regions. In northern Thai, Thotsaphon is Thasaphorn, Wanaprawet is Wanlaprawet; Kumarn is Kumaraban, Matsi is Mathi, and Chohkasat is Sakati (see Manee 1976, 47). I shall use the central Thai names, based on Gerini ([1892] 1976, 27). Because the number of verses is also relevant in jataka performances and totals the one thousand verses of the *Khathaphan* ("khathaphan" meaning one thousand verses), I list them below as well.

Chapter name	Translation	No. of verses
1. Thotsaphon	The Ten Blessings	19
2. Himaphan	The Himalaya Forest	134
3. Thanakan	The Donations	209
4. Wanaprawet	Entrance into the Jungle	37
5. Chuchok	Jujaka	79
6. Chulaphon	The Sparse Forest	35
7. Mahaphon	The Thick Forest	80
8. Kumarn	The Children	101
9. Matsi	Matsi	90
10. Sakabap	Indra's Words	43
11. Maharaat	The Great King	69
12. Chohkasat	The Six Royals	36
13. Nakornkan	The Return to the Capital	48

An additional challenge is transliterating northern and northeastern Thai since they are different dialects of Thai. The festival celebrating performance of the *Vessantara Jataka* is called Bun Pha Wet in the northeastern region. Although it is transliterated variously as Bun Phra Wet, Bun Phaves, Bun Phra Ves, Bun Prawet, and so forth, I shall call it Bun Pha Wet.

Generally I am using a modified form of the Haas system of transliteration. In the case of Thai proper names, I have followed their preferred transliteration whenever known, for example Manee (instead of Manii) Phayomyong. In other cases, I am using the transliteration by which someone has become known in English, for example Prince Vajiranana instead of Wachirayan. Similarly with temple names, I am using the most common English spelling, for example Wat Mahathat instead of Wat Mahathaat. Place names are also transliterated in various ways, so I have generally used the most common English spelling.

The regional designations of central, northeastern, and northern are themselves problematic, reflecting the political outcome of the formation of the modern country known as Thailand. The central region was once called Siam; the northern kingdoms have become known as the Lanna region, although the region was once also called western Laos. However, to simplify matters, I have chosen to use the contemporary designations for these regions.

Of Beggars and Buddhas

Introduction
Of Monarchs, Monks, and Peasant Masses

The *Vessantara Jataka* is celebrated as "the most famous story in the Buddhist world" (Cone and Gombrich 1977, xv). When I first read it as an undergraduate in 1971, I found the story appalling.[1] In it, a prince named Vessantara perfects the virtue of charity with ever-greater feats of generosity. I could admire him when he gave away gold coins, jewelry, and even his magical rain-making elephant, but I had serious difficulty with his decision to give away not only slaves but also his children and his wife. As an anthropologist grounded in studies of political economy, I hardly expected to become mesmerized by a myth. But it happened, and this book is the result.

The *Vessantara Jataka* is part of a broader collection of 547 *jatakas*, or moral parables about the previous lives of the Buddha.[2] In each jataka, the future Buddha is born in a variety of animal, human, semidivine, and divine forms; while perfecting a virtue necessary for his final enlightenment, he is born as the historical Gotama Buddha in northern India.[3] Retold for over two thousand years, the stories are entertaining. The Sri Lankan scholar Rajini Obeyesekere, warmly recalling her grandfather reading jataka stories from a leather-bound book by lamplight, describes these stories as playing an important role in "how we learned to be Buddhists" (1991, ix–x; see also Jones 1979, xi). Their importance is summarized in the words of a noted historian of religion, Frank E. Reynolds: "within the entire history of religions there is no sacred biography which has had a wider dissemination or made a greater impact" (1976, 37).[4]

Of all the hundreds of jatakas, the Buddha's incarnation as Prince Vessantara has been given pride of place as his penultimate earthly birth and is often called

Figure 1. Scene from Kumarn chapter: Vessantara gives his children to Jujaka. Vessantara convinces the children to come out of the lotus pond where they were hiding (*left*). Jujaka then departs with the two children, Kanhaa and Chalii (*right*). Temple mural at Wat Nam Bo Luang, Amphur Sanpatong, Chiang Mai, July 2013. Photo by author.

the story of the "Great Life" (*Mahachat* in Thai). Scholars have suggested that this story is "better known in Buddhist cultures than even the story of Gotama Buddha's own life" (Collins 1998, 333; see also Mizuno 1971, 171). Although fading into obscurity in India, it grew in popularity over the centuries throughout the Theravada Buddhist countries of Southeast Asia—namely, Sri Lanka, Burma, Thailand, Cambodia, and Laos.[5] Rev. Robert Spence Hardy, writing in the late nineteenth century, records that "the Sinhalese will listen the night through to recitations from this work, without any apparent weariness" ([1853] 1967, 101). Writing of Burma, Melford Spiro notes that the *Vessantara Jataka* is "the best known and most loved of all Buddhist stories," adding that it is "alluded to frequently in conversation, recounted repeatedly in sermons, and—even more important—regularly enacted in dramatic form as part of the standard fare of the itinerant Burmese repertory groups" (1970, 108, 359; see also Shway Yoe [1882] 1963, 294; Mi Mi Khaing [1946] 1956; Nash 1965, 114, 148, 295). In Cambodia, an eighteenth-century Khmer inscription refers to the popularity of its recitation among the laity at Angkor (Chandler 1996, 24); writing in 1902, Adhémard Leclère observes that the *Vessantara Jataka* is "certainly the most important, the most beautiful and the best known" (1902, 3; see also Harris 2005, 69-70; Hansen 2007, 88). Of Laos, John Holt writes that the *Vessantara Jataka* is "easily the most popular jataka" (2009, 40; see also Karpeles 1931; Condominas 1968, 93; Stuart-Fox 1998, 174). Writing of Thailand as late as 1987, Charles Keyes summarizes, "The 'Great Life' is known widely throughout Thailand to this day. . . . There is probably no Buddhist in Thailand beyond the age of ten or so who could not give at least a synopsis of the story, and many people especially in villages, can quote passages in the same way English speakers can quote parts of the Bible, or selections from Shakespeare" (1987, 181).

I first traveled to Thailand in 1974. My research in those days focused on the growing poverty and political tensions in the countryside. However, I recall seeing a modern operatic performance of the story in Chiang Mai, the largest city in northern Thailand, in 1977.[6] The performance focused on Jujaka, the beggar to whom Vessantara gave his children. I remember indignantly asking my companion (a friend who taught Thai literature) how a story featuring a beggar whose stomach explodes after he overeats could have any socially redeeming message. Where was the compassion for the beggar? What right did Vessantara have to give away his children and his wife, let alone slaves? How can anyone—particularly any woman—hold such an inhumane man as a moral exemplar? When my friend tried to tell me the story was funny, I was outraged. Focusing on Vessantara, I considered his acts of generosity as marked by an appalling callousness rather than an admirable charity.

My abhorrence of the jataka also meant I had barely noticed that, for all the scholarly discussions of the jataka's popularity, in fact its performances were becoming increasingly rare in the central and northern regions of the country.[7] Historically when monks recited the full jataka, it was a major event lasting several days, and the temples were decorated in grand style to re-create the ambiance of the forest where Vessantara gave away his wife and children. Although individual chapters were recited at funerals, the village in northern Thailand where I have spent the most time over the past forty years has never hosted a full recitation during this entire period. Nor (with a few exceptions) has any village in the surrounding area. Nonetheless, one still finds mural paintings of the jataka on the walls of most temples in Thailand, including in the villages where I have conducted fieldwork. Nationally the jataka is still being printed on special stamp editions, assigned in schoolbooks, and broadcast from time to time on television.[8] However, my Thai women friends also find Vessantara's decision appalling and as modern women showed no concern about the story's apparently growing irrelevance. An important transformation appears to be occurring unremarked.

Having prematurely decided that the *Vessantara Jataka* was an immoral oddity best relegated to the dustbin of history, I blithely ignored the obvious puzzles posed by both its former popularity and signs of its current transformations. In retrospect, I realize that men and women in the past were no less perplexed by it, if not horrified. As Richard Gombrich noted of Sri Lanka, Vessantara's decision to give away his wife and children not only "strikes us as excessive. It strikes the Sinhalese in the same way" (1971, 267).[9] Two Sinhalese monks flat out told Gombrich that "Vessantara was wrong" (1971, 267). An elderly Lao man whom Patrice Ladwig interviewed found Vessantara's escalating gift-giving "problematic and egoistic," explaining, "His drive for giving becomes a burden for other people and it produces considerable suffering. His excessive generosity is almost comparable to a kind of illness" (2009, 146). Many taxi drivers I have subsequently interviewed in Thailand also believed that Vessantara was wrong and that the jataka served as a lesson about wrongful giving.

Some scholars have tried to ameliorate the horror of Vessantara's acts by suggesting that they needed to be placed in the historical context of ancient India, which they characterize as a rigid patriarchy in which women and children were viewed as property (e.g., Cone and Gombrich 1977, xxi). This pseudo-explanation ignores both the text and the performance of the jataka. In the text, the scenes in which Vessantara gives away his children are prolonged and heart-wrenching. Indeed, as Steven Collins notes, "the Pali text here goes out of its way to emphasize the pathos of these scenes" (1998, 44). Numerous accounts of performances note that the audiences were in tears over the agony of Vessantara, his wife (Matsi), and their children (e.g., Pallegoix [1854] 2000, 253; Forbes 1878, 150; Winternitz 1933, 152; Ladwig 2009).[10] Monks are taught voice-modulation techniques to elicit emotional responses of admiration, awe, love, fear, calm, grief, suffering, and pity (Ladwig 2009, 146). One monk I interviewed in Thailand said that the chapter describing Vessantara's wife's profound grief upon learning her children are gone is widely known as the "Tearjerker Chapter" (Kan Riak Nam Taa).

Furthermore, the listening audience was overwhelmingly female. Unlike women in patriarchal societies, women in the Theravada Buddhist countries of mainland Southeast Asia have long held positions of considerable economic and political strength, owning property and managing businesses. Men typically marry into their wives' households (a post-marriage residence pattern known as matrilocality, or, more accurately, uxorilocality); inheritance is bilateral with a tendency toward female ultimogeniture rather than male primogeniture.[11] Despite my tacit awareness that women comprised the primary audience for performances of this jataka, and my recognition of the remarkable strength of women in mainland Southeast Asia, I had never forced myself to confront the contradiction between the text's apparent misogyny and its popularity, particularly among women.

My fascination with the *Vessantara Jataka* developed serendipitously. Planning to conduct research on changes in rural electoral politics, I got off the plane in Bangkok in 2004 and was greeted by newspaper headlines about a controversy over signs in northern Thailand prohibiting women from entering certain parts of Buddhist temples, ostensibly due to concerns regarding menstrual pollution. Since most of my fieldwork has been conducted in northern Thailand, I was aware of this prohibition. Having long hated those signs, I was quietly delighted to see a movement challenging them. The senator who raised the issue was from northeastern Thailand, where this taboo was not in effect. The senator found herself the subject of a cursing ceremony and was beset with death threats. She was forced to apologize for her ignorance of northern Thai customs, and she then resigned from the parliamentary committee on women, children, and the elderly.[12]

Although the senator's resignation may have quelled the immediate controversy, my curiosity was catalyzed; I had not realized this taboo was regionally specific. When I was back visiting friends in Chiang Mai province, I began asking them what they thought of the taboo; I encountered an entire spectrum of opinions. My village friends were far more skeptical of the taboo than my urban friends. While my urban friends argued for the importance of maintaining traditional beliefs, my village friends wondered why men whose habits included drinking, gambling, and womanizing were considered any purer than themselves; and, as they pointed out, what about Kotex and other such modern feminine hygiene products? Recognizing the intense passions the senator's simple query had aroused, I decided I needed a more neutral avenue to discuss the northern prohibition with its leading northern proponents. Reviewing hundreds of interviews I had conducted over the years, I began making a list of some of the differences I noticed between northern practices of Buddhism and those in other regions in Thailand.

My list included comedic monks called *tujok*. I remembered hearing tujok monks performing at northern Thai village funerals in the 1970s, sometimes in person but more typically through tape recordings. Villagers loved them, laughing uproariously at all the punchlines. Because *tu* is the northern Thai word for "monk," I assumed that tujok must refer to "monks who joke." Given my mistaken belief that *jok* came from the English language, I viewed this form of humorous preaching as a more recent development. Although the funereal tradition of listening to these tujok monks has largely been replaced by other types of entertainment, I began asking my village friends for more information about them. I was surprised to learn that these comedic monks were not modern but instead were part of a long-standing tradition related to northern Thai performances of the *Vessantara Jataka*. The much beloved tujok monks were none other than the monks who recite the Jujaka chapter of the *Vessantara Jataka*. Jujaka is the beggar who requests Vessantara's children; Jujaka is pronounced "Chuchok" in Thai, and through elision the term "tujok" results.[13] Suddenly I found myself contemplating not only the factors that had shaped northern feminist history but also the text I had so long reviled. Wrapped in an aura of sacral horror, the *Vessantara Jataka* had never struck me as funny.

The Journey Begins

Intrigued by the new interpretive vistas that were looming, I asked a village friend to check with other villagers at the morning market to see if anyone still had any of the old tujok tapes. She learned of a store in Chiang Mai city that still sold tujok tapes, and we immediately headed into town. The most famous of the tujok monks was named Luang Poh Bunthong. I proceeded to buy every tape of his that the store carried, most of which appeared to date to the 1970s. I had heard his tapes at funerals, but I had rarely understood the punchlines; at the time I had no opportunity to break into the roar of the listeners' laughter because my questions would have interrupted the flow just as the monk was moving on to the next story. Now I was able to stop the tape and ask my friends to explain the jokes. The stories were funny, but I was surprised by their bawdy and scatological humor. In retrospect, perhaps I should not have been so surprised since I had already heard fairly raunchy repartee between male and female *chang saw* singers at northern temple festivals—but those singers were not ordained monks!

As I began discussing these tapes with villagers, I learned that one of Bunthong's disciples was the abbot of a temple in a nearby village in Tambon Nongthong, Amphur Hang Dong; he was also known as a tujok monk. The next day a couple of village friends and I headed off to meet him. We were in luck since we caught the abbot, Phrakhruu Athong, on a quiet day. Evidently bemused by my fascination with tujok, the abbot generously provided me with an extended interview. To give me some sense of the poetic form of the northern Thai versions of this jataka, the abbot began demonstrating the operatic

Figure 2. Memorial shrine to Luang Poh Bunthong. The body of the famous tujok monk, covered with gold leaf, lies in the glass casket. In front are wax replicas of Luang Poh Bunthong and his beloved dogs. Wat Sophanaram, Tambon Don Kaew, Amphur Mae Rim, Chiang Mai, July 2011. Photo by author.

techniques behind the various styles of chanting. Soon he had me laughing in amazement. I could not believe my ears. As he described Jujaka's pillows made from chicken droppings and bamboo containers made to hold his wife's excrement, I found myself entering the provocative domain of village humor. Furthermore, the abbot was explicit that much of the humor had been toned down lest it offend modern urban audiences. Having been raised by a father famous for his recall of bawdy limericks unsuitable for polite company, I became increasingly fascinated with the abbot's account of this disappearing genre of village humor.

The *Vessantara Jataka* is divided into thirteen chapters, each with its own title. The story begins in heaven, when the god Indra realizes that the time has come for his chief queen Phusadi to be reborn on earth. In this chapter, called "The Ten Wishes" (*Thotsaphon*), Indra grants her ten wishes, which include giving birth to a Buddha and not having her breasts sag. Born to a chief queen on earth, Phusadi is married to King Sonchai in Jetuttara, the capital of the Sivi kingdom. Soon thereafter, she gives birth to Vessantara. From the moment of his birth, Vessantara wants to offer gifts, so his mother provides him with one thousand gold coins to give away. On the same day, a magical rain-making elephant appears in the royal stable. Vessantara continues offering gifts. At age sixteen, he marries Matsi, who becomes his chief queen in charge of sixteen thousand royal women in court. Matsi gives birth to a son named Chalii and a daughter named Kanhaa. When a drought causes famine in the neighboring kingdom of Kalinga, the King of Kalinga sends eight Brahmins to ask Vessantara for his magic rain-making elephant. Vessantara gives them his elephant. Under pressure from his outraged followers, King Sonchai sends Vessantara into exile, thereby concluding the second chapter (called *Himaphan*). The third chapter is called "The Donations" (*Thanakan*). Here Vessantara makes the people a huge offering known as the "Gift of the Seven Hundreds"; he then leaves for exile in the forest with Matsi and his two children.[14] In the next chapter (*Wanaprawet*), the royal family visits Matsi's kingdom; Matsi's father sends a hunter named Jetabutr to protect them while they live in the forest.

The setting now shifts to the impoverished kingdom of Kalinga, where we are introduced to *Jujaka*, the beggar, in the chapter with his name. When his wife Amitataa is teased by other village women, she asks Jujaka to get Vessantara's children as her servants. Reluctantly, Jujaka begins his journey, entering the forest where Vessantara and his family are living. Jetabutr's dogs chase Jujaka up a tree, but Jujaka is able to convince Jetabutr not to shoot him because he is a royal messenger. In the *Chulaphon* and *Mahaphon* chapters, Jujaka finds Ajuta, an ascetic, and tricks him into giving him directions to the home of the royal family in exile. In the chapter titled *Kumarn* (children), Jujaka is given the two royal children; he ties them up and leads them off into the forest. In the *Matsi* chapter, Matsi, who has been gathering food in the forest, returns home after being blocked by magical animals, learns that her children have been given away, and faints in shock. Vessantara restores her to consciousness and explains his actions. In the *Sakabap* chapter, the god Indra, disguised as Jujaka, requests Matsi but then returns her to Vessantara. In the *Maharaat* (great king) chapter, Jujaka and the two children find themselves back in Jetuttara, where the king pays Jujaka the handsome ransom Vessantara had set for them and feasts Jujaka. Jujaka dies from overeating, and the ransom is restored to the king. King Sonchai and Queen Phusadi are delighted to learn that Vessantara and Matsi are alive. In the twelfth chapter, called "The Six Royals" (*Chohkasat*), the king and queen set out with a large retinue to invite Vessantara and Matsi back to court; they all faint for joy at their reunion, so a red rain falls from the heavens to revive them. In the last chapter, called *Nakornkan*, the reunited family returns to the capital, jewels fall until everyone is knee deep in them, and everyone is happy. (For the full English translation, see Cowell [1895] 1957; Cone and Gombrich 1977, 2011; see also Gerini [1892] 1976.)

In the course of interviewing northern monks and villagers in earnest, I became increasingly aware that Jujaka was their favorite character. Although other chapters can also be performed, the Jujaka chapter has long been the main choice for funerals. Monks developed reputations for their specializations in specific chapters, but the most beloved were the tujok monks who performed the Jujaka chapter. Only tujok monks were set apart as a specific named category; they wore costumes and made grand entrances into temples. Evoking warm memories and laughter among older villagers as they recalled past performances, the tujok monks were held in high regard for their comedic abilities.

My academic training had certainly not prepared me to encounter Jujaka as a beloved character who brought joy and laughter to his audiences. The literature, based in the ancient Pali texts of the Theravada Buddhist canon, had focused on Vessantara and portrayed Jujaka as the cruel, frightening, and greedy villain. In the Pali version jatakas have codas that explain who each of the characters ultimately became during the historical life of the Gotama Buddha; the principal character (almost invariably male) is identified with the Buddha, other characters are his relatives or key disciples, and the villain is "always the schismatic monk Devadatta" (Cone and Gombrich 1977, xvi). Devadatta is understood to be the evil cousin of the Buddha who plotted to kill the Buddha and his own father. He is also believed to have created the first schism within the monastic order, itself one of the highest offenses in Buddhism. In the coda for the *Vessantara Jataka*, we are told that Jujaka will be reborn as Devadatta.

Prevailing scholarship about Jujaka follows the Pali coda, casting him in negative terms. Thus Charles Forbes describes him as "the villain of the piece" (1878, 149); L. Allan Goss as "the surly and greedy brahmin" (1895, iii); and Khin Thitsa as a "hideous creature" who caused children to tremble at the thought he "could be allowed to get his hands on the boy and girl" (1980, 20). Similarly, Vallaya Piyarat writes of the "villain-like Chuchok whose cruel treatment of the children often makes the listeners or the readers cry" (Sombat 1981, 194). Characterized as "scheming" and "vengeful," Jujaka is described by Nidhi Eoseewong as "a cruel, selfish, wicked, and heartless man. He is cunning, afraid of his wife, and a coward" ([1982] 2005, 221, 222). Furthermore, vernacular recensions of the jataka often add that he was reborn in hell.[15]

With possible portrayals of Jujaka now ranging from funny to frightening, I wondered if the northern interpretation was also typical of other regions of Thailand. Whenever I traveled to Bangkok and elsewhere in the central region and in northeastern Thailand, I asked people I met what they knew about Jujaka and the *Vessantara Jataka*. These random informal interviews resulted in three additional surprises. The first surprise was the number of people in the central region who not only had never attended a reading of the *Vessantara Jataka*, but could barely recall anything about this story without my prompting; this lack of familiarity was particularly true of the younger generations living in Bangkok. The second surprise was that there were significant differences in the actual performances of the jataka in each of these three regions, beginning with the simple fact that each region preferred to perform it in a different time of year.

The third surprise was that the northern portrayal of Jujaka differed dramatically from that of the central and northeastern regions. The central region, and to some extent the northeast, largely paralleled the negative academic portrayal. When I asked a central Thai monk and a northeastern monk who perform the Jujaka chapter how they came to their specialization, both told me it was because there were no other monks willing to perform this chapter. When I asked which chapters people were least eager to host, many central Thai monks and villagers replied that it was the Jujaka chapter; potential lay sponsors feared they would somehow become contaminated by Jujaka's demerit (*baab*), inauspiciousness, negativity, poverty, ugliness, and greed.[16] Several people explained that the practice of having lay sponsors draw lots to determine who would sponsor each chapter developed as a way to solve the problem of finding a host for the Jujaka chapter. Some monks told me that they cajoled lay hosts, assuring them that Jujaka was a *khuu baramii*, or partner, to Vessantara without whom Vessantara could not reach enlightenment. Even when Jujaka was seen as laughable, he was certainly not viewed as lovable. If Jujaka could be interpreted differently across regions, how many other aspects of the jataka's meaning also varied? These surprises in the story I had so long ignored now intrigued me. And so this book exploring regional variation across space and time was born.

Regional Variation in Space and Time

Most studies of the *Vessantara Jataka* have been undertaken by scholars of religious studies rather than anthropologists. Consequently, attention has centered on the text rather than the context of its performance. Furthermore, analysis has focused on the Pali text, in part because scholars viewed the Pali texts as more authentic than localized versions and in part because they believed that local texts did not differ from the Pali version.[17] Margaret Cone and Richard Gombrich, writing about the importance of the *Vessantara Jataka* in Sri Lanka and elsewhere in Southeast Asia, insist, "For all this area, then, the version presented in this book is the basic one; local versions are derived more or less directly from it, and do not innovate" (1977, xli). Similarly, Collins argues in his earlier work that "the many tellings of Vessantara's story do not seem to display the enormous variation, even in such basic features as plot elements, to be found in different tellings of 'the' Ramayana story" (1998, 538). Donald Swearer writes, "The *Vessantara Jataka* has been translated into the major Southeast Asian vernacular languages with minor changes in the text" (2010, 34). Writing of Thailand, Elizabeth Lyons concludes that the Thai version "differs only in a few unimportant details from the original Pali" (1960, 167). Similarly Patrick Jory, while noting the existence of "countless vernacular translations" of the *Vessantara Jataka* in Thailand, concludes that "when comparing versions of the Vessantara Jataka texts from different regions of Thailand one is struck by their lack of divergence from the same basic narrative" (1996, 24).

A contemporary wave of literature more grounded in anthropological approaches has highlighted the robust diversity of folklore. As the noted anthropologist Kirin Narayan observes, "Folklore, in its very nature, displays multiple existence and variation" (1989, 26). In South Asia, Paula Richman and others have described the diversity of narrative traditions of the Ramayana (see Richman 1991; Jaiswal 1993). Philip Lutgendorf (2007) has taken a single figure from the Ramayana complex, the monkey-king Hanuman, revealing an ever-expanding epic cycle that he calls the "Hanumayana." Furthermore, as A. K. Ramanujan (1991) comments, different tellings are neither totally individual stories nor divergences from the "real" version. Instead, each version is a "unique crystallization, a new text with a unique texture and a fresh context" (Richman 1991, 8). Significantly, as Wendy Doniger suggests in her engaging cross-cultural study of bedtricks: "When myths tell us what happened, they do not always tell us why the people in the story did what they did or how they feel about what happened to them. To this extent, they remain open and transparent and can be retold, within one culture or in several cultures, with several very different meanings" (2000, xviii).

There is some foundation to the argument for a certain uniformity of performance and interpretation in the *Vessantara Jataka*. In most recitations, the Pali recension is almost invariably recited together with the vernacular version; the maintenance of the Pali text arguably encourages a certain uniformity in the basic plotline of the story. As Nidhi points out, "the Vessantara Jataka is a 'sacred' Jataka. So the alterations that can be made to the story are much more limited" ([1982] 2005, 223). Contributing to the unique sacrality of the *Vessantara Jataka* is the fact that it is interwoven retrospectively into three events in the historiography of Gotama Buddha's life. The first mention occurs when the Buddha is being tested by Mara (the personification of evil) just prior to reaching enlightenment; the Buddha calls the earth to witness his generosity in his life as Vessantara.[18] The second reference occurs after he has reached enlightenment and goes to preach to his father and other relatives; as he prepares to preach, a miraculous red rain falls. The Buddha explains that a red rain had fallen before, when he was Vessantara. The final reference is when he returns after his enlightenment to visit his wife and reminds her of her past role in allowing him to give away all their possessions.

A further contribution to the sacrality of textual recitations of the *Vessantara Jataka* is the way the story is framed. In the Theravada jataka tradition, "the stage is set by a short 'story of the present' in which the occasion when the Buddha supposedly recounted the jataka in question is described. This staging is followed by the 'story of the past' which constitutes the jataka itself" (Reynolds 1997, 23). Each jataka ends with an explanation of how each character was reborn during the life of the historical Buddha (e.g., Jujaka as Devadatta). Even when the *Vessantara Jataka* is recited in local dialects, each chapter begins with a brief excerpt from the Pali version at the beginning of each chapter (*chunniyabot*), thereby adding to the sacrality of the recitation.

However, a new wave of scholarship is beginning a serious engagement with indigenous recensions, marking a shift from the prevailing paradigm of scholarship, which has hitherto ignored earlier evidence of local variation (Appleton 2010; Collins 2016). Already in the late nineteenth century, scholars noted significant differences between jataka collections (Feer [1865] 1963; D'Oldenberg 1893). Viggo Fausbøll remarked that a Burmese manuscript of the Maha Nipata, a collection of the ten jatakas that includes the *Vessantara Jataka*, offers a much enlarged text so different that he would "advise some scholar to give a separate edition of the Maha Nipata according to the Burmese redaction" (Winternitz 1928, 12).[19] A collection of some fifty jatakas believed to have originated in the Lanna kingdoms of northern Thailand contains additional stories different from those in the Pali canon.[20] Other jatakas include an indigenous Southeast Asian deity named Manimekhala, shipwrecks, and other Southeast Asian motifs that, Padmanabh Jaini suggests, "would never have been found in the canonical Jataka stories originating on the Indian mainland" (1989, 26). Comparing the stylistic transformations that occurred in Thai artistic depictions of the Buddha to those in Thai literature, A. B. Griswold wrote, "The old Siamese dramatists borrowed scholarly words from Sanskrit and Pali, but embedded them in Siamese syntax; they looked to the Ramayana and the Jatakas for their plots, but steeped their incidental descriptions in local color" (1953, 6).

Several Southeast Asian vernacular texts are more than mere variations in details of local color. Laos has a jataka called Phra Lak Phra Ram, which has elements of the Ramayana but is very different from the South Asian nexus (see Sahai 1996; Holt 2009, 58-60, 259-69; Kislenko 2009, 68; Wilson 2009; Bowers 2011). With the growth of interest in community culture and indigenous knowledge, scholars at regional teacher colleges and universities have begun studying local texts. Several analyses, written in Thai and hitherto overlooked by most non-Thai scholars, reveal regional variations on the *Vessantara Jataka* itself (e.g., Manee 1976; Prakong 1983; and Nidhi [1982] 2005; see Jory 1996 for a bibliography of Thai regional recensions).

In addition to geographical variation, evidence suggests that the jataka's popularity also varies across time. Its overall longevity has been buttressed by its incorporation into two interrelated prophecies, both of which were widely known. The first prophecy was popularized by the noted fifth-century Indian Buddhist commentator Buddhaghosa; he declared that Buddhism will deteriorate over time, only lasting five thousand years (*Digha Nikaya*, 26). As George Coedes remarks, it is a prophecy "with which all Buddhists are familiar" (1956, 96). The earliest known inscription explicitly linking the *Vessantara Jataka* with this prediction dates to 1357 CE and was made by King Lithai of Sukhothai kingdom. The Theravada Buddhist calendar begins on the day of Buddha's enlightenment; thus Thailand is currently in the year 2560 BE (Buddhist Era), or 2017 CE.[21] The inscription predicts that the decline of Buddhism would begin in 2000 BE (circa 1457 CE). In 2000 BE, according to the inscription:

> The Three Pitakas will disappear. There will be no one who really knows them, though there will be some who know a little bit of them. As for preaching the Dharma, such as the Majajati [Great Life or *Vessantara Jataka*], there will be no one who can recite it; as for the other Dharmajatakas, if the beginning is known the end will not be, or if the end is known the beginning will not be; and as for the Abhidhamma collection, the Patthana and the Yammaka [the last two books of the Abhidhamma] will disappear at that time. (Griswold and Prasert 1973, 99)

That this prediction was well known is reflected in the remarks of prominent monks of the nineteenth century, albeit with some slight variations.[22] Phra Wannarat, a senior monk involved in the ninth Council Tripitaka revisions in 1788-89 during the reign of Rama I, makes the link between Buddhism, the *Vessantara Jataka*, and government explicit; he writes, "When study of the scriptures declines, when it slips away, there will occur an age of vice and misery (Skt. *kaliyuga*) of the unrighteous people. When the king is without Dhamma the people, the ministers, for example, follow, and become without Dhamma in the same way" (Reynolds 1972, 54). The monk goes on to detail the stages of deterioration:

> When lay people are poor they cannot offer the monastic requisites and monks cannot look after their disciples. As study of the texts declines further, monks lose knowledge of the commentaries, then the canon itself. First the Abhidhamma is lost, leaving the Suttas and the Vinaya. Then the Suttas follow, beginning with Anguttara-Nikaya and ending with the Digha-Nikaya. Only the Vinaya and Jatakas remain. Conscientious monks will adhere to the Vinaya, but those who look to the acquisition of gain and advantage will be unable to exercise their rational faculties when reciting the Suttas and will know only the Jatakas. Like the Abhidhamma and the Suttas, the disappearance of the Jatakas takes place in sequence, beginning with the Vessantara, the most popular Jataka in Siamese tradition. Finally, the Vinaya is forgotten, and the last vestige of the Buddha's teaching is considered lost forever when there is no layman who remembers a four-line verse of the Buddha's words. (Reynolds 1972, 54)

Phra Wannarat's remarks are echoed in Prince Paramanuchit's edition of the Buddha's life, completed in 1845. Prince Paramanuchit, who became the supreme patriarch (*sangharaja*) of the monastic order in 1851, concluded his edition with Buddhaghosa's famous prediction, noting that Buddhism was destined to disappear in five thousand years after the Buddha's enlightenment in five equal stages: the decline of the scriptures, the decline of conduct, the decline of knowledge of the way and its fruits, the decline of asceticism, and the disappearance of the relics (Reynolds 1972, 134–35).

This bleak prophecy was generally linked to the second major prophecy about the coming of the future Buddha, Maitreya.[23] The *Phra Malai Sutra*, considered one of the three most important texts in Theravada Buddhism, is the primary medium through which the belief in the coming of Maitreya was popularized. According to this text, Phra Malai visited the hells and the heavens. When he was in the heavens, he met the Maitreya Buddha. Maitreya informed Phra Malai to tell people to listen to the *Vessantara Jataka* "in one night and one day" if they wished to be reborn during his coming. Accordingly, the *Phra Malai Sutra* is almost always recited just before the *Vessantara Jataka* itself, particularly in the northern and northeastern regions of Thailand. As one northern Phra Malai text of Maitreya's message explains:

> If anyone wishes to see me in the future, they should make extraordinary merit in the following way. Have them set their minds on listening to the *Vessantara Jataka Dhamma*. Have them listen in one day until it is finished, with the

customary objects of worship, that is, a thousand lanterns, a thousand lotuses, completely without lacking in any way, a thousand balls of rice. Have them invite the monks to preach the esteemed *Vessantara Jataka Dhamma*, all one-thousand stanzas. . . . The people should go together and listen to it in one night and one day until it is finished. When everyone follows these teachings, . . . they will see me. (Brereton 1995, 64; see also Griswold and Prasert 1973, 85; Collins 1993, 85; McGill 1997, 207)

The affiliation of the *Vessantara Jataka* with the survival of Buddhism and the arrival of the Maitreya Buddha buttressed the importance of the jataka. However, despite apparent safeguards for its longevity and despite the presumption of its unchanging appeal by many of its scholars, the *Vessantara Jataka* has undergone changes in its appeal over time.[24] In Thailand today, the northeast is the only region where the *Vessantara Jataka* is still being widely recited annually. Although it is hard to imagine a northeastern villager of any generation who is not familiar with the *Vessantara Jataka*, a majority of younger central Thai and northern Thai have never attended a performance and have almost no familiarity with the story. Urbanites regardless of region are less likely than villagers to know the story. Most younger Bangkokian looked at me in amazement when they learned of my interest in the *Vessantara Jataka*; they viewed the story as implausible and largely dismissed it as irrelevant. Many village elders with whom I sat at various village funerals in northern Thailand also had to be prompted to recall parts of the story that had become vague over the course of the passing decades. Clearly the scholarly paradigm about the importance of the *Vessantara Jataka* is in need of reconsideration.

Historical Agency

Recognition that the *Vessantara Jataka* is not uniform either in its interpretation or its performance opens new avenues of inquiry. Regional variation raises the issue of historical agency, providing an invitation to engage in an imaginative exercise to rediscover the people who were individually and collectively shaping regional shifts. Whose interests were being promoted in the shifts over the course of the jataka's long history? This engagement with historical agency has been missing in the prevailing text-based analyses of the *Vessantara Jataka*, which have centered on analyzing essentialized existential and ahistorical core meanings of the story. However, the readings of texts change as contexts change; sometimes new themes take precedence within a story and at other times the entire text fades into oblivion. Like many American mothers of my generation, I chose not to read my children Little Red Riding Hood, Hansel and Gretel, or the Strummelpeter stories, deciding instead to read Dr. Seuss's corpus and later J. K. Rowling's Harry Potter series.

Explorations of the rise and fall of texts over both space and time provide an avenue into history. If the *Vessantara Jataka* is not to be analyzed as an abstract, essentialized, universal expression of some element of the human condition but as a historically dynamic expression of ever-changing points of emphasis, who were the people responsible for these changes? Who had enjoyed tellings of the *Vessantara Jataka* and why? What points did the teller want the audience to understand? Whose interests were being promoted? Why has the story's appeal changed differentially across regions? How should we explain the process by which the single most famous and important story of Theravada Buddhist Southeast Asia is fading away in some regions? The *Vessantara Jataka* is still being recited throughout Southeast Asia, but its individual tellers and listeners have made decisions, big and small, that have reshaped the story in different ways over time and across regions.

In order to integrate historical agency into our analyses of the *Vessantara Jataka*, we can begin by considering the fundamental categories of social actors. Historians have generally categorized Theravada Buddhist societies of Southeast Asia into three main groups: the court, the monkhood, and the peasantry. Paralleling these social divisions, explanations of the story's popularity might be categorized according to those that emphasize its appeal for the monks, for the monarchs, and for the masses. Because Vessantara was both a member of a royal family and a future Buddha, scholarly attention has hitherto focused on the story's significance for the first two categories—namely, for the monkhood and for kingship. Explorations of peasant interests in participating in *Vessantara Jataka* recitations have been minimal and have tended to portray villagers as superstitious or utilitarian in their motivations. Were the interests of the monks, the monarchs, and the masses being served equally? Did these respective interests overlap or conflict?

Monastic Motivations

Religious studies scholars' analyses of what they have assumed to be a uniform text generally highlight the value of the jataka in supporting the monastic community. Although they argue that the *Vessantara Jataka* emphasizes the social virtue of generosity for the common good, their analyses ironically tend to focus on the value of renunciation for the benefit of the individual. As Larry McClung writes, the *Vessantara Jataka* "provides Buddhists with an important vehicle for the attempted resolution of a deep-seated conflict which prevails between the urge to pursue an ethic of individual salvation and the desire for human community" (1975, 36). Collins phrases this central tension as "a painfully honest confrontation of the difficulties of renunciation" and "the most subtle and successful attempt in Pali literature to infuse ascetic values and soteriological motifs into an ideal image of collective life in an ordinary, productive and reproductive society" (1998, 501). Cone and Gombrich suggest the story has a covert appeal for monks since, like them, "Vessantara has renounced all worldly ties, and in particular, family ties" (1977, xxvi).

Furthermore, the jataka supports the monkhood by encouraging parents to gift their sons and wives their husbands to the temple (Theravada Buddhist monks may enter the monkhood after marriage). Writing of central Thailand, Lauriston Sharp and Lucien Hanks mention the importance of gifting children in the *Vessantara Jataka* in connection with ordination; they write, "parents, by giving their sons to the temple, make greater merit than by any other single act of devotion" (1978, 143). Writing of Burma, Melford Spiro suggests that the *Vessantara Jataka* serves as "an impressive historico-mythological charter" that sanctions the decision to ordain (1970, 346).[25] Providing a provocative formulation, Spiro explains the tensions inherent in a husband's decision to ordain: "Simply to abandon one's family would provoke intense social disapproval in Burma.... If their wives were to protest their action, it is they and not their husbands who would become the objects of disapproval: how can they object to their husbands' search for salvation? . . . Rather than being disdained for shirking their obligation to their families, they are praised for having had the strength to cut their attachment to them" (1970, 346).

The jataka not only safeguards the recruitment of monks into the order but also legitimizes the alms needed to support them (Spiro 1970; McClung 1975; Brereton 1995). As Alfred Foucher suggests, the monastic community encouraged recitations of the *Vessantara Jataka* because it "is totally dependent upon alms—for food, clothing and medicines—and exalts all examples of generous givers in its preaching to the laity" (Foucher 1955, 331; see also McClung 1975, 11). Similarly, Bonnie Brereton observes, "for the Sangha [monastic order], which must rely on the generosity of the laity for its very survival, the *Vessantara Jataka* provides a convenient way of reminding the faithful of the preeminent importance of *dana* [gift-giving]" (1995, 65). Thus, as Keyes writes, "Ordinary people emulate Prince Wetsandon, not by giving their goods to anyone who asks for them, but by offering alms to those most worthy of receiving them, the members of the sangha" (1987, 181).[26]

Royalist Motivations

Among scholars with a more historical bent, the *Vessantara Jataka* has been portrayed as a mechanism to establish royal political legitimacy. Many Southeast Asian kings sponsored recitations of the *Vessantara Jataka*, often accompanied with spectacular displays of gift offerings. By generously supporting lavish recitations of the jataka and by drawing upon an implicit parallel between themselves as kings and Vessantara as both king-to-be and Buddha-to-be, monarchs could hope that the public saw them as incarnations of Vessantara and, implicitly, the Buddha. In his pioneering essay about the long-standing importance of the Emerald Buddha, Frank Reynolds highlights the importance of the *Vessantara Jataka* in the symbolism of political power. The Emerald Buddha was seen as the palladium of whichever kingdom came to hold it, not least because "the various princes of the kingdom swore their fealty to the reigning monarch who possessed it"; Reynolds notes that "at least from the time of the Bangkok period this ritual of changing the Jewel's adornments had come to involve, as a central element, the chanting of the Mahavessantara Jataka" (1978, 184).

Sombat Chantornvong explored the background of the earliest extant version of the *Vessantara Jataka* of 1482, which was believed to have been translated from Pali at the behest of King Trailok (r. 1448–88), ruler of the ancient kingdom of Ayutthaya. Sombat argues that the king's sponsorship of the translation was part of a "strategy that King Trailok used in establishing supremacy over the people of Sukothai, especially in legitimizing himself in their eyes as a pious Buddhist ruler" (1981, 192). Throughout this recension, the Buddha and Vessantara "are addressed by various names, all of which are very similar to King Trailok's" (1981, 196). Sombat also suggests that the story highlights as "deviant behavior" the angry demand that Vessantara be banished for giving away the magical rain-making white elephant. Sombat takes this demand as evidence of the people of the kingdom's brazen belief that the elephant belonged to them. According to Sombat, the text's ending indicated that "the ruler had a legitimate right to everything" and pointed to "the need to accept unlimited monarchical rule" (1981, 197). He concludes: "In short, the Maha Chat Kamluang appears to present the masses as ignorant and evil and the rulers as wise and benevolent. This kind of presentation is compatible with the political tradition of the day which not only demanded total loyalty on the part of the common people but also excluded them completely from any active political role" (1981, 198).

Forrest McGill provides further insight into the pressures King Trailok faced. King Trailok's reign coincided with the ominous prophecy made earlier by King Lithai in his inscription of 1357 predicting that Buddhism would begin declining in 2000 BE (1457 CE). In a variety of acts ranging from creating Jataka sculptures and constructing temples to staging his own ordination and sponsoring *Vessantara Jataka* recitations, King Trailok was seeking to link himself with Vessantara and "may have intended to present himself as a bodhisattva, or even, indeed specifically as Maitreya" (1993, 437–38).

Patrick Jory has also emphasized the role of the *Vessantara Jataka* as a royalist text in the early nineteenth-century Thai state, arguing that "the Vessantara Jataka was one of the most important texts in the premodern Thai State for the expression and dissemination of a political theory based on the concept of *barami* [charisma] and the exemplary figures of the *bodhisatta*-king" (2002b, 38). As Jory explains:

> The association between the Vessantara Jataka and Thai rulers can be traced back as early as the Sukhothai period, but it is in the early Bangkok period that the status of the Vessantara Jataka as one of the key texts expressing the political ideology of the Thai kingdom can be seen most clearly. In this period the kingdom's rulers, modeling themselves on the *bodhisatta*-king, consciously made use of the story to promote the idea that *barami* was inherent in the royal line itself, conflating the genealogy of the Buddha with that of the ruling dynasty. (2002b, 38)

Jory suggests that because of their utility as "the principal conduit of a conception of authority and social hierarchy," Thai rulers actively promoted recitations of the *Vessantara Jataka* (2002a, 913). In Jory's view, "The *Thet Mahachat* contributed to the creation of a cohesive cultural community" (2002b, 62).

Peasant Motivations

Kings and monks may have had vested interests in encouraging the propagation of the *Vessantara Jataka*, but did they succeed in promoting their agendas with the peasantry? Anthropological accounts have provided generally apolitical and utilitarian motivations for village participation in its recitation, ranging from otherworldly desires to make merit to this-worldly desires to safeguard rainfall. Anthropologist Charles Keyes provides perhaps the most expansive early insight into the range of meanings of the jataka for villagers, noting that the story "provides moral models for the most important social relationships: those of father and child, husband and wife, mother and child, ruler and subject, world-renouncers and people who remain in the world. Above all, it validates the supreme religious significance of the sacrifice of possessions through acts of generosity" (1987, 181). Stanley Tambiah writes that, as part of an annual village festival, the recitation "combines merit-making with secular interests," suggesting, "In terms of the agricultural cycle it reflects two themes—thanksgiving and looking forward to the next cycle. Occurring as it does in the middle of the dry season, it looks forward to the onset of rains" (Tambiah 1970, 161). Stephen Sparkes describes its performance as an "attempt to induce rain" (2005, 177). Similarly, Howard Kaufman, writing of a village in central Thailand, notes the recitation's association with boats (*krathong*) that are offered to river spirits to ask for health and wealth for the coming year. In Kaufman's village the focus appears to be less on Vessantara and more on Phrayar Naga, the naga snake. Villagers believe Phrayar Naga resides at the bottom of the canal by the village and, following in the Buddha's footsteps, has succeeded in reaching Nirvana. The legend of Phrayar Naga is told together with the *Vessantara Jataka* story depicting "the king who gave away his rain-producing elephant and went into exile, thus causing the rains to cease" (Kaufman 1960, 195-96). After both stories are told, villagers go down to the canal to float their krathongs, praying to the "Goddess of the River, *Maekhongkha*, and the King of Snakes, *Phrajanag*," to bring them health and wealth—and a winning lottery ticket (Kaufman 1960, 196).

These anthropological accounts provide primarily utilitarian motivations for these village performances without indicating whether villagers interpreted the jataka as affirming either monks or monarchs. What were the attitudes of villagers toward the court and the ecclesiastical hierarchy? Why did villagers— women in particular—enjoy listening to recitations of the *Vessantara Jataka*? While I accept the sober scholarly emphases on the importance of the *Vessantara Jataka* for monarchs and monks, the question remains as to why the story was popular among the peasantry. To the extent that the story is being told in a Buddhist context, the argument that jataka supports monastic interests has weight. However, despite repeated mention of the link between the *Vessantara Jataka*, the *Phra Malai Sutra*, and millenarian political movements, scholars have been remarkably silent regarding the political message of the *Vessantara Jataka* as interpreted by the peasantry.

Reasons for Decline

Furthermore, whatever the reasons that the *Vessantara Jataka* appealed to monarchs, monks, and the masses in the past, why have those reasons changed such that interest in the story has diminished in the present? And why has it diminished differently across regions? The scholars, monks, and laity I talked to throughout Thailand proffered a variety of reasons for this declining interest. Louis Gabaude (1991) notes that both criticism and defense of the *Vessantara Jataka* have increased in the last few decades, at least among urban and university intellectuals. One obvious factor is the negative reactions of feminists, who have openly denounced the way Vessantara has been held up as a moral exemplar for giving away his wife and children (e.g., Kornvipa 1989; Khin 1980). Some monks I interviewed did not want to preach the story because they felt it was implausible. One monk specifically objected to the absurdity of a beggar being able to outsmart royal guards. A female store owner in a northeastern city said that the younger generation is interested in video games and movies rather than ancient folklore, adding that young people prefer shopping in malls to sitting around listening to monks preach.

The most frequent reason I heard for this shift in interest centered on the growth of science and rationalism in the face of mythology and folktales. As a man with a PhD in engineering who runs a computer software business in Bangkok suggested to me, the belief in rational science was overcoming silly superstition. Yet any casual visitor to Thailand can see that Thai urbanites as well as villagers engage in a wide variety of ritual practices that can easily be considered "superstitious," including such practices as making morning offerings to territorial spirits (*chaothii*), consulting with geomancers to lay out their business offices, buying magazines in malls about amulets, and visiting monks to obtain lottery numbers. In the United States, celebrations of Halloween witches, Santa Claus, and the Easter Bunny have not only not died out but appear to be steadily expanding. Griswold's observation regarding divergent tendencies in Buddhist scriptures could no less apply to modern acceptance of the *Vessantara Jataka*: "On one hand, the rationalist could accept as metaphor and parable the most fantastic inventions of the pious. . . . On the other hand the mystic could read transcendental meanings into the most prosaic records, while the superstitious could pick up a few words from the Scriptures, use them out of context, and turn them into spells" (1953, 9).

If the growth of scientific rationalism and urbanism is not in itself a compelling explanation for the declining interest in the *Vessantara Jataka*, other people I interviewed suggested more mundane logistical considerations. Several interviewees in the central region mentioned the difficulty of finding monks who knew how to recite the various chapters. Another person mentioned the expense involved: for example, one of the famous monks from Petchabun was paid 100,000 baht to travel to Suphanburi province to recite only one chapter in a *Vessantara Jataka* recitation. A monk noted that lay organizers play an important role, but nowadays many laity do not know how to organize a *Vessantara Jataka*. When I asked northern monks why the *Vessantara Jataka* had declined in their region but not in the northeast, they suggested that northern performances involved greater expense and greater expertise. I do not find the expense arguments compelling since northeastern celebrations also involve considerable time, effort, and expense. Although the issue of expertise is relevant, the northeast has developed a center for training monks. In both the northern and northeastern regions, many of the younger generation of monks cannot read their indigenous scripts. As in northern Thailand, villagers in northeastern Thailand have faced similar issues in the use of a regional dialect, the decline in the number of monks and novices at local temples, and the rise of secular education; but northeasterners have maintained a strong recitation tradition. The reasoning behind these logistical explanations is circular; if monks and laity found recitations to be important, they would continue to support them.

Patrick Jory provides the most detailed and thought-provoking explanation for the declining popularity of *Vessantara Jataka* recitations. Analyzing the jataka in terms of its importance for monarchs, Jory explains the story's decline as a result of political shifts in court attitudes during the reign of King Rama V (r. 1868-1910). The modern Chakri dynasty was founded by Rama I in 1782. Jory argues that the early Chakri kings, like their earlier premodern predecessors, found the *Vessantara Jataka* a useful bulwark of its political legitimacy and thus the *Vessantara Jataka* remained "one of the key texts expressing the political ideology of the Thai kingdom" and a "discourse of authority" (2002b, 38, 63). However, Jory suggests that during the reign of Rama V, "the process by which the Jatakas were displaced from their formerly central position in popular Buddhist teaching began" (2002a, 892).[27]

Four major reasons for this historical change in royal statecraft can be found in Jory's analysis. First, with the expansion of a more stable administrative bureaucracy the state no longer depended on oaths of allegiance and other such public rituals to govern. Second, given the growing presence of European observers, the nineteenth-century Thai court was increasingly embarrassed by the mythological content of Buddhist legends. In its defense of Buddhism against Christian missionizing, the court sought to emphasize the life of the historical Buddha over the jataka stories. Jory notes that King Rama V provided an introduction to a collection of thirty jatakas in 1904 in which the king drew upon the work of the British Pali scholar T. W. Rhys Davids to argue that the jatakas should be understood "as mere 'tales' (*nithan*), which, moreover, were 'pre-Buddhist' in origin" (Jory 2002a, 894). The overall objective of the king "was to remove the Jatakas from orthodox Buddhism.... No longer acceptable as stories of the Buddha's former lives, the Jatakas were now to be read either as parables with a moral, or for those with more scholarly interests, as folktales (*nithan boran*) containing a wealth of information about how ancient peoples of foreign countries lived" (Jory 2002a, 897). The king even flaunted the ancient prediction about the future of Buddhism, suggesting that the *Vessantara Jataka* was most likely to be the first to disappear rather than the last (Jory 1996, 100).

A third and related reason was the expansion of the Thammayut sect, itself a movement that foregrounded science and reason. The Thammayut sect was founded by King Mongkut (Rama IV), during his days as a monk. King Mongkut came to the throne in 1851. During his reign as king, the Thammayut order became increasingly influential. As Colonel Gerolamo Emilio Gerini explained, "Members of the Dhammayuttika-nikaya [Thammayut] or orthodox congregation . . . do not as a rule hold recitals of the Maha Chat or any other Jataka story, because they contend that such tales cannot have been uttered by the Buddha, but must be the work of commentators. Their chief argument is based on the fact that no allusion to events in former births is ever met with in the sacred texts which they regard as the pure world of the Great Teacher" ([1892] 1976, 26).

A fourth reason was active court suppression of jataka recitations in the face of a growing number of millenarian revolts at the turn of the twentieth century. Jory sees the *Vessantara Jataka* as a double-edged sword. While its political ideology supported the moral authority of rulers, its performance "also enabled local figures to take advantage of the same concepts of authority and thus threaten the control of the Bangkok kings" (Jory 2002b, 62). The ambiguity in the political discourse of the *Vessantara Jataka* made it possible not just for kings but also for local rulers, local monks, and other local leaders to lay claim to being incarnations of the future Buddha as well; such claims provided the justifications for revolts against the crown. Jory suggests that "up until the period of the Fifth Reign, the religious and cultural affairs of the rural hinterland had not seemed to be a major issue of concern for the Thai court" (Jory 2002a, 910). With the increase in the number of revolts in the countryside, the court would no longer have found the *Vessantara Jataka* an effective discourse of authority. However, in Jory's royalist reading, the jataka did not serve as a peasant critique of royal power but rather as a legitimation of competing claims to the throne.

Jory's explanation does much to provide a laudable sense of historical context to explain changes in the jataka's popularity; indeed, this book owes much to his serious engagement. However, Jory's analysis masks three complicating issues. First, Jory presumes a top-down flow of political opinion-formation without a full consideration of the perspective of the peasantry. Just because courts or local rulers sought to buttress their political legitimacy through ritual does not mean they succeeded. The occurrence of peasant revolts both before and during the early Chakri Dynasty suggests the possibility that political legitimacy was often, if not always, problematic. Thus, even before the expansion of the administrative bureaucracy, oaths of allegiance and other such public rituals were never sufficient to suppress public unrest. Second, as will become clear in the next chapter, the Chakri court does not appear to have opposed recitations of the *Vessantara Jataka* per se and indeed has continued to support public recitations even up to the present day.[28] Furthermore, oaths of allegiance and other state rituals continue to serve as an important form of modern statecraft (see Bowie 1997 for fuller discussion of state rituals and efficacy). Third, Jory's emphasis on efforts of the Bangkok court to suppress *Vessantara Jataka* recitations does not explain regional variation. While Jory has conducted pioneering and important work in the use of the *Vessantara Jataka* in Thai statecraft, we need to find a fuller explanation for its rise and variable demise.

Of Rabelais and Comedy

I believe that a closer re-reading of relevant court edicts suggests the court was concerned with *comic* recitations, a position that should not be conflated with court support for *serious* recitations. Already from the beginning of the Chakri Dynasty, evidence suggests that the court's interpretation of how the *Vessantara Jataka* should be performed differed markedly from the peasantry's. Court edicts themselves reveal both the widespread popularity of comic performances

Figure 3. Jujaka's funeral procession. Excerpt from temple scroll showing Jujaka, who evidently died happy. From Sisaket province, dated 1967. Photo courtesy of Thomas Kaiser, Völkerkundemuseum der Universität Zürich.

and the attendant royal condemnation that, as Jory himself notes, can be traced back to the very first of the monastic regulations issued by Rama I in 1782:

> At this time the entire populace of the kingdom is holding recitations of the Vessantara Jataka. However they do not respect the story as part of the Dhamma. They listen only to the *comical* poetry, which is of no benefit to them. Some of the monks who recite the story have not studied the Tipitaka. They know only the parts, which have been put into song-verse (*kap klorn*), which they then recite in a *comical and obscene* manner. They are interested only in fame and riches. They have never desired to study and pass on the knowledge of the Dhamma. This is damaging to the religion and encourages people to be careless in teaching the Dhamma. Such people will suffer long torment in the four hells....
>
> So as of this time the king orders that monks who give sermons and the people who listen to the recitation of the Maha Chat Jataka must recite and listen to only the Pali canonical verses and the Commentary.... The recitation of and listening to sermons in song-verse or the expression of *buffoonish* words for *comic* purposes is strictly forbidden. (Jory 2002b, 59, emphasis mine)

The king also notes that monks who preach using "comic and vulgar speech [*thoi kham talok kanorng yap cha*]" will not meet Maitreya in the future; they will only receive the full merit and meet Maitreya if they preach "the full Pali text and commentary" (Jory 1996, 38). The king's regulation was addressed to all royal officials and the monastic authorities "both in Bangkok and in the kingdom's First, Second, and Third-class cities of the Western, Eastern, Southern, and Northern regions of the kingdom, and 'everywhere'" (Jory 2002b, 59). Violators of the law, along with their relatives, were liable for punishment (Jory 2002b, 59). The king evidently objected not to recitations of the *Vessantara Jataka* but to comedic performances. Why? If the court condemned comedy, what was the politics behind their concern?

Rama IV similarly denounced "buffoonish recitations" of the *Vessantara Jataka* in his colorful decree in 1865. I quote it in some detail so that readers can contemplate the royal critique for themselves:

> It is the traditional custom of Siam . . . to hold recitals of the Maha Chat. . . . By so doing, the supporters of these exhibitions think to perform a meritorious work, and deem the money spent upon them, to be as a tribute of honour paid to religion.
>
> However, there is no lack of people who fail to see and believe that the practice of having such *farcical* shows can be really meritorious. Such ones

censure the practice, and question how merit can possibly be derived from *buffoonish* recitations of the Maha Chat and from the treasure and valuables squandered upon them.

Now, here is the story. One preaching hall had remained deserted for nearly a whole season, no recital of the Maha Chat having been held in it. A layman felt sorry for this, and started to go around from house to house asking the people to take up participation tickets. . . . At this juncture, a person belonging to the class of dissenters above spoken of, came forth and said: "How can merit accrue from holding *farcical* recitations of the Maha Chat? In my opinion the money collected for such a purpose could be better employed in buying fuel to burn dead dogs' carcasses with. No regret would be felt for money devoted to such a useful end, whilst the same cannot be said of money spent upon *buffoonish* exhibitions of the Maha Chat." (Gerini [1892] 1976, 57, emphasis mine)[29]

The king in this edict suggests that monies would be better spent "in honouring the members of the clergy who zealously observe the disciplinary rules of the order and are true upholders of the prestige of religion; or in paying a tribute of gratitude and veneration to one's parents and aged relatives and benefactors; or in assisting the poor and relieving invalids; or in making roads and footpaths, building bridges and hospices; or in any other philanthropic work." Rama IV goes on to suggest that monks involved in buffoonish exhibitions are parasites "seeking in holy orders a means of earning a livelihood." He continues, "Such parasites, as soon as they have received in alms enough candles studded with silver coins, forsake the religious life, take a wife, and become drunkards and gamblers." He concludes that such donations contribute to "demolishing true faith, and the practice must therefore be deplored." According to Gerini, the king's edict had some effect: "since that time the exposition of the Maha Chat in temple grounds and homely circles has become more dignified" ([1892] 1976, 25).

However, comedic performances continued over the course of the nineteenth century despite these royal edicts and opinions. In 1917 the supreme patriarch, Prince Vajiranana (Wachirayan), despite initial efforts at prohibition, assumed a more conciliatory stance "in which he recognised that a song-like *thamnorng* [rhythm] encouraged certain kinds of people to listen and to make merit, and that as long as the recitation was intelligible and the reciting monk maintained his monastic dignity, such preaching was acceptable" (Jory 1996, 39). Official objections to comic performances of the *Vessantara Jataka* continued well into the twentieth century, ironically suggesting their continuing popularity. Thus in 1937 the Ecclesiastical Council (Mahatherasamakhom) issued another regulation forbidding bawdiness "as well as comic behaviour which is damaging to monastic dignity" (Jory 1996, 40).

As evidenced in the multiple royal edicts seeking to suppress it, humor was clearly a major component in the popular appeal of the *Vessantara Jataka* throughout Thailand. We know from the sangha inspectors who traveled in the central regions in the early twentieth century that the jataka was "very popular among local people" (Kamala 1997, 30).[30] In 1886 Mary Cort highlighted the importance of humor, writing that the natives "choose priests who are good talkers and can tell stories to make the audience laugh" (1886, 117). Throughout the nineteenth century, when the court was trying to suppress comedic recitations of the *Vessantara Jataka*, the court itself was sponsoring its own state performances. Consequently I would suggest that the court took umbrage at the displays of humor but not at the jataka itself. However, the reasons for the court's objections to humor are unclear. In the eyes of King Mongkut, comedic recitations of the *Vessantara Jataka* made a "burlesque of the life of him whose career they were intended to honour" (Young 1898, 324). The later regulations suggest a concern for "monastic dignity"; however, earlier generations of monks had evidently considered the use of humor to teach the dharma as legitimate. What was so objectionable about comedy?

Scholars from Sigmund Freud and Henri Bergson to Mikhail Bakhtin and others have tried to analyze humor, but its roots remain elusive. Compounding the difficulties of analyzing humor cross-culturally is the problem that "many comic effects are incapable of translation from one language to another, because they refer to the customs and ideas of a particular social group" (Bergson [1911] 2005, 4).[31] Nonetheless, humor often lays bare the cleavages and faults in society, sometimes merely expressing shared frustrations and other times hopes for change. In Rabelaisian Europe, peasant humor mocked "the official and serious tone of medieval ecclesiastical and feudal culture" (Bakhtin [1965] 1984, 4; see also Thompson 1974). Such folk humor "makes no pretense to renunciation of the earthy" (Bakhtin [1965] 1984, 19). James Peacock's work on the *ludruk* performances in Indonesia provides an example of working-class humor occasioned by cross-class interactions (1987). Donna Goldstein (2003) provides insight into the absurdist and black humor used by women in Brazilian urban shantytowns in the face of trauma and tragedy, and Steve Lipman (1993) describes the use of humor during the Holocaust. Even in the face of death, "gallows" humor emerges. Similarly, James C. Scott has written of humor as a "hidden transcript" (1990). A long-standing literature on tricksters—from the coyote in the Navajo tales to Brer Rabbit in the African American slave community and the bawdy Uncle Tompa in Tibetan tales—reveals comic characters who dare to challenge the most powerful figures in society (Radin [1956] 1972; Dorje 1997; Brennan 2003, 73; Dembicki 2010). Indeed, there is a growing literature noting the role of humor in political brinkmanship (e.g., Feinberg 1971; Townsend 1992; Jenkins 1994; Sanders 1995; Boskin 1997; Hart and Bos 2007; Krikmann and Laineste 2009).

The recent translation of the once popular tale *Khun Chang Khun Phaen* by Chris Baker and Pasuk Phongphaichit (2010) serves to remind us that nineteenth-century Southeast Asian audiences enjoyed a bawdy sense of humor that puritanical audiences of today find shocking. The court may have sought to suppress the sexual and scatological elements in a religious ceremonial occasion in order to maintain respectability in the eyes of European dignitaries and puritanical American missionaries. If the nineteenth-century performances contained irreverent references to members of the court or the monastic order, the king's concern with humor may have been less about Victorian sexual respectability than it was about control over the monastic community and political security. Formal recitations in court settings may indeed have been intended to glorify divine kings, but popular performances may have mocked royal and ecclesiastical pretentiousness. In one of the few surviving nineteenth-century descriptions of humor, Ernest Young suggests that not only was popular humor bawdy, but it had an edginess that came from political critique. Describing the humor in *likay* performances, Young writes, "The buffoonery is excellent, but the language is nearly always coarse. Current events are burlesqued, and foreign residents with pronounced mannerisms get caricatured" ([1898] 1982, 170).

As various scholars have noted, villagers believed that by listening to the *Vessantara Jataka* they would improve their chances of being reborn in the time of the Maitreya Buddha, a time of social justice and compassion for all. Grounded in his royalist reading, Jory sees the jataka as providing legitimacy for rulers, be they actual or aspiring. But read as an anti-authoritarian performance associated with millenarianism, the *Vessantara Jataka* is less a means for local leaders to portray themselves before the masses as incarnations of Vessantara than it is a comic expression of peasant frustration against administrative abuses of power. The *Phra Malai Sutra*, which was often read before *Vessantara Jataka* recitations, has passages that served as humorous critiques of those in power. For example, corrupt or unjust rulers were reborn "with huge decayed, foul-smelling testicles that hang down to the ground" (Kamala 2003, 305).[32] Similarly, a corrupt government official was reborn as a hungry ghost: "He had testicles that were as huge as water jugs. They hung way down to the ground like a shoulder bag. Rotten and putrid, bloated, and stinking, they were like slimy snails. Whenever he wanted to go somewhere [the hungry ghost would] fling his testicles over his shoulder, stagger under their weight, and reel from side to side. Whenever he wanted to sit down, they'd get pinched between his legs, and he'd have to stand up, and then sit down on top of them" (Kamala 2003, 306).

The *Traiphum* has similar colorful passages suggestive of peasant political critiques and the hopes for future retribution. In its descriptions of the hells awaiting those who commit wrongdoings, the very first hell listed is the Vetarani hell for the rich, who possess "property and men and slaves" because they "harmed others and took their property by force." The description is lengthy, but a brief excerpt provides an overview:

> The guardians in the Vetarani hell have clubs, large knives, lances, swords, spears, and all kinds of weapons for killing, stabbing, shooting and beating, all of which are made of fiery red iron, have flames that shoot upward like a fire in the sky, and blaze without ceasing. The yama guardians hold these throwing and stabbing weapons; they chase the hell beings, throw at them, stab them, and beat them with these weapons. These beings suffer great pain and anguish that is too much for them to bear.
>
> In this hell there is a large river called Vetarani in which the water is extremely salty. When the hell beings flee and try to escape, the river has in it a tangle of intertwining rattan stems and vines. The rattan has thorns as huge as hoes that are formed of fiery red iron and are constantly aflame. When the hell beings flee into the water they come against the thorns of the rattan, and their bodies are cut to pieces just as if someone was taking a very sharp knife and cutting them everywhere. Under the rattan vine are huge, long spikes made of red fiery iron. The flames burn the bodies of the hell beings like the fire burns trees in the middle of the forest. . . . They suffer great anguish. (Reynolds and Reynolds 1982, 71–73)

There is a similar hell for "those who are ordered by a ruler to collect taxes from his subjects, but collect more than is prescribed"; they are reborn as hell beings who "live in a large river full of feces with a terrible smell. . . . At a certain point, not being able to restrain themselves any longer, they take the feces for food and drink, and do so every day" (Reynolds and Reynolds 1982, 77). While the vivid descriptions of hell presented in the *Traiphum* appear to be intended to impress its readers with their horror, one can also imagine how they might be integrated into comic routines.

Similarly echoing such anti-authoritarian interpretations in the present, Phra Thepwethi (also called Prayut Payuttho, Ratchaworamuni) observes that the jatakas mention instances of people demonstrating against an unjust ruler. This monk suggests that if a monarch causes difficulties for his subjects and fails to uphold the ethical principles appropriate for a king (the *dasarajadhamma*), the jataka stories invite the people to rise up and protest, forcing the monarch to reconsider his actions and edicts. Thepwethi maintains that these references can be regarded as "an origin of the contemporary idea of demonstrating. . . . This is the Buddhist system of government" (Jackson 1993, 90; see also Aung San Suu Kyi 1991). Incidents in the *Vessantara Jataka* such as Vessantara's gift of the magical rain-making elephant to representatives from the neighboring drought-stricken kingdom can be seen as examples of his generosity to the disadvantaged masses. Vessantara's father's decision to expel Vessantara from his kingdom can be portrayed as the result of bad political advisers in his court who had no sympathy for the plight of the poor—or as the result of an ignorant populace. Thepwethi's interpretation inverts the pro-royalist reading of Sombat.

Understanding the politics of humor is an underexplored avenue into history. The fact of royal and monastic efforts to suppress this humor raises the possibility that the court and monastic orders were themselves the comedic targets. Any of the jataka characters could have conceivably been turned into comedic foils. Even the tragic figure of Matsi can occasion a humorous moment, as when the monk stops his wailing to ask his audience for money for Matsi's coffin since she appears on the verge of death. In another example that might seem heretical today, Vessantara himself might have been made a target. Mary Grow, in her analysis of Thai dance drama, describes comic routines in which the monarch, sporting the headdress of a checkered snake, plays with the Thai term "*chao lok*." As Grow explains, "*chao lok* means 'ruler of the world,' yet in slang it is a euphemism for the phallus." The pun thereby "[exposes] the hidden passions and illicit behavior of a seemingly flawless ruler" (1996, 48).[33] Perhaps the entire *Vessantara Jataka* was performed as a comedy in which the supergenerous Vessantara was contrasted with the super-grasping Jujaka, and each character is exaggerated to provoke a discussion of the Buddhist middle path of moderation. Although we must allow the possibility that comedic traditions developed differently across the Theravada Buddhist regions, evidence based on the northern Thai performances suggests that the humor was centered not on the revered Vessantara but primarily on the irreverent figure of Jujaka. The survival of the northern portrayal of Jujaka provides a window into the humor among the peasants of the nineteenth century, and in turn it raises the question of why the comedic tradition continued to be robust in the northern region but not in the other regions.

Overview of This Book

This book is a travelogue of my journey in search of Jujaka, as he in turn searched for Vessantara. The serendipity of a newspaper headline back in 2004 led me on unanticipated trips through the central, northeastern, and northern regions of Thailand. By paying attention to Jujaka, I reconstruct a comedic, peasant-based reading of the *Vessantara Jataka* to add to the sober monastic and monarchical readings already extant. By embedding the text in its historical context, my reading revives the story of the tensions between monks, monarchs, and the masses and transforms the *Vessantara Jataka* from an essentialized homogeneous text into a cudgel brandished by rich and poor in their struggles to shape society, at both the village and national levels. Understanding the historical processes that molded the interpretations and performances of the *Vessantara Jataka* helps to provide an explanation of its regional divergences in Thailand. Thus the politics of humor is an important element in understanding both the vicissitudes of Thai society and the *Vessantara Jataka*.

My approach is interdisciplinary, combining my long-standing interest in history and political anthropology with research in folklore and religious studies. Since my first trip in 1974, I have lived in Thailand for a total of some eight years. Most of my time has been spent in villages in northern Thailand, but I also lived in Bangkok for two years and spent nearly a year in Khon Kaen in northeastern Thailand in 1996–97 as a Fulbright Scholar. These earlier stays have enabled me to develop a wide network of friendships to draw upon for this research. After preliminary interviews with current and former tujok in the summer of 2004, I conducted further interviews in northern Thailand in the summer of 2005. I spent the summer of 2009 interviewing monks and villagers in northeastern and central regions; I conducted more interviews in March 2010, and again in the summers of 2011 and 2013–15. I also collected vernacular recensions, tapes, and VCD recordings of recitations. Thus this book draws on primary interviews, archival sources, DVD/VCD recordings, photographic collections, websites, vernacular textual studies, and secondary sources as well as in-person observations of *Vessantara Jataka* performances in northern, northeastern, and central Thailand. All quotations from Thai printed materials, tapes, performances, and interviews are my translations.

I divide this book into two main parts. Part I, divided into three chapters, focuses on regional variation in the performances and interpretations of the *Vessantara Jataka* in the central, northeastern, and northern regions, respectively. Chapter 1 focuses on the central Thai court and the central region. I argue that the court supported jataka recitations in state rituals but defeated humor by authoring texts that portrayed Jujaka as terrifying. By foregrounding the boat imagery of the Kumarn chapter, the jataka became more aligned with the political and metaphysical emphases of the Thammayut movement. The court met with some success in implementing its interpretation in the central region. In chapter 2 I turn to northeastern Thailand, where villagers have maintained their tradition of annual recitations, albeit in a subdued form in which humor has been largely diverted. The northeastern emphasis on the Nakornkan chapter, family reunification, and village unity embeds a very ambiguous attitude toward the state, reflecting a de facto detente established between the villagers and the state. In chapter 3, I describe the northern interpretation, highlighting both its focus on the Jujaka chapter and its broader delights in the exploits of the Jujaka character. Rather than glorifying royalty, the northern emphasis on Jujaka enables monks to address the earthly, non-royalist challenges facing villagers in everyday life.

In part II, also divided into three chapters, I describe the historico-political process by which each region came to develop a different interpretation of the *Vessantara Jataka*, and I bring our understanding of the jataka up to the present. Because comedic performances of the *Vessantara Jataka* endured in their most robust form in northern Thailand, we are able to gain insight into the broader peasant imaginaire of the nineteenth century.[34] In chapter 4 I argue that in the northern imagination, the comedic Jujaka was understood as a trickster whose exploits provided opportunities for not only instruction in morality but also critiques of earthly kings. Once performances of the *Vessantara Jataka* are interpreted as anti-authoritarian critiques embedded in a historical context of millenarian revolts, the court's desire to suppress comedic recitations becomes understandable, not merely as deference to bourgeois morality but also as a means of addressing threats to its political security.

However, the court was positioned quite differently in each of the three regions. The Bangkok court was able to exert its influence in central and northeastern Thailand much earlier than in the northern region. Because performances of the *Vessantara Jataka* were primarily in the hands of monks, the court sought to gain control over the monastic order. Chapter 5 outlines the expansion of the court's control in the central, northeastern, and northern regions, showing how understanding the differences in this expansion helps to explain not only the differences in humor but also the differential decline of performances in each region over the course of the twentieth century. In chapter 6 I summarize the ongoing transformations in *Vessantara Jataka* performances, describing its new relevance for the promotion of wealth, tourism, and cultural heritage. In evaluating the jataka's future transformation, I will return to the feminist concerns that initially prompted my explorations and suggest that the jataka has a wide range of possible conservative and progressive interpretations. If understanding the politics of humor reveals a historical intersection of the agency of kings, monks, and peasants, the jataka's future may well depend on its interpretation by the modern generation of women.

As we pack our bags to embark on this journey through space and time, let me review some preliminary assumptions. First, given that the sources currently available allow us to travel back in time little more than a century, I am basing my assumption that comedic recitations were widespread by the early nineteenth century on the following: common sense, the passing remarks of late seventeenth-century European visitors to Ayutthaya, nineteenth-century court edicts, and the few surviving bawdy temple mural paintings. Furthermore, I am assuming that the Jujaka character is the primary focus of this humor.

Second, I regret that our journey does not include the south. The reasons for this omission are a lack of sufficient information in existing secondary sources and my own lack of any particular expertise in the south. However, if I were to venture some preliminary guesses, I would anticipate more similarities with the central region than either the north or the northeast. The first sangharaja of the central Thai court in Thonburi was a monk from the southern province of Nakhon Sithammarat; the Thonburi edition of the *Tripitaka* (the Theravada Buddhist canon) was copied from the texts from Nakhon Sithammarat; King Rama III's mother was from a southern Muslim noble family; and the recitation of the jataka in Nakhon Sithammarat is today a major tourist event held during Buddhist Lent on Wan Sart, as is common in the central region.[35]

Third, the *Vessantara Jataka* has many tellings in a range of media, from postal stamps to mural paintings, from illuminated manuscripts to school textbooks and children's cartoons,[36] from versions that are read silently to versions that are performed for listening audiences, from versions told by grandparents in the privacy of homes to mass public recitations in temples, from versions performed by monks to versions performed by theater puppets, from versions performed with live audiences to versions recorded on DVDs and sold globally. In all three regions, monks recite two versions of the jataka, one in Pali (called the *Khathaphan*) and one in vernacular Thai, the dialect varying with the region. This book focuses on regional variation in the vernacular tellings in which monks "read" the jataka, some chanting the words written on the page, some chanting from memory, some following the words, some abridging the story, and some expanding upon it.

Finally, a brief note is in order on my methodology with regard to textual recensions and performances. I can best describe my method as "pointillism," an approach in painting of placing dots of color on a canvas. These dots seem random when viewed up close but form recognizable patterns when seen from a distance. There is no "authentic" jataka text or performance. Even the same performer never fully replicates a previous interpretation. Indeed, as Justin McDaniel notes, "monks have not felt obliged to accurately relate a story handed down from the Pali canon and commentaries. Instead, their story changes with each retelling" (2008, 129). Yet when various texts and renditions of them are compared in each of the three regions we will visit, overall patterns emerge. In developing my portrayal of overall regional patterns, I am drawing not only on sample textual recensions but also on scores of interviews with monks and villagers in each of these areas. For each region I draw on a primary text to illustrate more generalizable patterns: in the central region that primary text is the "court" version; in the northeast the primary text is my translation of recorded excerpts of a recitation I attended; and in the north I draw on my translation of tapes recorded by the north's most famous tujok, Luang Poh Bunthong.

We are now ready to begin our journey into history.

Part I

Diversity in Humor

1

Central Thailand
Humor Defeated

This part of the book begins in central Thailand, where glimpses of Jujaka and his comedy are fleeting, disappearing behind the bedazzling glamour of royal recitations of the *Vessantara Jataka* at formal state functions. The jataka was once very widely popular in the region. Late seventeenth-century European visitors to Ayutthaya note "how far the People are infatuated with such Fables," including the story in which the Buddha "even gave his Wife to a poor Man that begged an Alms" (Tachard [1688] 1981, 291–92; see also Gervaise [1688] 1989, 129, 140–41). Its popularity continued well after the court was re-established in Bangkok. Writing in the late nineteenth century, Gerini notes that it is "not uncommon to see a rush of people at some temple of the Mahanikaya congregation in order to attend the premier of some one of such productions" ([1892] 1976, 25). Gerini, although disdainful of the "unscrupulous" theatrics deployed, provides a rare description of the "sorts of tricks calculated to excite laughter in the multitude":

> The blaring of trumpets, the ringing of bells, the whistling of birds in the recesses of the Himavanta forest, the noises of a storm and the pealing of thunder were imitated almost to perfection and given after each Pali distich with a flourishing of many whimsical adjuncts, to relieve the monotony of the entertainment. This then took more the character of a *pochade* of Christmas mummers than of a solemn religious ceremony. The sole object was to obtain effect, for as soon as the new literary production met with public approval its author and expounder became famous and the exhibition in general request. ([1892] 1976, 25)

Ernest Young also provides a scornful description of popular recitations, viewing them as having "degenerated" into theatrical performances "accompanied by pantomime and song." Nonetheless, his description provides some sense of the excitement and creativity these performances generated, as he explains that "new versions were given; the rhythm of the original poem was altered; and temple vied with temple, and house with house, in the introduction of novelties that would attract large audiences" ([1898] 1982, 324).

Much has changed over the course of the twentieth century. Central Thai audiences today hold their hands in the formal *wai* position of respect as they listen to the sacred recitations; their expressions are solemn, meditative, and emotionless. At a public recitation I observed at Wat Samien Nari in Bangkok in the summer of 2013, the temple committee had even invited the central Thai monk who was famous for his performance of Jujaka. With the exception of inattentive school children who were giggling at each other's jokes and oblivious to the monk, the audience was not laughing. The audience I observed at another recitation at Siriraj Hospital was similarly solemn. The expectation that a performance of the *Vessantara Jataka* be enjoyable has clearly faded among modern central Thai audiences. This chapter will argue that despite scholars' suggestions that the court opposed jataka performances, the Thai court has in fact played an important role in promoting formal recitations while successfully defeating humor. Thus the decline in the jataka's popularity is better explained by the lack of humor in the now dominant courtly textual version and the aftermath of the transition from absolute to constitutional monarchy in 1932.

This chapter is divided into four sections. The first section presents evidence showing significant court involvement in recitations from the founding of the Bangkok dynasty in 1782 to the present. The second section notes the important role of members of the royal family in shaping a stately, sober interpretation of the jataka. By downplaying the Jujaka chapter and foregrounding maritime imagery in the Kumarn chapter, the court provided a more metaphysical interpretation of the jataka, portraying it as a boat to cross the sea of suffering. These two sections rely heavily on the account of Colonel Gerolamo Emilio Gerini, an Italian who spent twenty-five years in Bangkok (1881–1906) and whose account I consider particularly reliable since it was proofread by none other than King Rama V himself.

The third section describes recitations and interpretations in central Thailand, highlighting their overall similarities with those of the court in Bangkok. The concluding section notes the decline in the overall popularity of *Vessantara Jataka* recitations in the central region, attributing this decline both to royal

Central Thailand • 41

Figure 4. Jataka performance in honor of the birthdays of the Thai king and queen. The monk recites a chapter in a forest setting, surrounded by mounds of coconuts, banana stalks, lily pads, money trees, and pyramidal offerings made from flower blossoms. Siriraj Hospital, Bangkok, July 20–22, 2011. Photo by author.

success in eradicating humor and the weakened position of the aristocracy following the revolution of 1932. This chapter shows how the Bangkok court succeeded in damping down the laughter Jujaka might have elicited, but for the reasons why it objected to this humor we will have to track Jujaka into other regions in subsequent chapters.

Royal State Performances

Although some have argued that court support for the *Vessantara Jataka* ended by the late nineteenth century, this section will show that court support for formal recitations has been maintained into the present. State recitations at the royal temple of Wat Phra Kaew continue to this day, and a state-supported recitation also occurs at Phutthamonthon, a national Buddhist park located west of Bangkok. The court was also involved in public recitations at Wat Phra

Kaew and in chapter recitations by novices; these recitations continued well into the twentieth century but appeared to have declined after 1932 with the transition from an absolute to a constitutional monarchy.

Wat Phra Kaew (Emerald Buddha Temple)

The importance of the *Vessantara Jataka* in statecraft is made clear by the maintenance of the long-standing tradition of its triannual recitation at the royal court temple. The court temple of the modern Thai kingdom is Wat Phra Kaew, the popular tourist destination located in the compound of the Grand Palace in Bangkok. This royal temple has long been the site for the most important state rituals for the Bangkok court. Today, an excerpt of the jataka is recited three times *during* Buddhist Lent each year at Wat Phra Kaew, notably by lay officials and *not* by monks.[1] The three occasions are the beginning of Buddhist Lent, the middle of Lent (*wan sart*), and at the end of Lent (*wan ohk phansaa*) (Gerini [1892] 1976, 23).[2] I would suggest that the association of the *Vessantara Jataka* recitation with the Emerald Buddha is the result of the convergence of two earlier traditions: (1) the tradition of the recitation of the *Vessantara Jataka* at the royal court temple of Ayutthaya and (2) the tradition of its recitation for the Emerald Buddha.

State recitations can be dated at least as far back as the Ayutthayan court. According to Gerini, King Songtham, a former monk and accomplished poet who ruled Ayutthaya from 1611 to 1628, wrote a version of the *Vessantara Jataka* designed for *thamnong suat*, or chanting style (*Mahachat Khamluang*). Thereafter court lay officials chanted his version at the royal court temple at Wat Sri Sanphet in Ayutthaya. When the court was moved to Bangkok, court officials and pupils of royal schools recited this version at both Wat Phra Kaew and Wat Sri Sanphet every holy day. However, during the reign of Rama V, the recitations were reduced to three (Gerini [1892] 1976, 23-25). According to Khun Somchai Kuakoon, who is himself one of the lay specialists (*kharawaat*) involved in chanting, most of the Ayutthayan text was lost when the city was sacked, and only eight sections of the Mahaphon chapter survived. Consequently at Wat Phra Kaew today, only the surviving eight sections of the Mahaphon chapter of the *Vessantara Jataka* are recited.[3]

Today the recitation is entwined with the worship of the Emerald Buddha. Considered the palladium of the modern Thai kingdom, the Emerald Buddha was captured from Vientiane, Laos, in 1778 by the future Rama I and brought to Thonburi, where it was initially enshrined in the palace temple of King Taksin.[4] After Rama I took the throne in 1782, he moved the court from Thonburi to Bangkok, located on the opposite side of the Chao Phraya River.

He then had the Emerald Buddha relocated and enshrined at Wat Phra Kaew in the compound of the Grand Palace in Bangkok in 1784. Obviously recitations for the Emerald Buddha would not have occurred in the Ayutthayan kingdoms since these kings never possessed the image. Although the *Vessantara Jataka* was likely recited at the Hor Phra Kaew temple in Vientiane, the recitation in Laos may have occurred during Bun Pha Wet, the usual timing for *Vessantara Jataka* recitations in Laos. Following a lunar calendar, Bun Pha Wet usually occurs around March, whereas Buddhist Lent generally falls in July–October. Consequently it appears the modern practice of reciting the *Vessantara Jataka* during the rainy season at Wat Phra Kaew in Bangkok is an amalgam of the Ayutthayan practice of reciting the jataka at the most sacred royal temple and reverence for the Emerald Buddha itself.

The ceremonies for the changing of the Emerald Buddha's robes follow a different schedule from the ceremonies for chanting the *Vessantara Jataka*. Initially there were only two seasonal costumes; these were made for the Emerald Buddha by King Rama I—one for the summer season and one for the rainy season. King Rama III (r. 1824–51) had a third costume made for the cold season.[5] The ceremonial changing of the robes today takes place three times a year, at the beginning of each season: the rainy season, the cold season, and the hot season. The chanting of the *Vessantara Jataka* only coincides with the changing of the robes for the beginning of the rainy season; it is not chanted on the occasion of the other two robe changes. Although the king (and now the crown prince) performs the robe-changing ceremony, the king is only present for the first of the three occasions during the rainy season when the excerpt from the *Vessantara Jataka* is chanted (see also Wells 1939, 93). In the past, court officials organized the jataka recitation at Wat Phra Kaew, but this role has now been turned over to the Religious Affairs Department (Krom Kaan Saasanaa). On the days when the king or his representative comes, the lay reciters begin chanting in the morning so some of it has already been completed by the time the king arrives. On those days, the chanters wear white *jongkraben*-style pants and white dress jackets with white cloths across their chests. On days when the king is not in attendance, they wear simpler white pants and shirts. Chanting the excerpt today takes less than two hours.

Public State Recitations

In addition to the triannual formal chanting of an excerpt during Buddhist Lent by lay officials, a second tradition appears to have developed at Wat Phra Kaew over the course of the second half of the nineteenth century—namely, a public recitation by monks of the full thirteen chapters. These recitations were held during the rainy season, toward the end of Lent. I stumbled upon this now defunct annual monastic recitation by accident. In my search for people to interview about *Vessantara Jataka* recitations at Wat Phra Kaew, I had gone to the Grand Palace inquiring about who might be knowledgeable about "*thet Mahachat.*" Because I had read about annual *Vessantara Jataka* recitations for the changing of the Emerald Buddha's robes, I was quite surprised when I was repeatedly told by staff that annual recitations are no longer held and indeed had ended "decades ago." I was finally given the name of a former staff person, an elderly man who had worked there since 1937. He insisted that the recitation of the *Vessantara Jataka* had not been held annually or in association with the changing of the robes for as long as he could remember.[6] However, I later learned that the main organizer of the recitations at Wat Phra Kaew was the lay leader (*makhathayok*, also called *huanaa nakthaet*) of Wat Prayoon (or Wat Prayurawongsawat).[7] I wondered why Wat Prayoon came to play such an important organizational role. Wat Phra Kaew is not a temple with monks, so of course any monastic recitation would involve monks from elsewhere. Wat Prayoon was built in 1828 by the powerful Minister in charge of the Royal Treasury, Foreign Affairs and Defense, Somdet Chaophraya Borom Maha Prayurawong (Dit Bunnag, also known as Somdet Ong Yai). In 1832 the monastery was declared a royal monastery by King Rama III under the name of Wat Prayurawongsawat. (Wat Prayoon is its shortened form.) Prayurawong played a very important role in Prince Mongkut's ascension to the throne as the King Rama IV. Prayurawong died in 1856 at the age of sixty-eight. Of his forty-seven children, many held positions of high rank.[8] Since Wat Prayoon only became a royal temple in 1832, it is unlikely it was involved in organizing annual monastic recitations at Wat Phra Kaew before then (although the court itself may have organized such performances directly). Recitations may have begun during the reigns of Rama IV or Rama V, since this period marked the height of the Bunnag family's power. It is possible the recitations began during the period when Rama V took the throne as a young boy and when Chao Sri Suriyawongse, Prayurawong's son, was serving as regent, perhaps as a way to provide stability in this transition period.

These recitations appear to have ended by the 1930s. When I asked Phra Rajathammawaathii, a senior monk at Wat Prayoon, why the recitations had ended, he said that when the main lay organizer at his temple died, no one else was able to continue organizing the recitations. Clearly this explanation is insufficient; other lay organizers could have been found. I suspect that the demise of annual monastic recitations at Wat Phra Kaew is correlated with the economic pressures on the court budget during the 1920s and intensified by the

Great Depression of 1929–30, as well as political pressures following the People's Coup of 1932. For both economic and political reasons, the new government likely wanted to curtail this quasi-royalist recitation.

Special State Occasions

In addition to the triannual lay recitation and annual monastic recitations at Wat Phra Kaew, the court sponsored particularly lavish recitations on special state occasions. One such occasion was the founding of the new capital in Bangkok in 1782. Given that Rama I's predecessor, King Taksin, was deposed, one can imagine a political period of uncertainty. The 1782 recitation was on a grand scale, drawing explicit comparisons to the "Gift of the Seven Hundreds" and the dramatic almsgiving of the Ayutthayan king Prasat Thong in 1639. The "Gift of the Seven Hundreds" is a reference to the Thanakan chapter in which Vessantara offers seven hundred elephants, horses, chariots, beautiful women, well-trained slaves of both sexes, cows and bulls (Cone and Gombrich 1977, 24). The year 1639 marked the millennial anniversary of the Chulasakarat calendar, which began in 638 CE.[9] Faced with dire prophecies predicting the "end of the ages" and questions about his legitimacy, the Ayutthayan king performed a symbolic version of Vessantara's offering by giving one hundred items from each of seven categories: elephants, ponies, carts, male slaves, female slaves, gold and silver catties (Gerini [1892] 1976, 33; Baker et al. 2005, 156–57, 243–44). Rama I gave on a lesser scale than King Prasat Thong, but the amount was nonetheless apparently impressive. In addition, the king and his relatives showered the assembled crowds with limes containing "lottery tickets, consisting of slips of palm leaf inscribed with the name of the donor or donors and the designation of the articles, either in nature or correspondent value in cash, to which the recipient of the tickets is entitled" (Gerini [1892] 1976, 33). Given the circumstances of Rama I's succession to the throne, one can easily see the grand distribution of gifts not only as part of an effort in merit-making but also in establishing the new court's political legitimacy.

Special state recitations also took place in 1805 and 1807. Gerini does not explain the circumstances prompting these recitations, but he provides details of the 1807 recitation and notes that it surpassed the 1805 ceremony. The recitation began on November 7 and lasted two days. It took place in the Grand Palace, with three senior priests each reciting one-third of the Pali *Khathaphan*.[10] The king attended, together with "the royal family, the court and ministers of the realm, the wise men (*kravijati*), the purohitas of the royal household and the astrologers." The throne hall was "gaily decked with conical umbrellas, flowers of the most brilliant hues and sweet fragrance; gorgeous lustres and candleabra, giving it a highly picturesque appearance." The raised platform where the monks sat was also decorated with flowers and "the golden and silver trees of tribute sent by the Malayan, Cambodian and Laosian States recognizing the suzerainty of the King of Siam" (Gerini [1892] 1976, 37).

Although the decorations and the performance inside the throne hall would only have been witnessed by participants inside the court, the spectacular offerings would have been visible to the broader public. On the first day, as each monk completed his reading, the king presented him with "a set of robes and priestly requisites, besides a quantity of sweetmeats, fruits and other presents." Each monk was then "escorted with great pomp to the barge designed for him." The gifts were loaded into one of three canopied royal barges "decked with innumerable hanging lamps, gay makara flags (Chinese dragon standards), which was moored at the royal landing, each waiting to convey in turn one of the three officiating high-priests to their monasteries." Each senior monk was then accompanied "by a large retinue of other boats to the temple, where the offerings were taken out of the barge and carried to his cell" (Gerini [1892] 1976, 37).

On the second day, the gifts were no less extravagant. On this day, the thirteen chapters were recited in Thai. The supreme patriarch (*sangharaja*) who resided at Wat Mahathat recited the first chapter, and Phra Phanarat of Wat Pho recited the final chapter (Gerini [1892] 1976, 36). Different members of the royal family assumed responsibility for preparing the *krajaats*, or offering baskets, for each of the thirteen monks.[11] The king's eldest son supplied the offerings for the first and last chapters, the king's second son provided the gifts for the second chapter, and other princes and princesses provided gifts for the remaining chapters (Gerini [1892] 1976, 37, 63).[12] In addition to the krajaat, the king gave the monks gifts that included bedsteads, large brass bowls, boats, palanquins, sedan chairs, covered howdahs, and uncovered elephant seats replete with mahouts, as well as money and clothing for each of the thirteen chapters. As each monk completed his chapter, "the musical band consisting both of string and brass instruments, Malay drums, sankha shells, etc., struck up a lively strain" (Gerini [1892] 1976, 37). They were then escorted in a grand royal procession, either in palanquins or in boats, back to their temples.[13]

The thirteen krajaat baskets were gigantic. Each krajaat was a pyramidal structure comprised of five or seven layers, thirty-three feet wide at the bottom and as much as forty-seven feet in height. At the base were wicker baskets "with dry food, boiled rice and sweetmeats prepared in the best style." Around the upper edge were monks' robes folded up in white cloth "in the shape of conical umbrellas, sprays, twigs and flowers," or displayed so as to represent flags and banners. Eight companies of body guards (*tamruat*) and government serfs (*phrailuang*) had erected sheds to protect the krajaat from the sun and rain. One of the krajaats, prepared by a prominent palace lady, included "a slave youth still wearing the top-knot, who was to be presented as a servant to the priests" (Gerini [1892] 1976, 37).

According to Gerini, the enormous krajaat were "the prominent feature of the festival." He describes the reaction of the public as follows: "The people assembled in large crowds to see the krachats [krajaat]; all beholders were raising up their joined hands in act of praise and admiration, exclaiming sadhu, sadhu (well done! hurrah!) and rejoicing in their hearts at the sight of the great act of merit accomplished by the king. The elders, who had in their childhood witnessed similar exhibitions at Ayuthia, said they never beheld krachats of so sumptuous and imposing a character" (Gerini [1892] 1976, 37).

As Gerini himself writes, his account "gives an idea as to what high importance the recitation of the Maha Jati [Mahachat] acquires in Siam when it becomes a State ceremony" ([1892] 1976, 37). Writing at the end of the nineteenth century, Gerini remarks that even though the Thet Mahachat ceremony was "not so general and popular as in the days of yore," it was still held annually, the temples were still gaily decorated with five varieties of nymphoea flowers, and it "[ranked] among the important religious performances to be witnessed in the country" ([1892] 1976, 34). King Rama III included in his coronation ritual an imitation of Vessantara's act of giving away his son (Nidhi [1982] 2005, 200). Another grand recitation took place in 1882, on the occasion of the one hundredth anniversary of the founding of Bangkok.[14] In addition to these ostentatious state occasions, the aristocracy supported recitations at the various royal temples throughout Bangkok and in other towns in the central region.

Thus evidence indicates that recitations of the *Vessantara Jataka* have remained an important element of royal statecraft. The practice of court representatives chanting an excerpt at Wat Phra Kaew continues to the present. Although less lavish than in the nineteenth century, royally sponsored recitations have been re-established at Phutthamonthon, a government park opened in 1955 in celebration of the 2,500th year of the Buddhist Era. According to a senior staff member there, recitations of the *Vessantara Jataka* began there in about 1990 and are held during Buddhist Lent.[15] In 1991 the jataka was recited in honor of Crown Princess Sirindhorn and in 1992 in honor of Queen Sirikit's sixtieth birthday (Jory 1996, 5n22). Members of the royal family, notably Princess Sirindhorn, continue to host chapters. Thus in 1995 the princess hosted the Matsi chapter in memory of her grandmother. In 2005 she hosted the Maharaat chapter in honor of her fiftieth birthday. In 2006 she sponsored the Maharaat chapter in honor of the king's sixtieth anniversary on the throne. In other years she has sponsored chapters in honor of her father's and mother's birthdays, supporting recitations of Nakornkan, Kumarn, and Chohkasat. Recently Princess Chulabhorn came, hosting the Jujaka chapter. Different government agencies work with the National Ecclesiastical Council (Mahatherasamakhom) to organize these major state recitations.

Novice Recitations

Further evidence of royal support of the *Vessantara Jataka* is exemplified through novice recitations. Unique to the central region, these ceremonies feature novices who returned to their parents' homes to recite a single chapter from the *Vessantara Jataka*.[16] The timing "for this simple but impressive ceremony" was typically in October or November, just after Buddhist Lent. The ceremonial reading "was performed with great pomp in every household in past generations" and would "[confer] pleasure on [the] parents" (Gerini [1892] 1976, 34–35). The logic underlying the custom, Gerini suggests quite plausibly, "seems to owe its origin to Buddha having pronounced the Vessantara jataka in the midst of an assembly of his relatives and friends." He continues, "This is the reason the Vessantara jataka and *no other* is selected for the novice to rehearse on such occasions" ([1892] 1976, 34; see also Young [1898] 1982, 336–37).

Although novice recitations were once widespread, they survived the longest among royalty and other elite families. As Gerini observes in 1892, "this custom, which up to forty or fifty years ago was quite general and strictly adhered to by every family whether rich or poor, has gradually declined, and nowadays its observance is limited to a few of the noblest and wealthiest families of the realm" ([1892] 1976, 34). Similarly, Ernest Young, writing in 1898, remarks: "With the exception of the public state recital of the poem, it is now only recited in connection with the novitiate of the eldest sons of rich parents. The poor no longer ask their friends to visit their houses to listen to the thousand stanzas. . . . The honour of thus repeating the old story belongs now to the eldest son, except in the case of children of royal birth, for each of whom a public recital is held" ([1898] 1982, 336–37; see also Fournereau [1894] 1998, 123; Lyons 1960, 168).[17]

The novice normally recited only one or two chapters (*kan*) (Gerini [1892] 1976, 34). According to Phya Anuman Rajadhon, "There is a certain kan or part of its story which has a popular and favourite melody and one which the father of the novice wishes his son to learn and recite. When he has mastered the kan with its melody, he is invited to give a recitation of that kan at his parents' house. It is a great day for there is gathering of the family, also of friends and neighbours to hear the recitation" (1988, 193). According to Young, the novice may recite even less: "As the novice has not had time to learn the whole poem, he only delivers the first few lines, the rest being repeated by monks of longer standing, who have it all by heart" ([1898] 1982, 336-37; see also Gerini [1892] 1976, 34).[18] At the conclusion of the ceremony, "offerings of food and robes are ostentatiously distributed to those priests who have given their services" (Young [1898] 1982, 336-37). The offerings are prepared "for the boy in whose honour the celebration is held" (Gerini [1892] 1976, 34). Upon completion of the recitation, the novice then "distributes these offerings among his brethren and the elders of the temple" and, even more remarkably, "also to his young relatives and friends of the laity" (Gerini [1892] 1976, 34).

In the case of the crown princes, the ceremonies took place at the royal chapel in the Grand Palace (*phra thinang song tham*) (Gerini [1892] 1976, 36). The young novices were brought to the chapel from the monasteries at which they were residing (Gerini [1892] 1976, 35-36).[19] The 1866 account provides a poignant description of the prince-novice's arrival by state coach at the chapel, noting his father, the king, "came forth to meet him, and taking him in his arms made him alight; then led him by the hand up to the royal chapel" (Gerini [1892] 1976, 36).

When a crown prince performed his novice recitation, the ceremonies were extraordinarily lavish and very public spectacles. Accounts remain of all three of the crown princes—namely, Prince Mongkut (later Rama IV) in 1817, hosted by his father, King Rama II; Prince Chulalongkorn (later Rama V) in 1866, hosted by his father, Rama IV; and Crown Prince Vajirunhis in December 1891, hosted by his father, Rama V (Gerini [1892] 1976, 34-36).[20] Interestingly, Gerini remarks that the 1817 performance "had never in former reigns happened on such a magnificent scale" ([1892] 1976, 35). Unlike the trays and wicker baskets used in other novice recitations, the krajaat for the 1817 recitation was "colossal"—namely, "a conical seven storied structure like a Siamese royal umbrella or canopy of state" (Gerini [1892] 1976, 35). With "the Court, the nobility and the people assembled in large crowds," these lavish krajaat, "splendid to behold," were restricted for use only by novices who were heirs apparent (Gerini [1892] 1976, 35, 63). The offerings for the 1866 and 1891 novice ordinations were even more spectacular, the framework for both structured as Chinese junks.

Such novice recitations suggest that the *Vessantara Jataka* recitations continued to be an important part of the lives of both members of the court and other elite families well into the twentieth century. Writing in the mid-twentieth century, Phya Anuman notes that "many Kings and Princes of the present dynasty, have, in the past, entered the Faith as [novices] and have performed such a recitation of the Great Birth for the monarchs, their august forefathers," but adds, "this custom is seldom done nowadays" (1988, 193–94). A senior monk in Suphanburi recalled that parents were still hosting novice recitations in the 1950s. The noted Buddhist intellectual Sulak Sivaraksa (1933–) informed me that he himself recited a chapter for his parents when he was a novice.[21]

Establishing the Court Text

A survey of royal performances of the *Vessantara Jataka* suggests profound royal interest in supporting annual recitations at the court temple of Wat Phra Kaew, in both lay chanting and monastic readings. King Rama IV, despite his role in founding the Thammayut reform sect, recited the Matsi chapter for his novitiate and wrote editions of several chapters, including the Sakabap chapter, which was recited by his son when he became crown prince at his own novice ceremony. Similarly, King Rama V, despite his modern attitudes regarding administration and philosophy, continued to support recitations during his reign. He had his son recite a chapter as crown prince for his novitiate in 1891 and asked his half brother to recite a chapter on the occasion of the one hundredth anniversary of Bangkok in 1882. Although Thammayut temples generally did not perform *Vessantara Jataka* recitations, the royally supported Mahanikai temples continued to do so.[22] Consequently, the evidence does not demonstrate an obvious pattern of decline in royal support for recitations of the *Vessantara Jataka* over the course of the nineteenth century. Instead, the court took steps to establish an approved edition of the jataka, with members of the court actively involved in writing most of its chapters. This court version provided little room for comedy, presenting the jataka as a serious metaphysical text. As this section will show, the court appears to have sought to gain control over the jataka's core message by portraying it as an otherworldly text about escaping suffering rather than a this-worldly celebration of bawdy humor.

Court Authors

Court interest in the *Vessantara Jataka* is indicated not only through official support for recitations but also through the court's role in developing a definitive text. Of the thirteen chapters that comprise the *Vessantara Jataka*, all but three were written by members of the Bangkok court, including King Rama IV himself. No complete court text of the *Vessantara Jataka* apparently survived the sacking of Ayutthaya, so various poets, primarily princes affiliated with the court, worked together to reproduce all thirteen chapters. Chaophraya Phrakhlang

(Hon),[23] Minister of Finance and Foreign Affairs under Rama I, wrote editions of the Matsi and Kumarn chapters; a subsequent version of Matsi was written by Prince Kromsomdet Phra Bamrap Parapak, a son of Rama IV (Gerini [1892] 1976, 54).

Prince Paramanuchit Chinorot, a son of Rama I who later became supreme patriarch of the Buddhist sangha, played a particularly important role. In the version used in state recitations, Prince Paramanuchit wrote or edited at least seven chapters: Thotsaphon (chapter 1), Himaphan (chapter 2), Thanakan (chapter 3), Wanaprawet (chapter 4), Maharaat (chapter 11), Chohkasat (chapter 12), and Nakornkan (chapter 13) (Gerini [1892] 1976, 54). Prince Paramanuchit also produced a version of Chulaphon (chapter 6) (see Nidhi [1982] 2005, 219–20).[24]

King Rama IV himself—despite being the founder of the Thammayut order and having denounced buffoonish recitations—composed editions of three chapters—namely, Wanaprawet (chapter 4), Chulaphon (chapter 6), and, most notably, Sakabap (chapter 10). His edition of Sakabap was recited by his son, Rama V, upon his ordination as a novice and was also recited by Crown Prince Vajirunhis on his ordination as a novice in December 1891 (Gerini [1892] 1976, 60; see also Nidhi [1982] 2005, 208–9).

Government interest in the *Vessantara Jataka* continued into the early twentieth century. The role of Rama IV and other high-ranking members of the aristocracy can be seen in the compilation published as the "standard" by the Department of Education in 1910 (Nidhi [1982] 2005, 207) and the related compilation recently published by the Munithi Hortrai in 1990. The Munithi Hortrai adopted the following recensions:

1. Thotsaphon   Prince Paramanuchit Chinorot
2. Himaphan   Prince Paramanuchit Chinorot
3. Thanakan   Unnamed; Wat Thanon
4. Wanaprawet   King Rama IV
5. Jujaka   Unnamed; Wat Sangkrajai (Phra Thepmuni [Duang])
6. Chulaphon   King Rama IV
7. Mahaphon   Phra Thepmoli (Klin)
8. Kumarn   Chaophraya Phra Khlang (Hon)
9. Matsi   Chaophraya Phra Khlang (Hon)
10. Sakabap   King Rama IV
11. Maharaat   Prince Paramanuchit Chinorot
12. Chohkasat   Prince Paramanuchit Chinorot
13. Nakornkan   Prince Paramanuchit Chinorot

Boat Symbolism and the Kumarn Chapter

In comparison with the Pali version and versions from other regions of Thailand, the royal version of the *Vessantara Jataka* differs in its emphasis. In Chaophraya Phrakhlang's version, the boat imagery in the Kumarn chapter is greatly elaborated. In this chapter, the two children flee and hide in a lotus pond when they learn of Jujaka's intention to take them to be his wife's servants. As can be seen in the following passage, in the Pali rendition, the boat imagery is very brief. In the Pali version, Vessantara follows their footprints to the pond and calls out:

> Come hither, my beloved son, my perfect state fulfil;
> Come now and consecrate my heart, and follow out my will.
> Be thou my ship to ferry me safe o'er existence' sea,
> Beyond the worlds of birth and gods I'll cross and I'll be free.
> (Cowell [1895] 1957, 5:282)

This boat imagery is dramatically expanded in Chaophraya Phrakhlang's variation of this scene. Although written in the early nineteenth century, this version has become the "official" one. Nidhi has done a close comparative reading of Chaophraya Phrakhlang's and an older version, which Nidhi argues dates from the late Ayutthayan period found in Phetchaburi. The importance of the boat metaphor is already evident in the Phetchaburi text (see Nidhi [1982] 2005, 216). Thus Chaophraya Phrakhlang was expanding upon not only the Pali but also the Phetchaburi version by adding even greater maritime detail to the already extensive passage involving boat imagery.[25] In one very long section, the central Thai text describes a junk's hull, mast, rigging, flags, cargo, and encounter during a monsoon while on the high seas (Nidhi [1982] 2005, 217). Gerini also highlights the growing symbolic importance of the boat imagery over the course of the nineteenth century, concluding humorously:

> As a matter of course new features were gradually introduced into modern versifications of this passage of the Maha Chat; and in a measure, as shipping progressed, the golden Vessel of the Law was also improved in fittings and appearance. From King Song Tham's reign, when it was depicted as a Chinese junk, down to the present time, it passed through numerous transformations, and became successively a square rigged vessel, a frigate, a paddle-steamer, a screw-steamer, and an iron-clad; and it would not be at all surprising in some contemporary or future refashioner of the poem should describe it as a torpedo-boat or a submarine vessel. ([1892] 1976, 50)

Figure 5. Krajaat built as a Chinese junk for the novitiate of the crown prince in 1891. Part of the elaborate maritime display erected for the occasion next to the palace, the fifty-meter-long wooden krajaat was a replica of the masonry junk jedi located at Wat Yannawa, Bangkok. With two jedis as its masts, the boat symbolizes the means to enable humans to cross the sea of suffering. Photo on display at Wat Yannawa, Bangkok, July 2015. Rephotographed by author.

The importance of the boat imagery of this chapter is also highlighted in aspects of its performance. The Kumarn chapter is chanted in a special style called *lae Yannawa* (boat chanting), serving to further emphasize the importance of the boat imagery and underscore the children as the ship that will carry their father over the sea of suffering (Manee 1976, 62). When the crown princes held their public recitations, the offerings were presented in the form of junks. For the 1866 ceremony of the crown prince, the krajaat was "in the shape of a symbolical ship, built after the style of a Chinese junk or *samphao*" (Gerini [1892] 1976, 35). Set up in front of the Grand Palace, it was "the admiration of the people at large, who assembled in crowds to see it" (Gerini [1892] 1976, 00). Gerini provides the following detailed description: "The junk was intended as a support or basement for the krachats which were three in number and stood in the place of the masts. One towering seven storied krachat was substituted for the main mast, and two smaller ones of five tiers for the fore and mizen masts. On deck were disposed stalls replete with goods after the manner observed on board the junks which formerly came to trade with Siam." These goods included "sweatmeats, cold eatables, fruits, Buddhist priests' requisites and implements, in large quantities." To make sure the offering boats would be widely viewed, the king "directed that theatricals or 'Lakhons' should be added to the programme, so as to render the pageant more attractive" (Gerini [1892] 1976, 35–36).

For the novice ceremonial in 1891, the boat was even larger than in the 1866 version. Descriptions are provided by Ernest Young, Lucien Fournereau, and Gerini. Young notes, "A huge junk was erected on the grass, and its sides were totally covered with boxes of cigars, boxes of sardines, and tinned provisions. The cabins and hold were filled with eatables" ([1898] 1982, 337). In addition, Gerini points to "a numerous fleet of minor craft of all descriptions; of fishes both real and fantastic; and marine monsters, all made of or filled with eatables and other offerings tastefully arranged" ([1892] 1976, 36). Fournereau describes a long palisade made of sugarcane and enclosing a public exposition, "a curious retrospective history of shipbuilding in Siam"; he elaborates:

> The traveler who visits this strange enclosure at least believes that he is transported to the island of pleasure, of a gastronomic past: a lighthouse of sugar throws its electric light on ice fields of sweet things. All around the junk and its accessories runs a small barrier of edible things and cakes and at the end opposite of the lighthouse, a crenellated wall, flanked by donjons of matchboxes, closes the enclosure.[26]
>
> The remainder of the terrain is overcrowded with fabulous or mythological animals, dragons, griffins, sharks, the smallest of which are six meters long. A gigantic swordfish made of sardine cans opens its eyes formed by American stopwatches and moves its fins made of Japanese platters.
>
> The junk, fifty meters long, produces a complete illusion. All kinds of gifts overload it from the front to the back. On the false bridge stand wax figures in natural sizes, chairs and furniture of the same material; on the poop deck a niche launches a slender Phra Chedi in to the sky. Along the masts and the ship's rail electric lamps illuminate this terrestrial vessel the hull of which is overflowing with fruits, areca-nuts and coconuts.
>
> The lower part of the hull below the line of flotation is made of sugar cane. Let us still indicate the steam launch, a masterpiece of ingenuity, given that the construction materials consist of paper, rags, matchboxes and tinplates.
>
> Summing up, this spectacle is most picturesque at night when it is animated

by this rainbow-colored and shouting crowd which applauds and claps their hands like a herd of children. ([1894] 1998, 122-25)

Nidhi argues that the expansion of the boat imagery was an indication that the jataka was being interpreted "less as a religious sermon and more [as] a piece of literature." Explaining that Chaophraya Phrakhlang was making full use of his own direct experience of the junks leaving the port of Bangkok, Nidhi suggests that this change "reflects the greater confidence in human ability which is characteristic of the thinking of the upper class generally in the early Bangkok period" ([1982] 2005, 218). In Nidhi's view, Chaophraya Phrakhlang "added metaphors from *this* world which results in a considerable weakening of the other-worldly meaning" ([1982] 2005, 218). I would like to offer a different interpretation—namely, that by expanding the boat imagery in the text, the jataka becomes more firmly linked not only with scientific maritime advances and global trade but also with the metaphysical message of a more philosophical tradition of Buddhism being encouraged by the court and its intertwined Thammayut reform sect.

The comparison of worldly suffering with ocean imagery is widespread in Buddhism, "the stormy ocean of continued existence or transmigration" from which the soul "is only able to escape by following four sublime courses or paths (*ariyamagga*) leading to the dipa, the 'island' of Arhatship and thence to Nirvana, the 'Further Shore' (*Para*) where salvation is attained by a release from existence" (Gerini [1892] 1976, 44). *Yana nawa* is the "water-vehicle" of salvation and has gained a symbolic place in Siamese art. At Wat Pho, the "golden vessel of the Law" is depicted as a Chinese junk, or samphao, on the Buddha's foot (Gerini [1892] 1976, 47). Wat Yannawa has an enormous masonry junk that was built by order of King Rama III; it has two jedis as its masts.[27] The symbolism was also repeated in the boat replicas used as public krachat beginning at least as early as the celebration of the crown prince's novice ordination in 1866. In sum, the boat is "the vehicle which will enable human beings to cross the ocean of rebirth, affliction, and death, and reach a safe and peaceful haven" (Gerini [1892] 1976, 48). Its elaboration in both text and performance can be seen as a combination of the court's growing dependence on the junk trade and on King Mongkut's interest in combining science with philosophical insights in Buddhism through the use of nautical imagery.

A subsequent passage in the Kumarn chapter establishes the link between the this-worldly ship and the transcendental ship. Gerini provides the following summary text of this passage:

My children, my dear ones, your father scarcely sees your faces in the broad light as yet. You must come forth, and learn of the golden ship your father devises to build. He will take as her deck the ten perfections accumulated during one hundred thousand kalpas [eons]; the eight successful attainments in the path of charity and other meritorious practices, as pilots steering on a straight course across the ocean of worldly existence. Of the three jewels (i.e. Buddha, the Law and the Order) he will make three sublime masts; of his virtuous behaviour and high morality, her excellent sails and awnings; of the superior virtues he has practised and perfected for ages (i.e. his steadfast and true resolve to attain Buddhahood), her hull. Moreover, he will take the four sublime truths to be the hour glass that will tell the watches of day and night whilst the ocean is being crossed. He will take the star of truth as the guide of the ship's course; the modesty that deterred him from sin as the windlass; his meritorious actions, as shipmaster and mate; and out of his unflinching determination and unswerving resolution he will make the rudder which shall keep the ship on a straight course.

Do ye be attentive now, my children! Your father will load this ship with all that is required to accomplish the journey, that is, the seven constituents of Buddhahood; he will erect amid ships a royal throne for himself adorned with the seven gems of the scriptures and canopied by a gold and jewelled pavilion.

Crowds of Devas [deities] will sing his praises and extol his universal science; the golden ship will meanwhile weigh anchor and glide off majestically on the billows. Although thousands of impetuous surges may rush against her bulwarks and the immense violence of the wind of desire and lust try to stay her course and drive her back to this world, the ship will yet keep on going and will overcome all dangers, and lo! Your father will effect his escape from the realm of ignorance, error and see it no more.

Such is the transcendental ship and it now must appear clearly before the mind, my dear Chali, that only with a ship like this will it be possible for me to cross. ([1892] 1976, 49-50)

Fournereau provides more details of the 1891 novitiate of the crown prince, which further suggests that the boat imagery was selected deliberately as a metaphysical metaphor. The four-day event began with reading the jataka ([1894] 1998, 122-25). On the second day, the crown prince held a lecture on the allegory represented by the junk as a krajaat, explaining that the junk is a "symbol of the journey of all men towards Nirvana" (Fournereau [1894] 1998, 123). On the third day he held a sermon in which he elaborated upon the four noble truths. On the final day Fournereau says there was a lottery for the materials of the junk and its contents, which were "distributed among the monks" ([1894] 1998, 123). Ernest Young states that "the whole vessel was broken up, and its contents distributed amongst the poor and the hospitals ([1898] 1982, 337). Gerini writes that the gifts, "though intended exclusively for the young Prince," were donated by him "partly to the relief of the sufferers from a recent cyclone in one of the Southern provinces of the realm, and partly to the hospitals and other charitable institutions of the capital" ([1892] 1976, 36). In the crown prince's actions one can hear the echoes of his grandfather Rama IV's exhortation that the money spent on buffoonish recitations would be better spent helping the poor. The young prince's generosity would likely have been seen as reinforcing the message of Vessantara's generosity to the poor. In his sermon and his generosity, the prince made the association of the boat imagery with the theme of transcendence explicit. Even today, the association is widely recognized.[28]

Other Royal Chapters

Other chapters of especial significance for royal recitations were the three chapters that were most likely recited by novices, namely Sakabap, Chulaphon, and Mahaphon (Gerini [1892] 1976, 27, 35). Of these three, Sakabap appears the most important. Although Rama IV had recited the Matsi chapter for the celebration of his novitiate as crown prince, he specially wrote a recension of the Sakabap chapter to be recited by his son Chulalongkorn for his novice recitations as crown prince (Gerini [1892] 1976, 35-36). As king, Chulalongkorn had his son Vajirunhis recite this same chapter for his novice recitation in 1891 (Gerini [1892] 1976, 35-36). He also asked his half brother, Prince Vajiranana (Wachirayan), to recite this chapter as part of the 1882 Bangkok anniversary celebration (Reynolds 1979, 53).

In part, the relative brevity of these chapters was a reason why they were often chosen for novices. For his novitiate, Sulak Sivaraksa had recited the Chulaphon chapter. When I asked him why, he laughed and replied, "Because it was short!"[29] These chapters are indeed among the shortest ones; Chulaphon has thirty-five verses, Sakabap has forty-three verses, and Mahaphon has eighty verses. Compared to longer chapters such as Thanakan, with 209 verses, or Himaphan, with 134 verses, these chapters are relatively short; however, they are not the shortest. (See the list of chapters on page oo: Thotsaphon, with nineteen verses, is the shortest, and Chohkasat has thirty-six; see Gerini [1892] 1976, 27, 35.)

However, more importantly, only certain chapters were considered appropriate for members of the royal family to recite. In general, according to senior monks who are themselves involved in royal recitations today, princes only performed stately, majestic chapters that had slower cadences (*riap riap, thamnong chao*). One senior monk mentioned chapters such as Thotsaphon, Himaphan, Sakabap, or Nakornkan were appropriate for princes. Another senior monk said members of the royal family (*chya phawong*) would recite the Sakabap, Chulaphon, and Wanaprawet chapters. Chapters such as Kumarn and Matsi were inappropriate because they show high emotion, as were the Jujaka or Maharaat chapters because of their comedy. Chapters such as Chulaphon and Mahaphon were also acceptable because of their flowery descriptions of nature; as Nidhi remarks of court literature in general, "The crux is not the story or plot but the poet's ability to weave fine words and images" ([1982] 2005, 13). Another possible factor in their association with royalty is that in chapters such as Thotsaphon, Wanaprawet, and Sakabap, the god Indra is speaking; the noble words of the powerful Indra were likely considered as more appropriate for members of the royal family to recite than those of the covetous Jujaka.

Jujaka Chapter

The court appears to have wasted no time in establishing a court version of the Jujaka chapter. Court concern with bawdy comic recitations of the *Vessantara Jataka* can be documented back to Rama I. We can presume that the Jujaka chapter was of particular concern. The court version of the Jujaka chapter also dates back to the reign of Rama I. Although the text is often referred to as the Wat Sangkrajai version, its likely author was Phra Thepmuni (Duang), both because he was abbot of the temple at the time and because he was known for his performances of the chapter (Damrong 1918; Manee 1976, 24-25). Phra Thepmuni was himself a monk whom Rama I frequently consulted. Furthermore, Rama I's chief consort, Chaochom Waen, played a major role in the temple's establishment.[30] Waen, the daughter of the King of Vientiane, became a consort of Rama I in 1779, in the days before he became king, when he was leading a military campaign against Vientiane. After a major altercation between Rama I and his queen over Waen, Waen became his chief consort and oversaw palace affairs.[31] Consequently, the selection of the abbot of Wat Sangkrajai as the author of the problematic Jujaka chapter was likely not accidental but instead suggests the deep concern of the court with this chapter.

Phra Thepmuni's rendition of Jujaka portrays him as evil and very disgusting. The tone of the chapter is not humorous. Amitataa is portrayed as filial and tragic, a woman who views herself as a slave (*thaat*). Even the scene of the village women attacking Amitataa is filled with pathos rather than humor; the village women question the integrity of her parents, commenting that parents usually try to do well by their children and not marry them off to the likes of such a despicable old man. They malign her by suggesting that she must have made an offering to the gods at the wrong time such that an old black crow flew off with them before they reached the gods, or she made incorrect offerings to the gods, or she spoke badly with monks or someone who was an arahant. They suggest she would be better off dead than having to live under her current circumstances.

Senior monks I interviewed stated explicitly that not only was humor inappropriate for chapters recited by members of the royal family, it was also inappropriate for royal recitations at court. They explained that there were two main types of recitations: royal and popular. The *thamnong luang* style uses more formal language, a more languorous recitation style, and often includes the accompaniment of a *piiphaat* ensemble.[32] Furthermore, royal readings are tightly structured; each monk must stick to the time allotted him. Royal performances do not include comedy (*luuklen*) because, as one senior monk stated explicitly, it would be "inappropriate to have joking in a royal performance for a king or other member of the royal family." By contrast, when these same monks perform for regular audiences, they use a style called *thamnong lae*, in which the vocabulary is changed to make sure the audience can understand the words. As one monk explained, instead of royal or formal words for "to eat," *sawoej* or *raprathaan*, they use informal words such as *daek* and *kin*. Several monks indicated that they felt their audiences would not approve of any joking. One taxi driver from Nakhon Nayok, responding to my query about whether any central Thai monks made jokes part of their recitations, stated that monks were not supposed to chant that way and should instead "preach as the Buddha had taught that it should be done" (*thet baep phraphutthachao sohn wai*).

Popular Performances

If court performances were formal and centered upon a maritime metaphysical metaphor, how did the public interpret the *Vessantara Jataka*? In this section, I will suggest that, given overall similarities in the way the jataka has come to be performed in the central region, the Bangkok court was relatively successful in implementing its more metaphysical interpretation. The overall pattern in recitations of the *Vessantara Jataka* in the central region shares many similarities with the court form in such matters as timing, offerings, favored chapters, de-emphasis of Jujaka, and lack of humor.[33]

Although the Bangkok court developed an increasingly negative attitude toward bawdy humor, early nineteenth-century court literature itself had erotic

Figure 6. Jujaka chapter: bawdy village scene. An early nineteenth-century central Thai cloth painting with bawdy vignettes showing Amitataa being ridiculed by village women, villagers fighting, and Jujaka with Amitataa. Paint and gold on cloth. Gift from Doris Duke Charitable Foundation's Southeast Asian Art Collection. Object Number 2006.27.81.3. Asian Art Museum, San Francisco.

elements portrayed in "wondrous scenes" (*bot atsachan*).[34] Although Nidhi suggests that they had faded from Thai upper-class literature even before the influx of Victorian morality from the west, "once western Victorian morality had come to totally dominate the upper class in the second half of the nineteenth century, wondrous scenes completely disappeared from upper class literature" ([1982] 2005, 32; see also Pasuk and Baker 2011). Nonetheless, bawdy literature rife with "wondrous scenes" continued among folk poets. As Nidhi explains:

> Sexual activity is a rather major part of folk literature. Many forms of singing such as boat *phleng*, harvest *phleng*, courtship *phleng*, Korat *phleng*, and *phleng thepthong* (a kind of popular verse-play) are about flirting and courtship between men and women, and refer to sexual activity by using metaphor. . . . In folk literature, metaphors about sexual activity employed on the one hand comparisons with nature such as bees, flowers blooming, and rain, and on the other hand, comparisons with everyday life such as transplanting paddy, pounding rice, and weaving cloth. ([1982] 2005, 29–30)

Similarly, surviving Buddhist temple murals throughout Thailand include "scenes of flirting, courting, and more-or-less explicit depictions of lovemaking" (Brereton and Somroay 2010, 69). A temple painting dated to 1670 at Wat Chong Nonsi in Bangkok depicts a humorous scene of a couple pounding rice together as a mischievous boy is poised to ensnare the man's genitals in a noose (Napat and Gordon 1999, 7). Surviving Ayutthayan mural paintings suggest that Amitataa and the village women was a favorite scene; Wat Chong Nonsi features "a hilarious depiction of a near-riot when Amitataa is drawing water from the village well. One lady is so vigorous in her protest against Amitataa's anti-social behaviour that she is tumbling head first down the steps of the front porch" (Napat and Gordon 1999, 14; for more on Wat Chong Nonsi, see Anonymous 1982).[35] Other depictions show the village women mooning Amitataa. However, these visual memories disappear from the formal recitations.

Timing: During Buddhist Lent

Unlike other regions where recitations during Buddhist Lent were considered to be inappropriate, recitations of the *Vessantara Jataka* in the central region frequently occurred *during* Lent or immediately following the end of Lent. The recitation of the excerpts of the *Vessantara Jataka* at Wat Phra Kaew took place during Buddhist Lent. Mary Cort notes that krajaat festivities were usually held in the seventh Siamese month, and she describes a ceremony in August 1883 (1886, 61–62). Monks and laity I interviewed indicated that recitations of the *Vessantara Jataka* in the central region were most likely to take place either on Wan Sart or Wan Thewo (also called Wan Tak Bat Thewo), both festivals occurring during Lent.

Wan Sart appears to have been the preferred date in the central region for recitations of the *Vessantara Jataka* and occurs on the fifteenth waning day of month ten of the Thai lunar calendar, or circa September–early October (Anuman 1961, 96; 1988, 190). On this day hell opens, releasing the ghostly spirits (*phii*).[36] With the dead returning to the human world, merit made for them is believed to be especially effective on this day. In the famous nineteenth-century account of the *Vessantara Jataka* in *Khun Chang Khun Phaen*, the recitation was held at a temple in Suphanburi on Wan Sart (Baker and Pasuk 2010, 65). At Bangkok's Wat Suthat and Wat Arun the *Vessantara Jataka* is performed annually on Wan Sart. Thonburi's Wat Suwannaram holds the *Vessantara Jataka* every year on this day. An abbot in Samut Sakorn said that his temple no longer performed the *Vessantara Jataka*, but that it was usually performed on Wan Sart. It is also one of the three days the jataka is chanted at Wat Phra Kaew (Gerini [1892] 1976, 23).

Many other central Thai temples host *Vessantara Jataka* recitations on Wan Thewo. Wan Thewo falls the day after the end of Buddhist Lent, on the first day of the waning moon of lunar month eleven (circa October).[37] This festival marks the day that the Buddha returned from heaven after preaching to his mother, who had died shortly after his birth. When the Buddha returned to earth, thousands of people presented food to him and his disciples. In remembrance of this day, devotees make special food-offerings to monks. In many areas, people bring a Buddha image down from a hill, imitating the Buddha's descent from heaven (Anuman 1986, 69). Bangkok's Wat Mahathat holds its recitation on Wan Thewo. Wan Thewo is a big festival in Uthai Thani, Uttaradit, and Suphanburi, as well as provinces in the south. Photos from Muang Klaeng in Rayong province taken in the late 1960s show Wan Thewo being celebrated with townspeople dressed as ghosts, animals, the god Indra, and other deities to represent the hells and heavens (Tesabaan Tambon Muang Klaeng 2009, 56, 126, 144, 321, 327, 353).

Convenience also factors in. Wat Pho holds its annual recitation before the end of Lent.[38] At Bangkok's Wat Chaichanasongkram the *Vessantara Jataka* is recited over a two-day period before the end of Buddhist Lent; they choose a holy day (*wan phra*) that is followed by a Sunday so that people have time to join. In explaining the general preference to hold recitations during Buddhist Lent, one monk suggested that there are many monks gathered at temples during Buddhist Lent, so there are more monks available for recitations. Another monk suggested monks are not able to beg for alms (*bintabatr*) in the rainy season; furthermore, many of the novices are poor and need to focus on their studies, so the performance helps support them.

However, there were also central Thai temples both in and outside of Bangkok that held their recitations after Buddhist Lent. Kaufman, writing of Bangkhuad in Bangkapi district (25 kilometers northeast of Bangkok) in 1953, notes that the *Vessantara Jataka* is recited as part of Loi Krathong (November) (1960, 195). Jane Bunnag observed a partial recitation in Ayutthaya in February 1967 as part of a fund-raiser to complete an ordination hall (1973, 117-18). An abbot in Chanthaburi (Wat Klang) said they host the *Vessantara Jataka* every December. Another abbot (Wat Dorn Taan) in Chanthaburi said they hold their annual *Vessantara Jataka* reading in January, adding that most temples in Chanthaburi hold it after Lent. The explanations for why recitations were held after Lent were also varied. Phya Anuman suggests that "the reason why it is usually performed after the Lent is obvious. For during the period October to December, food especially fish and prawns, are in abundance, and the people, in particular the countryfolk, have a comparative leisure time" (1988, 190). Another monk suggested they did not hold their recitations during Lent because the audience flees if it is raining (Wat Klang, Chanthaburi).

Maitreya Ignored: Beyond Twenty-Four Hours

Among the central Thai temples that held their *Vessantara Jataka* recitations during Buddhist Lent, many spread their chapter recitations over a period of days or weeks. This extended pattern is a dramatic contrast with the northern and northeastern belief that the recitation must occur within a twenty-four-hour period. A taxi driver from Nakhon Nayok related that a chapter of the *Vessantara Jataka* was performed on holy days (wan phra) throughout Buddhist Lent, beginning on Wan Khao Phansaa and taking three months to complete. A taxi driver from Chachoengsao also provided an account of recitations that extended throughout Buddhist Lent. Wat Lahaan in Nonthaburi also does a chapter each holy day. Some wats recited a chapter each week, but on a Sunday, when people have time. Phra Vijit provided a historical description of such an expanded recitation from Ayutthaya, involving multiple temples and villages; I recorded our conversation in my notes: "He was born in Ayutthaya where the rice grew twice as tall as people. During the growing season, there was nothing for people to do, so they had time to go to temple. The *Vessantara Jataka* was generally not recited all at once, but rather 1-3 chapters were recited on a given holy day [*wan phra*]. . . . A group of temples along a given river way would get together and divide up the sponsorship of various chapters, so it wasn't recited all at one single temple. Each temple took a turn to host the reading of a chapter.

Whichever temple was hosting, villagers from the other communities would all arrive by rafts and boats. The jataka was recited each year. In the central region, the reading fostered community co-operation by having multiple communities and monks working together."[39]

While some temples stretch the reading over the entire period of Buddhist Lent, other temples divide the reading over several consecutive days (e.g., Anuman 1988, 190). At Wat Suwannaram in Thonburi the recitation takes three days. The first day the thousand verses are done in Pali, with only short Thai summaries. The Thai version begins on the second day, with the final chapters recited on the third day. On the final day they also hold a ceremony to distribute the sacred water (*nam mon*), and they give away the bananas, coconuts, and other offerings to the attendees. Similarly, at Wat Chaichanasongkram in Bangkok the *Vessantara Jataka* is recited over a two-day period before the end of Buddhist Lent; they choose a wan phra that is followed by a Sunday so that people have time to join in. They recite the first six chapters in Pali in the morning, followed by the Thai version in the afternoon; on the second day they recite the remaining chapters in Pali and the respective chapters in Thai in the afternoon. Interestingly, because this is historically a Mon temple with many Mon supporters, they recite one chapter—namely, the Wanaprawet—in Mon rather than in central Thai. At Bangkok's Wat Mahathat, the recitation lasts three days, each day beginning about 10:00 a.m. and ending about 6:00 p.m. A monk at Wat Prayoon commented that the recitation may be completed in just one day since in the modern era people are busy, or it may be spread out over two to three days.

In the Hua Hin region, in the past these performances were done in stages over the course of three consecutive days. The recitation typically began in the evening and lasted from 5:00 to 8:00 p.m., when the first two chapters were recited. Then everyone went home to bed. The next morning began about 4:00 a.m., and two more chapters were recited before breakfast. After a pause for breakfast, two more chapters were recited. After a break for lunch, two more chapters were recited from 1:00 to 5:00 in the afternoon. After everyone had dinner, another two chapters were read and then everyone went home to sleep. On the third day, the recitation again resumed at about 4:00 a.m., following the same pattern until all thirteen chapters were completed. Nowadays it is becoming much more common to finish the recitation in one day, using just a few monks; this format is not because of any belief about seeing Maitreya but simply because of the time constraints of people's work schedules. In this abridged format, the monk explained, three monks may take turns getting through the first six chapters in the afternoon and the remaining seven chapters in the evening.

It is unclear how the central Thai pattern of extended recitation developed. Nonetheless, it is easy to imagine that the court would have found this pattern preferable to the pattern in the other regions since it undermines the association with the millenarian Maitreya, who told people to listen to the jataka from beginning to end within a twenty-four-hour period. It is ironic that many temples are now undertaking single-day recitations, but merely for logistical reasons.[40]

Number of Monks

Whereas in the North the number of monks is fixed at thirteen for the thirteen chapters and in the northeast may range as high as fifty or more, in the central region the number of monks was generally lower. In Gerini's account of the 1807 state recitation, three senior priests recited the Pali *Khathaphan* on the first day, with thirteen reciting the thirteen Thai chapters ([1892] 1976, 37). Kaufman notes five monks recited the jataka he observed during his fieldwork (1960, 195). Abridged versions are also becoming more common in the central region, further reducing the number of monks involved. However, even when the full jataka is performed, most central Thai recitations still involve fewer monks. Thus at the recitation in 2009 at Wat Mahathat, one of the principal temples in Bangkok and home to a Buddhist university, five monks recited all thirteen chapters; the reading was held over three days, and selected monks read more than one chapter (monks were invited from Wat Pho, Wat Prayoon, Wat Samien Nari, and Wat Saamphrayar). At Wat Suwannaram, some ten monks were invited from various Bangkok temples, some monks chanting more than one chapter. At Wat Prayoon, the number of monks varied from three to thirteen. Outside of Bangkok, in Chanthaburi province temples recited the abridged format with as few as two monks summarizing the story. One Chanthaburi monk recalled that in the past monks specialized in certain chapters and were carried in for the recitation (*haam*). A monk in Chanthaburi (Wat Dorn Taan) said they invite five to six monks, each of whom recites two to three chapters; monks may come from as far away as Bangkok. A taxi driver from Chachoengsao who also said that a monk may recite more than one chapter, so that fewer than thirteen monks need be invited, added that a person is not considered a full monk unless they have received kathin robes and recited the *Vessantara Jataka*.

Many central Thai monks and members of the laity denied that monks specialized in specific chapters, commenting that it was difficult these days to find monks knowledgeable in any of the chapters. The abbot at Wat Dorn Taan, Chanthaburi, denied that, with the exception of the Matsi chapter, which required a softer voice, specific chapters called for special voices.[41] By contrast, several senior monks in Bangkok said that monks needed particular kinds of voices for certain chapters: a big voice (*siang yai*) for the Maharaat chapter; a soft voice (*siang lek*) for the Kumarn and Matsi chapters; a lovely voice for the Mahaphon chapter (*siang numnuan, phairoh*); and a voice like an old man (*siang khon kae*) for the Jujaka chapter.

Lay Sponsorship

Unlike northern Thailand, where individual chapters are sponsored in accordance with one's year of birth, in central Thailand sponsorship occurred in one of three ways: through invitation by a monk or temple committee member, volunteering, or drawing lots. Although some members of the laity did not want to host the Jujaka chapter, Wat Suwannaram avoided the problem by inviting individuals to serve as host, a request the monk I interviewed said the laity was not likely to refuse. Taxi drivers from Suphanburi and Samut Sakorn said they drew lots (*jap salak*) to see who would host the various chapters. A taxi driver from Nakhon Nayok said people hold a lottery to see who will host which chapters. A taxi driver from Chachoengsao said that hosts would reserve (*jong*) their chapters but were not supposed to reserve the same chapter two years in a row. At Wat Klang and Wat Dorn Taan in Chanthaburi, the temple committees organize the sponsorship, with people reserving chapters. (Here hosting the same chapter two years in a row is allowed.) A similar pattern is followed at a temple in Hua Hin, where reservations are made on a first come, first serve basis. In cases where multiple villages cooperate to host a conjoint reading, representatives of each village get together and draw lots to determine which village will sponsor which of the thirteen chapters (according to another Chachoengsao taxi driver).

Offerings: Quest for Status

The central Thai performance style does not appear to have placed particular emphasis on the skill of the monk reciting or on the temple decorations but more on the competitive grandeur of the public offerings. As in other regions, in central Thailand (according to the monks and members of the laity I interviewed) the temple is decorated to look like the Himaphan forest with sugarcane, bananas, and coconuts.[42] Many interviewees also noted offerings and decorations of fruit, perhaps reflecting the fact that central Thailand has so many fruit orchards. No one recalled ever having seen cloth scrolls or mazes, which typify the northeastern and northern regions, respectively. By comparison with the other two regions, the temple decorations in the central region were relatively simple and basic.

In central Thailand, emphasis seems to have been placed on the lay offerings that were brought in a procession by the lay hosts of a given chapter, traveling either by boat along the riverways or through the village or town. Unlike in northeastern Thailand, where the villagers unite to form large processions, in central Thailand the sponsors of each individual chapter formed competitive and separate processions. An abbot I interviewed in Samut Sakorn (whose temple has not held recitations for as long as he could remember) told me that in the past he had heard that members of the laity arrived by boat with their offerings and all of their relatives in tow, in a competition to see who had the largest following. Phya Anuman (1888-1969) provides a similar description with the caveat that already at the time of his writing (circa mid-twentieth century), "You will not be able to see such things as I describe in present-day Bangkok or in other progressive towns" (1988, 195). He notes that once it has been determined who is hosting the various chapters, "Each owner vies with the other for the performance." Often more than one family may join together, creating a sense of "bustle and merriment" as everyone helps with the cooking and the decoration of the offering baskets (krajaat). The offering basket is typically "a big basket made of bamboo in the shape of a huge blooming lotus flower with its many coloured paper petals pasted on, together with other decorations," and it is sometimes so big "that it takes a number of persons to carry it in a procession from the house to the wat" (Anuman 1988, 195). The basket was typically filled with food, sweetmeats, and fruits, while other items such as monks' robes were carried on other special trays. Phya Anuman continues, "There will be crowds of people along the route to witness the procession. If you are a wealthy man and your offerings are mean, there will be gossip in the village and you will 'lose face,' which psychologically, you do not desire. If there are many wealthy owners of different kans or parts of the recitation, it will be a great day. For there will be competition among themselves as to whose offerings and procession are the best and most costly because everyone wants to 'gain face' as much as possible" (1988, 195).

One of the only nineteenth-century accounts of a *Vessantara Jataka* recitation that occurs outside of Bangkok is found in the famous epic tale *Khun Chang Khun Phaen*, a version of which was recently translated into English by Chris Baker and Pasuk Phongpaichit (2010). This account provides insight not only into the grandeur possible in the lay offerings but also its comedic possibilities. The performance takes place at Wat Palelai in Suphanburi. The wealthy Khun

Chang is asked to host the Kumarn chapter, both because of the chapter's importance and because the chapter offerings are among the most grandiose. Khun Chang wants to impress the heroine, Phim, but Phim is in love with Khun Phaen. The heroine's mother will provide the offerings for the Matsi chapter. Each lay sponsor will parade through the town with the chapter offerings.

Our heroine's elegant offering is described in some detail. Its decorative elements—such as the lion that blocked Matsi's return—mirror the key events in the chapter and its inclusion of Hindu-derived deities intimate court Brahminical influence:

> Phim Philalai summoned the servants. "Make the betel for the episode for me. Go and fetch betelnut, pan leaf, and cotton."
>
> They brought many papaya to slice and carve, added color to make the figures bright and attractive, and set up the whole display as a mountain range.
>
> The carvings included a lion with a full face, standing looking majestic; Lord Brahma in a votive pose; Lord Indra soaring through the air holding a crystal; and Lord Narai mounted on Garuda, swooping across the sky. "Carry them along for everyone to appreciate." The servants set off immediately, and put them on display at the sala. The lay faithful crowded around to look. "Oh they did everything and so beautifully!" "All that hard work was certainly not wasted!" (Baker and Pasuk 2010, 70)

The pompous Khun Chang's offering provides a comic contrast. The carvings in his offering have nothing to do with the content of the Kumarn chapter; they include flowers, which typically symbolize love, surrounding a papaya carving of vultures eating a corpse! The display completed, Khun Chang orders his servant to carry the offerings in a noisy procession along the road so that people will see it, and he adds, "Be careful with the offerings. If you drop or lose anything, I'll kick you along like a ball" (Baker and Pasuk 2010, 69). The offerings sent off to the temple, Khun Chang then turns to bathing and dressing himself. Despite being old and ugly, Khun Chang tries his best to look attractive in order to woo the young and beautiful Phim. He then leaves his house and struts off "with his head in the air, nodding in greeting to bystanders." Once at the temple and at the appropriate time for the recitation of his chapter, Khun Chang orders his servants to present the offerings to the monks: "Pile up the offerings for the episode—all the taro, potato, white sugarcane, red sugarcane, watermelon, pomelo, maduk, mafai, chamot and wheel sweets, red sticky rice, touchstone sweets, clam sweets, and big melons. . . . Bring in the monks' robes and bowls, the mats, mattresses, seats, and cushions! And don't hide away the betel tray for the episode! Place it out in front of the salver with the triple robes" (Baker and Pasuk 2010, 71–72). Despite Khun Chang's best efforts, his hopes are dashed. The monk who is supposed to recite the Matsi chapter is taken ill and replaced by a talented novice. The novice is also interested in Phim and in a mildly erotic—and by modern standards wholly inappropriate—scene is able to enchant her such that at the end of his recitation, Phim removes her beautiful shoulder cloth and offers it to the novice. The romance continues, and I shall recommend the reader pursue the famous folktale for all the ensuing complications. However, Phim's prayer for her merit-making is also intriguing, for it reveals her conscious intentions; she prays, "I salute the almighty power. I offer alms. May I have rank and servants into the future, and be rich and joyful in every way" (Baker and Pasuk 2010, 75).

Phya Anuman provides one additional element of the offerings made in central Thai recitations that I have not encountered in the northern or northeastern village performances—namely, the offering of a pig's head. I have seen such offerings at wai khruu ceremonies for central Thai theater troupes and at major ceremonies at royal Buddhist temples in Bangkok.[43] According to Phya Anuman, this offering of a pig's head takes place early in the morning at the time that the first chapter is being recited. As he explains:

> It has been the custom that the presiding monk must be the abbot of the wat where the recitation takes place. Apart from the usual offering there must also be offered, a boiled pig's head complete with its four legs and tail, and a "Bai Sri Pak Cham," a sort of ritual—boiled rice in a big earthen bowl. Nobody can give me a reasonable explanation of this offering, except that it is merely a tradition and a custom. Here I venture a conjecture. It is a custom among well-to-do people to have a "Bai Sri" and a boiled pig's head, as an offering to the guardian spirits . . . of the place, when an important undertaking is to be carried out and a successful issue is desired. This has nothing to do with Buddhism but is a survival of the belief of primitive days. The guardian spirit of the place where an important undertaking is to take place must be propitiated before-hand. The boiled pig's head with the four legs and tail is nothing but a supposedly whole pig. It is easy to hoodwink the unseen, if you think so. Now you will understand why the abbot is the first person to perform the recitation for the abbot himself is the tangible guardian of the place. (Anuman 1988, 198; see also Manee 1976, 59)

Offerings of pigs' heads are often associated in Thailand with Brahminical rites. Court Brahmins played important roles in such royal rituals as coronations, royal weddings, oaths of allegiance, and the first ploughing ceremony. They also make astrological calculations for auspicious times for various ceremonies and undertakings. Even today Brahmins officiate at the ploughing ceremony, the anniversaries of the king's birthday and coronation, and the changing of the seasonal robes of the Emerald Buddha at Wat Phra Kaew.[44] Additional occasional royal ceremonies in which Brahmins are involved include the king's acceptance of a new white elephant, the birth of a royal child, a royal cremation, and so on. Among ordinary townspeople in the central region, Brahmins may be called upon to perform a variety of rites, such as the setting of a spirit house, the laying of a building's foundation stone, weddings, pre-ordination ceremonies, and various other occasions at homes, offices, schools, and shops. Many Buddhist rites are performed in conjunction with Brahmin priests, including even the installation of a Buddha image (the *phutthaphisek* ceremony). Thus the offering of the pig's head suggests officiants may be making a symbolic link to the court.

I did not ask systematically if the chapter offerings correlated in specific ways with the respective chapters. Anuman's description of the offering of the pig's head as part of the inception of the recitation suggests this possibility. The offerings described in *Khun Chang Khun Phaen* suggest that the lavish offerings were not only supposed to be spectacular but reflected in some manner the content of the specific chapter. A monk in Chanthaburi, after I thought the interview was over and was making small talk, unexpectedly mentioned that the foods offered to the monks varied according to the chapter. He said that for most chapters the monks were given *khao tom*, ground sticky rice steamed with sugarcane and coconut fillings. However, there were two exceptions: the monk who chanted Matsi was offered fruits in recognition of her role in the forest, and the monk who chanted Jujaka was given dried food because, after all, Jujaka had to go on a journey.[45]

Broader Central Thai Reading

The central Thai interpretation of the *Vessantara Jataka* in villages and towns beyond the court is notable for three aspects. The first is the shared emphasis placed on the Kumarn chapter. The second is that many central Thai monks and laity did not even mention the favorite chapters of the other two regions. Remarkably, one monk I interviewed in Chanthaburi explicitly told me that neither the Jujaka nor the Nakornkan chapter was of any particular importance; such a remark would have been unimaginable in northern or northeastern Thailand. Third, central Thais manifested a greater diversity—or lack of consensus—of favorite or most important chapters. A monk at Wat Dorn Taan, in Chanthaburi, said simply that people preferred to sponsor the chapters chanted during the day.

Overall, the most important single chapter in the central Thai reading of the text is the Kumarn chapter. The expanded text of the Kumarn chapter suggests its importance to royalist readings of the jataka. However, its importance appears to have been widely shared throughout the central Thai region. Longstanding public awareness of this chapter may date back to the former court custom, which lasted into the reign of Rama IV, of having the vice-king travel upcountry to receive offerings of lotus flowers (Gerini [1892] 1976, 37, 62); the lotus flowers likely represented the lotus pond in which the two children hid.[46] However, most people I interviewed did not highlight the chapter's metaphysical meaning but rather its focus on the children and in particular the bond between the mother and her children. One woman in Chanthaburi said that everyone's favorite chapter was Kumarn and the people in the audience often cried thinking of the poor children hiding in the pond. A monk in Bangkok highlighted an earlier part in the chapter, commenting, "The Kumarn chapter is the most famous. It is read with a very sad voice. The focus is on the bond between a mother and her children. The mother dreams about her children, wakes her children up and teaches them how to take care of themselves. She then heads off into the forest."[47] It is easy to imagine the tugs on the heartstrings of mothers in the audience.

The second most frequently mentioned chapter was the Matsi chapter, a favorite throughout Thailand. When Rama IV was a novice, he recited the Matsi chapter for his father (Gerini [1892] 1976, 35). The Maharaat and Nakornkan chapters were also mentioned, although with far less frequency than in northern or northeastern Thailand and with far less frequency than either the Kumarn or Matsi chapter. Thanakan was another chapter mentioned in the central region as a favorite. Two monks even went so far as to say that Thanakan was the main chapter. Not one single person whom I interviewed in the north or northeast mentioned Thanakan as being particularly important, and certainly not as being a favorite.

Mahaphon is another chapter frequently mentioned by monks and laity in the central region as one of their favorites. In this chapter Jujaka wanders in the forest and encounters Ajuta, the ascetic. The Mahaphon chapter was one of the three chapters that young novices were most likely to recite for their families and relatives (Gerini [1892] 1976, 27). Most people today emphasize its vivid reconstructions of nature. Several people mentioned that it is enjoyable because of its many birdcalls.[48] One monk told me that the monk who recites this chapter should have a lovely, delicate voice (*siang numnuan, phairoh*) in order to replicate the beauty and sounds of nature.[49] Kamala also notes, "The preacher of this episode had to be good at describing the forest poetically: its trees, streams, and wild animals—tigers, deer, songbirds" (2003, 7). With its descriptions of nature, one can speculate that rural audiences enjoyed the familiarity of the forest into which they would go to seek mushrooms, bamboo shoots, or kindling on its edges and honey, beeswax, animals, or wood in its inner depths. Alternatively, one can speculate about the appeal of the romance of nature and the deep forest to an urban population that rarely (if ever) ventured far from town.

However, one can also reconstruct a more comedic interpretation of the Mahaphon chapter that may have explained its popularity in the past. A senior monk who actively teaches how to recite this chapter to other monks and novices said he assigned it to novices because it is difficult and uses many different voices, from the gentle sounds of nature to the old man's voice of Jujaka and the booming voice (*siang raeng*) of Ajuta. As he demonstrated the voices, he brought the text to life. One monk famous for his recitations of the Mahaphon chapter was Ajarn Son Suwannasuk (1865-1932), the abbot of Wat Palelai in Suphanburi. In Kamala's description of the reason for his popularity one can begin to imagine an engaging and even funny encounter between Jujaka and the ascetic:

> When he was a young monk he had trained to preach the Vessantara Jataka. He could perform all episodes of the Vessantara, although he is said to have been at his best in the Mahaphon, the episode in which the brahmin Jujaka traveled alone through a great forest in order to reach Prince Vessantara's hermitage.... Whenever he took on the character of the vile brahmin who deceived the hermit he met in the jungle, Ajan Son drew great crowds. Once the preaching hall was so overcrowded that the sala (pavilion) collapsed. (Kamala 2003, 7)

Attitudes toward Jujaka

Although the modern attitudes toward Jujaka in central Thailand are mixed, they are more negative than positive. Of seven senior monks I interviewed in Bangkok, six had negative associations with the Jujaka chapter and character; the remaining monk had a more neutral description. People in the central region I interviewed outside of Bangkok had more ambiguous attitudes, but in no case was there the warm chuckle that accompanied the mention of Jujaka's name in northern Thailand. Instead of remarking on the comic timing skills required of a monk reciting the Jujaka chapter, monks focused on the ability to sound old.

A senior monk in Bangkok remarked that although the audience enjoyed listening to this chapter, no one wanted to be its host because everyone hated Jujaka: he was a cheater and liar (*khon niyom tae mai mii khrai yaak pen chaophaab, kliat Chuchok, tua kong*). Other members of the laity did not want to host the chapter because they were afraid they would become poor like Jujaka. Another senior Bangkok monk commented that he had heard that in the old days many women did not like hosting the Jujaka chapter because they were afraid that they might also get an old husband (*klua ja dai phua kae*). Yet another senior monk said members of the laity did not have a problem with the Jujaka chapter since they thought it might help them get rich and get a young wife (*tham hai ruai, ja dai mia sao*), but that it was difficult to find monks willing to perform the chapter. A monk in Thonburi remarked that hosts were not happy if they had to sponsor the Jujaka chapter, but they avoided the problem by inviting sponsors to host specific chapters, an invitation the laity was not likely to refuse. Another Bangkok monk assured me that the laity liked Jujaka because he became rich, but that monks themselves did not want to recite this chapter in part because it was a difficult chapter to perform and it involved a lot of acting, but also because one had to be able to replicate the voice of an old man. As one senior Bangkok monk added jokingly, "So it is not a good chapter for handsome monks."

Dr. Manop (Phrakhruu Winaithorn, Wat Pho, Bangkok) is possibly the most famous of the Jujaka monks in central Thailand. As he explained to me in a lengthy interview, he became interested in Jujaka because no one ever wanted to chant that chapter, yet it was necessary for a complete *Vessantara Jataka* recitation.[50] He tried to find people to teach him, but they had all died. Monks and laity were concerned that they might end up poor like Jujaka. When he indicated his interest in learning to perform this chapter, a senior monk commented, "Aren't you afraid of becoming impoverished" (*mai klua aaphab ryy*)? He said he used to think this way too, but then he changed his mind. He studied with Maha Fai,[51] who was originally from Nakhon Sawan but was then residing at Wat Ben, whose style imitated likay performances . He also studied with Ajarn Saiyan at Wat Welurachin in Thonburi; although not specifically a specialist in Jujaka, he had a funny style. He also spent time with beggars and listened to their music (*plaeng khoh thaan*). Dr. Manop now performs the Jujaka chapter at recitations held at the most famous of Bangkok's temples, including his own temple, Wat Mahathat, and Phutthamonthon.

Central Thai monks generally followed the text. Dr. Manop has written his own sections for Jujaka, in which he elaborates on the kinds of foods that

Jujaka's mother wanted to eat while she was pregnant. He has not gone further both because time is restricted and because many in the audience will complain that to go beyond the text (*nohk ryang*) is not authentic and therefore inappropriate. Another senior monk explained that when he is performing the formal *kamluang* version, he sticks to the script. However, he said there was more opportunity for humor in the *lae* form since monks could make faces and be more creative. He himself has written a version in which a smelly, drooling Jujaka, with his nose and hands eaten away by leprosy and his back bent over like a sea shell or a Volkswagen, eats seven pots of food.

Outside of Bangkok, among those whom I interviewed from the central region, the view of Jujaka was decidedly mixed. A taxi driver from Chachoengsao told me that people did not like Jujaka because he was always asking for things. An abbot in Chanthaburi said the audiences enjoyed the Jujaka chapter as it added flavor (*tham hai mii lot chaat*), but monks did not want to learn how to recite it (*mai mii khrai yaak rian*). A Mon abbot in Samut Sakon said that Jujaka has a funny body and is a reincarnation of Devadatta; he recalled beggars coming by boat during the recitation singing a song called "Waniphok" (unfortunately he could no longer remember the lyrics). Many people assured me that Jujaka was necessary because without Jujaka there would be no story. Several said Jujaka was not funny. An abbot in the town of Chanthaburi said that Jujaka was funny, and he had heard in the past that there were monks who wore white beards and carried yam bags and canes; he added that *baab* (demerit) and *bun* (merit) go together like black and white. Several said that people like Jujaka because Jujaka was hardworking and good at getting money (*haa ngen kaeng*).[52] Several people mentioned the existence of Jujaka amulets to help people make money (of which more in chapter 6). Another monk said that Jujaka should not be understood as a bad character; after all, he made it possible for Vessantara to become the Buddha (*chuai sang baramii*). Although a few people viewed Jujaka as a comic figure, the reasons that central Thais gave for their positive view of Jujaka tended to focus more on Jujaka as hardworking and good at making money. This portrayal is very different from the vaudevillian portrayal of Jujaka in the northeast or the beloved figure in the northern Thai portrayal.

Attitudes toward Amitataa

The portrayal of Amitataa is also varied, but she is generally portrayed as an obedient daughter and a good wife. A monk in Chanthaburi saw Amitataa as a good example of a dutiful daughter (*katanyu*) who helped her parents when they had no other way to repay their debt to Jujaka. Another monk at another temple in Chanthaburi praised her for being hardworking, saying the other village women were lazy and therefore jealous of her; but he also believed she went astray (*sia*) when she wanted Vessantara's children. Some monks used the village women as an example of how jealousy is wrong. A monk in Hua Hin described her as industrious. One senior monk in Bangkok used Amitataa to discuss virtue and parenting.[53] Many monks and members of the laity commented that her misfortune in having to marry Jujaka resulted from her old karma (*kam kao*) from her previous life playing itself out. As one villager explained, "Maybe she had not made merit properly back then; maybe she was naughty when the monks were making alms rounds. And so she ended up with a husband who looked like a toad [*khankhohk*]." Others portrayed Amitataa in a negative light, as "a young but bad-tempered, scolding wife" (Anuman 1988, 188).[54]

Various portrayals can be used to heighten the audience's disdain for Jujaka. In cases where Amitataa is a shrew, the audience can dislike both Jujaka and Amitataa. In cases where Amitataa is filial, she serves to heighten audience aversion to Jujaka. In some nineteenth-century central Thai recensions, an emotional scene is added to the brief Pali text. In this version, the parents meet with their daughter while Jujaka is waiting outside; the mother explains why they must surrender their beautiful daughter to this old man and end her hopes for a bright future (Damrong 1918). The tone is emotional and heart wrenching rather than comic; Jujaka appears covetous and disgusting. Similarly, Nidhi describes an Ayutthayan version in which "the Ayutthaya author of the recitation version of the Mahachat creates a whole scene of conversation between the Brahmin father and mother of Amittada and Jujaka, so that the giving away of their daughter does not appear too heartless" ([1982] 2005, 226).

Chapter Diversity

Thus a perusal of the favorite chapters in central Thailand reveals an emphasis on the Kumarn chapter and the metaphysical imagery of a boat crossing the sea of suffering, a wide diversity of chapters considered to be important, and a de-emphasis of the Jujaka chapter. Although opinions of the Jujaka chapter show some variation, they indicate significant reluctance among the laity to serve as its sponsors and among monks to serve as its performers. Priority appears to be given to the chapters that were most likely to have been endorsed by the court, including those most likely to be performed by young princes at their ordinations.

A recitation of the *Vessantara Jataka* held July 20–22, 2011, in honor of the king's eighty-fourth birthday and the queen's seventy-ninth birthday, provides some interesting, though not conclusive, contrasts regarding preferred chapters in contemporary Bangkok. The occasion was a fund-raiser held at Siriraj Hospital, the hospital where the king had been residing for some time. A board announced the amounts of money raised, divided by chapters. The total amount was 28,289,116 baht.[55] The three lowest earners were the Pali *Khathaphan* (at 1 million even), the Maharaat (at 1,006,000), and Jujaka (at 1,007,080). Most chapters, including Kumarn and Matsi, were in the 1,000,000 baht range. However, the highest earning chapters were Chohkasat (at 5,168,809), the Nakornkan (at 3,072,060), the Himaphan (at 3,015,440), and Sakabap (at 3,001,800). Himaphan is one of the chapters considered appropriate for royalty; Chohkasat and Sakabap are both chapters in which the god Indra appears, and Chohkasat has the word for king (*kasat*) explicitly in its title. I saw many in the audience wearing skirts from northeastern Thailand; they may have boosted the donations for the Nakornkan chapter. A similar fund-raiser in northern Thailand would likely have the Jujaka and Maharaat chapters at the top of the leaderboard, together with the *Khathaphan* and Nakornkan.

The Decline of *Vessantara Jataka*

Reviewing the history of performances of the *Vessantara Jataka* over the course of two centuries reveals dramatic changes. The French Bishop Pallegoix, who lived in Bangkok from the 1830s to his death in 1862, while writing of burlesque theater performances, describes the *Vessantara Jataka* as "a very touching story . . . which the monks preach each year, so as to make their listeners weep" ([1854] 2000, 122, 217, 253–55). Various sources, including the kings' edicts, inform us that bawdy comedic recitations were once widespread in Bangkok and central Thailand more broadly.[56] Already by the late nineteenth century, Ernest Young suggests that what was once a "universal custom" had become "chiefly a state ceremony performed in special places" ([1898] 1982, 324).[57] Similarly, novice recitation, once popular among all classes, became a custom of elite families.

This general decline of popular recitations in the central region may explain why anthropologists working in central Thai villages beginning in the late 1940s failed to include detailed descriptions of *Vessantara Jataka* recitations in their accounts. Beyond a passing mention that "in one of the more popular Jataka tales it is related that King Wessantara gave away his wealth, his kingdom, and finally his children" (1978, 143), Lauriston Sharp and Lucien Hanks make no mention of *Vessantara Jataka* recitations in their book.[58] Also writing of the same village (Baan Chan), located thirty-one kilometers northeast of Bangkok, Herbert Phillips makes no mention of *Vessantara Jataka* recitations. Similarly, Barend Terweil, writing of a village near the town of Ratburi, mentions that sermons often included episodes from the jatakas, and he makes repeated mention of the Phra Malai sermon but no explicit reference to the *Vessantara Jataka* or its recitation; furthermore, he notes that "at present . . . very few monks know how to chant Thai texts in the proper traditional manner and the story is not told any more" ([1975] 2012, 251).[59] Ajarn Kingkeo Attagara, in her dissertation on Ban Nai in Chonburi province, provides a list of village rituals but does not mention any recitations of the *Vessantara Jataka* (1967, 68–70).[60] Kaufman is one of the few anthropologists to provide even a minimal description of the ceremony, which appears to be primarily focused on Phrayar Naga (1960, 195). Jane Bunnag remarks on a "general decline in lay support" and an "increasingly general lack of enthusiasm for spending lavishly to support the Sangha; an attitude which is correlated with the growing interest in Western ways and material culture" (1973, 128). Thus the urban temple's recitation of the *Vessantara Jataka* was intended to raise 800,000 baht to complete the bot, but only realized 5,885 baht (1973, 118).

My own efforts to determine the frequency of *Vessantara Jataka* recitations suggest that in contemporary central Thailand, only a minority of temples still hold *Vessantara Jataka* recitations. It is held annually at major royal Bangkok temples of the Mahanikai order such as Wat Suthat, Wat Mahathat, Wat Pho, and Wat Suwannaram. However, the overall trend is toward greater decline. Wat Prayoon, which used to hold *Vessantara Jataka* recitations every year, now only holds it in "some years." At a temple I visited in Chanthaburi, I was told that the temple had not hosted a *Vessantara Jataka* recitation in at least thirty years. An herbal healer in Chanthaburi said that he has never seen it performed, adding that young people have no interest in it. At another temple in Chanthaburi (Wat Dorn Taan), where recitations are currently held, I was informed that *Vessantara Jataka* recitations had died out but were revived about thirty years ago. An abbot of a temple in Samut Sakorn said he had never seen a performance at his temple. A monk in Hua Hin said his temple no longer hosts the *Vessantara Jataka*, but an association (*krum sorn pariyatthitham*) founded in 1982 sponsors it each year and uses the money raised for good causes, such as pencils and other school supplies. A taxi driver from Suphanburi said he cannot remember his village ever hosting it. A taxi driver from Ayutthaya who had ordained for one Lent in Lopburi knew the *Vessantara Jataka* story from school but had never heard it recited. Some members of the laity even went so far as to deny that the *Vessantara Jataka* is recited in any temples in their province.

How should this dramatic pattern of decline be explained? The argument that statecraft had changed with the development of an administrative bureaucracy is not convincing since, as we have seen, the court and now the state have continued to support annual recitations. Similarly, the utilitarian desires of the villagers for prosperity, good crops, and good health remain in the present day. Three reasons for the observed decline seem more compelling.

Firstly, the world depression in the late 1920s had a huge impact on the central region. Lauriston Sharp and Lucien Hanks describe the impact on their village near Bangkok, writing that "from 1930 to 1945 Bang Chan underwent fifteen years of travail. The decade of easy living had ended. A new period began as prices for padi sagged and dropped" (1978, 145). More and more villagers pawned their land, such that "owners became renters and renters became hired laborers" (Sharp and Hanks 1978, 147). This economic decline would have obviously impacted all religious ceremonies since even cremations were being delayed (Sharp and Hanks 1978, 146). The central region appeared to have been experiencing hardships even before the Great Depression. In 1912 the *Bangkok Times Weekly Mail* reported that "a number of landowners in Bangkok are doing what they never had to do before—buying rice here and sending it to their tenants in the country who have nothing to live on" (*BTWM*, July 23, 1912). Another report records, "Very few people in Bangkok can afford to give alms every morning to the monks, and it is not unusual for priests to have to traverse a whole street before reaching a house where food is still distributed. . . . The cessation of almsgiving is not due to any great slackness of religious principles on the part of the people . . . but is wholly owing to the present high price of rice. Formerly the palace ladies used to send out alms every morning sufficient for nearly four hundred priests. This has also ceased" (*BTWM*, August 3, 1912).

Second, the replacement of the absolute monarchy with a constitutional monarchy in 1932 appears to have had a significant impact on a range of Buddhist ceremonies. Many members of the aristocracy had homes and landholdings outside of Bangkok; they supported local temples and local ceremonies. These local performances would have provided opportunities for local elites to display impressive krajaat offerings. After 1932 many of these princes went into exile, had their assets confiscated, or otherwise experienced economic hardships. Furthermore, the post-1932 governments sought to prioritize educational, economic, social, and administrative development over religious ritual. As Virginia Thompson summarizes the changes, "Festivals are dying out; and though the Buddhist Lent and Kathins continue to be observed, government schools for the first time in 1933 failed to honor Wan Phra, the Buddhist equivalent of Sunday" ([1941] 1967, 640).

Third, the court pressure to eliminate humor from the popular performances appears to have been another factor. As Phya Anuman observes, "The religion of the intellectual and of the mass . . . is not exactly the same" (1988,

193). Noting explicitly that the humor is focused in the Jujaka chapter, Anuman comments that popular recitations contained drollery and vulgarity upon which "the orthodox people frown" (1988, 193). He remarks that there are usually only the chapter sponsors and "a few old people" for the first chapters in the early morning, but there will "gradually be more people in the congregation in the succeeding kans until the fifth kan describing the scene of Jujaka, the aged Brahmin mendicant and his shrew, the young and beautiful wife." Anuman continues:

> There is much drollery and humour which naturally attracts the people. If the reciting monk is well known for his wit and humour, the place is packed to the utmost, for people from far and near, come to hear the recitation. The young men will ask for encores and more money contributions will willingly be made.... In former days such recitations with additions of drollery and humour in some cases overstepped the limits of modesty and were distasteful to cultured minds. Through the progress of time such things are now seldom to be found, for moral ideas have changed, but the need for humour is still there with the folk. While here in Bangkok the recitation in some wats has the tendency to be more prosaic and has become monotonous thus depriving much of its psychological value of display and ceremony which the mind needs as well. (1988, 199)

With a more orthodox emphasis on the Pali *Khathaphan*, one monk commented that the monks just read the words in Pali, with neither the monks themselves nor the audience knowing their meaning. Explaining that the audience was basically just listening to gain merit, he remarked that "the better the monk, the faster they could recite the Pali and the happier the audience was." Phya Anuman also observes that the Pali recension did not appeal to the masses:

> Although the hearing of such sacred words recited may give rise to mystical feelings, the people do not understand them and their emotions are not satisfied. The people want something more. They want to hear the voice of their favourite presiding monk, to hear his melodious voice which is familiar to them, for many are able to recite too. They want to live in love and hate, in happiness and sorrow, to be sad or to be in humour, and to raise their imaginative mind to a higher plane and ideal, which the various characters of the story manifest. Hence the reciting of the Pali Thousand Stanzas only, does not appeal to the masses. (1988, 191)[61]

Court disdain for humor in sacred performances, the growing influence of Thammayut monks, the Great Depression, and the aftermath of the political revolution of 1932 contributed to a significant decline in the number of temples holding *Vessantara Jataka* recitations. By the 1930s, it appears that the majority of central Thai temples were no longer holding recitations. By contrast, *Vessantara Jataka* recitations were continuing apace in northeastern Thailand. Why did performances continue in the northeast to the present day? We now turn to northeastern Thailand, where significant differences in the performance and interpretation will become apparent. From humor defeated we will find signs of humor diverted.

2

Northeastern Thailand
Humor Diverted

Although performances of the *Vessantara Jataka* have declined dramatically in the central region, recitations continue to be performed annually in most villages in the northeastern region.[1] Tracking Jujaka into northeastern villages is at once easy and difficult—easy because the story is so deeply embedded in the fabric of everyday village life and difficult because Jujaka masquerades as multiple personas. In the twelve-month lunar calendar of rituals, northeasterners have a month explicitly titled "Bun Pha Wet," or the "Merit-making for Vessantara" (*pha* is an honorific and *Wet* is an abbreviation from Wesandorn, the Thai pronunciation of Vessantara).[2] Typically falling in February–March, its importance is remarked by nearly every anthropologist who has conducted fieldwork in northeastern villages. Stanley Tambiah, writing of the village in Khon Kaen where he conducted his fieldwork in 1961, concludes Bun Pha Wet is "the grandest merit-making complex of ties in the village" (1970, 160). Thomas Kirsch, who conducted his fieldwork in 1962–64 in Nakhon Phanom, described it as the favorite and most elaborate of village annual ceremonies (1967, 154, 298).[3] In 1983 anthropologist Yukio Hayashi asked inhabitants of a village in Khon Kaen to rank thirteen annual rituals; villagers overwhelmingly ranked the Bun Pha Wet as the most important (2003, 121).[4] Leedom Lefferts and Sandra Cate have conducted by far the most extensive study of Bun Pha Wet. Having traveled to over two hundred temples in northeastern Thailand, Lefferts states unequivocally that Bun Pha Wet remains "the most important merit-making event of the ritual calendar" (2006/7, 100; see also Brereton and Somroay 2010, 30; Lefferts and Cate 2012).

More than just an annual celebration, the jataka permeates villagers' everyday lived environment. In ordinary conversations, a person who generously gives

Figure 7. Escorting the royal family to the village temple. After a ceremony inviting the royal family to return, monks and villagers prepare to process the scroll back to the village temple. Vessantara and Matsi ride the elephant. Made of burlap and decorated with flower garlands, the elephant has a large red and white penis. Village in Khon Kaen province, March 2010. Photo by author.

something away can be described as "having Vessantara's heart" (*jai Pha Wet*); a virtuous, long-suffering wife is said to be like Matsi; and children who listen to their parents are equated with Kanhaa and Chalii (e.g., Ladwig 2009, 142). Those who are stuffing themselves or eating noisily can be described as "eating like the brahmin" (*kin yang phraam*), that is, like Jujaka. Kirsch found that just during the period of his fieldwork, even beyond the festival, "the story of Vessantara was also portrayed by school children of the village on one occasion, and was performed (at the villagers' request) by traveling folk-players on two occasions" (1967, 38). A cave in Nakhon Phanom is known as "Tham Pha Wet," or Vessantara's cave (Kamala 2003, 31). One group of northeasterners, the Phu Thai, even believe themselves to be descendants of the father of Vessantara (Kirsch 1967, 36–38, 140).[5] Koichi Mizuno remarks that people in the northeastern village he studied were more familiar with Vessantara than the Buddha (1971, 171). The jataka is usually the only jataka depicted in temple murals (Brereton and Somroay 2010, 30). The jataka's pervasive presence in the local imagination is revealed in a well-known story about how Matsi saved the life of Ajarn Chop, one of the most famous meditation monks of the northeast. In 1930, when he was meditating in Udonthani, his mother came to visit. While she rested, Matsi appeared to her. Excited, she called to her son to come, just as a tree crashed on the spot where he had been sitting (for details, see Kamala 2003, 31).

The festival usually lasts three days, with the jataka itself being recounted on the final day. Because of its correlation with the Maitreya Buddha, northeasterners believe very strongly that the recitation of the jataka itself must begin and end within the same twenty-four-hour period. A complete recitation of the jataka begins in the early morning and ends late in the night. However, today the dominant format is an abridged version called Hok Kasat, or "The Six Royals." One monk I interviewed estimated that about 80 percent of *Vessantara Jataka* recitations in the northeast now are Hok Kasat performances. This abridged format lasts approximately three to five hours. The monks, typically three in number (*saam thammaat*, or "three pulpits"), use narrative interspersed with dialogue to tell the story, mixing stylized chanting with more normal speaking. In the Hok Kasat version I observed, one monk performed Vessantara's dialogues, another monk performed Matsi's dialogues, and the third monk performed the roles of King Sonchai and Jujaka; the monks summarized the remainder of the story largely through narration. Such Hok Kasat monks are usually virtuoso performers who specialize in this form. With the exception of the Hok Kasat abridgment, the rest of the celebration has remained largely unchanged; thus, the recitations of the *Phra Malai Sutra* (*Malai Myyn* and *Malai Saen*), the *Sangat*, and the Pali *Khathaphan* are recited as before (see Lefferts and Cate 2012, 56–57). Some elements, such as the village processions, have even expanded.

Booking monks during the month of Bun Pha Wet is challenging since they do numerous recitations during this period—often more than one in a single day. Using cell phones to coordinate their arrivals, monks involved in a full jataka performance typically recite a few pages of a given chapter and then leave to go to the next village. Hok Kasat monks are performing over a period of several hours, so they are unlikely to schedule more than one or two performances on a single day. One monk escorting me to interview a famous monk in Ubon remarked that my timing was fortunate; if I had come during the month of Bun Pha Wet, this monk would have been so busy that he would have had no time for an interview. Lefferts photographed the calendar of one famous preaching monk; he was booked solid over the weekends from Friday to Monday for over a month. The weekend I met him, he had four recitations to perform, traveling in one weekend from Selaphum district in Roi Et province to Nam Phong district in Khon Kaen and performing a recitation in Petchabun that Monday (I interviewed him in his car while he was en route).[6]

In this chapter, I will argue that Bangkok penetration into the northeast resulted in a kind of detente in which northeasterners maintained many elements of their performances but accommodated pressure from Bangkok by diverting the risqué elements in their humor to apolitical vaudeville. I divide this chapter into three main sections. In the first section, I lay out the northeastern emphasis on the Nakornkan chapter of the Bun Pha Wet. As we have seen, central Thai interpretations of the *Vessantara Jataka* tend to foreground status hierarchy and the metaphysics of boats; the northeastern interpretation highlights themes of family reunification and village well-being. Although northeasterners are more likely than central Thais to find some humor in Jujaka, he is not their central focus.

In the second and third sections, I explore the political ambiguity of the northeastern performance by focusing in particular on presences and absences. The second section suggests that northeasterners safeguarded their traditions by at once defying and accommodating the Bangkok court, conducting a royal procession with a democratic tone, portraying a comic Jujaka, and maintaining their Maitreyan emphasis. Despite the pro-royalist appearance of the royal procession, I will argue that its emphasis on family reunion is not necessarily evidence in favor of the acceptance of the legitimacy of earthly rulers: it can also be seen as a form of critique. Although the humor in the modern performances appears apolitical, evidence of absences suggest the possibility that the northeast acquiesced to many of Bangkok's concerns. The third section considers the muted humor, the virtual erasure of Amitataa from the story, and the apparent deletion of much of Jujaka's wandering. In addition to my own interviews and reading of secondary sources, the argument in this chapter owes much to discussions with Leedom Lefferts and Sandra Cate; indeed, Leedom accompanied me to the Hok Kasat performance I describe in this chapter.

Points of Emphasis in Northeastern Performances

In central Thailand the court developed the *Vessantara Jataka* into a state ritual that served to highlight the lavish offerings of individuals, reinforce social hierarchy, and impress a passive public. By contrast, the Bun Pha Wet as celebrated in the northeast is egalitarian and highly participatory. It has long been a time in which all the village households worked together and celebrated with friends and relatives from throughout the region. Accordingly, the northeastern festival has developed very different emphases—namely, themes of family reunification and village harmony.

The Nakornkan: Family Reunification

Unlike in central Thailand, where the Kumarn chapter became the primary focus, the main focus of the northeastern Bun Pha Wet is the Nakornkan and its theme of family reunification. Villagers and monks I asked overwhelmingly replied that Nakornkan was their favorite chapter. When I asked why, villagers explained that this chapter emphasized the family's return home and the audience felt happy that the whole family was reunited. In addition to the final Nakornkan chapter, many monks and villagers mentioned the Matsi chapter as one of their favorites, often remarking that a talented monk with a beautiful voice (*siang phroh*) would have the audience in tears. Indeed, the two chapters fit together in the northeastern reading, the agony of separation in the Matsi chapter heightening the joy of reunion in the Nakornkan chapter.

I was struck as I listened to a Hok Kasat version by how intensely the monks emphasized the anguish of the family breaking up, mirroring the agony in prolonged, operatic wailing. The performance began with a protracted dialogue between Indra and his chief queen, Phusadi, in heaven; Indra had to convince her the time had come for her to be reborn on earth as a human since Phusadi did not want to be separated from Indra. The story then proceeded in summary form until the announcement that Vessantara was to be banned from the kingdom. Vessantara hardly had any dialogue at all; his longest speech occurred in the scene where he says he does not want Matsi to suffer with him in the forest. Although not named as a favorite, this scene is part of the Himaphan chapter. Out of the five-hour performance, this chapter, in which King Sonchai banishes his son and Matsi decides to follow her husband, took a full forty-five minutes.

The focus was on Matsi, first as she convinced Vessantara that she would not stay in the palace but join him in exile, and then as she convinced Queen Phusadi and King Sonchai of the same point. The monk who performed the role of King Sonchai lamented that was he losing not only his son but also his daughter-in-law and his grandchildren; he asked Matsi to remain in the palace so she and his grandchildren would not have to face the dangers of the forest. The monk who dramatized Matsi gave an amazing performance, singing with stylized wailing and without taking a breath for virtuoso lengths of time. I was in awe. Refusing to change her mind, Matsi then took her leave from King Sonchai in another protracted emotional operatic soliloquy. The tension was at one point eased by a comic aside in which Matsi indignantly informs the audience that she was not about to stay and become King Sonchai's wife.

Matsi continued to play a major role in the remainder of the performance, with another long episode of stylized wailing reoccurring in the Matsi chapter itself as the monk re-created Matsi's grief at the loss of her children. Matsi's heart wrenching agony was clearly being dramatized in order to set the stage for the joy of the reunification. As several northeastern monks explained, the listeners feel sorry for Matsi (*songsaan*). She is a woman who has complete love for her husband and children. She did not need to go into the forest with Vessantara when he was banned, but she chose to stay with him so she could help him. She is the perfect wife. Her importance in the northeastern interpretation is reflected in the annual parade in Roi Et, where a large group of women form a contingent, each holding hands with two children.[7]

This theme of family reunification parallels the celebration as a time when village families and friends reunite. As Lefferts explains, "It is a major occasion during which villagers extend invitations to relatives, friends, work associates, and acquaintances to visit and see the village at its best" (2006/7, 102). Writing of the 1960s, William Klausner observes that "villagers come from near and far, and there is much visiting of old friends and, on the part of the young, making new friends" (1993, 47). A villager in Sakon Nakhon recalled that "elderly people from other Lao villages in Sakon Nakhon often came at that time to stay in his village wat to observe the Eight Precepts and listen to the recitations" (Kamala 2003, 245). A central Thai sangha administration official who traveled to Korat in 1934 and criticized the performance for being too "crude and noisy" noted that there were some three hundred villagers in the audience (Kamala 1997, 35). In order to accommodate the large number of guests, the host villagers prepared lodgings for their guests from neighboring villages; these lodgings were typically made of bamboo, thatch, and coconut fronds (Sommai and Dore 1991, 43; 1992, 90).

As Lefferts and Cate suggest, these festivities tie in with the Nakornkan, replicating the chapter's description of the court "celebrating the prince's return from exile" (2012, 48). The atmosphere is convivial. Walking through the village at the festival I was observing, I saw circles of families and friends chatting, drinking, and sharing laughs. Adding to the merriment, villagers usually hire outside performers as entertainment. In earlier times, there was often a performance by *morlam* singers. By the 1980s, Khon Kaen city had a traveling movie agent who brought the film equipment to the villages in a large truck; Hong

Kong kung fu movies were especially popular (Hayashi 2003, 133). Villagers used to construct their own wooden stages, but "today outside professional performers bring their own stages, loud-speaker systems, and curtains" (Lefferts 2006/7, 102). For the Bun Pha Wet celebration I saw in 2010, the temple committee had organized a traveling likay troupe to perform at night; during the day there was a fair replete with a large inflatable bouncy castle, a shooting gallery with prizes, a sort of merry-go-round, and a trampoline.

Bun Pha Wet is an occasion when villagers working in Bangkok or elsewhere are likely to return home.[8] As the poorest region of Thailand, the northeast has the highest rate of outmigration. In the past their sons and daughters migrated to Bangkok as pedicab drivers and domestic servants (Textor 1961; Keyes 1967, 36–40; Mills 1999). Writing in 1967, Keyes notes that in a village in Mahasarakham province, "49 percent of the men 20 years of age and over or 67 percent of the men between 30 and 39 had worked in Bangkok" (1967, 38). Although initially men migrated in search of work, increasingly women also began migrating to Bangkok; today many of Bangkok's taxi drivers and factory workers come from the northeast. Mary Beth Mills writes of a village she studied in which temporary and circulating migration to Bangkok, especially by unmarried youth, involved "nearly three-quarters of the community's 200 households" (1999, 28). Nonetheless, Mills notes that migrants she knew "retained close ties with people in the countryside, visiting at least once a year or more" and almost all "had plans to return home" (1999, 149). As Lefferts writes, "For many, the festival is a homecoming" (2006/7, 100). In this context, the northeastern emphasis on the Nakornkan becomes particularly poignant, as villagers celebrate the royal return as an emotional meta-language of their own family and village reunification.

Unifying the Village Community

Monks and laity I interviewed are quite explicit that one of the major purposes of the Bun Pha Wet is to foster unity among villagers. Even in its abridged form, the celebration of the *Vessantara Jataka* requires considerable cooperation. As one villager explained to Cate and Lefferts, "The whole village is owner of the festival" (2012, 169). In addition to preparing food for all the friends and relatives, households must organize the temple decorations and share financial costs. As Lefferts writes:

> The Bun Phra Wet requires extensive planning: the temple and village committees agree on a date a month or more in advance and discuss the amount of monetary assessment to be levied on each household; a contract is signed with

one or more performing groups; and the lay head of the wat committee (*tayok wat*) contacts monks from outside the community and invites them to participate. At least two weeks before the festival, specific groups of people begin to prepare the requisite accouterments: elderly men weave bamboo baskets; elderly women prepare a thousand betel nut chews, a thousand hand-rolled cigarettes, a thousand balls of rice, and other prescribed items. The tayok wat pulls out of storage the nine long flags that are flown in the wat and locates the bamboo poles that hold them. (2006/7, 102)

Villagers contribute labor to decorating the temple grounds, turning it into the mythical "royal space, appropriate to welcome the prince and the Buddha-to-be" (Lefferts and Cate 2012, 49). Outside the hall where the monks will recite the jataka, villagers erect nine poles with long flags, one at the entrance of the temple and the remaining eight at the eight cardinal points (Lefferts and Cate 2012, 49). Inside the temple hall, villagers re-create the royal forest hermitage (*rajawat*), decorating it with banana tree stalks, sugarcane stalks, coconuts, flowers, wasp nests, and the like. One or two large jars of water, representing the pond where the royal children hid, are filled with lotus flowers, fish, turtles, and mud. At the recitation I observed, villagers festooned the temple hall in strings with birds and fish woven from banana leaves, strings of colored paper with old audiocassette tape forming tassels, strings of plastic straws cut into short lengths and interspersed with bits of colored paper, and strings onto which rice had been glued. The baskets that each household had prepared were set on a shelf that surrounded the rajawat. Villagers also helped prepare the thousand wicks, which were then formed into thirteen candles, the number of wicks in each candle dependent upon the number of the respective verses in each chapter. Each candle would be lit as its corresponding chapter was read and the wax dripped into one of the pots of water; after the ceremony villagers could take this sacralized water (*nam mon*) home to bless their homes and family (although at the recitation I observed, almost no one did so). (For further details, see Manee 1976, 52–53; Cate and Lefferts 2012, 176–77; Lefferts and Cate 2012.)

Because the recitation was also an important occasion to raise money for their village temple, monks and villagers also worked together to organize a temple fair. The temple fair included not only secular forms of public entertainment, but also various booths staffed by local monks and novices to raise money with such enticements as selling gold leaf to apply to a statue of the Buddha and raffling objects donated by villagers, merchants, and others (*soi daaw*; see Lefferts 2006/7, 102).

Number of Monks

Further contributing to the unifying and democratic character of the northeastern performance is its pattern of drawing upon large numbers of local monks and novices. Unlike in other regions of the country, here it is not uncommon for a full recitation to involve as many as forty to fifty monks and novices, each reading a few pages. Thus Klausner writes, "It is customary to have fifty or more monks come and participate in this festival, as the chanting is very taxing, and the more monks there are, the less each individual monk will have to chant" (1993, 47). In Tambiah's account, villagers invited twenty-six monks from surrounding temples to join those at their own temple (1970, 168). At Ubon's Wat Mongkol Kowithaaram in 2009 they invited fifty monks; another temple in Ubon invited sixty monks. Monks in Khon Kaen described a similar pattern, generally inviting thirty-five to forty-five monks from many different temples in the area. Each monk chants for some ten to thirty minutes. A shorter chapter may involve three or four monks, and longer chapters may involve many more. The decision about the number of temples (*sai kii wat*) and the number of monks to invite is made by the individual temple committees. Very often novices are invited to do the opening *Sangat* or *Khathaphan*. This democratic format serves to help bind village temples in the region into a strong social network.

Given the large number of monks and novices being invited, the emphasis was less on operatic excellence than on broad participation. Unlike the north, the northeast does not associate particular monks with specific chapters.[9] Although the proliferation of the Hok Kasat version has changed this democratic format, villagers have maintained elements of this pattern by having local monks from their own and adjoining temples recite the other affiliated texts that comprise the full northeastern complement. In the village recitation I observed, villagers had invited about a dozen monks to receive morning alms. A local senior monk chanted the *Phra Malai Sutra*, and four local novices raced through the *Khathaphan* in Pali, all four reading simultaneously in a delightful cacophony. We all empathized with the lone novice who was the last to finish his assigned verses.

Selection of Sponsors: Lottery

In contrast to the central Thai pattern in which considerable attention was focused on the lavishness of the individual offerings, the northeastern offerings for the monks were relatively modest and offered conjointly on behalf of the village as a whole. A typical donation for an ordinary monk reciting verses for the ceremony is currently about 300-500 baht, but a monk known for his preaching talents can receive significantly more. A Hok Kasat monk may be invited for an initial donation of 1,500-2,000 baht. At the Hok Kasat performance I observed, the three monks each received an offering of 2,000 baht, a sum agreed upon in advance and given to them on behalf of the village as a whole; the three sponsors of the monks received no formal public recognition, although their identities were known to the villagers themselves. During a monk's performance, the audience members often get up and put additional money into his bag, particularly if he "has hit a few 'high notes' or held a sound for a long time" (Klausner 1993, 48). At large events, a monk may receive as much as another 5,000 baht in his bag. In addition to spontaneous offerings from the audience during the performance, monks may include a special request for donations for their character. During the recitation I attended, villagers made much smaller donations into their bags, in amounts ranging from 1-100 baht. "Jujaka" also begged for additional money from his audience, provoking chuckles and more contributions.

In general in the northeast, the hosts of each chapter are drawn by lottery (*jap salak*) or by people volunteering to host.[10] Villagers are responsible for providing an offering to whichever monks recite the particular verses in the chapter they have drawn. Since individual monks were not reciting designated chapters, there was no need to have lay sponsors for specific chapters. Instead a lottery was held for gifts for the local monks and novices involved in chanting the related texts. At the recitation I observed, while the dozen or so monks and novices were eating their morning meal, a bowl was passed around among the laity. Everyone kept drawing names until all the slips of paper were gone. Because there was little time to prepare any specific gifts, the offerings were simple. Offerings for novices and monks consisted of only a few necessities, although whoever drew the name of the abbot was likely to prepare a somewhat more substantial gift. The offerings were presented unobtrusively after a given monk or novice had completed his reading and was leaving. The only exception to this pattern of simple offerings was the "random" offering (*kan lon*), an additional overflow offering for which villagers parade through the village soliciting extra donations.[11] Unlike the central Thai performance, in which the chapter offerings were a competitive form of public display for status by individual donors, the northeastern celebration focused more on village unity and shared responsibility.

The Three Processions

Also contributing to the unification of the village are the three processions that form part of the normal structure of northeastern Bun Pha Wet celebrations.

Each of these processions is an invitation to various personages, invisible and visible, to join the recitation. Typically, the first day features the procession inviting Upakut; on the second day the procession inviting Vessantara and his family takes place; and the third day features the procession of one thousand balls of rice, which serves as a de facto invitation to the villagers themselves.[12] Rather than proceed to the temple as individuated sponsors of a given chapter, the village comes together to parade as a group. Participation in the three processions, each historically a unique component in the northeastern performance, is open to everyone.

Inviting Upakut

Typical of northeastern recitations is the invitation to Upakut (Upagupta).[13] Villagers have various explanations, albeit interrelated, for who Upakut is. Upakut is widely associated with "protecting the village and ensuring the rains" (Tambiah 1970, 161; see also Kirsch 1967; Sparkes 2005, 177, 184-92; Lefferts and Cate 2012, 51). For many villagers Upakut is a Naga, or serpent spirit, who lives in the water and is invited to safeguard against murder, storms, and lightning that Mara might cause; Mara is variously understood as the king of demons, the Buddha's enemy, and a signifier of death (Tambiah 1970, 170). In another interpretation, Upakut is believed to be the monk whom King Asoka called upon to preside over a gathering of one thousand monks to eliminate doctrinal differences; at the time Upakut was meditating in water (Tambiah 1970, 170). The most colorful explanation was provided by two elderly ritual specialists: "Phraa Uppakrut was a novice who lived in the water of the swamp (in a subterranean town). He was the son of Buddha and his mother was a mermaid. It is said that once the Buddha forced his semen ... into the water and a mermaid swallowed it, became pregnant and gave birth to Uppakrut. He was subsequently ordained as a novice (or monk) and lives in the water, for he is a mermaid's son" (Tambiah 1970, 169).

Regardless of his origins, Tambiah notes that informants were agreed that Upakut is the enemy of Mara and is invited to the Bun Pha Wet in order to safeguard the proceedings. One village elder explained, "Whenever a big ceremony is undertaken, he must be invited to ward off dangers caused by Praya Marn [Mara]," adding, "When we make merit, we invite Phraa Uppakrut to come so that he will prevent fighting and killing and damage by fire" (Tambiah 1970, 170). Sommai Premchit and Amphay Dore also suggest that Upakut is invited to prevent Mara from interrupting the ceremony (1992, 87). Thus, as Tambiah summarizes, "In the villagers' statements continual references are made to rain, long life, good health and absence of conflict" (1970, 172; for further discussion, see Tambiah 1970, 168-78; Lux 1971; Strong 1992; Sparkes 2005, 185-86).

The invitation of Upakut in effect marks the formal beginning of the ceremony. Tambiah provides one of the earliest scholarly accounts of this part of the ritual. Since villagers believe Upakut lives under water, they form a procession to a nearby body of water (*byng*) such as a pond or swamp. Inviting Upakut involves the following list of ritual paraphernalia: "a monk's bowl, a set of monk's yellow robes, umbrella, a pair of monk's sandals, two small images of the Buddha, *karuphan* (made of various kinds of flowers), puffed rice, two banana-leaf trays containing locally made cigarettes, and a kettle" (Tambiah 1970, 162–63). Tambiah continues:

> All these articles were placed on a cushion which rested in the centre of a wooden sedan chair. The procession actually started from the *wat* compound and was led by three monks, who were followed by elderly leaders (*phuu thaw*) carrying the sedan chair. Then followed a large body of villagers—men, women, and children. Guns were carried, and music was provided by a bamboo flute and drums. Conspicuous were the flags with pictures of Nang Thoranee (goddess of the earth), a mermaid, a crocodile, etc.[14] . . . The procession, after passing through the hamlet, headed for a pond in the paddy fields. The ponds selected must have water all the year round. (1970, 162–63)

At the pond, a village elder invited Upakut "to come and be guardian of the ceremony." The elder threw puffed rice on the sedan chair. Guns were fired several times, drums were beaten, and the people shouted "Chaiyo." According to Tambiah, the guns were intended to frighten off Mara, and the word "chaiyo" proclaimed their victory. The kettle was then filled with water from the pond and placed on the sedan chair. In Tambiah's account, Upakut appears to have been symbolically represented by the water in the kettle; several other accounts suggest that Upakut is represented by a stone placed on a tray or even a novice or monk (e.g., Sommai and Dore 1992, 94; Strong 1992, 172). When the Upakut procession arrived at the temple, the villagers circumambulated the temple hall (*sala*) three times. The flags were placed near the pulpit; the kettle and other paraphernalia were placed on a shelf in the corner of the sala (Tambiah 1970, 162). Other observers provide a similar account of villagers setting off firecrackers, firing guns, and playing musical instruments as they processed back to the temple (Manee 1976, 51; Sommai and Dore 1992, 94; Sparkes 2005, 186).

At the ceremony I observed in a Khon Kaen village, the invitation of Upakut occurred in the morning rather than in the late afternoon, and at the river that flowed by the temple rather than outside the village at a pond.[15] Nonetheless, it was very similar in principle to the invitation ceremony described by Tambiah. As the monks were eating their morning meal, villagers began assembling the things needed to invite Upakut: his statue, an umbrella, a begging bowl, sandals, robes, a tea pot, candles, and flowers. The procession of villagers, led by the head of the lay community (*thayok wat*), headed down the steps to the river landing. No monks were involved. The lay leader performed the invitation ceremony. Instead of stones, he used a statue of Upakut. At the completion of the brief ceremony, instead of firing guns or lighting firecrackers, villagers beat a large gong. The thayok wat who was carrying the Upakut statue led the procession of villagers up the stairs from the river. The procession was mainly women, many of whom were dancing as they walked. We danced around the sala three times. The thayok wat then climbed up on a preaching chair to place Upakut, his umbrella, and other paraphernalia up high in the back left corner facing the altar. After some announcements, which included remarks by the abbot about his plans for future building, this phase of the ceremony was complete and we returned to our village hosts for breakfast around 9:00 a.m.

Villagers' concern with safeguarding harmony and unity against Mara raises questions about their implicit views about the potential sources of conflict or evil. At the most mundane level, one can easily imagine youth getting into arguments with youth from other villages; I recall many such fights at alcohol-infused temple festivals I have attended. Tambiah also suggests that the Upakut is defending Buddhism "by reconciling theological differences in the sangha" (1970, 171); as one reflects back on history, one can reconstruct the possible tension that existed as villagers' traditional religious praxis came into increasing conflict with the central Thai Thammayut reform order. It is also perhaps not too much of a stretch to imagine that for nineteenth-century villagers fearful of the next military campaign, their prayers for protection included protection from the Bangkok state itself. Thus in their invitation to Upakut—this ambiguous mix of naga, novice, and court-appointed negotiator—villagers express their hope that their community might be in harmony with nature, the monastic hierarchy, and the state—and thereby safe from drought, schism, and war, respectively.

Scroll Procession: The Royal Return

A major element widespread throughout the northeast—but not a part of traditional recitations in northern or central Thailand—is the invitation of Vessantara and Matsi to return to the kingdom and the correlated procession of the scroll (Mizuno 1971, 171; Manee 1976, 51-53; Sommai and Dore 1992, 87; Hayashi 2003, 132; Sparkes 2005, 188). This phase of the ritual begins outside of the village where villagers gather to hold a ceremony in which they invite Vessantara and Matsi to return. Carrying a long cloth scroll, the villagers then parade through the village, ending at the temple. These scrolls are a key symbol of the Bun Pha Wet; Lefferts and Cate have documented their widespread use throughout the northeast.[16] About a meter wide and some 25–45 meters in length, "even today, almost every village temple in northeastern Thailand owns at least one of these scrolls" (Lefferts 2006/7, 99; see also Cate and Lefferts 2012, 170). The scroll is so representative of northeastern Bun Pha Wet celebrations that the scroll parade scene has even been painted into the wall mural of a recently built temple in Khon Kaen city, which itself does not even hold *Vessantara Jataka* recitations.

Described as "murals on the move," Sandra Cate and Leedom Lefferts have conducted by far the most detailed studies of this hitherto neglected folk art. The importance of the Nakornkan chapter is reinforced in the scroll since this chapter typically "receives by far the most space"; one scroll devoted "almost 35 percent of its length to this one section" (2012, 172,174). However, as they point out, the scroll "has meaning beyond its immediate function of visually recounting the *Vessantara Jataka*," but it is in effect an embodiment of Vessantara and the royal family returning to the city, with the villagers serving as their entourage. As Lefferts explains, "The scroll itself becomes the prince and his family, invited by the villagers and guided by them from the forest to which they had been exiled into this village, transformed into a city (*muang*), and into the wat, transformed into a palace (*wang*)" (2006/7, 101).

Making the parallel between the mythological time of the Nakornkan and the real time of the present even more vivid, many villages have expanded the procession beyond the scroll itself. Very often villagers are dressed up as Vessantara, Matsi, and other figures from the jataka, the royal figures often making their return on elephants, real or fake. Klausner provides an account of a northeastern village (probably Ubon) from the 1960s: "The monks in their bright saffron robes lead the procession. It is a colorful sight. However, perhaps the most imposing sight of the process is the 'white elephant' of Prawaed. The villagers spend quite a few days in making a gigantic elephant out of bamboo and white cloth. It is usually a realistic facsimile, even to the last detail of an extra large cucumber dangling between the elephant's hind legs. The elephant is pushed along on a cart" (Klausner 1993, 47; see also Manee 1976, 52–53).

The colorful procession I saw in Khon Kaen village in March 2010 began in the late afternoon of the day before the jataka recitation. Around 3:30 p.m. Leedom and I made our way through the village to the pond on its outskirts, where Vessantara and Matsi were to be invited to return. We caught up with a life-size elephant covered with brown burlap except for its white and gold tusks and its large red and white penis. Freshly decorated with flowers, it carried a covered howdah on its back. We joined a cast of characters in rented likay costumes, drummers, monks, and an ever-growing crowd of villagers. Soon the thayok wat arrived by bicycle carrying in his basket a small Buddha image intended to represent Vessantara.[17] Mats were spread out on the ground next to the pond, the monks sitting with their backs to the pond and the villagers facing the pond. With the Buddha image and the scroll before him on one tray and a second tray with flowers and two lit candles, the thayok wat read the invitation to Vessantara from a small book. Afterward the monks chanted and the audience chanted in response. The ceremony completed, the village children who were representing Vessantara and Matsi, dressed in colorful rented outfits, climbed up a ladder to get into the howdah on the elephant's back.

The procession was now ready to begin. The elephant carrying Vessantara and Matsi led the way. Next followed Jujaka with the two royal children bound by ropes. The two children also wore fancy rented costumes. The villager playing Jujaka, a samlor driver the rest of the year, wore white *jongkrabaen* style pants with a pillow stuffed under his blue T-shirt; he carried a white shoulder cloth, white bag, and cane. He danced *lamwong* style, mock hitting the children as the parade moved through the village.

The scroll procession was next and portrayed the story in reverse. Monks led the scroll parade, holding the Nakornkan scene. Villagers held the rest of the scroll, which concluded with a scene representing the first chapter, the scene of the Buddha's enlightenment during which he recalled his life as Vessantara, and scenes from the *Phra Malai Sutra* in which Phra Malai visits the heavens and the hells.[18] Following the scroll were large numbers of villagers. There was a contingent of middle-aged dancing housewives, wearing flowers in their hair and matching flowered shirts and northeastern-style skirts (*phasin*). Next came a contingent of male drummers, many of them in flowered shirts that matched those of the housewives. Following behind the drummers was an array of musicians, some with cymbals, one with a keyboard, and another with an unusual Thai style wood carved electric guitar; these latter instruments were plugged into a loudspeaker system mounted to a cart. Along the route inside the village, people had set up chairs with plastic water jugs and cups so that all could quench their thirst in the heat. Some threw water on us as we walked past; even the ice cube that landed in my collar felt refreshing in the heat. As we passed by the shops near the temple, one of the shop ladies threw handfuls of candies into the passing crowd, bringing about squeals of laughter as children dove and jumped to get them.

When the procession arrived at the temple, the scroll was carried around the sala three times. Since it was impossible to parade the burlap elephant over the rough ground around the sala, its riders dismounted and joined the circumambulating group. Villagers apparently often hold mock debates about whether or not Jujaka should be allowed to enter the temple grounds but conclude that he should be allowed since "he's really a Buddhist."[19] On the occasion I observed, Jujaka joined in the circumambulations. As they entered, some villagers placed small offerings into the nine baskets located at the bottoms of flagpoles around the sala.[20] Then the scroll was mounted on the walls surrounding the sala. A monk seated in a preaching chair recited the *Phra Malai Sutra*, setting the stage for the recitation of the *Vessantara Jataka* to follow the next day. Villagers then went home for dinner, returning in the evening for the show performed by traveling entertainers and other temple fair attractions.

Procession of the Thousand Balls of Rice

The day of the recitation begins with another occasion for a shared village procession—namely, "the procession of the thousand balls of rice" (*hae khao phan kohn*). The procession serves in effect as the final village announcement. The thousand balls of rice represent the thousand verses of the *Vessantara Jataka*. The procession I saw in 2010 was similar in principle to that described by Tambiah, but with some differences in detail.[21] The procession began at about 4:00 a.m. on the morning of the day the *Vessantara Jataka* was to be recited (the temple fair had ended and the performers were packing up). The thousand balls of rice had been arranged into a single beautiful arrangement comprised of a pyramidal cone with one thousand sticks of bamboo about two feet in length, on the end of each of which jiggled a small ball of sticky rice. The arrangement had been prepared in advance and had been placed in the center of the temple sala on a fancy gold-painted preaching chair (*thammart*). While it was still dark, a small nucleus of villagers assembled at the temple. Two men carried the arrangement through the streets of the village, the white rice balls bouncing up and down with each step, casting a beautiful contrast against the dark streets. Behind them followed a small contingent of noisy drummers, men with cymbals, and a man playing the same apparently homemade electric wooden guitar attached to amplifiers on a cart. As the procession passed by village homes, more and more villagers joined in (though not as many as during the Vessantara procession the day before since many young people who had attended the fair were still sleeping and others were preparing breakfast for their families and guests). After arriving at the village temple, the procession circumambulated the sala three times, and the arrangement was then returned to its former position in the sala.

With the monks and audience now assembled, the lay leader chanted an invitation to the thewada and spirits of deceased ancestors "who have not yet moved to the spirit world" to join in listening to the *Vessantara Jataka* (Lefferts and Cate 2012, 57). As Lefferts and Cate summarize, "Past and present beings of the water, the heavens and of the earth are now assembled" (2012, 57). A monk then chanted the *Sangat*, beginning with the current date as told in the number of years that have passed since the Buddha reached enlightenment. The *Sangat* explains the occasion of the Buddha's enlightenment when the earth goddess (Mae Thoranii) bears witness to the merit he had accumulated in his previous life as Vessantara by sending a flood.

On the occasion I observed, the *Sangat* took place at about 6:00 a.m. It was followed by the recitation of the *Khathaphan* by four novices, each of whom was sitting in one of the four decorated preaching chairs. Since the *Khathaphan* is in Pali and the novices were reading simultaneously, no one understood much of it. When the *Khathaphan* was completed, the monks were offered breakfast. All of us who were at the temple then ate breakfast together. We then waited for the Hok Kasat monks to arrive.

The three monks arrived at the village temple shortly before 11:00 a.m. The villagers offered them food, and we ate after the monks had finished. At about noon, the recitation began. Their performance was impressive, a mix of narrative and dialogues between characters. The performance took about five hours to complete, with the monk who was performing Vessantara taking breaks from time to time to talk quietly on his cell phone or smoke a cigarette. Some chapters were given in brief summary form, and other moments were turned into extended dialogues. When the end of each chapter was announced, a villager sounded the gong. As a new chapter began, joss sticks and the appropriate candle with wicks corresponding to the number of verses in the chapter were lit. Since the Hok Kasat version abridged various chapters, candles accumulated as some chapters were zipped through in a matter of minutes.

Unlike the central Thai interpretation, in which emphasis is placed on the children in the Kumarn chapter, the clear emphasis in the northeastern interpretation is on family reunification and village solidarity. Rather than grandiose displays of individual offerings, the emphasis is on drawing the village together as a unified whole. This difference in emphasis is also reflected visually in the scrolls, the panels concerning Vessantara's gift of the children and Matsi's return to the hermitage being "only of middling importance" (Cate and Lefferts 2012, 172). This royal reunification occurring in the jataka no doubt parallels the joy villagers are feeling at the reunification of their own families for the recitation.

Political Ambiguity: Signs of Defiance and Accommodation

Given the significant difference in emphases between the central Thai court and northeastern interpretations of the *Vessantara Jataka*, the question arises of the Thai state's position in the peasant imaginaire. How did villagers view the state? If Bangkok was trying to reshape or suppress jataka performances, is there any evidence that they were successful in the northeast? Assessing the extent of central Thai influence involves knowing more about historical indigenous practices. Unfortunately, such a historical reconstruction, due to the lack of sources, involves considerable speculation. On the one hand, to the extent that northeasterners maintained a very different tradition in their celebration of the *Vessantara Jataka*, their maintenance of their customs or refusal to modify their recitations could be construed as evidence of their independence and even as a form of defiance. Indeed, Pranee Wongthet suggests that the jatakas helped the Laotian prisoners of war who were resettled in Prachinburi in eastern Thailand "to achieve new awareness and hope in a new society, a society in which they had to accept the status 'captives'" (1989, 24). On the other hand, to the extent that the Bun Pha Wet was altered to be more in accord with central Thai values, northeasterners could be seen as accommodating Bangkok. In this section, I will explore three elements of ambiguity: the royal procession, the portrayal of Jujaka, and the timing of the performance. Positioned between defiance and accommodation, each hints at the possibility that northeasterners maintained their independent interpretations while accepting compromises with the Bangkok court.

The Royal Procession

As is borne out by the importance placed on the Nakornkan chapter, for northeasterners the return of Vessantara and his family "is the core meaning of the festival" (Lefferts 2006/7, 103). What is the political subjectivity being expressed by northeasterners in the Bun Pha Wet? If the theme of family reunification, celebrated in the Nakornkan chapter, resonates with the villagers, are villagers generalizing from the royalty whose reunion is being celebrated in the jataka to earthly royalty? Cate and Lefferts suggest that for participants, the scroll becomes "far more than a 'representation' of the story; it provides the means by which the community transforms itself into the subjects of the Prince" (2012,

174). By processing the scroll, celebrants are "actively becoming subjects of the Prince accompanying his return" (Cate and Lefferts 2012, 178). As one monk explained, "the spirit of the Prince is 'in the cloth'" (Cate and Lefferts 2012, 174).

The northeastern emphasis on the return of Vessantara and his family would appear to support a pro-royalist interpretation. The incorporation of national symbolism in many northeastern performances provides further support. Nationalist messaging is interwoven into the modern performances in the northeast: "In Northeast Thailand this procession also demonstrates that today's citizens now come to agree with today's ruler and his kingdom. Flags—both the Thai national flag and the yellow flag of Buddhism—are ubiquitous during this festival along the route of the procession" (Cate and Lefferts 2012, 178–79).

However, interpreting the political subjectivity inherent in the northeastern interpretation is complex. In a region whose political allegiance has long been under suspicion by the Thai state, the ubiquitous flags also raise a sense of "the lady doth protest too much, methinks." The northeast is comprised largely of war captives force marched into the region from Laos at the beginning of the nineteenth century.[22] Their resistance to the Bangkok administration was made manifest in various revolts, the most famous being the millenarian "Holy Men's Revolts" of 1902. In the nineteenth century, it is doubtful that northeastern war captives were sponsoring recitations of the *Vessantara Jataka* in order to celebrate the legitimacy of the Bangkok court. It is possible the court promoted recitations hoping to portray itself as the chosen government of the people, but it is unclear how effective this approach would have been. Few northeasterners would have seen the lavish gifts offered when the *Vessantara Jataka* was being performed in Bangkok; if they had, it is not known what their reaction might have been—awe or outrage at the extravagance in the midst of widespread poverty.

The generations of impoverished northeasterners who sought work as domestic servants, factory workers, or taxi drivers in Bangkok were often mocked as unsophisticated country bumpkins and turned into stock characters in many national television shows; these portrayals often comprised themes in northeastern morlam and country songs (*luuk thung*). Their loyalty and identity as "Thai" citizens has even been called into question (e.g., Keyes 1967; Mills 1999). During World War II the northeast was an important base for the Free Thai movement (e.g., Haseman 1978; Wimon 1997; Sorasak 2005). The region has a history of electing socialist candidates and over the course of the twentieth century became a stronghold of the Communist Party of Thailand. Accordingly, the region was subject to numerous communist suppression campaigns during the 1960s and 1970s (Morell and Chai-anan 1981; Bowie 1997; Kasian 2001).

The region remains the poorest in Thailand. Today the northeast is a bulwark of the "red shirt movement," many members of which are increasingly critical of the institution of the monarchy and its accumulated wealth.[23] Many northeasterners today hold great admiration for King Bhumiphol; however, their admiration is not based upon his support for recitations of the *Vessantara Jataka* or a royalist ideology reinforced by the jataka but instead on his efforts over the decades to provide relief from their poverty. Faced with the dangers of having their village labeled as "communist," it is not inconceivable that earlier generations of villagers sought to couch their struggles for social justice within a framework that affirmed their loyalty to the nation. A similar argument can be made for villagers now being labeled as "republican" at a time when charges of lèse majesté can lead to prison terms (see Streckfuss 1995, 2011; Thongchai 2012).

Cate and Lefferts broach the political message, suggesting that "the Bun Phra Wet constitutes also a festival of allegiance: the people have acquiesced and accepted this Prince as their future King" (2012, 178). However, accepting Vessantara as their future king is not necessarily the same as accepting an earthly ruler as their legitimate king. Thus the royalist imagery raises the question, in whose kingdom did the northeastern villagers imagine themselves? Did villagers presume an isomorphism between the divine and the earthly, between the village realm and the national realm? The possibility exists that villagers may have been envisioning a divide between the future imagined ideal and the present earthly reality, either as two dissociated realms or as associated realms in which the former is used to critique the latter.

In part analyzing the jataka's political resonances depends on how one interprets the manner of Vessantara and Matsi's exile and return. If one believes Vessantara was virtuous by helping his drought-ridden neighbors, then the courtiers or populace who pressured King Sonchai were in the wrong and Vessantara was unjustly banished. If one believes Vessantara was wrong to give away the rain-making elephant, then he deserved his punishment. The decision to invite Vessantara back to their village kingdom can be understood accordingly as the result of recognition by the court, courtiers, and/or populace that they had made a mistake. Alternatively, the invitation can be understood as the result of the people's willingness to forgive Vessantara for his mistaken overzealousness.

In socialist Laos, where the king was deposed in 1975, the jataka is widely celebrated and Vessantara is portrayed as having made a mistake. As a former longtime monk explained to Patrice Ladwig:

As a king, Vessantara has responsibility for the kingdom and all the people living in it. They pay taxes, are his subjects and the kingdom flourishes until he gives away the magic white elephant. Although the elephant was born on the same day as Vessantara, it's strictly speaking not his personal property. It is the *ming-khwan* [magic symbol; essence] of the kingdom and it is necessary to protect it and make the rice fields fertile. The elephant is the property of the people. Vessantara knows that, but still gives it away without any conditions when the Brahmins from the other kingdom beg for it. The people are right to demand his dethronement, because he has acted in a highly irresponsible manner. A king cannot simply do what he wants to do, he has to care for the people and listen to them. That is sometimes the problem with kingship. (2009, 151)

Another man that Ladwig interviewed also portrayed Vessantara's decision to give away his wife and children negatively, saying:

If you think about the difficulty of his decision, what options did he have? He also loves his wife and children, but he also wants to attain enlightenment. He acts incorrectly in some sense in order to advance on the path of enlightenment. I pity him for that, but through this big sacrifice he becomes the Buddha and will be able to show humanity the way out of suffering. And in the end, when he was Vessantara, he was a being with much merit, but still a human, and as humans we sometimes fail. (2009, 153)

For Ladwig, the audiences show pity and compassion for Vessantara. As he explains the Lao interpretation, "An exemplary figure that is human without producing suffering and carrying out acts that are at least ambivalent is probably more accessible for the listener than a completely perfected being" (2009, 153). Northeasterners seem to share the view of their fellow Lao across the Mekong River that Vessantara may have made mistakes; even in one of the scrolls Lefferts and Cate studied, two court ministers remark to each other, "Phra Wet should not have given away his two royal children" (2012, 136).

In the central Thai murals depicting the Chohkasat chapter, Vessantara's parents invite the royal couple to return (Lefferts and Cate 2012, 91). By contrast, Lefferts and Cate note that northeastern paintings "emphasise the role of the citizens in extending the invitation to Phra Wet to return to govern his kingdom"; northeastern artists usually depict "citizens, soldiers, or ministers" who "march to the forest to negotiate his return to the kingdom and then parade triumphantly back to the temple" (2012, 4, 91).[24] Lefferts and Cate suggest that this democratic interpretation is grounded in long-standing traditions of popular involvement in local government:

> Until the state-administered reforms established centralised control of the ordination, promotion, and titles of monks, village laity in this region exercised considerable control over their local wat, even choosing their own abbots in a tradition that one government inspector of the period identified as *samoson sommut* (authority based on popular consent). Perhaps echoing this tradition, in the performance of Bun Phra Wet, monks and laity alike have interpreted to us the relationship between the citizens and their king—the act of sending him into exile and then requesting his return—as the workings of *prachathipathai* (democracy). (2012, 55–56)

Supporting this more democratic world view is evidence from northeastern temple paintings. Bonnie Brereton and Somroay Yencheuy suggest that the early twentieth-century temple murals in the central and southern regions of Thailand reflect a hierarchical world view, with villagers "relegated to genre scenes found only on the periphery." By contrast, they suggest that northeastern murals are "radically different in that the landscape they portray is a democratic one, in which commoners and their activities occupy all levels of the composition" (2010, 47).

Furthermore, it should be noted that the idea of elective rather than hereditary kingship is not new in Buddhist philosophy, but rather comprised its core. Thus the *Aggana Sutra* describes how after disorder among human beings reached its highest point, people "selected from among themselves 'the handsomest, the best favoured, the most attractive, the most capable' and invited him to be king in return for their contribution of 'a proportion' of their rice" (Tambiah 1976, 13). If villagers did follow millenarian leaders, it may well have been because, in accord with the *Aggana Sutra*, they had elected them. Even in modern times the carryover of the Bun Pha Wet appears to contain an ambiguous message about monarchy, given that republican red shirts and kingless socialist Lao still celebrate readings of the *Vessantara Jataka*.

Vaudevillian Jujaka

The northeastern portrayal of Jujaka is similarly ambiguous in that he is both despised and comic. Many monks and members of the laity I interviewed had negative associations with Jujaka, suggesting that the dominant central Thai portrayal was also influential in the northeast. Thus northeasterners commented that Jujaka was a bad person, that it was difficult to find monks willing to perform his role, and that the laity had mixed feelings about sponsoring this chapter. A monk in Ubon observed that he mollifies distressed sponsors of the Jujaka chapter by explaining that Jujaka is very clever and reminding them that Jujaka is an important part of the story. Another monk in Khon Kaen noted that while the listening audience enjoys the humor of Jujaka, many think hosting Jujaka will bring them demerit (*baab*); he also explains to the unhappy hosts that Jujaka is part of the story. When I asked one monk who specializes in the role of Jujaka in the Hok Kasat performances how he came to learn this role, he replied, "Because no one else was willing to do it. Everyone wants to be Vessantara or Matsi!" He added that actually the Jujaka part is harder to perform than the other characters because one has to be able to make one's voice sound like that of an old man.[25] This negativity is reflected in the debates over whether Jujaka should be allowed to enter the temple at the end of the scroll procession.[26]

Yet many northeasterners also view the Jujaka chapter—if not Jujaka himself—as comic. It is difficult to present a "traditional" northeastern depiction of Jujaka because the performance has undergone such dramatic changes in the process of its abridgment to the Hok Kasat form. In the Hok Kasat performances, which dominate the Bun Pha Wet performances of today in the northeast, Jujaka is typically portrayed as a vaudevillian character. Although Jujaka is not terrifying, as in central Thai portrayals, he is also not beloved, as in northern Thailand. Given the court's concern with comedic recitations of the *Vessantara Jataka*, the portrayal of Jujaka as comic rather than terrifying suggests a certain measure of northeastern defiance. However, as the following description of the Jujaka chapter suggests, the laughter the modern Jujaka provokes appears apolitical. This apolitical comedy suggests the possibility that the court had gained some measure of control in the northeast.

In the Hok Kasat performance I attended in March 2010, Jujaka played a central role and provoked laughter on multiple occasions. The dialogue centering on the Jujaka chapter comprised a prominent part of the overall performance. Out of the five-hour performance, the Jujaka chapter lasted about fifty minutes. One monk took the role of narrator and Jujaka; a second monk took the role of Jujaka's friend with whom Jujaka entrusted his money and the role of Amitataa. The narrator began the chapter, informing the audience that those who listen to this chapter will be rewarded with big clumps of bananas, abundant vegetables, and other good things. As a comic aside, he adds that bad things will happen to those who are not listening.

The Jujaka monk then begins the chapter with a description of Jujaka's mother's abnormal pregnancy, during which she was always eating; he humorously enumerates in operatic style that she ate seven bushels of vegetables,

Figure 8. Bawdy scroll scene from Jujaka chapter. This excerpt shows Amitataa being taunted by village women and Amitataa with Jujaka. Village in Khon Kaen province, March 2010. Photo by author.

thirty pans of chopped buffalo meat (*laap khwaai*), three plates of chopped chicken (*laap kai*), plates of chopped oxen meat (*laap wua*), and more. Her pregnancy lasted ten months and she was in labor for seven days. She no sooner delivered Jujaka than she died. Jujaka's father then took over raising him, but he died. Then a series of relatives all took over the responsibility of raising him: paternal grandparents, maternal grandparents, paternal aunts and uncles, and maternal aunts and uncles. All died, and so Jujaka ended up at the temple. But he caused conflict at the temple and was expelled. These events are not in the Pali version or in the central Thai court version.

Jujaka thus began his life as a beggar. The monk then sings in operatic style a poetic sequence in which Jujaka begs for goods that rhyme with the names of the cities to which he travels next: Jujaka set off for Laos, where he asked for glasses (*kaeo*), and then traveled to Muang Maeo. There he asked for a musical instrument (*phin*) and traveled to China (*jin*). In China he asked for a comb (*wii*), then traveled to Lopburi. There he asked for chicken (*kai*) and traveled to Chiang Mai. There he asked for mats (*sat*) and traveled to Korat. He asked for pillows (*mohn*) and traveled to Yasothon, and so on. The monk then says that Jujaka has now arrived in the midst of the audience and wants money. Audience members then begin going up to the monk and dropping coins or bills into his bag. When I approach, the monk says, "Thank you very much" in English, again getting a laugh from the crowd of listeners. As villagers come up, he blesses them with such remarks as "Now you will go to heaven, your water buffaloes will be beautiful and fetch a good price, you will be rewarded with 10,000 or 100,000 baht." None of these events are in the Pali version or in the central Thai court version.

Jujaka then arrives at his friend's house. An exchange follows when his friend asks who is at the door and Jujaka replies, "Bak Sui." (*Laughter since we were not expecting that name.*) His friend (the role played by another monk) finally recognizes him after several exchanges and invites him in to relax and have a smoke. The friend then comments that Jujaka is looking like a westerner with lots of money, asking how he made his money and suggesting that perhaps he had become rich selling coconuts. Jujaka says he has a sophisticated strategy. (*Laughter.*)

Jujaka then explains that he has 400 *kahapana* to entrust. After some to and fro about 400 kahapana being equivalent to 400 baht, the friend suggests that Jujaka should put that money in a bank. After all, Khon Kaen has banks. Jujaka says banks are a big hassle and one has to have all kinds of papers, such as household registration forms and birth certificates. No one has recorded his birth and he has no birth certificate. (*Laughter.*) The friend then says that if he is to take Jujaka's money, then they will need witnesses, and so they should proceed to the kamnan's house. The occasion for the visit to the kamnan is a setup for an absurd series of puns. The kamnan is named Joi; his wife, the Village Head, is named Mitr, and their daughter, the Assistant Village Head, is named Jat. Having these three administrative titles in the same household is already implausible, so the setup alone gets laughs. But when the names are pronounced together, the result is *JoiMitrJat*, which in effect means "completely and utterly vanished," intimating what will happen to Jujaka's money. Some banter follows about when Jujaka will return to claim his money, whether at 2:00 a.m. or 3:00 a.m. Jujaka then heads off to continue begging.

Jujaka returns to reclaim his money. "Hello, anyone home?" The friend comes to the door and refuses to believe his eyes. Jujaka says he wants his money back. "Oh, you want your money? How do you want your money? In Lao kip or Thai baht?" Jujaka, growling, replies, "Thai baht of course."

The friend then explains: "Times were bad, my water buffalo had no offspring, and the crops failed. So I had to buy rice. And then my daughter wanted a red skirt for New Years. She went to the market and came home. She told me that she had seen you at the market. She said she saw with her own eyes that you were hit by a car and died. I believed her and so I used up the rest of the money making merit for you."

"But I'm not dead. My money is gone?!"

"I thought you were dead, so I made merit for you."

"How would I get any merit? I'm not a ghost [*phii*] yet." (*Laughter.*)

"My money is gone [*Ngen kuu mot*]." (*He begins crying.*)

"Well, crying won't get your money back." The friend then introduces a plan for compensation, asking Jujaka if he has a wife. When Jujaka says no, the friend then says he has three daughters. The audience knows that normally only one daughter is mentioned, so this remark draws laughter. There is some back and forth about what a good deal three daughters for 400 baht is. The three daughters are a setup for a series of risqué puns. The friend proceeds to describe his oldest daughter, who is a school teacher in the government system and teaches private lessons on weekends. Jujaka replies that she would be fine, that it would be good for him to have a smart wife since he is stupid (*byyk*). The friend then says her name is Khruu Tuai, with a series of alternative mispronunciations, which ends with *khuai tru*, which might mean "my water buffalo" (northeastern pronunciation) or "my penis." The friend adds that "it" could be sold for several thousand baht. (*Laughter.*)

The friend then describes his second daughter, who works as a servant for a Chinese storeowner in Khon Kaen. Because she is so light skinned, the Chinese merchant calls her Aa Maa, Aa Moi, Aa Mao, and Aaa, shifting the pronunciation of the words through the word for pubic hair (*moi*) and ending up with Ow Maa, meaning "to take" and also "to have sexual intercourse with a dog." (*Laughter.*) Jujaka screams in dismay, hollering that he just wants his money. (*More laughter.*)

The friend then changes the tone, saying that he was just joking. He had another daughter named Thong Amitataa, but Jujaka would have to talk to her himself. The friend then calls for his daughter, calling her a variety of names from Thong (Gold) to Ii Laa (Last-Born) and Taa, the last name setting up the next joke. Jujaka asks for her name. The monk, acting out the role of Amitataa, replies, "My name is Tukhataa [doll]," with overly effeminate intonation. (*Laughter, since no one was expecting that answer.*) Jujaka asks if she will take him for her husband (*ow ai pai pen phua?*). She replies, "But you are so old." Jujaka starts hollering again, "Just give me my money." The friend intervenes to say that his daughter is only sixteen years old and that Jujaka should use a magical formula to win her over. Jujaka does so and the friend comments that the magic seems to have taken effect. (*Laughter.*) The couple take their leave, Jujaka saying, "Good-bye my buddy [*sio*]." The friend replies, "Now you are not my buddy, but my son-in-law." (*Laughter.*) Jujaka and his bride get into a car and repair to Jujaka's village.

From this point on, the tone shifts from vaudeville spoken in dialect to a summary of the main points of the narrative, done in operatic style. The narrative hints at the poetic form of the longer textual version. The Jujaka monk explains that Jujaka can hardly wait for dark to fall and wishes that he were young again. He expresses his desire in a literally flowery poetic form:

Smell the fragrance of *dohk chik*	Reminds one of the old home [*baan lang*]
Smell the fragrance of *dohk khang*	Reminds one of *dohk waa*
Smell the fragrance of *dohk champaa*	Reminds one of the old place [*baan kao*]
Smell the fragrance of *dohk khaatkhao*	And one is young forever.

This pattern follows a common poetic form of the last word rhyming with the last word of the next line (e.g., *lang* with *khang*; *waa* with *paa*).

The monk summarizes the remaining story in the chapter—namely, that Amitataa encountered village women who were upset with her because their husbands were jealous of Jujaka; that Amitataa returned home and told Jujaka she would no longer leave her house; that Jujaka offered to do all the household chores; and that Amitataa refused since her mother told her it would bring demerit (*baab*) if her husband did domestic work. Consequently Jujaka sets off in search of Vessantara's children. Thus ends the fifth chapter called Jujaka, with its seventy-nine verses. The monk then instructs that the gong be sounded to mark the end of the chapter, concluding with "Amen" (*Sathu*).

It is difficult to assess whether this vaudevillian humor was a long-standing component of the northeastern oral version or a recent addition. This version is certainly a significant expansion upon both the Pali and central Thai tellings. Based on contrived setups of names or words with alternative meanings, its humor is centered on the dialogue between Jujaka and his friend. Jujaka does not appear to be particularly terrifying, but rather more like any other frustrated villager who wants his money back. This telling has no particular didactic purpose. It is not a satirical look at politicians or monks. While slightly bawdy, its humor is not critical of the state or the sangha. However, accounts of northeastern morlam singers refer to the political innuendo possible in vaudeville. So the tame comedy of the present remains an ambiguous inroad into the past.

Maitreyan Timing

When compared to central Thailand, northeastern Thailand maintained its own traditional form of Bun Pha Wet, as is evident from its differing emphases on chapters (Kumarn versus Nakornkan), numbers of monks (few versus many), and types of processions (hierarchical display versus democratic unity) that I have already described. Another important difference was the respective timing. Unlike central Thailand, where the recitation is often held during Buddhist Lent, in northeastern Thailand the *Vessantara Jataka* is almost always recited during "Month Four" (February–March).[27] The celebration is not associated with a particular day but can occur any time during that month to facilitate the large numbers of villages that are holding recitations. Increasingly, the celebrations are being scheduled on weekends since many of the younger generation have jobs during the workweek. Consequently, some Bun Pha Wet are held somewhat earlier or later than Month Four.

Furthermore, villagers in the northeast believe that the recitation must be completed in a twenty-four-hour period. Villagers are explicit in explaining that this belief is based in the Maitreya Buddha's own admonition to Phra Malai. The recitation of the *Phra Malai Sutra* is an integral part of the Bun Pha Wet. Phra Malai's journey to heaven and especially to hell is reproduced on nearly all the temple scrolls (Lefferts and Cate 2012, 57). As a dedication panel on a 1959 scroll states, "Phra Malaithera recommended that people keep the Five and Eight Precepts and listen to the sermon on Phra Wet so that they could meet Phra Sri Ariya [Maitreya]. In the next life, one will meet the meritorious person. After leaving this world, one will go to the gem city of heaven, truly" (Lefferts and Cate 2012, 8).

The Bangkok court was likely particularly worried about millenarian revolts linked to the Maitreya Buddha. Given that the central Thai court would have been interested in breaking the link between the jataka recitation and millenarianism, one might expect the court to have sought to alter the timing in the northeast. To the extent the court sought to change the timing and to the extent the northeasterners refused to change it, the maintenance of the twenty-four-hour exhortation, the reading of the *Phra Malai Sutra*, and the non-Lenten timing suggest the possibility of northeastern defiance. However, the possibility that the northeasterners accommodated Bangkok's concerns to some extent is suggested by the form of the *Sangat*, in which monks state the number of years that have passed since the Buddha reached enlightenment. As Coedes explains, "Formerly it was the custom of the Siamese priests to begin their sermons with a reference to the exact number of years, months, and days that had passed since Parinirvana and the number of years, months, and days still to run before the predicted ending of the five thousand years" (1956, 108). However, Rama V had this practice ended, decreeing that "henceforth monks should not begin their sermons by declaring the exact time in years, months, and days that had passed since the Enlightenment and the time remaining until the year 5,000" (Reynolds 1972, 135). As Coedes writes, "King Chulalongkorn, considering that this continued reference to the danger that menaced religion was irksome, and after having consulted the Supreme Head of the clergy, who was himself critical of this announcement of the disappearance of the Doctrine, simply suppressed any reference to the years to come, retaining only a mention of the time that had passed since Parinirvana" (1956, 108).[28] The contemporary *Sangat* recited in the northeast no longer refers to the number of years until the arrival of Maitreya, instead describing only the number of years that have elapsed since the Buddha reached enlightenment.

Provocative Absences: Hints at an Earlier History

Although the presence of elements in the northeastern celebrations—such as the royal procession, a comic Jujaka, and Maitreyan timing—is ambiguous, the absence of other elements further suggests northeastern accommodation toward the central Thai court's efforts to reshape northeastern cultural practices. Although northeasterners maintained many elements of their traditional Bun Pha Wet, there is also evidence to suggest that northeastern religious practices did change, perhaps voluntarily or perhaps in reaction to growing administrative pressure. Brereton and Somroay note that central Thai aesthetic views increasingly shaped northeastern practices: "As outsiders from the capital, many of them tended to denigrate the local people and their cultural forms. Consequently, and not surprisingly, village abbots often failed to see the value of local Buddhist art and architectural styles and encouraged their replacement by Bangkok-influenced models" (2010, 6).

If Bangkok's artistic aesthetics came to replace indigenous traditions, one would also expect to see central Thai values shaping religious practices as well. In addition to his dislike of comedic recitations of the *Vessantara Jataka*, Rama IV banned northeastern morlam singing from the capital in an 1865 proclamation because of its destructive influence on traditional Siamese musical genres; he justified his reasoning by wryly appealing to superstitious beliefs—namely, that morlam singing affected the rainfall and was responsible for poor rice yields. Although it was likely only enforced in the central region, the king issued a request that "all Thai who remain loyal and grateful to him . . . stop performing the Laokaan [bamboo reed instrument]." To give this request more weight, he added, "Anyone who disobeys this proclamation will be taxed" (Miller 1985, 38–39; see also Raikes 1988, 21–22).

The Bangkok court sought to consolidate its control over the region through more than direct military suppression. The Thammayut monks residing in northeastern temples made efforts to change local practices of Buddhism. The ecclesiastical head for the Thammayut order in Ubon enforced strict standards of behavior on monks under his control, "forbidding participation in indigenous rituals such as the rocket festival (*bun bangfai*), boat-racing, drum-beating competitions, and horse raising" (Taylor 1993, 51–52). His successor, Ubalii, a northeastern monk who studied in Bangkok and had become abbot at Wat Supat in Ubon, found the behavior of the undereducated rural sangha to be unsatisfactory. In his report for Monthon Isan, Ubalii noted that villagers still preferred to spend their time listening to the Mahachat tale, which they believed earned them merit, rather than adhering to "doctrinal tradition" (Taylor 1993, 64). As local administrators were increasingly replaced by central Thai officials, one would expect to see increasing central Thai influence. In this section I will highlight three intriguing absences that hint at the possible success of state efforts to control recitations of the *Vessantara Jataka* in the northeast: the lack of bawdiness, the erasure of Amitataa, and the abridgement of Jujaka's adventures.

Bawdiness Restrained

Although there is some bawdy humor in the modern performances of the Jujaka chapter in the northeast today, it appears relatively tame in comparison with other northeast festivals, most notably the Rocket Festival. A hint that the northeastern performance of the Bun Pha Wet may have been toned down comes from Klausner's work. He notes that in comparison with the bacchanalian celebration of the Rocket Festival, the Bun Pha Wet is more subdued; Klausner even suggests that the Bun Pha Wet is set apart from other village rituals because "there is none of the drinking or dancing which is usually found in village festival life" (1993, 47). While the Bun Pha Wet certainly has drinking and dancing nowadays, it may be that in comparison with other northeastern festivals, it was more heavily monitored during the twentieth century.

Temple murals provide further hints that the northeastern celebration of Bun Pha Wet was once more bacchanalian. Thus at Wat Ban Yang in Mahasarakham province, the Great Departure scene, when the Buddha leaves the palace to pursue enlightenment, depicts the palace concubines with exposed breasts and genitalia. At Wat Khon Kaen Nya in Roi Et province, the flood scene at Buddha's enlightenment portrays Mara's soldiers being consumed by fish, drawn with exaggerated genitalia protruding from the fishes' mouths (Brereton and Somroay 2010, 69). Depictions of village ritual processions show "the men sometimes wrapping their legs around the women or fondling their breasts — the women resisting, acquiescing, or sometimes reciprocating" (Brereton and Somroay 2010, 69-72). Village scrolls are themselves often quite ribald.

The northeastern region is hardly devoid of bawdy humor. One simply needs to consider the water-cannon-like penises ejaculating streams of water all over onlookers during the Rocket Festival, another event associated with rain-making and village health. In my incarnation as a prudish westerner, I was shocked when I attended my first Rocket Festival in the 1970s. Klausner provides a description:

> On the day preceding the actual shooting of skyrockets there is much gaiety in the village with song and dance, drinking and a great deal of sexual by-play with risqué songs, crude sexual pantomimes, boys dressed as girls, and phallic symbols waved about and shot at girls from slingshots attached around the boy's groin. In the usually peaceful and restrained setting of the Wat, there is a late afternoon drunken dance parade about the temple hall with the completed skyrockets on view for all to admire. The reeling parade, danced almost exclusively by men, weaves around the sala and is a colorful spectacle with male costumes varying from the traditional tartan-like plaid sarong to a borrowed dress or skirt and a bandana tied around the head and grapefruit stuffed in the appropriate places. (1993, 43; see also Tambiah 1970, 285-311; Akin 1992)

Monks were also directly involved in the festivities, and if the rockets they made turned out to be duds, they could even be "thrown unceremoniously into muddy fields" (Klausner 1993, 42, 45).

Even today one finds phallic imagery incorporated into many village religious practices. Mary Beth Mills has written about how villagers became concerned about a rash of unexplained deaths among northeastern migrant workers in Singapore and elsewhere. Blaming these deaths on "widow ghosts" (*phii mae mai*), rural communities throughout the northeast erected large, carved wooden penises on village gateposts and at the entrances of most houses to ward off these deadly female spirits (Mills 1995, 245). Similarly, one finds penis-shaped amulets (*palad khik*) throughout the northeast. Blessed by monks, men often wear these on strings around their waists as protection against loss of virility and physical vitality (Mills 1995, 251). I found a large variety of palat khik for sale in varying sizes in a northeastern store selling Buddhist paraphernalia. As the popularity of morlam singers attests, bawdy humor is not shocking to northeastern villagers (Compton 1979; Miller 1985).

There is evidence of state involvement in policing the Rocket Festival in recent decades. As Klausner notes, "The dangers inherent in the Bang Fai [Rocket] festival are recognized to the extent that the District Headquarters must be advised of the date of the festival and permission asked to hold it. Usually, at the villagers' request, two or three policemen will be stationed in the village during the festival" (1993, 45). Similarly, in his description of the changes made by government officials in the Rocket Festival, Rabibhadana Akin writes, "The villagers report that the Governor has prohibited the display of phallic symbols and other similar sexual objects such as figures of copulating animals or human beings" (1992, 15).

A sense of how the worlds of ritual and politics can interconnect is provided in Akin's account of their interactions in the town of Yasothon, which has become the most famous of the tourist destinations since the tourist board began promoting the Rocket Festival in 1972. Official involvement has changed the style of dancing and the decorative patterns of the rockets to be "more like those of Bangkok and the Central Region"; the focus has shifted to nagas shooting water rather than phallic images (Akin 1992, 19). One can also see the sociopolitical shifts in the route of the processions, which originally began at the temple and went to the guardian spirit shrines; when the statue of King Chulalongkorn was erected in 1988–89, the procession added this new destination (1992, 18). Akin provides further insight into the wide-reaching changes that have been occurring: "Since Bun Bang-Fai in Yasothon has become a national event, the Governor, the highest national representative in the province, has become the Chairman of the Organizing Committee and has a great deal of weight in the way the ceremony is organized. In 1992, Commander of the Second Army was the Chair Person of the Ceremony. . . . Earlier (prior to 1966, or 1977, or 1987 according to different sources of information), the Municipal Authority was the main organizer of the ceremony" (1992, 17).[29]

If the Rocket Festival is only being subdued in recent decades, it is possible that the Bun Pha Wet came under tighter government control even earlier given its closer association with Maitreya and millenarianism. The colorful and bawdy celebration of the *Vessantara Jataka* that still takes place each year in the remote northeastern province of Loei may provide a hint into how Bun Pha Wet may have been celebrated in the nineteenth and early twentieth centuries. The Bun Pha Wet at Dansai is a time when "thousands of people head through the streets for what becomes a chaotic fertility festival, many participants in the

Figure 9. Phiitaakhon ghosts on display at Dansai Folk Museum. Wat Phonchai, Amphur Dansai, Loei province, July 2009. Photo by author.

parade carry phallic water guns and comically over-sized wooden penises with them."[30] The celebration is primarily known for its ghosts called *phiitaakhon*.[31] Although no one really knows the meaning of this term, the two most frequent explanations are that it is abridged from "ghosts following people" (*phii taam khon*) or "ghosts with human eyes" (*phii taa khon*).

These phiitaakhon ghosts are part of the contingents of alcohol-infused dancers in the royal procession to welcome Vessantara and Matsi back to the city. These ghosts are not mentioned in the Pali text. Some people suggest that they were awoken from the dead by all the cheering of the city folk when they learned of Vessantara and Matsi's return. Another explanation is that they are supposed to frighten evil spirits away. According to Jetjaras na Ranong, the men who dress as phiitaakhon "believe that donning this attire will spare them from illness in the years to come" (2009). These ghosts are portrayed by village men wearing fabulous masked costumes. The masks are made from the woven bamboo containers that are usually used for steaming sticky rice (*huad*); these rice baskets are attached to coconut-tree trunks and carved into elongated faces with horns and prominent long noses, painted in wild designs. The body of the costume is comprised of strips of cloth that hang from head to toe. The dancers wear strings of noisy bells around their waists and dance around brandishing swords or large penises with tips painted bright red. The headdresses in particular can easily take a month to make and involve considerable artistry; indeed, local stores are now producing them for sale to tourists. The masks are stunningly beautiful and are often made in secret to hide the identity of the mask's maker. After the festivities they are also supposed to be thrown in the river; in fact, most families, including the owners of the guesthouse I stayed at in Dansai, keep theirs for the next year (or increasingly sell them to tourists).[32]

Joining in the parade are also contingents of semi-naked men in blackface and covered with leaves. They are said to represent wild, primitive forest people who, it seems, had befriended the royal family while they were living in the forest; they carry bamboo poles, which they use to pound the ground as they walk. There are also ghosts, wearing costumes made in the yellow cloth associated with monks' robes (see Jetjaras 2009). In addition, the parade includes two giant phiitaakhon, one male and one female, considered to be ancestral figures.[33] Made from bamboo and towering over everyone else, each is replete with explicit and prominent genitalia. At the end of the festival, the giant male and female phiitaakhon are thrown into the river. None of these colorful characters are in the Pali version.

The festival takes place over three days, usually in June (in the seventh month of the lunar calendar), but before Buddhist Lent (Jetjaras 2009; abbot).[34] As elsewhere in the northeast, the festivities begin when the Upakut is invited from the Mun River, which flows through the town. On the second day, the phiitaakhon assemble and form a bacchanalian procession, thrusting their phalluses at onlookers as they escort Vessantara and his family back to the city. The dancers go from house to house collecting food, which they bring to the temple to feed the novices and other temple guests (Dansai Mss). The jataka is recited on the third and final day. Vessantara has traditionally been represented by a Buddha image and is followed by four monks carried on litters to represent the four branches of Buddhists (monks, nuns, laymen, and laywomen).[35] In response to encouragement to create a better attraction for tourists, a procession of people dressed in royal costumes to represent Vessantara, Matsi, and the two children has been added, replete with entourages of royal attendants following them.

The festival is associated with rain, water, and fertility. A monk representing Vessantara is carried on a palanquin around the temple of Wat Phonchai. Villagers try to shake him from his litter, adding, "If they fail, then the coming year will be fruitful with plenty of rainfall; if they succeed, there will be drought" (Dansai Mss). Also in the parade is a man representing Chao Poh Kuan, a local ancestral figure, riding on a homemade rocket; if this rocket is successfully launched, "there will be lots of rainfall in the coming year" (Jetjaras 2009). According to an official at the Dansai Folk Museum, the festival is held to honor this ancestral spirit of the Dansai district, in the belief that if it is not held, people will get sick and the rains will not fall. Interestingly, Jujaka is not a featured character in the Dansai procession.

A hint that Jujaka may have played a larger role in northeastern *Vessantara Jataka* recitations comes from Baan Nongkathao in Amphur Nakhonthai, in Phitsanulok, located in a region influenced by both northern and northeastern cultural practices. In this region, Jujaka is considered the most important chapter. Consequently their parade does not include Vessantara, who is considered to be in the temple, but instead highlights Taa (Grandfather) Jujaka, portrayed as a drunken old ghost (*phii pret*); his human belly has exploded from overeating but his spirit lives on. With his face blackened to look ghost-like, the local actor wears yellow monastic robes (*phaa jiiworn*) and carries a monk's bag. During the procession, Jujaka chases young women and children. After the procession, his costume is burned. Whoever performs the role does not want others to know lest his children get teased. At one point the local kamnan thought it was inappropriate to have Jujaka wearing monastic robes, so he had the costume changed. However, the rain did not fall much that year and so the garb was restored. Now using money from the tambon council, each year the community makes bigger offerings so the ghost of Jujaka will finally die; they hope to teach him to learn to give and not only take (Pathom 2013). That this version of Taa Jujaka was once more widespread is suggested by parallels with a similar performance in Sukhothai.[36]

Against this broader backdrop of bacchanalian and bawdy village festivals, the Bun Pha Wet comes to appear relatively sedate. The Bun Pha Wet may always have been more sedate than other northeastern rituals. On the other hand, it is possible that the phallus-enriched *Vessantara Jataka* of Dansai was once more widespread throughout the northeast, dramatizing the power of the Buddha's words to subdue the wildest of spirits. As the examples I have described in this section suggest, the Bun Pha Wet of the nineteenth century may well have been much bawdier, but it became more subdued as northeasterners accommodated central Thai sensibilities.

Amitataa Erased

Another feature of Bun Pha Wet performances that suggests they were toned down is their virtual erasure of Amitataa. The bawdiest scenes are likeliest to occur in the scenes of Jujaka's marriage to Amitataa in the Jujaka chapter, in the descriptions of Jujaka's relationship with Amitataa, and the relationships of other village women to their husbands. Remarkably, northeastern versions, both abridged and long, provide little description of Amitataa's life and character. In the Hok Kasat version I described, Amitataa is barely mentioned. She goes with Jujaka because she has been duped by his love magic. Manee Phayomyong has compared various regional texts of the *Vessantara Jataka*. Manee also notes the diminutive role of Amitataa in the northeastern texts, even in comparison with the central Thai version. In the northeastern textual versions, the village women are upset that their husbands are complaining about them and so they meet at the pier, where they verbally attack Amitataa, teasing her for having pert young breasts but an old man for a husband (Manee 1976, 275).[37] According to Manee, this scene in the northeastern versions is shorter than those of all four other regions. In the central and southern Thai versions, Jujaka postures about how he will bring the village women to court if Amitataa will only tell him which one was so mean. Amitataa receives her greatest elaboration in the northern version.

The overall insignificance of Amitataa in the northeastern version is tellingly revealed in the nineteenth-century mural painting of the jataka at Wat Thung Sri Muang, in Ubon. As I scanned the walls, I was surprised to realize that the mural does not even include an image of Amitataa; Jujaka himself first appears in the mural in a tree. Significantly, the mural is housed in an ordination hall (*ubosot*) constructed by Chao Khun Phra Ariyawongsachan Yanawimon Ubon Sangkhapamok (Sui), the chief ecclesiastical officer, around 1829, in the reign of King Rama III. Ariyawongsachan had originally resided at Wat Saket, in Bangkok, but moved to Ubon. He subsequently had a footprint of the Buddha moved from Wat Saket to Wat Thung Sri Muang and built the ordination hall to house it. The hall itself is built in a mixture of Bangkok and northeastern styles. This erasure of Amitataa strongly suggests possible central Thai censure since the scenes in which she is involved are the bawdiest.

More direct evidence of possible state involvement in shaping the Jujaka chapter comes in a bizarre addition found in a pre-1970s northeastern edition that Manee examined. Amitataa is often portrayed as threatening to torment Jujaka by flirting with other much younger men in order to convince him to search for Vessantara's children (Manee 1976, 264-65, 266, 271). In this particular northeastern version, Amitataa, in her efforts to convince a cowardly Jujaka, develops a typology of four kinds of soldiers. The four types of soldiers are: (1) the type who are men in name only but are not willing to fight and start shaking in fear at news of a battle; (2) the type who go into battle but are terrified; (3) the type who fight but flee when they lose; and (4) the type who fight until they have attained victory. Amitataa continues, "All are called soldiers, but the first type are the vilest, like you who are just as cowardly" (Manee 1976, 267-68). State influence likely underlies this rousing militarist argumentation.

Hints that Amitataa once had a greater role in the northeastern village version remain in the Bun Pha Wet scrolls and village temple murals. As Brereton and Somroay note, the scene of Amitataa and the village women is a favorite of temple murals. They are quite bawdy and serve to generate sympathy for both Amitataa and Jujaka. Brereton and Somroay provide the following comparison with central Thai representations of this scene: "While in Central Region murals the neighbors' antics are limited to pinching the unfortunate young woman, in Isan they go much further. At Wat Ban Yang, they insult her by 'mooning' her, lifting their *phasin* (skirts) to expose their bare buttocks. At Wat Sanuan Wari, they not only lift their skirts but also urinate at her. Such portrayals evoke sympathy toward Amittada and Chuchok, who, rather than being monochromatic icons of good or evil, are tinged with a range of moral, human hues" (2010, 72-74).[38]

The way Amitataa is portrayed helps to set the emotional reaction to Jujaka. The northeastern portrayal varies from victim to shrew. In the Hok Kasat version, where Amitataa was given love magic, much of the potential pathos is removed. Northeastern monks and villagers I interviewed, with only one exception, said that Amitataa was a model of filial virtue who sacrificed herself to help her parents (as did a generation of northeastern girls who went into prostitution or married older foreign men). In one of the scrolls Lefferts and Cate studied, when Amitataa returns home crying, Jujaka asks, "Did the young men who recently left the monkhood harass you by trying to touch your breasts, my dear wife?" Amitataa replies, "No, that's not the case, pot-bellied old man" (2012, 119). Although Amitataa is not mentioned again in the Pali version, the scroll that Lefferts and Cate studied includes a touching remark when he is about to die from having gorged himself: "In his agony he moans, 'Oh, I miss my dear wife Amitataa so much'" (2012, 137). However, her overall insignificance is reflected in the fact that several northeastern taxi drivers I talked to did not even know who Amitataa was.

Jujaka's Adventures Abridged

When northeastern performances are compared with northern performances, differences emerge; the northern performances do not typically emphasize (1) the invitation of the Upakut,[39] (2) the scroll and the invitation to the royal family to return, and (3) the procession of the thousand balls of rice, each of which is typical in northeastern performances. Nonetheless, the northeastern and northern recitations share several elements, most notably the recitation of the *Phra Malai Sutra* and the belief that the recitation must be completed within twenty-four hours in order to meet Maitreya Buddha. Similarly, when the northeastern textual versions are compared to the northern versions, interesting parallels emerge. Overall, Manee Phayomyong finds that the northeastern versions have more in common with the northern versions than the central or southern texts. While the central and southern texts contain considerable royal terminology and were intended to include members of the court in their audiences, the northern and northeastern texts contain less royal terminology and are therefore more accessible to village audiences (Manee 1976, 244). However, the northeastern texts have more royal words and Pali words than the northern texts. Indeed, Manee surmises that the author of one of the northeastern texts was likely a monk who had studied a high level of Pali since it included so many Pali words (1976, 244, 266). Nonetheless, although the northeastern versions have some fancy royal words, they are largely composed in ordinary language and make many references to northeastern everyday life. The northern version has the least amount of royal vocabulary; as Manee writes, "The northern version portrays Jujaka more like an ordinary person, with no fancy words so it is easy for audiences of all types to follow" (1976, 244).[40]

Comparing the northeastern textual versions with the northern versions reveals further interesting similarities and also intriguing differences. Both regions offer a comic portrayal of Jujaka. Both regions expand the Jujaka chapter beyond the Pali or central Thai versions. However, although these creative elaborations in the northeastern versions echo those we will find in the northern versions, they appear to have been abridged in the northeast in comparison to their greatly expanded form in the north.

Both regions develop an earlier life story for Jujaka of events before he appears in the Pali text begging. In the Hok Kasat version of the Jujaka chapter I heard, the monk makes mention of Jujaka's mother's abnormal pregnancy, during which she was always hungry; of Jujaka's father and relatives, who tried to raise him after his mother's death; and of a stay at the temple, which led to him being evicted because he was such an impossible temple boy. With no other sources of support, Jujaka then begins a life of begging. The monks describe a begging journey for Jujaka, listing items he wanted and destinations to which he wandered before he ever accumulated the gold he left with Amitataa's father. Similarly, northeastern temple murals provide evidence of a longer prehistory for Jujaka, noting that he had to flee his home near the city of Benares, which burned down "because of his bad deeds" (Lefferts and Cate 2012, 22). Another Hok Kasat monk who specializes in the Jujaka character said that he sticks to the text, but he also includes a description of how hungry Jujaka's mother was during her pregnancy.

Both regions enrich the scene between Jujaka and his debtor beyond the Pali version. Although the Hok Kasat monks I heard expanded on the conversation between Jujaka and his friend, the northeastern long textual versions that Manee studied in the 1970s contain little elaboration. When Jujaka reappears to reclaim his gold, the northeastern parents give their daughter right away, without the humorous cajoling and sweet-talking of the northern Jujaka (Manee 1976, 226–28). Unlike the Pali or central Thai versions, both the northern and northeastern versions often describe the sorry state of Jujaka's home; nonetheless, the northeastern versions do not have the level of comic detail typically found in the northern version (Manee 1976, 225). However, beyond this brief fabrication of an early life for Jujaka, the northeastern monks I interviewed said they did not elaborate upon the text any further or create new adventures for him. None I interviewed had heard of northeastern monks creating an extended wedding performance, and none were familiar with the extended description of Jujaka's house, replete with a pillow made from chicken excrement, or the various other elaborations we shall encounter when we meet the northern Jujaka. One monk indicated that he would be concerned that the audiences would disapprove of such elaborations since they would go significantly beyond the text.

The Jujaka chapter concludes with the encounter between Jujaka and Jetabutr, the hunter. Again, in comparison with the northern version, the northeastern version is far less elaborated. Manee also notes a difference in tone between the two regions. In the northeastern version, the passage is humorous because Jujaka is inappropriately arrogant, trying to intimidate the hunter into sparing his life, saying, "Listen Jetabutr, I [*rao*/also *kuu*] am not an ordinary person, but an important royal official of the kingdom. I am a royal ambassador of King Sonchai. And not just any ambassador, but the one King Sonchai trusts to find his son and daughter-in-law to invite them to return home" (Manee 1976, 230–31).[41] In the northern version, Jujaka is rendered comically pathetic, groveling and using royal terminology not for himself but for addressing the hunter.

The northeastern and northern versions of the Maharaat chapter, in which Jujaka meets his death, include significant additions to the Pali, central, and southern versions. All four regional versions contain descriptions of how Jujaka overate, in each case including details about local foods. Thus in the southern version Jujaka not only eats southern foods but also uses chopsticks (Manee 1976, 249–51). Both the northern and northeastern versions provide long lists of village delicacies, village commonplaces, and village favorites rather than dishes known to the Bangkok court. (For lists of northern and northeastern foods, see Manee 1976, 254–57.) Both regions highlight Jujaka's lack of manners as he stuffs himself. Further attesting to the popularity of this scene among northeasterners, Lefferts and Cate write, "During our fieldwork, while examining scrolls, onlookers recited from memory the numbers and kinds of foods Chuchok is offered" (2012, 90).

Both the northern and northeastern versions expand upon Jujaka's death scene. Lefferts and Cate note that northeastern monks often play up this scene, as the audience eagerly anticipates an explosion of sound (2012, 90). Similarly, Brereton and Somroay note the frequent inclusion of Jujaka's demise and funeral scene in northeastern temple painting, explaining: "Chuchok's demise is often depicted with great fun and gusto. Isan painters seem to relish portraying how his uncontrolled craving leads him to consume such a massive amount of food that his stomach bursts open, causing him to die. One way to do this is to draw a bystander pointing to the Brahman and his bulging midriff. A clever caption can add even more emphasis to this crucial incident . . . *thong phram taek tum tai*, 'the Brahman, his belly bursting open with a bang, bit the dust'" (2010, 72, 75). Jujaka's death scenes often receive elaborate rendering in the scrolls as well. As Lefferts and Cate comment, "Sometimes, an X-ray view of his stomach shows how rapidly Chuchok ate his meal; it contains half-chewed and broken chicken parts" (2012, 90). They also describe a modern scroll from southern Laos showing how "exploding intestines force Chuchok into the air, blood and various food parts fly in all directions, killing and wounding bystanders, even those dressed in modern attire" (2012, 90). However, the northeastern textual version is much shorter than the northern accounts.

As if overeating and an explosive death scene were not enough, northeasterners also frequently include Jujaka's funeral scene. In temple murals, "Often a procession is seen carrying his body in a sling or a coffin to the cremation site, accompanied by monks and laypeople. He lies face up with his hands tied together on his chest in a *wai*, the customary gesture of respect" (Brereton and Somroay 2010, 61, 67). In some cases, the portrayal of the funeral is itself funny.

The northeastern versions also often include an abbreviated version of Jujaka's problematic funeral arrangements. Thus these northeastern versions mention that they take the body into the deep forest with krathing bulls and rhinoceroses, crossing over a deep river (Manee 1976, 260). They try to find a monk to conduct the funeral, first inviting the head of the sangha (*sangaraja*), but he says he has a stomachache; they invite other monks, but they complain of not feeling well (Manee 1976, 260).[42] They finally find an old monk, who, in accordance with custom, uses his stick to hit the coffin. In an inversion of custom, the old monk tells Jujaka to turn his face to hell (Awejii) and to stop thinking about his wife, Amitataa (Manee 1976, 262). In the scroll that Lefferts and Cate translated, in addition to a painting showing a monk standing over Jujaka's cremation pyre, the following is written: "A monk recites an invocation over Chuchok's body, 'You must not be among the merit-making group that will go to heaven. You must humbly accept your fate and go to hell, Uncle Brahmin'" (2012, 139). As we shall see in the next chapter, this funeral scene is also to be found in the northern versions, but with far greater elaboration.

The fact that the northeastern and northern tellings share so many comedic elaborations beyond the Pali and central Thai versions makes the abridgments in the northeastern version intriguing. Were the northeastern versions once even more similar to the northern version? Were greater comic elaborations deliberately deleted? The virtual erasure of Amitataa in the northeastern versions lends support to the possibility of central Thai censure.

Reading through the kind of humor presented in the modern performances of the *Vessantara Jataka* of the northeastern region does not explain why the Bangkok court was so intent upon suppressing comedic recitations. Cate and Lefferts imply that the mere preservation of the Bun Pha Wet in the northeast reveals an uneasy political truce between the descendants of northeastern war captives and the Bangkok court when they write, "Isaan residents have devised a means by which they can continue to perform their preferred story—Phra Wet, instead of the Life of the Buddha—while still being loyal subjects" (2012, 179).[43] The northeastern performance's egalitarianism, its emphasis on family unity, its possible emphasis on elected leaders, and its desire for the social justice of Maitreya all hint at political resonances. Jujaka is not the main character or the main chapter in the northeastern telling; Matsi and the theme of family reunification are far more important. But the restrained bacchanalianism, the erasure of Amitataa, and the textual parallels with the northern versions suggest that the northeastern performances may once have had more in common with those of the north. Even vaudevillian diversions can mask political resonances.

If indeed, as I have suggested in this chapter, the court succeeded in influencing northeastern performances, perhaps the northeastern Jujaka was once not so tame. So our search for danger posed by comedic recitations continues. Hints from the northeast suggest we may find a livelier Jujaka if we continue our journey into northern Thailand.

3

Northern Thailand
Humor Delighted

Our journey in search of Jujaka has now brought us to northern Thailand. Like the travelers who were amazed to find the ruins of Angkor Wat buried in the forest, we can delight in finding scattered jewels of laughter that Jujaka broadcast in his wake during his wanderings through the mountain valleys in this region. The *Vessantara Jataka* has had a long, vibrant history in northern Thailand; historians such as Prince Damrong Rachanuphab have even suggested it developed in northern Thailand and only spread later to the central Thai region (Damrong 1919). According to Prakong Nimmanhaeminda, there are over 120 Lanna versions of the *Vessantara Jataka*, some arguably over three hundred years old (Prakong 1983, 7).[1] This tremendous variety suggests not only the importance of the *Vessantara Jataka* in northern Thailand historically but also that it has been a living and dynamic tradition. When the northern versions are compared, the chapter with the most variation is the Jujaka chapter (Manee 1976, 258–59; Prakong 1983, 54).

As reflected in the diversity of its Jujaka chapters, humor in recitations of the *Vessantara Jataka* has survived in its most elaborated form in the region of northern Thailand. Much of the humor is Rabelaisian, which, as Bakhtin explains, makes "no pretense to renunciation of the earthy" and celebrates the material bodily principle through "images of the human body with its food, drink, defecation, and sexual life" ([1965] 1984, 18, 19). Recognizing the performance as one "which to some Westerners would seem to transgress the boundaries of respect," Charles Keyes provides a rare first-person account of a tujok performance that took place during a funeral of a prominent abbot in 1973: "On Saturday evening, a well-known monk from Mae Rim near Chiang Mai

Figure 10. A northern village performance. A village woman gives the chapter offering to the monk. Behind her is the tripod in which her fellow chapter sponsors are seated as part of the syyb chataa. A banner and lantern are decorated with animals representing the twelve-year birth cycle. Sacral strings and paper cutouts of elephants and horses hang on the string grid overhead throughout the temple viharn. Photo courtesy of Yuwa Tambon Council, Amphur Sanpatong, Chiang Mai, November 2006.

delivered a two-hour version of the Jujaka story from the *Vessantara Jataka*. For the whole two hours, he had the audience in stitches as he made ribald remarks about the love of the old Brahmin, Jujaka, for a young pretty girl, as he described, with imitations of conversations, how this young girl grew into an avaricious bitch and how Jujaka, constantly plagued by flatulence (noted with appropriate sound effects), strived to do his wife's bidding" (1975, 54).[2]

In the days before radio and television, the monks involved in the recitation of the *Vessantara Jataka* were much like the local rock stars of their generations. As the noted northern intellectual Manee Phayomyong remarked in an interview with me, "People would discuss the monks as they do singers today."[3] Specific monks became famous for their performances of specific chapters. Among these monastic stars, the tujok was the most celebrated.[4] Sometime before World War II, performances of the *Vessantara Jataka* began to decline (Ferguson and Shalardchai 1976, 131; Manee 1976, 50; Swearer 1978, 3; Sommai and Dore 1992, 85; Brereton 1995, 83). Although a variety of factors contributed to this decline, tujok monks themselves foregrounded the sensitivity of bawdy humor.

This chapter is divided into three parts. The first section highlights key elements of northern Thai performances of the *Vessantara Jataka*, providing evidence of the important role of Jujaka. The second section explains how tujok monks expanded upon the basic plotline of the Pali text, primarily by creating a series of adventures for Jujaka in his journey from his life as a scorned village beggar to his death as an honored court guest. The chapter concludes by suggesting that understanding Jujaka's importance in northern Thai interpretations presents evidence of a non-royalist reading of the *Vessantara Jataka* and lays the foundation for an anti-royalist reading; both readings are grounded in the profane realm of the everyday life of commoners.

This chapter owes much to Luang Poh Bunthong (1934-2007) of Wat Sophanaram (T. Don Kaew), in Mae Rim District.[5] Of all the northern monks involved in performances of the *Vessantara Jataka* in recent decades, none was more famous. Most Jujaka monks throughout Thailand today have either heard of or been influenced by him, and the best known tujok monks performing in northern Thailand today are his students. Indeed, his tapes were the ones I heard in the late 1970s being played over loudspeakers at village funerals; the attention of the rapt audiences was interrupted only by communal guffaws each time he delivered a punchline. A gifted storyteller, he had a phenomenal sense of comic timing. One of his former students, a well-known tujok today, remarked that Bunthong only needed to say a few words and his audiences were already laughing. Born the fifth of six children to parents who were landless agricultural laborers, Bunthong attributed his talent to his ability to remember humorous folktales (*jia*) from his childhood. As he recalled in his interview with me, he used to love listening to the monks' stories. In those days monks would stay overnight with the laity during funerals. His mother would have to chase him home at night whenever there were funerals.

Over the course of his life, Bunthong had been invited to preach in every tambon in Chiang Mai province and many beyond. His performances of the Jujaka chapter survive to the present day through his recordings, which are still being sold and are even now accessible on the Internet. As a mark of how beloved he was, Bunthong's body has been preserved in a special pavilion in his temple. At the outer entrance is an enormous, gold-covered statue of him, standing. Off to one side by a tree are quasi-life-size replicas of Jujaka with his cane, holding Amitataa's hand; they appear to be coming to pay homage to Bunthong. Inside the pavilion is a lifelike effigy of Bunthong sitting with two of his favorite dogs, behind which Bunthong's body lies covered with gold leaf in a glass casket. Scores of villagers still come daily to pay him their respects.

There are very few written accounts of northern recitations of the *Vessantara Jataka* in English, but three northern scholars have provided accounts in Thai: Manee Phayomyong (1976), Prakong Nimmanhaeminda (1983), and Sommai Premchit (2001).[6] Manee (1930-2009) himself was famous for his performances of the Maharaat and Nakornkan chapters before he disrobed in 1962.[7] In addition to these works, this chapter is based upon interviews with four current or former tujok monks (including Luang Poh Bunthong, who was undergoing kidney dialysis but generously made time to meet me); tapes I obtained of Luang Poh Bunthong's performance of the *Vessantara Jataka* (these tapes were likely made in the 1970s); my own observation of part of a *Vessantara Jataka* performance in Hang Dong district;[8] photographs taken of *Vessantara Jataka* recitations in San Patong district of Chiang Mai province held in 2006 and 2009, respectively, each organized by the local tambon council; tapes and photographs of a *Vessantara Jataka* recitation held in the town of Lampang in 2008 and organized by the Lampang branch of Mahachulalongkorn Buddhist University; and various interviews with monks, former monks, and lay organizers in Chiang Mai and Lampang provinces.

Points of Emphasis in Northern Performances

In this section I will summarize the evidence regarding the historical importance of the *Vessantara Jataka* in the northern region and highlight key features of its northern performances. As will become clear, the northern recitations were explicitly linked to the Maitreya Buddha, and many of its unique performative elements serve to emphasize the character of Jujaka.

Historical Importance

Evidence suggesting the importance of the *Vessantara Jataka* in the north dates back at least to the fourteenth century.[9] An inscription dated 1361 compares the Sukhothayan king Lithai to kings in three jatakas, including Vessantara (Griswold and Prasert 1973, 163; Skilling 2008, 70). Jataka scenes found at Wat Si Chum in Sukhothai also date to this period.[10] A Sukhothai inscription dated 1380 records, "They listened to the Dhamma of the Dasajati [Ten Jatakas]" (Wray 1972, 117; see also Skilling 2008, 70). In 1519 the reigning king consecrated a Buddha image and listened to a version of the *Vessantara Jataka* that he had commissioned (Prakong 1983, 6; Veidlinger 2006, 87). By the fifteenth century, Chiang Mai had become a major center of Buddhist studies; this period has been described as the "Golden Age" of Lanna literature (Veidlinger 2006). Chiang Mai is also believed to be the source of the Paññāsa-*jatakas*, a collection of an additional fifty stories recorded during the fifteenth or sixteenth century beyond the 547 jatakas in the Pali canon.[11] As noted by Jaini, these additional jatakas reflect "the penchant of Buddhist storytellers to embellish old canonical tales with new elements drawn from the indigenous cultures of their own native regions"; since more than half of Paññāsa-*jatakas* are "variations on the theme of extreme charity," Jaini also suggests they were inspired by the *Vessantara Jataka* (1989, 23, 25).[12] The importance of listening to the jataka is reinforced by the many early nineteenth-century *Anisong Vessantara* texts catalogued by Coedes; these texts "are often bound with copies of the *Vessantara Jataka* and extol the great merits to be attained by listening to this text" (Veidlinger 2006, 142).

The association of the *Vessantara Jataka* with the prophecies regarding the future decline of Buddhism and the coming of Maitreya also appears to be long-standing. Epigraphs from King Lithai, the ruler of Sukhothai from 1347 to 1368, suggest that he was "deeply concerned about the implications of the prophecy on future generations in his kingdom" (Griswold and Prasert 1973, 84; see also Brereton 1995, 67). In an inscription dated 1357 the king explicitly mentions his concern that in the future there will be no one left who can recite the *Vessantara Jataka* (Griswold and Prasert 1973; Brereton 1995, 69). Other inscriptions from this period link the recitation of the *Vessantara Jataka* "to the idea that the disappearance of the jatakas is one of the stages in the decline and disappearance of the Buddha's teachings" (Skilling 2008, 70). A northern Thai king's 1426 inscription records that he "devoutly wishes to behold the Lord Sri Ariya Maitri [Maitreya]"; numerous fourteenth- to sixteenth-century inscriptions contain similar passages (McGill 1993, 435). Although some have argued the *Phra Malai Sutra* emerged first in Burma, other scholars suggest its origins lie in the northern Thai kingdom of Chiang Rai (Brereton 1995, 39). Regardless of its origins, it is clear that for centuries the *Vessantara Jataka* was recited annually in temple ceremonies, evidently with the goals of both preserving Buddhism and providing the opportunity of beholding Maitreya at the time of its demise.

Chapter Specialization

The most important character through which to understand the appeal of the *Vessantara Jataka* in northern Thailand is Jujaka. When I asked northerners to name their favorite chapters, by far the most frequently mentioned were the Jujaka and Maharaat chapters; of these two chapters, the Jujaka chapter was the most beloved. Donald Swearer notes that audiences "may request encores, particularly when a skilled, charismatic preacher recited the fifth chapter" ([1995] 2009, 36). Other chapters mentioned were the Kumarn (highlighting the part when the children are beaten by Jujaka) and Matsi chapters, with a few including the final chapter, the Nakornkan. Paralleling these favorite chapters, Prakong finds that the greatest textual variation across versions occurs in the Jujaka, Kumarn, Matsi, Maharaat, and Nakornkan chapters; the chapter with the most innovations is the Jujaka chapter (1983, 7, 54). Similarly Manee, in his comparison across four regions, concludes that the northern Jujaka is by far the most elaborated (1976, 258–59). This textual diversity reflects the creative license given to tujok monks to innovate.

Monks in northern Thailand developed reputations for expertise in reciting specific chapters.[13] Thus monks with deep booming voices specialized in the Maharaat and Nakornkan, thereby replicating the majestic royal processions. Monks with high soft voices specialized in the Kumarn, Matsi, and Sakabap chapters, thereby replicating the voices of the children and mother. The Chohkasat chapter was usually read by a young novice (Manee 1976, 45). Monks with a sense of comedic timing specialized in the Jujaka chapter. Other chapters were not as specialized; very often the abbot of the sponsoring temple performed the opening or closing chapter as much for reasons of convenience as honor since these chapters were both likely to be recited in the wee hours of the morning. Although northerners will note the ability of the monk who recites the Matsi chapter to reduce the audience to tears, the Jujaka chapter was considered the most difficult to perform because tujok monks were expected to be funny and had to continually find new ways to entertain audiences with their wordplay.

Regardless of their chapter specialization, monks would apprentice themselves for extended periods of time with a monk who had already established a reputation for a given chapter. The preaching style varied from province to province; for example, Chiang Mai's style is somewhat slower and more elongated than Phrae's (Manee 1976, 46). Monks I interviewed said it would take weeks and months to learn how to sing a given chapter. Since there were no microphones in the old days, monks had to be able to project their voices so that the audiences inside and even outside the temple could hear them. Manee Phayomyong describes his training when he was a novice in 1944 in Mae Rim district in Chiang Mai. Although northern monks were asked to recite only one chapter during an actual performance, Manee practiced by reciting the entire jataka. As he explained, "I started reciting at 7 A.M. [and] gradually I began to lose my voice. Yet I kept it up until I reached the final chapter. By then it was 6 P.M. and my voice was completely gone. For seven or eight days, I had no voice" (Kamala 1997, 31–32).

Lanna monks traditionally recited their chapters from a raised pulpit in which they were not visible to the audience.[14] According to Prakong, monks were to recite behind a curtain or other concealed space so that their facial or body movements would not distract from the narrative (Prakong 1983, 4). Manee explains that these pulpits enabled monks to assume a variety of postures better amenable to fulsome chanting than the position one generally sees today when monks sit cross-legged behind a fan: "In this dhamma booth the monk could sit comfortably, since he could look out but the audience could not see him. He did not have to be dignified. He might remove his robes, put his hands over his ears, open his mouth widely, or tap his hands on the floor to aid his rhythm. [Instead of sitting on the floor] most preachers preferred to squat. My teacher told me squatting lets the testicles hang naturally, so the preacher has no constraint in projecting his voice loudly" (quoted in Kamala 1997, 32).

Monks who developed fame for their operatic ability were in great demand. As a measure of their status (and possibly their ability to reap significant financial gain), Manee observes: "Often, monks with lesser skill are jealous and seek to ruin the preacher by using black magic [*khun sai*]. So a good preacher must possess magical knowledge for self-protection. He must learn to recite sacred mantra for self-defense as well as to attract people with goodwill. He must tattoo protective amulets on his body for the same reason. He must always keep certain kinds of amulets or magic cloth [*pha yan*] to make him invulnerable" (Kamala 1997, 33).

Tujok-Jujaka

In northern Thailand, the special status of monks who performed the Jujaka chapter was highlighted by the fact that they traditionally dressed up to look like Jujaka. No one I interviewed in the northeastern or central regions had ever heard of monks dressing up in costume, be it for recitations of the *Vessantara Jataka* or any other sermon. In northern Thailand, the only occasion for which monks wore costumes was for performances of the *Vessantara Jataka*, and even then only the monk who performed the Jujaka chapter dressed up. Many tujok monks carried a walking stick, with a bag or a bamboo container over their shoulders. Some even donned a beard and a white wig. Given that monks have their heads and eyebrows shaved, sporting hair would indeed have been shocking to outsiders. One older villager even recalled seeing a tujok monk when he was young chewing betel and letting some betel juice drip down his mouth.[15] Nowadays in contemporary northern Thailand, it would be considered highly inappropriate for monks to dress up in costumes. Luang Poh Bunthong maintained the tradition but modified it. He continued to bring the Jujaka costume with him, and, although he no longer wore it, he would put the bag, cane, beard, and wig in the front of the temple hall (*viharn*) for people to see as they entered. As Luang Poh Bunthong explained to me:

> In the past there were monks who dressed as Puu Phraam [Grandfather Brahmin, i.e., Jujaka]. They had a bag, with a bamboo salt container. They would wear a beard and walk with a cane. They wore their yellow robes underneath. The more one dressed like Puu Phraam, the more people liked it. But it is not allowed nowadays. If a monk did this today, it would be in the headlines of the newspaper as totally inappropriate. They would print a photograph. People would say, "Look at this. Look how he is dressed! As a Buddhist, is this appropriate?" Things change with each period. It's not against the vinaya, but is considered inappropriate [*phit malayaat*]. Monks are supposed to be revered, and so now it is seen as lowering one's status because one has self-interests to gain from the villagers, in other words, the monk wants to get rich. But in the past, they didn't think like this. The better the costume, the more people liked it.[16]

Tujok monks were also known for making grand entrances into the temple grounds, a practice not associated with any other monk. Several villagers described the tujok entrances as a competition to see who had created the best costume and had the most dramatic entrance. The tujok's arrival was eagerly anticipated. Because the Jujaka chapter was generally performed in the late morning, there was typically a large crowd of children milling around the temple grounds. When the tujok monk arrived, a cry would go out, "*Tujok maa laew!*," "the Tujok has come." Often the tujok would walk into the temple and chase after the giggling children, waving his crooked cane at them. Some tujok entered with two children tied to ropes to represent the royal children; one of my closest village friends, a woman who is now in her midsixties, giggled as she recalled being chosen to perform the role of Kanhaa as a young girl. Other tujok playfully threatened to hit village children who had come to watch. Some tujok entered the temple holding leashes with several dogs, the dogs representing the thirty-two dogs who chased Jujaka up a tree, as typically detailed in the northern recitations. One tujok in Lampang even entered with a group of children who had been dressed up to look like the thirty-two dogs in the story; the "dogs" then had fun chasing as many of the onlookers to or up whatever trees were nearby. Monks and laity explained these dramatic entrances as deliberate strategies intended to heighten interest. Unlike in the northeast, where the temple entrances focused on Vessantara, or the central region, where the temple entrances focused on the individual chapter offerings, in the north the grand temple entrance was made by the tujok representing Jujaka.

Mazes

The importance of Jujaka in northern Thai recitations of the *Vessantara Jataka* is further reinforced by the construction of elaborate *wongkot* (mazes).[17] The term refers to the mountainous region in which Vessantara and his family traveled in exile (Khao Wongkot, or Crooked Mountain). While it might be assumed that the villagers are retracing Vessantara's steps, evidence suggests that northerners are in fact retracing Jujaka's path. At many of the entrances to the northern mazes, Jetabutr the hunter—or sometimes Ajuta the hermit—is represented, sometimes on simple cardboard and sometimes in elaborate papier mâché forms. Jetabutr is the hunter the king of Jeta had assigned to guard the entrance to the forest, and Ajuta is the hermit living deeper in the forest. Jujaka had to trick both in order to find out where Vessantara and his family are living.

The mazes are quite complicated, with numerous dead ends. Some are constructed from bamboo, and the more elaborate are made of wood. Although a simple maze may be waist high, most mazes are taller than a person. Apparently in the past some were even constructed with roofs. In the old days, villagers traveled into the forest to gather all the necessary raw materials, which they then had to haul back to their villages. Its actual construction also involved considerable village cooperation. The maze design itself is quite intricate, as I realized when one villager who had designed his temple's maze generously offered to

Figure 11. The maze. Villagers inspect the finished maze. Photo courtesy of Yuwa Tambon Council, Amphur Sanpatong, Chiang Mai, January 2009.

share his blueprint with me. At the center of the maze that I walked through was a Buddha image, which I was told represented Vessantara. In the maze in which I found myself lost, children, teenagers, and parents alike were clearly enjoying the challenge. Wandering through the maze highlights the journey that Jujaka undertook and is intended to draw young people to the temple.

Syyb Chataa

Preparations for full *Vessantara Jataka* recitations are extraordinarily elaborate and involve large numbers of people working together. The decorations usually begin at the entrance to the temple compound. As is typical of recitations in other regions, the temple itself is decorated with banana trunks, lengths of sugarcane, lanterns, and a large jar with fish swimming under lotus leaves; these items symbolically represent the forest in which Vessantara and his family were exiled and the pond in which Vessantara's children initially hid from Jujaka. As in other regions, northerners also prepare a large bowl of water to be sacralized in the course of the ritual. The thousand verses of the Pali text are also represented visually, the temple typically decorated with one thousand small wax candles, paper flags, and sticks of incense. However, the number one hundred is also frequently invoked. Northerners will commonly decorate the interior of their temples with paper cuttings of horses and elephants, and Sommai and Dore report seeing cut-outs of one hundred oxen, buffaloes, and male and female servants (1992, 79). Some villagers said these paper cuttings represent the gifts of the hundreds that Vessantara made before his departure into exile, but most said it represents the ransom Vessantara set for his children before allowing them to leave with Jujaka.[18]

Unlike other regions, northern temple decorations often include a tripod within the rajawat, or royal fence inside the viharn. The chapter hosts sit under this tripod. The tripod is associated with the *syyb chataa*, or life-lengthening ceremony also typical of the northern region. The tripod is draped with sacral strings that are connected to a network of strings ultimately leading to the Buddha image on the altar and the string held by the monk as he recites a given chapter. Throughout the viharn myriad additional sacral strings hang in a grid overhead, also leading from the Buddha image on the altar and the monk in the pulpit to the individual listeners. As Sommai and Dore observed: "The white cotton cord not only surrounded the ritual enclosure, but also formed upon it a kind of woven ceiling made of perpendicular lines. From this one end of cord about 1.50 meters hung down, which lay people would fasten around their head while sitting inside the enclosure and listening to the reading of the *Vessantara Jataka*" (1992, 84).

Timing

Northern Thais share the belief with northeasterners that the *Vessantara Jataka* must be recited within twenty-four hours and that audience members who listen to the entire recitation will be reborn in the time of the Maitreya Buddha. The *Vessantara Jataka*—either in its entirety or as individual chapters—is performed on three different types of occasions in northern Thailand: (1) the second month Full Moon Festival (Dyan Yii Paeng), which occurs in November after Buddhist Lent; (2) a special temple festival called Tang Tham Luang (great dharma presentation); and (3) special occasions such as funerals and housewarmings.[19] In the north, there is widespread agreement that the *Vessantara Jataka* can be recited any time *except* during Buddhist Lent. Since most, if not all, northern Thai temples recited the *Vessantara Jataka* for Dyan Yii Paeng, common sense suggests that most recitations for Dyan Yii Paeng drew upon the monks and novices at their own temples. Konrad Kingshill describes how in the village where he conducted his fieldwork monks practiced weeks in advance of Dyan Yii Paeng (1976, 153). Since the northern textual version is already amusing, one can imagine the audience's enjoyment from a reading by even a moderately talented monk. This practice appears to continue to varying degrees. One abbot assured me his temple performs it every year at Dyan Yii Paeng; when I pressed him to say who had recited the Jujaka chapter in recent years, he explained that they only recite one chapter.[20] Other monks said the *Vessantara Jataka* used to be performed at every northern temple but has since died out.

Funerals are another major occasion for which a monk may be invited to perform a reading of a single chapter, most often the Jujaka, Kumarn, or Matsi chapter. Indeed, Prakong Nimmanhaeminda notes that for her own father's funeral, none other than Luang Poh Bunthong was invited to perform the Jujaka chapter (1983, 4; see also Keyes 1975, 54). A particular version of this chapter was used as the foundational text from which the reciting monk would then create his own variations, adding asides as teaching examples or songs for amusement. I have attended several funerals during the 1970s at which the tapes that Luang Poh Bunthong had recorded were played over the loudspeakers; indeed, the first time I learned of the existence of tujok was at these funerals. More recently, I attended a funerary reading of the Matsi chapter, the chapter chosen both because the local village monk was known for his excellence in performing it and because one of the relatives knew I was writing about the *Vessantara Jataka*. Prakong suggests that the Kumarn and Matsi chapters served to distract the mourners from their own grief by calling attention to that of the characters in the jataka (1983, 4). The Matsi chapter also offers not merely a distraction but an opportunity to affirm Buddhist teachings about life as suffering and about the need for detachment. Prakong suggests that Jujaka was a particularly popular chapter for funerals because it provided a way both to entertain guests and to counter the sadness among friends and relatives, a reason substantiated by villagers I interviewed. Funerals are the most important of an individual's life cycle rituals, and relatives are proud if the deceased's funeral draws a large number of guests, even though many of them may not even know the deceased.[21] Since funerals routinely last several days, multiple monks could be invited to perform different chapters on different nights.

Individual chapters were also performed on other special occasions, such as housewarmings, auspicious day celebrations (*wan mongkol*), temple construction celebrations (*ngaan boi*), ordination hall consecrations, and ordinations (Manee 1976, 50; Prakong 1983, 4). Although *Vessantara Jataka* recitations for novice ordinations were once common in the central region, no one had heard of this practice in the north. Northerners I interviewed indicated that the Nakornkan chapter was considered most appropriate for housewarmings since it parallels

Vessantara's return home. Single chapters could also be recited for syyb chataa ceremonies (e.g., for life-lengthening ceremonies for individual people, homes, temples, villages, or cities). One monk said that the Thotsaphon chapter was considered most appropriate for such occasions.[22] Single chapters could also be performed as a way to raise money for temple construction projects (Manee 1976, 50).

The major event at which full recitations of the *Vessantara Jataka* take place, the Tang Tham Luang, is a rare and special occasion. A given temple may go many years without organizing such an event.[23] Although they can last as long as seven days (Manee 1976, 45), the full performance of the jataka in its varying forms usually takes two days. On the first day, the Pali version (*Khathaphan*) is recited, together with the *Phra Malai Sutra* (divided internally in the north into *Malai Ton* and *Malai Plai*). Also recited are the *Anisong Vessantara* and *Khaiwibaak Vessantara* (Sommai and Dore 1992, 80).[24] On the second day the thirteen chapters of the vernacular version are performed, involving thirteen different monks (or novices); this recitation must be completed within twenty-four hours.[25] These major performances often included drumming competitions to encourage surrounding villages to participate. These large events were usually associated with the completion of some major new addition to a temple or to raise funds for major temple expansion.

Lay Sponsorship by Birth Year

Unlike in the central or northeastern regions, where chapter sponsors may vary, in the north one's birth year determines one's sponsorship. In the north, each chapter is correlated with one of the birth years in the twelve-year cycle. Thus I am born in the Year of the Tiger and would therefore become a sponsor of the Thanakan chapter. Although everyone is expected to listen to all chapters, when the chapter associated with one's birth year is being performed, one is generally careful to attend. As one monk noted, the audience changes as people born in different years sit under the strings to gain the blessings transmitted through them from the monk sitting in the pulpit. The primary chapter sponsors sit under the syyb chataa tripod, but everyone else participates through the web of sacred strings. The last, or thirteenth, chapter is for everyone.[26]

The chapters and birth years are correlated as follows:

Thotsaphon	Rat
Himaphan	Ox
Thanakan	Tiger
Wanaprawet	Rabbit

Jujaka	Dragon (Nguu yai; great serpent)
Chulaphon	Snake
Mahaphon	Horse
Kumarn	Goat
Matsi	Monkey
Sakabap	Rooster
Maharaat	Dog
Chohkasat	Pig-Elephant
Nakornkan	All (Sommai and Dore 1991, 35)[27]

When an abbot or temple community decides to host a Tang Tham Luang, the abbot will typically convene a meeting with the lay leader (*makhathayok* or *ajarn wat*), temple committee, and laity to select the date and determine the primary chapter hosts (Manee 1976, 48). The chapter hosts are responsible for inviting the monk who will perform the chapter. In the past the invitation to the monk was made in person, accompanied by an offering with flowers, but nowadays hosts often simply invite the monks by phone. The chapter hosts are also responsible for providing the monks a copy of the relevant chapter in advance so they have time to practice their performance; in the past this text may have been newly copied by hand for the occasion, but today print versions can be bought (Kingshill 1976, 276; Manee 1976, 48). During the actual performance, the chapter hosts present their offerings to the monk after their chapter has been read; the monk responds with a blessing.[28] At the end of each chapter, a gong may be sounded and firecrackers set off; in more elaborate performances, a small orchestra may provide musical interludes to mark the transitions (Manee 1976, 48).

Jujaka's Extended Journey

Northern Thai textual scholars have remarked on the significant elaboration and variation in the Jujaka chapter of the *Vessantara Jataka*. The great number of innovations in the Jujaka chapter results from both its role as a favorite chapter and the inherent demands of comedy. A simple recitation of the northern written texts of the Jujaka chapter even by inexperienced monks likely generated laughter, given its extended rhyming patterns and wordplay. But for monks with the gift of comic timing, the possibilities for humor were considerable. As tujok monks explained, simply accentuating certain sounds could be funny. For example, in the scene when Jujaka is attacked by dogs, the northern variations often go so far as to name and describe as many as thirty-two dogs who attack

Jujaka; Luang Poh Bunthong, simply by the manner in which he said "*tua*" to refer to each dog, provoked laughter. Even monks who had apprenticed with another tujok monk did not necessarily recite the chapter the same way. As one monk who had apprenticed with Luang Poh Bunthong explained, "Preaching is not like singing; it is not possible to preach exactly the same way. Each person develops their own style. For example, when Tu Lung Thong [Bunthong] has barely started, everyone already starts laughing. If I tried to imitate his style, it wouldn't work, people wouldn't laugh. Tu Lung Thong is the absolute master at doing this. He barely starts talking and people want to laugh. Even me, I've listened to him telling the same stories ten, twenty times and I still find myself laughing."[29]

Unlike in northeastern Thailand today, where modern humor primarily consists of bawdy puns, in northern Thailand humor was generated by creating ever-new episodes in which Jujaka overcame obstacles in his journey to reach Vessantara. Luang Poh Bunthong often incorporated pop culture into his performances, drawing on villagers' knowledge of likay performances (a form of folk theater) and contemporary hit songs, generating laughter in part through the audience's surprise that a monk might be familiar with current popular songs. (In American culture, this kind of incongruity would be analogous to an older priest who raps.) Although some comic incidents occurred in the Maharaat chapter, where Jujaka dies from overeating, most of the comic developments were in the Jujaka chapter. There was considerable variation from tujok to tujok, with some sticking close to the text while others created new comic obstacles. However, the most popular tujok monks were known to experiment with new elements in their performances.

Inventing Episodes

Some sense of the comedic range the figure of Jujaka afforded tujok monks can be gleaned by following the adventures of Jujaka through the Jujaka chapter. In the Pali form, this chapter is a mere seventy-nine verse lines in length. In the hands of a tujok monk, this chapter expanded severalfold as they invented new episodes in Jujaka's life. To understand the extent of the northern elaborations, we can consider the first paragraph of the Pali version of the Jujaka chapter:

> At that time, in the kingdom of Kalinga, and in a brahmin village name Dunnivattha, lived a brahmin Jujaka. He by quest of alms having obtained a hundred rupees deposited them with a certain brahmin family, and went out to get more wealth. As he was long away, the family spent that money: the other came back and upbraided them, but they could not return the money, and

so they gave him their daughter named Amittatapana. He took the maiden with him to Dunnivittha, in Kalinga, and there dwelt. Amittatapana tended the brahmin well. Some other brahmins, young men, seeing her dutifulness, reproached their own wives with it: "See how carefully she tends an old man, whilst you are careless of your young husbands!" This made the wives resolve to drive her out of the village. So they would gather in crowds at the river side and everywhere else, reviling her. (Cowell [1895] 1957, 270)

Tujok monks generally began their recitation of the Jujaka chapter with an initial formal chant in Pali (*chunniyabot*), which the audience was not likely to understand but which reminded the listeners of the sacrality of the text. Although Jujaka was invariably portrayed as an old Brahmin beggar, the details of his personage varied. The Pali version of the Jujaka chapter provides no physical description of Jujaka other than the fact that he is old. However, in the Kumarn chapter, Vessantara's young son provides the following description:

> His foot is huge, his nails are torn, his flesh hangs sagging down
> Long underlip and broken nose, all trembling, tawny-brown,
> Pot-bellied, broken-backed, with eyes that shew an ugly squint
> All spots and wrinkles, yellow-haired, with beard of bloody tint
> Yellow, loose-jointed, cruel, huge, in skins of goats bedight,
> A crooked and inhuman thing, a most terrific sight;
> A man, or monstrous cannibal? And canst thou tamely see
> This goblin come into the wood to ask this boon of thee?
>
> (Cowell [1895] 1957, 283-84)

All the Thai versions make clear that he is ugly.[30] But while the central Thai court version emphasizes how frightening he is, the Lanna versions delight in providing an image of Jujaka that is so extreme it becomes comic. All five Lanna versions Prakong studied describe Jujaka as having feet with leprosy, wrinkled skin, skin covered in red and black spots, drooping lips, a crooked nose, crooked teeth, drooping eyelids, blinking eyes, a beard, a back that is crooked like an elephant's, and a big stomach. In addition, he is often described as smelling like a vulture, with a body like a ghost (*phii*). When he laughs, his stomach jiggles. He looks like a ghost, but his stomach is too big. His eyes roll up, and his eyelids droop down past his nose. When he laughs, he drools (Prakong 1983, 43). In a comic scene where Jetabutr is trying to figure out what he is seeing in the tree in one of the northern versions, Jetabutr says, "Maybe it is a *phii tamoi* (a ghost that flashes), but it isn't flashing. It may be a monkey but it has no tail. It could be a deer, but they don't climb trees. It could be a wild chicken, but it doesn't have feathers. It could be a person, but it doesn't look like one, so it must be a *phii phraai* ghost!" (Prakong 1983, 44).

In his taped version of the Jujaka chapter, Luang Poh Bunthong skipped over the details of this description by mentioning Jujaka's alleged enormous dimensions and joking that they might represent lottery numbers. Instead he chose to create a scenario in which Jujaka was living in one of the hells. He described Jujaka making the rounds of various cemetery ghosts, in the hope that one of them would agree to become his parents so he could be reborn in the world of humans. Playing with a rhyming pattern in which the last syllable of the line rhymes with an individual's name, Luang Poh Bunthong created the following passage:

Bai haa Lung Ai, Lung Ai bo ao	He went to Lung Ai, Lung Ai refused
Bai haa Lung Mao, Lung Mao ko bo byy	He went to Lung Mao, Lung Mao said no
Bai haa Lung Tyy ko pan	He went to Lung Tyy, who sent him on
Bai haa Ui Chan.	To see Ui Chan
Bai haa Ui Chan, Ui Chan ko klua	He went to Ui Chan, but Ui Chan was afraid
Bai haa Ui Bua, Ui Bua ko bo dai.	He went to Ui Bua, Ui Bua wouldn't agree
Bai haa Lung Ai . . .	He went to see Lung Ai . . .
Kuu le bya.	Whew, I'm tired of this![31]

After the laughter subsided, Luang Poh Bunthong shifted from a chanted rhyming pattern into a more conversational narrative about how no one wants to be around difficult people. He concludes that ultimately Jujaka is reborn with his former mother, who is very poor.

Jujaka's imagined childhood is another opportunity for tujok monks to invent episodes, describing how he is a difficult child and how his mother has to steam lots of rice for him (e.g., Prakong 1983, 54–59). Because his parents find him so difficult, Jujaka is then sent to live with the abbot at the village temple. Luang Poh Bunthong then uses the occasion of Jujaka at the temple to segue into a series of funny stories centering on the theme that temples get all the difficult children and rejected animals. These stories of Jujaka as a temple boy or novice end with Jujaka being too difficult even for the abbot to deal with; he then is sent back home for his parents to cope with (these stories likely resonated with the trickster stories discussed in the next chapter). His parents — and sometimes a long list of other relatives — then die and Jujaka becomes a beggar.³² In some other Lanna versions Jujaka was not always poor; instead he is portrayed as having lived in a large city called Saawaphii, but after his home was burned down in a fire and he lost all his food and possessions, he had to leave in sadness and finally arrived at Thunwit (Dunnivittha) in poverty (Manee 1976, 225).³³ The northern versions then return to the plot in the Pali version in which Jujaka accumulates several bags of gold, which he then leaves with a couple whose daughter is Amitataa.

Unique to the northern region, many tujok monks create an elaborate wedding ceremony for Jujaka and his bride, drawing upon villagers' often bawdy cultural associations with a form of witty courtship repartee known as *joi* and *soh*. To gain some sense of these cultural associations, the following is a widely known *soh* about the magical properties of semen:

Namyaa Kaeo Taa Laai	The fluids of Kaeo Taa Laai (male name)
Khao waa yaa maa nae	They say it is reliable
Bo jai yaa kae	It is not a medicine
Bo jai yaa khang	It doesn't cure mouth sores
Pen yaa dii-o	It's a strengthening medicine
Pen yaa kamlang	It's a powerful medicine
Khao bo dam	It's white, not black
Chat dii wiiset	It's really quite magical
Namyaa Kaeo Taa Laai	The fluid of Kaeo Taa Laai
Ja taetiam bai	It can be compared
Myan yang makuajtaet	To that of a papaya
Yaa yang nii	This kind of medicine
Man dii wiiset	It's really quite magical
Kon man taeng thang lum	When it enters at the bottom
Man thyng bong thang bon.	Things get big at the top (i.e., pregnancy).

Although monks even in the past were never likely to go as far as the raunchier soh verses, they nonetheless ventured to the edges. Some tujok developed a section where Jujaka badgers his bride's parents for more money, using the old language of poetic couplets (*pen khao pen khrya*).³⁴ In his taped version, Luang Poh Bunthong describes the wedding guests (everyone from beggars to medical doctors, some of whom were thin as rhinoceroses and others of whom were as tall as dachshunds) and their gifts (inappropriate gifts ranging from baby cribs to funerary hangings [*thung saam hang*]).³⁵ After the meal, Luang Poh Bunthong described the post-prandial merriment, setting the scene of a master of ceremonies coordinating a range of different styles of singing (e.g., *soh chiang mai, soh phra lor, soh saelemao*). In his taped version, Luang Poh Bunthong performed seven different songs. I have included three songs to give a sense of their range from more Buddhist themed to more bawdy. The following song draws on more traditional imagery of the heavens and produces a laugh from the audience mainly because of the incongruity of a sacred Buddhist theme in a secular folk song format:

Phiinong sathaa hao maa phattana	Laity, we have come to develop/learn
Ow suan kuson pai naa	To take the merit
Kuson suan bun khunthan	The kusol and bun of giving
Thii phiinong wongwan paa kan dai kit	That our kinship circle has in mind.
Khoh hyy dai pyyt pai kyyt sawan	May all of you be reborn in heaven
Thyng neraphan thii hong chan faa	The highest levels of nirvana
Tok mya chao hyy pen khaonai	If you get there early let it be for breakfast
Tok mya kwaai hyy pen phaensya phaenphaa	If you get there later let it be clothing
Tok mya yam laa hyy saphaokham	If you arrive at dusk let it be a golden boat
Nam ow fuung ow waa	Bring your friends
Bandaa phiinong	And relatives
Thaa khong khaet hong pai kyyt sawan.	To be born in heaven.
Thyng neraphan chan faa 9 hong.	To the ninth level of heaven.
Khoh hyy thyng thii neraphan	May you reach nirvana
Anan ja pen yoht (f).	That is the peak.
Ooh la naa nong la naaj. Swaj!	Ooh la naa nong la naaj. Swaj!

Another song is about the *hong kwan* ceremony, which calls the thirty-two aspects of the soul (*kwan*) together; this ceremony is not strictly Buddhist but is very common in Thai village life.[36] This song begins with some deliberately pseudo-Pali words and then concludes by moving the khwan elements to inappropriate new locations in the body:

Ah ja jai soo. Ah ja jai yo.	"Pseudo-Pali."
Ah ja nai wanni	Today
Ko maa pen wan dii bo sao	Is an auspicious and not a sad day
Poh Naan ja hong khwan chao	Poh Naan will call your khwan
Jong riip raeo maa	So come quickly

Khwan aeo hyy yai maa yuu thii thohng	Have the waist khwan move to the stomach
Khwan nong khyyn maa yuu thii khaa	Have the calf khwan move to the thigh
Khwan hua kaesa hyy yai bai yuu thang kon.	Have the head khwan move to the butt!

The following song ventures into the bawdy. For added comedic effect, Luang Poh Bunthong performs it in the Phra Lor style, to create a "cool [*chumchyyn*] atmosphere." It is a more formal, languorous style, but the content is clearly much more raucous:

Laelaeliu bai sutchan saai taa	Laelaeliu, One can see him coming
Kin sulaa maa mao khao baan	Entering his home drunk
Loi loi. . . . [flute part].	[Flute imitation].
Khrohpkhrua thyng man bo khang	He didn't care about his family
Man tae moh man tae haai	He broke pots and vessels
Thaa mia man lon khao pai	When his wife arrived
Man pia phom mia man wai nen	He grabbed her tightly by her hair
Yang maa tukh ok	Why such pain in her breast
Yang maa tukh jai	Why such pain in her heart
Wan waai niipnaen.	She was very upset.
Panyaa kankaen	She couldn't think clearly
Sia mia man yuam tem kam.	Then the wife grabbed a big handful [i.e., his testicles].
Phutthoo tho tham	In the name of the Buddha and the dharma
Naa man byyt yao yao.	His face grew long.

Luang Poh Bunthong then shifts to a spoken aside: "He was in agony. His wife had grabbed hold of his . . . [*deliberate pause*] shirt collar. Remember, ladies, you don't have to be afraid of your husbands. They have birth certificates. You also have birth certificates. Just grab their . . . shirt collars. They will pay attention." Clearly neither Luang Poh Bunthong nor the audience was thinking of shirt collars during his pregnant pauses. Although the song selections I have translated are specific to Luang Poh Bunthong, other tujok monks followed this same pattern, singing whichever songs they made up or thought might be considered funny by the audience.

After the wedding, Jujaka and his bride move to Jujaka's village (this does not conform with the dominant uxorilocal post-marital residence patterns among Thai villagers). The description of Jujaka's home generally highlights its poor construction. Thai village homes have long been built on pillars, very often made of teak for maximum strength and resistance to termites, and with a minimum of six pillars to ensure stability. However, tujok typically characterize Jujaka's home as rickety, built on only four pillars. That this expansion on the Pali text was widespread among tujok throughout northern Thailand is suggested by one of the few surviving nineteenth-century northern Thai mural paintings of the *Vessantara Jataka* at Wat Lampang Luang; unlike temple painting in other regions of Thailand, this mural shows Jujaka's home with these four stilts. The following is an excerpt from one tujok description of Jujaka's home, performed with a low, authoritative, chanting voice:

Hyan Puu Phraam thao 4 sao	The house of the old brahmin had 4 pillars
Khyyn maa wai	Climb up into it, it would sway
Yoh yae yong yaeng yong yaeng	To and fro, back and forth
Maa hang ten kwaeng jon phoh wai	A dog wagging its tail would make it sway
Siang maeo ai jon phoh shwai	The sound of a cat coughing could make it collapse
Ow thii wai thung kham bo dai	Nowhere to hang a bag of gold.[37]

Adding to the humorous description of Jujaka's home were often passages describing the wood from which it was built, typically wood that villagers would know was totally inappropriate. In a version retold to me by a temple leader in Lampang, not only was the house built on four wiggly stilts, but the stilts were made of *mai bao*, a wood villagers know is not strong enough to be used for house building (see also Prakong 1983, 60).[38] Some tujok went on to describe the scene that met Amitataa's eyes when she entered the rickety home, noting pillows made from chicken shit (*khii*), the lack of furniture, and the like.

Developing Amitataa

The way Amitataa is portrayed helps shape the audience's emotional bond with Jujaka. In the Pali version, Jujaka's receipt of Amitataa as his wife is very abridged.[39] As we have seen, central Thai versions expanded on the Pali plotline by portraying the daughter as a tragic victim of the cruel Jujaka. In the northern versions, Amitataa becomes a more important figure than in the central or northeastern versions. Tujok versions generally represent her as the epitome of a virtuous wife (much like Matsi) who is badly treated by the other women of the village. As one tujok monk explained to me, "Amitataa was someone who was modest [*sanguan tua*]. She was a good wife, swept the house, made the meals, got water, got firewood, gave him his toothbrush, washed the clothes—she took care of the old Brahmin. She was not like so many boys and girls today who aren't doing their duty."[40] However, northern portrayals of Amitataa give her a wider range of motivations. Some versions portray Amitataa as a passive victim whose parents were forced to give her away to repay their debt. Other versions portray Amitataa as a heroine, the idealized filial daughter who wanted to help her parents and volunteered to become Jujaka's wife. Yet other versions portray Amitataa as conniving, selfish, or shrewish. Thus Prakong includes variations in which Amitataa volunteers to marry Jujaka because she imagines him to be rich and, given his age, likely to die soon, leaving her his fortune (1983; Swearer describes her as "young and selfish" [1978, 3]; see also Swearer 2009, 36). In the performance Charles Keyes observed, the young pretty girl "grew into an avaricious bitch," and Jujaka is a henpecked husband who "strived to do his wife's bidding" (1975, 54).

When Amitataa returns home, upset by the village women's comments, Jujaka asks which women were involved. Part of the humor is in the details of the portrayals of villagers. Listeners would be able to readily identify these traits with the petty foibles and characteristics of individuals in their own villages. The women are named using the Lanna prefix "*Ii*," which denotes close familiarity and is generally used for fellow villagers the same age as or younger than the speaker. (The prefix has derogatory connotations in central Thailand, another reason why urban middle-class central Thais tend to be shocked by northern versions.)[41] The women are then described by their physical features, occupations, or private love lives, including details that would be known within a village but generally not shared with outsiders. In the process of listening to the characterizations of the village women, we become voyeurs observing the private—and imperfect—lives of people in Jujaka and Amitataa's village. Amitataa's tormentors included such women as the following:

> Ii Johm, the wife of Brahmin Nong,
> Ii Phii Phrai, the wife of Brahmin Yii
> Ii Yuang, the wife of the brahmin with the eyes that roll
> Ii Khambang, the one whose husband is afraid of everything
> Ii Crooked, the wife of Brahmin Puurok,
> The foreign woman [*kulawaa*][42] with the blinking eyes
> The sweet-talking woman whose heart is always frustrated
> Ii Sii, the one who likes to have lovers
> The black-eyed woman whose husband abandoned her years ago

Ii Phii Phai, the one who sells *miang* [fermented tea]
Ii Jiklik, the one who sells fermented fish sauce,
Or maybe the fruit seller or the seller of fermented soybeans.
(Prakong 1983, 15–16; see also Manee 1976, 319–20)

The depiction of Jujaka learning about how cruelly the village women have treated Amitataa provides other opportunities for comic expansion. In one variation, Jujaka offers her various medicines so that her injuries can heal (Prakong 1983, 24). In other variations, Jujaka offers to extract punishment from the village women, but then he cannot decide what a suitable punishment might be. Should he ask for a certain flower or some fermented fish paste? There is no point in asking for a horse because he does not know how to ride it and is afraid the horse might bite him. There is no point in asking for a flute because he does not know how to play it. He thinks he might want a fishing net but then he cannot decide if it should be big or small (Prakong 1983, 46). In other variations he is portrayed as unbelievably solicitous, willing to do all the chores that village women normally perform, such as getting up early in the morning, steaming rice, sweeping homes, drawing well water and washing clothes, activities that males typically did not perform.[43] His actions can be portrayed as an entirely wonderful demonstration of his love for Amitataa or his pathetically desperate desire to keep his young wife happy.

After Amitataa convinces Jujaka to travel to ask for Vessantara's children, tujok monks often have fun describing a farewell scene. Jujaka is portrayed in a manner intended to evoke empathy, as extraordinarily tender toward his wife and very fearful of embarking on his new journey. He makes comically detailed preparations for Amitataa to help her cope in his absence. He fetches water and fills every container in the house—not just water pots but matchboxes, salt containers, spoons, eggshells, duck shells, oyster shells, and the like (Prakong 1983, 47). He collects firewood, gathering not just dried wood but also tree branches, tree roots, tree bark, and even grass that was not dry (Prakong 1983, 47). While the Pali text also describes his preparations for departure and his tears upon leaving, the tujok version below provides an example of similar, if earthier, preparations:

An waa Puu Phraam thao	And the old brahmin
Man ko dai thung hor khao laeo	Got his bag with rice packed up
Laeo man ko dai long hyan lao	And climbed down from his home
Deo tam suung tam suung	Walking down up down up
Pai thyyng pratuu baan	He got to the gate

Lio lang sang mia man waa	Turned to his wife saying
Haa plaa salaat mii thii pak pratuu	If you want *salaat* fish, it is by the gate
Haa pleathuu ko mii yuu thii hing	If you want salted fish, it is on the shelf
An myyng phii klua klua	If you fear ghosts,
Myng khai io, hyy pai io sai chong bon hua	If you want to pee, pee through the house floor hole
Thaa yaak khii ja khii sai bong mai bohk mai sang	If you want to shit, shit in the bamboo containers
Jon kalaman tem sak 4–5 bohk	Until you have filled all 4–5 containers
Jon poh ja klap maa	Until I return.
Kalanaan thyy.[44]	Amen.

Whereas the Pali text focuses on Jujaka's arrival in Vessantara's kingdom, the tujok monks' versions have Jujaka wandering all over, traveling to such places as India, Japan, Vietnam, the United States, and any other locations with which the tujok might be familiar. Typically the tujok incorporates a few words from the language of each locale. Passing reference may be made to Jujaka's wife as she wonders what is taking him so long. Only at the end of this international digression does the tujok version return to the standard plotline, in which Jujaka finally ends up in Vessantara's former home to learn where Vessantara can be found.

Tricking the Royal Guardians

Although Jujaka's quest to find Vessantara provides numerous opportunities for tujok monks to invent scenarios, all versions—including the Pali text—highlight two major events: Jujaka's forest encounters with Jetabutr the hunter and with Ajuta the hermit (*rysii*). Jujaka must trick both of them into giving him directions in order to find Vessantara and the royal family who are living in exile deep in the mountain forest. Of these two events, by far the most elaborated is the scene with Jetabutr, the guard who had been assigned by the Jetan king to protect the royal family. Jujaka's encounter with Jetabutr begins when Jetabutr's guard dogs corner him up a tree. The northern tujok monks enjoyed elaborating this moment, finding many opportunities for comedy as Jetabutr tries to figure out what kind of strange being is in the tree and as Jujaka seeks to convince Jetabutr not to kill him. They also have fun with the dogs that chase Jujaka up the tree, which typically number thirty-two in the northern versions.[45] A common expansion is giving the dogs individual names and characteristics.

For added humor, the dogs may be given Lanna names that villagers typically might use for their dogs (Prakong 1983, 65). Luang Poh Bunthong developed a scenario, recited in a rhyming pattern, in which Jujaka was falling from tree branch to tree branch until he mistakenly grabs hold of a dead brittle branch.[46] Ending the stylized rhymes, Luang Poh Bunthong continued, using his normal voice:

> It was a really big branch, but it just couldn't take his weight. It broke, *khwaek*. Both the branch and Puu Phraam [Grandfather Brahmin—i.e., Jujaka] fell crashing down; neither could help the other. The branch called out to Puu Phraam the whole way down. The branch landed in a stream, *swaa*. Puu Phraam landed in a *yaakhaa* patch [*khaa* is thatch for roofing that grows in tall thick clumps], boom. The dogs all chased after Puu Phraam, big ones, small ones, male ones, female ones.
>
> One of the dogs was pregnant, but still chased after the rest. She ran into a tree with terrific force; out came three pups. So there were two males and two females; four dogs if you include the mother—after all, she was a dog too. . . . So there were these four dogs too. The mother didn't seem to notice. She kept on, running after the rest. Her pups tried to follow her, yelping. But they couldn't see where they were going because their eyes hadn't opened yet. They were ferocious. It was in their blood. Just like people or chickens. Some people just like fights, so they get small pups to try to fight. Or chickens. Chickens can be really fierce. A fellow was getting rich breeding fighting cocks. One day he was in his house and he heard the female making nesting noises, top tap top tap. So he went to see what was happening and he spied the eggs, already fighting. Not even born. It's in the blood. So the pups had their mother's instincts. There they all were, howling and chasing after Puu Phraam.
>
> Puu Phraam scrambled up the nearest tree he could find. He cried to his mother and father, "Mother, Father, I'm in a bad situation. Looks like I will die. Father, Mother, come here and I will help you." He got it backwards of course; usually one asks one's parents for help. That's what happens when you are really panicked. You get all confused. Like the fellow who went into town to buy things. [Here there follows a series of digressions about what happens when people get confused.][47]

Another elaboration is the process of capturing the thirty-two dogs, with the explanation that the dogs could not all be tied up in the same place because they might get into fights with each other. The following is an abbreviated example in which the "tua" is elongated for humorous effect:

Tua thii nyng pai mat ton basa<u>lang</u>	The first dog was tied to salang tree
Tua thii <u>song</u> ow pai mat ton mak<u>khaam</u>	Second dog tied to a tamarind tree
Tua thii <u>saam</u> ow pai mat ton mai <u>khii</u>	Third dog tied to khii wood tree.
Tua thii <u>sii</u>...	The fourth dog... and so on.

But lest the pattern become monotonous by now for the listeners who have already heard several of these rhyming patterns, Luang Poh Bunthong ended his list abruptly, saying, "It will take us all day to tie up these dogs. So let's skip the rest."

Another variation is to pursue a scenario in which Jujaka hurts his leg during his journey; he then has various encounters with alleged doctors who suggest various improbable remedies and find various ways to cheat him out of his money. Yet another digression is to have Jujaka upset because he lost the bag he was carrying when he was under attack by the dogs; the items he has lost can range from his medicinal bag in which he kept a lump of chicken droppings to cure his boils (*fii*) to silk cloth he was saving to wear at a temple festival (*boi luang*). Another alternative is to have Jujaka bemoaning the loss of the various foods that allegedly were in his bag, such as salted fish, collard greens (*phak kaat*), cabbage, sour bamboo shoots, *kaeng bon* (stew made with buffalo skin, a village favorite), tadpoles, or crispy rice cakes topped with sugar frosting. Precisely because most of these typical village foods were not likely to actually be taken on trips, they were good for a laugh (see Prakong 1983, 23–24). In some cases, he laments the loss of the bag because Amitataa wove it for him (Prakong 1983, 25, 29).

Whatever the range of variations, the tujok then returns to the main plot of the story, convincing Jetabutr that he is a messenger sent by the king to bring Vessantara and his family back to the palace. In his encounter with Jetabutr, Jujaka can be portrayed as quaking in fear as a humble peasant or feigning imperiousness as an alleged royal messenger; each extreme provides opportunities for comedy. In the end, Jujaka is able to overcome Jetabutr's fears that Jujaka's intentions are evil and tricks him into disclosing the whereabouts of the royal family. Jetabutr feeds him and gives him directions how to find Ajuta. The successful deception of Jetabutr brings the Jujaka chapter to an end. Following Jetabutr's directions, Jujaka then continues deeper into the forest, where he meets Ajuta, the rysii. Ajuta is also worried that Jujaka harbors evil intentions, but Jujaka is also able to convince him to reveal the forest path that will lead to the royal family (this scene typically receives little elaboration by tukok monks). With these two important roadblocks successfully overcome, Jujaka is now able to find Vessantara and request the royal children.[48]

The Death Scene

The subsequent chapters follow the basic plotline of the Pali version, with the exception of the death scene in the Maharaat chapter, in which Jujaka is rewarded for bringing Vessantara's children back to their royal grandparents. The portrayal of Jujaka's funeral in the Pali version consists simply of the words "The king arranged for his funeral" (Cowell [1895] 1957, 299). Far more than in the northeastern versions, in the northern versions the last meal and final funeral become an opportunity for extended comedy. In some versions, beautiful, young, bare-breasted female servants are feeding him; in other accounts he eats alone without any company (Prakong 1983, 49–50). Tujok monks typically expanded the section in which Jujaka is gorging himself, adding details of all that he was eating.

Jujaka is typically portrayed as overcome by desire, sometimes quasi-vulgar, sometimes overly innocent, and sometimes worthy of empathy. When the courtiers ask if he would like more to eat, Jujaka replies, "If there is more, I will have more." In some versions, Jujaka tells everyone that he is full, but people force him to keep eating, goading him on with such remarks as "What, you're not my friend! You don't like this dish?" Jujaka is portrayed as a hapless village buffoon who does not know what to do; after all, he did not want to hurt anyone's feelings (*kraengjai pyan*). Some versions emphasize that he is someone who has never eaten good food, with such details as "at home if he and Amitataa had vegetable soup with shrimp, Jujaka would eat the head, his wife would eat the tail and they would keep the body to eat for dinner." So now presented with so many delicacies, Jujaka stuffs himself, eating everything they bring him, sometimes using two hands at once. A sample list might include village favorites and delicacies, with accounts of his reactions to these dishes interspersed. For example:

> He ate *laap khwaaj*, duck stew [*kaeng khae bet*], mushrooms, roasted fish, *khaep muu* [pork rinds]
> His upper lip curled up,
> He ate *kaeng ohm* [pork stew], sour sausage, a dish sweetened with sugarcane.
> His eyes rolled up.
> He ate insect delicacies, he drank sweet juices. . . .[49]

After overeating, he feels sick, his stomach as big as a palm-sugar jar (*haitaan*). He wants to defecate, but he cannot. He wants to vomit, but he cannot. He wants to urinate (*thohk*), hoping to feel better. He holds his stomach all night in pain. In all five Lanna versions that Prakong studied, King Sonchai's

Figure 12. Jujaka in the palace. Jujaka, naked, is being fed by palace women while fondling their breasts. From nineteenth-century (?) painting from Wat Jaroen Muang, Amphur Phan, Chiang Rai, August 2015. Photo by author.

courtiers discuss giving him various medicines. The medicines or the dosages are all suggestions that villagers would know was inappropriate, such as three bags of an herbal laxative (*saloht*), a dosage villagers would know was far, far too much (Prakong 1983, 24–25).[50] In the Lanna versions, Jujaka appeared to die not just from overeating but also from too much medicine. After giving him various medicines, none of which helped, the courtiers then decided to fetch a doctor. However, their efforts were to no avail:

Went to the doctor at the head of the irrigation dam, who said he was not free
Went to the doctor with the very large head, who said he was busy doing nothing
Went to the old one, who said the medicine he was making was not yet ready
Went to the doctor with white hair, who said don't bother me
Went to the doctor who weighs palm sugar and found he had died
Went to see Doctor Kaeo, who would be difficult
Went to see the doctor with betel in his mouth, who said don't ask me.
Went to see Doctor Saanhai, who said he didn't know the directions
Went to see Doctor Yii, who asked, "Who sent you?"
Went to see Doctor Ai, who had also died
Went to see Doctor Chang Kaeo, but he was having a fight with his wife . . .
Went to see the doctor with the scar on his head, but he was clearing his fields
Went to see the *khwan* (soul) doctor, but he had parasites
Went to see the doctor at the market who had a cough
Went to see Doctor Khambai, but he was fixing the fence around his house and couldn't come
Went to see the foreign doctor, but he had fled to his fields
Went to see Doctor Hora, but he was *lomphong*[51]
Went to see Doctor Sohnhong, but he had been bitten by a dog.

(Prakong 1983, 50; see also Manee 1976, 258)

All of this is in a rhyming pattern in which the last word of each line of verse rhymes with the fourth word of following line.

These various remedies are unsuccessful and eventually Jujaka's stomach explodes. In Luang Poh Bunthong's variation, he details the damage caused by the explosion:

> Puu Phraam was very hungry and began eating. He leaned over the table, grabbing food from all directions and stuffing it into his mouth. He didn't offer any food to anyone else.
>
> | *Khop khaa bet yuu laalaai* | He ate duck legs crunch crunch |
> | *Khop khaa kai yuu luup luup* | He ate chicken legs, munch munch . . . |
> | *Kin jon mot kaeng mot thuaj* | Until all the dishes and bowls were empty |
> | *Kin mot thuaj mot jaan* | All the bowls and plates were clean. |
>
> The food had nowhere to go. His stomach was growing fatter and fatter. It looked like a balloon. And then it exploded. The blast killed many in the vicinity:

Khon thao daai pen 20	The old people who died numbered 20
muu pen bao pen sao daai pen 200	The teenagers who died numbered 200
muu noi noi daai pen 1000	The children who died numbered 1,000
muu thii lon bo tan, nap bo dai.	And it was impossible to count the numbers who couldn't run fast enough.

Fortunately there were no monks in the area, otherwise they might have been killed in the blast as well. That is what happens when one eats alone. As the Buddhist saying goes, *Nekasii rapthesukang* . . . [Pali], or *kin khon diaw, haa pen sukh mai dai*: "One is not able to find happiness if one is the only one eating." It's like the middleman [*naai naa*] who is supposed to share the profits with others, but steals the money all for himself. He is not going to be happy for long; he might even get himself killed.[52]

Even after Jujaka's death, the tujok continue to create humor in posing various challenges regarding his funerary rites and the question of where to cremate him. If they cremate him near the water, it might harm the fish, tadpoles, and other water creatures; if they cremate him near the termite mound, it might affect the mushrooms; if the site is too close to trees, it might affect the leaves; if it is near homes, that would also be inappropriate; if it is too near a path, people will be afraid to pass by; if it is too near the coconut tree, the coconuts might not be sweet; if it is near the palm tree, the palm fruit might be small. The site cannot be too close to the well because people will drink the water; it cannot be too near the gardens because the vegetables would be disgusting; if it is in the forests, the snakes will bite them; if it is too near a temple, people will fear that the temple is haunted; if they cremate his body at the cremation grounds, the spirits (phii) will hate them; if they cremate him near water, it might harm the fish. With the concern about the fish, the list of concerns comes full circle, implying a never-ending circle (Prakong 1983, 52). One former tujok who enjoyed this scene said he ended the list by just burying him wherever; after all, in those days people didn't cremate bodies, they buried them!

Another problem is finding porters to carry his body. As with the absurd wedding gifts, absurd medicines, and the like, the procession taking Jujaka's body for the final rites is comprised of deformed people and led by a blind man. As Luang Poh Bunthong tells the story:

Once Puu Phraam had died, the attendants went to inform Phrayar Sonchai. He hadn't even been in town overnight. That happens to people, you know.

They win the lottery and go off and party and get drunk; then they run into an electricity pole and die before they ever get their money.

So they told Phrayar Sonchai that Puu Phraam had died. They began to prepare the body, but they didn't know where to take it. They were afraid if they buried it near a squash field, the squash might all die. If they buried it near the rice field, the rice might all die. One of the elders said they should take the body deep into the forest, the place where vulture droppings had piled up as high as one's thigh and crow droppings had piled up as high as one's knee [see also Manee 1976, 259].

So they set off, carrying Puu Phraam's body bouncing along, bumping into tree branches and vines along the way.

Ow khon khaen hak tii kong	A person with a broken arm hit the drum
Ow khon taa pong maa tii kom	A person with bulging eyes hit a kom
Ow khon khaen ngong maa top swaai	A person with a crooked arm banged cymbals
Ow khon khaa yaeng maa pao pii tae thalae kham	A person with a bad leg played the flute
Ow khon tii kong nam pai tum tum	The drummer led the procession, tum tum
Ow khon taa sum maa nam thang	A blind man led the way
Ow khon taa fang maa baek khae.	Blind men carried the litter
Dii bo dii wae, man ko wae	Stopping where they shouldn't
Thii bo dii pai, man ko pai.	Going where they shouldn't
Ow khon hua saai maa saphaai thung 3 hang	A bald man carried the 3-tailed cloth
Kap thung hoh khao.	With a bag for his food.

The bald person was a good choice because when it gets dark, he has a spotlight built in, 12 volts no less![53]

Yet another problem is finding monks who are willing or able to perform the ceremony. In Luang Poh Bunthong's version, by the time the procession reaches the cemetery, they realize they have forgotten to invite any monks. So they travel all over looking for a monk to perform the funerary rites (*hap bang sakun*), but when the monks hear it is for Puu Phraam, they do not want to go:

Pai nimon tuchao wat tai, ko bo mya	Invited a monk from a southern temple, he refused to return.
Pai nimon tuchao wat nya ko waa	Invited a monk from a northern temple, he said

klua phii Puu Phraam <u>lohk</u>	he feared Puu Phraam's ghost would haunt him.
Pai thang tawan<u>ohk</u>,	Went to the east [temple],
ko waa pen <u>fohk</u>	who said he had ulcers.
Pai thang tawan<u>tok</u>,	Went to the west [temple],
ko waa khaa kra<u>dang</u>.	who said his legs were paralyzed.
Pai haa tujao Lan<u>chang</u>,	Went to find a monk in Lanchang,
ko bo <u>pai</u>	who also refused.
Nimon tujao <u>Thai</u>,	Invited a central Thai monk
"mai pai yom.	who said politely
Atthamaa mai pai" [*refined voice*].	"I will not go." [*laughter*][54]

They finally found a monk who was willing to go, named Tu Chiidok. But he wasn't much of a monk. He didn't know how to do any of the blessings. When he went begging, instead of having rice put into his bowl, he put his bowl into their rice. He told people to take his cane. When he arrived at the funeral, people were stunned. "What kind of a monk is this? He must be Puu Phraam's younger brother!" Others said, "Well, he's wearing yellow robes. So what if he's fat? It's not like he's harming anyone else."

The monk poked his stick in the pile of firewood a few times, poured some lustral water and mumbled something or other, but he didn't know any of the chants. He hit the coffin[55] and said "*Fang tham nyy. Namo Puu Phraam daai la phaophong wongsa.* Listen Puu Phraam, listen to the dharma. You have died and left your kin. Your spirit doesn't have to remain here and worry about the food and other offerings. You can leave those things for me. *Kusalathamma* [Pali] *a la la khaa pen netnaai* . . . a la la la, my legs are getting numb."

Then the monk gave the blessing to Puu Phraam, "*kosakoodula Puu Phraam.* Hey, Puu Phraam, I will tell you the path to follow to heaven. Bend over with your back to the heavens and your face looking toward hell [the reverse of the usual chant]. If you fall and land in a good place, get up and get moving right away. If you fall and land in a bad place, just stay there for a long time." What kind of a blessing was that! He really didn't know what he was doing! If anyone did a blessing like that for anyone else, people would chase him away from the cemetery as fast as he could go. So then they cremated his body [*phao phii saak*].[56]

This description of a funeral is at odds with many of the key ceremonial features of the normal village ritual, most notably the suggestion that Jujaka go to hell rather than the expected encouragement to pay respects to the Phrathaat Chulamani in the heavens. In some northern versions, the tujok may invent scenes typical of village funerals, in which some attendees play chess, some play checkers, some play cards, some tell stories, some are doing nothing but chewing *miang* and eating the royal feast, some beat gongs all night long, and some watch the *mahorasop* entertainment (see, e.g., Prakong 1983, 27). With his death, Jujaka's role is over and the northern versions of the *Vessantara Jataka* return to the Pali plotline.

The Jujaka character allowed tujok monks to make a wide variety of points, centering on greed, jealousy, desire, and impermanence. Most monks noted the obvious point that Jujaka is greedy and never satisfied; even when he has bags of gold he wants more, and his unabashed greed ultimately leads to his death from overeating. One monk said Jujaka also demonstrates the importance of having children to take care of elderly parents since he was an old man without extended family to take care of him. One monk praised Jujaka for being industrious and thrifty and for having a responsible plan for the future (Prakong 1983, 54). Because of his thrift, he was able to get a young, beautiful wife. Alternatively, wanting a young, beautiful wife led to his downfall. Other monks say that Jujaka illustrates the Buddhist principle of impermanence because his money did not last, his happiness with his wife was short-lived, and he ultimately died (Prakong 1983, 54-59). Similarly, monks discuss the four pillars of Jujaka's wiggly, unstable house as being impermanent and made of the elements of air, earth, water, and fire (Prakong 1983, 64). The village women demonstrate the problems of jealousy. The thirty-two dogs are used to represent components of our bodies such as the heart, lungs, kidney, and saliva, which are our enemies since they get old (Prakong 1983, 66). It is even possible to say that Jujaka died happy, his dreams of beautiful women and unlimited food having been met!

Thus, unlike other tellings that focused on Vessantara or Matsi, the northern Thai versions placed a particular emphasis on Jujaka. Indeed, one tujok monk explained to me that Jujaka was the key to understanding the jataka, saying, "In the end I will say we have to understand the meaning of the brahmin, we have to crack this shell. He is a form of the problem of desire. If we have much *kilesa* [inappropriate mental attachments leading to greed, hatred, delusion, and the like] we must keep being reborn in suffering, like the brahmin."[57]

Village Morality in Everyday Life

The previous two sections have shown the importance of Jujaka in the performance of the *Vessantara Jataka* in the northern region. In contrast to analyses that have emphasized the role of the *Vessantara Jataka* as a royalist panegyric, an analysis of the northern performance that foregrounds Jujaka over Vessantara suggests its importance as an engagement with the problems in everyday village life. In contradistinction to anthropologists who have suggested the jataka was important to villagers for secular purposes such as rain-making, its more important purpose seems to have been teaching the dharma through humor. Luang Poh Bunthong's humor drew upon a profound knowledge of village life, with an earthiness and an overlay of a nostalgia for a life that was fading away. As this section will show, primary emphasis is on the challenges facing villagers in everyday life, particularly in three sets of social relationships that were important historically—namely, those between husband and wife, parents and children, and monks and novices.

Non-Royalist Egalitarian Ethos

The humor in the northern recensions draws upon everyday village life. As Prakong finds in her textual analysis, the Lanna versions incorporate numerous elements of local cultural practices (1983, 14). The delight villagers evidence in their enjoyment of Jujaka's adventures is in large part due to their recognition of shared experiences. The Jujaka chapter itself provides opportunities for references to village foods, village dress, everyday activities such as washing clothes and fetching well water, and the foibles of villagers (e.g., the jealousy of the village women toward Amitataa; Manee 1976, 319-20; Prakong 1983, 17-18). Prakong suggests that northern texts are more interested in actions—who is doing what, when, where, and with whom—than in poetic descriptions of nature. For example, she notes that the description of nature that is twelve lines long in the central Thai version of the Mahaphon chapter is only two lines long in the Lanna versions (Prakong 1983, 74; see also Nidhi [1982] 2005, 13).[58]

The central Thai version, written by members of the court with the king and other royalty and court officials as the intended audience, contains considerable elegantly poetic words and a vocabulary associated with the language of the royal court. Thai has a very complex system of pronouns, which become even more intricate in royal court language. When addressing or referring to the king, court language involved lengthy honorifics. Thus the word for "I" becomes "the dust under the soles of your royal feet" (*tai faa laohng thulii phra baat*). By contrast, the Lanna versions were written by commoners and monks to preach to villagers and other commoners; the language in the northern versions is simple, non-reverential, and easy to understand. In the northern versions, the word for king is kept simple and may even be a single word (e.g., *kasat*). Villagers refer to themselves and each other as *kuu* and *myyng*, vocabulary that is commonplace but viewed by non-northerners as vulgar. When he is talking with Matsi, Vessantara calls himself simply husband (*kuu phii*), using a term that would seem shockingly colloquial in a court context (Prakong 1983,

76). Similarly, the northern references to Vessantara's royal elephant are straightforward, whereas in the central Thai version the elephant becomes "the elephant decorated with jewels sending shimmering rays for all to behold" (Prakong 1983, 73; for detailed comparisons of sample central and Lanna passages, see Prakong 1983, 72–73).

Members of the royalty are not elevated but portrayed in no less earthy terms than villagers. When Luang Poh Bunthong was describing Phusadi's ten wishes, which included her desire not to have breasts that sagged after her pregnancies, he told several stories about the usefulness of sagging breasts, which could be interpreted as even a critique of Phusadi's wish for ever-perky breasts. He prefaced his stories by apologizing to all the gods and goddesses and everyone else listening to him, but adding, "It is in the text, so I'm in trouble if I talk about this and I'm in trouble if I don't."[59] Asking the audience, "Why did she want this?" Luang Poh Bunthong continued:

You know the saying,

Phoh hang ko kaeo	Stare at the figure, it's perfect
Phoh aeo ko krom	Stare at the waist, it's round.
Pyyt phoh _____ [hua nom]	But lift up _____ [the blouse]
Myyn thung yaa kae.	[The breasts] are like medicine sacks.

Herbal doctors used to carry their medicines around in old sacks tied to their waists. I was once preaching in a *miang* forest. An old lady came up to me and said, "It's just fine if they [breasts] hang. Why? Because if you are in the forest gathering *miang* leaves and it starts raining and thundering, I can just stick my cigarettes and matches under them and they'll stay dry. Otherwise they'd get wet. In there is like a little cupboard." Everything has its own advantages and disadvantages. They may not be beautiful to look at, but they are useful.

There was a mother pounding chili paste and her children were crying for milk. She didn't want her kids to come in front of her because she was afraid the chilies might get in their eyes. But she could feed them from the back. Sort of like plugging in an electric cord; it was a long cord too. They could just suck away.[60]

Similarly, Luang Poh Bunthong did not hesitate to compare Vessantara's premature birth by the roadside with a bowel movement:

Some people think it is not appropriate for royalty to deliver on the side of the road. But labor is not something one can control; if the baby wants to be born, that's just the way it is. There are some things one just cannot control. Death is one. You can't tell someone, "Stop dying." You can maybe prolong the death with oxygen or whatever, but that's it. You can't stop the death. Going to the bathroom is another, particularly shitting. It's impossible to stop it, no matter who you are. Can even be dangerous. As they say,

Kin kaeng banam	Eat squash stew
Jep thohng oi oi	Get a small stomachache
Kin kaeng manoi	Eat manoi stew
Mae man, mii nai kapfai?	Wife, where are the matches?! [i.e., matches to go outside to the toilet in the dark].

Even I'm the same way. There I am walking with my legs crossed, I have to go so badly. Even my hair stands on end. When I can finally go, it just explodes. I'm so happy. Take a few steps, whoops, have to go again. This is just not something one can forbid.[61]

Husband-Wife Relations

Luang Poh Bunthong spent considerable time discussing problems in the relations between husbands and wives. Expanding on the jealousy of the men when they saw how well Amitataa treated Jujaka, he commented in earthy terms: "You know the saying, 'Holding shit is better than holding a fart [*kam khii dii kwaa kam tot*].' You should praise your own wife, not someone else's. Shit you can smear on your face; you can't do anything with a fart. If you complain about your own wife and praise someone's else, they will be upset. If you just want to complain about something, that's one thing, but don't bring someone else's wife into the picture."[62]

Even the scenes involving royalty are used as opportunities to discuss village matters. In the scene where Matsi expressed her desire to accompany Vessantara into the forest, Luang Poh Bunthong embarked on a lengthy digression about relations between husbands and wives:

Are we like Phra Wetsandorn and Nang Matsi? Do we love each other and are we willing to eat dirt and sand [*kin din kin saai*, an expression referring to enduring poverty and other hardships] together until we die? . . . At first people swear they are willing to eat dirt and sand until they die, but after a few years they are ready to eat kindling and pound brooms [*kin lua dam yuu*, i.e., throw things at each other]. As the saying goes:

Yam mya hak nam som pen waan	When in love, sour is sweet
Yam bo jyyibaan, namtaan ko waa som.	When miserable, sugar is sour.

Just like the old people say, "When in love, smiles all over." Even though there may be hundreds of people around, they only have eyes for one person. . . .

Youths . . . will happily take the girl wherever she wants to go. Or they will walk their motorcycles alongside their girl. They walk her up to the front of her home. But they don't dare to go in; the old tiger [*sya thao*—i.e., the father] might be waiting. They just hang around, until the girl has showered, gone to bed, and turned out all the lights. Only then do they finally go home. As long as the houselights are still on, they just stand there guarding the gate. "I was worried whether you were all right." As he goes home, he is thinking of her the whole way back.

Once they are married, the wife can't even get her husband to accompany her to the kitchen to soak the rice overnight.[63] Before he'd escort her wherever she went. "Husband, please, I beg you. Will you go with me to the back of the house?" "What, are you afraid of dying? Do you think some ghost is going to strangle you on the way?" As they say, "*Ton rak, dohk sok (soksao)*—the stem of love, the flowers of misery." At first they say, "I love you like the sky." He might even have it written on the back of his shirt. At first the boy is *thephabutr* [god]; the girl is *thepthidaa* [goddess]. "Your skin smells so sweet. In this world there is only you. I can't live without you. If you die, I die."

Then they get married and pretty soon the thephabutr is a monkey [i.e., a deceitful bastard] and the thepthidaa is a dog [i.e., a bitch]. "*Sya wohk thao*, old monkey. When will you meet with a fatal accident?"

There was once a woman who liked to drink. Her husband came home drunk. "What, drunk again, old man [*puu thao*]," she says angrily. He's in a good mood. He just says sweetly, "I brought a little home for you. Would you like some?" "Of course," she snarls.

If you curse at your husband and call him a monkey, how can you be a thepthidaa? Since when did goddesses marry monkeys? Have you ever heard them announce at the temple Mr. Monkey and Mrs. Goddess donate 20 baht? If you call your husband a monkey, then you must be a monkey too. How could it be otherwise? It must mean at night you are sleeping with a monkey. Your children, whose children are they? That monkey's!

The husband calls his wife a dog. Before she was a goddess, but now's she an old dog. And what are you if you call your wife a dog? Are you a god? You're a dog right along with your wife. Who steams your rice and makes your chili paste? That dog! You're eating your food together with a dog. The rice that dog steamed is being offered to the monks. The monk doesn't know anything about your private affairs. So he's not a dog. Why would he want to be a dog with everyone else? So that's what happens over time. At first they were all angels; suddenly they are monkeys and dogs living together. . . .

Everyone needs to be supported, both men and women. There are some men who, when their wives make them dinner, have nothing good to say, they complain that it is too spicy, too bland, too salty, too sweet. It doesn't have to be exactly to your liking. Then the wife is unhappy.

The same with men. When they come home, bring them cool water and a cool towel to refresh themselves; then you can get whatever you want from them. There are drunk husbands who stubbornly refuse to go home. Five, six men can't drag him through the door. But if his wife speaks sweetly and strokes him gently, "Husband, come inside." She has two fingers in his pantloops. It doesn't take much. She can just guide him into the house like one guides chickens into the coop. But if you get mad at him out there, he's likely to get violent. Wait until he's inside.[64]

Luang Poh Bunthong returned to this theme of husband-wife relations, using the occasion of Matsi reassuring Vessantara when he was afraid of the approaching army to encourage couples to be supportive of each other:

Mothers and fathers [*poh ohk mae ohk*], learn from this. If one of you has a problem, the other should reassure them. If the husband is sick, the wife should take care of him. If the wife is sick, the husband should take care of her. Don't abandon each other when there are problems. . . .

Some couples are too much. The husband loses 100 baht, and two years later the wife is still bringing it up. And another water pot is broken. "I said not to bring it up." There goes the water pot. There goes the water dipper. Let it rest after it is over. No need to go over it again and again.

"The knife is chipped." "Never mind. There are lots of people who can repair it." The next morning the husband finds the knife with the chip, "Hey, who used my knife?" "But I told you about it last night." "Well, I didn't know you meant the blade side." And that's how trouble starts. Be kind and considerate of each other. Just like Phra Wessandorn and Nang Matsi.[65]

Parent and Child Relations

Luang Poh Bunthong also included stories about the problems between parents and their children, particularly when the parents are elderly. One example is about a son and his short-tempered father.

The story is as follows. If the father got mad with his son, he wouldn't speak to him for days at a time, sometimes seven to eight days at a stretch. Now, listeners, this isn't right. Parents and elders, all of you who have children, you must remember that kids are still just kids and don't know as much. If you get angry with your kids and stop talking to them, then who will talk to them? As mothers and fathers, you should be teaching your children. If they do something wrong, then be democratic and have compassion. If you get angry, just be angry for a short time. You are the adults and you should understand their feelings too. If you stop talking, misunderstandings are likely to result. So this is the story of a father who goes overboard, when he got angry he wouldn't talk to his son for weeks, even a month at a stretch.

One day the father wasn't talking to his son because he was angry with him. He and his son were sitting there, eating breakfast. [*Laughs.*] They were eating breakfast together, but there was no conversation because the father refused to talk to his son. The father was wearing his farmer pants [*taeo sadoh*] and squat-sitting on his haunches. But his pants had a rip, right in the crotch. He was just sitting there eating, with all on display. The son didn't know what to do. He couldn't say anything to his father, because his father wasn't speaking to him. He was afraid of his father's reaction, because his father might get even angrier with him. A good deed might not meet with a good ending.

But the son couldn't concentrate, since every time he looked, there were his father's genitals in full view. What to do? He grabbed a stick and began talking to it, saying, "Father, I'd like to poke it [*ji*]." The father didn't respond; he just kept on eating. The son repeated to the stick, "Boy, oh boy, I'd sure like to poke it." The father thought the son wanted to poke at some of the food. Finally he couldn't stand it and told his son, "So good ahead and poke it." [*Pause.*] They obviously were thinking about very different things. [*Laughs.*]

"You say you want to poke it, but you don't. It's not going anywhere." The son goes out to the kitchen and grabs a stick with roasted chilies on it. In those days they ate on *khantok* [a raised tray]. The son put his stick under the khantok tray and began poking, each time poking the stick further and further under the tray.

All of a sudden the father let out a scream, and fell backward. His legs knocked over the tray and the food went flying. He stormed over to the water pot, exclaiming, "See what kids are like these days." He was really angry now. So please remember, whoever is right or wrong, please talk it through. If you don't talk to your children, terrible things can happen.[66]

In Thailand, elderly parents remain in the care of their children, most typically their youngest daughter. Very often there is tension. In the segment depicting Jujaka's efforts to be reborn, Luang Poh Bunthong described "people who don't think that there is anything about themselves they need to change," adding that "Puu Phraam was like this, so no one wanted to help him be reborn." He takes the moment to characterize old people who are always complaining about the younger generation:

Not that I am criticizing old people around here; I'm talking about old people far away. The old guy hasn't even gotten out of bed and he is already grumbling, *baem baem baem*. In the cold season, the kids are all sleeping peacefully, but he calls them to wake up. When they don't wake up, he's angry, lamenting, "This is so terrible. I just want to die [*kuu khai daai, yangnii lamlya*]."

Kuu khai daai	I wish I were dead
Pen nok pen nuu	To be a bird or mouse
Pai jap khing mai duu phoh suu	To climb on a tree branch to watch
Suu ja luk myadai.	To see when you will finally wake up.

But if he actually became a bird or mouse, the kids would probably shoot him with their slingshots! Wherever they are, they complain. If they are downstairs, they complain that it's too dirty so they can't sleep. All night they grumble. So then someone helps them upstairs. They complain again that it's too dirty and they can't sleep. They are tucked into their mosquito net in the bedroom. The fan is turned on. And they still complain that they feel itchy. Other people can sleep just fine. [*Laughs.*][67]

In another scene, Luang Poh Bunthong does a riff on unidentified people who are turning old people into fertilizer:

I've heard that old people have been made into fertilizer. So I've been told. Depends on the season. In the rainy season and hot season, they don't hunt them. But during the cold season it is easy to hunt them. It's hard to find them in the hot and rainy season, but in the cold season they are all either sitting by fires keeping warm or out sunning themselves to stay warm. So they catch them and take them to the fertilizer factory. Once there, they have the old men go off to the right and the old women off to the left. They use the old man fertilizer for the slow growing trees, like lamyai, mango, linchee, durian, rangsat. The old woman fertilizer is used for the fast growing annual crops like cabbage and *phak kaat* [greens]; that way they grow really fast. They [the crops] are tired of hearing all the complaints and so they grow fast. They called it *pui laeng*, rapid growth fertilizer, that's all from the old lady fertilizer. From early morning, they hear *baem baem baem baem*, complaining.[68]

Monk-Novice Relations

There is a wide repertoire of stories making fun of the relationships between monks and novices. In the past many villagers ordained their sons as novices in the village temple to ensure their education. The northern villagers' respect for the monastic order was reflected in the fact that monks who disrobed and returned to village life carried the title *Naan* as part of their village name; villagers who had once been novices were called *Noi*. With the rise of secular education this tradition is fading away. Nonetheless, most villagers can still recall the time when temples were full of novices, a time described to me by one former novice when there were so many novices trying to eat at the same time that they had to reach their arms in sideways. Inevitably the tensions between abbots and novices created opportunities for comic descriptions. Most children were sent to the temples to get an education, but problem children were sent to the temple in the hope that the abbot could reform them. Luang Poh Bunthong also made jokes about temple life, using the invented scenario of Jujaka being an impossible child as the excuse for the diversion:

> What is it about being a monk? We never get the good kids. The kids with high IQ and lots of knowledge, the parents keep to raise themselves, paying school fees, etc. The bad ones get sent to the temple. You've all heard parents saying, "If you are this lazy, why don't you go to the temple?" It's like I'm supposed to be the head of a party of the lazy. I don't like to talk about this, because it's very personal. [*Laughter.*] . . .
>
> Some parents scold their children, "Go to the temple if you just want to sit around [*sabaai yang tu*]." But who says monks live well? They think just because we don't have to buy a home to live in or food to eat that monks live well. I don't disagree that this is true; I accept it like a man [*luuk phuuchaai*].
>
> I don't have a problem with rice; I have a problem with the other dishes. Whatever the season, that is what we get. When it is *phak la* season, we eat phak la the whole time. When it is bamboo season, we eat bamboo the whole time. It's not that it isn't good, but it gets to be too much. The nutritionists say that bamboo has no nutritional value; it's mainly good roughage to get the bowels moving. As I see it, bamboo shoots have no hormones. You can tell from me, for example. I've eaten lots of bamboo shoots and I just get balder and balder.[69] In *phak kaat* season, it is nothing but phak kaat. Nowadays, ever since we started having local agricultural officers [*kaset tambon*], we get phak kaat all year. They call it Green Siam [*khiaw Sayam*]. Today it was *khiaw sayam sai muu hippii* [greens with hippy pork]. If you are wondering what hippy pork is, it is pork with pigskin that they never finished removing all the hairs from. The long hairs are still hanging there.
>
> There was once a central Thai monk. . . . The village headman decided he wanted to get rid of the monk. But he didn't want to be too obvious about it. What to do? He went around to all the villagers and told them, "This monk is

like the others. He loves *phak kaat joh* [a classic village dish, greens boiled with tamarind seeds]. If everyone makes him phak kaat joh, he will stay with us a long time." So all seventy households made phak kaat joh to send to the temple, seventy platefuls, thirty-five for breakfast, thirty-five for lunch. The next day another seventy, the day after another seventy.

He couldn't take it anymore. He had the novices form a barrier in front of the temple. Each held a large stick. . . . Pretty soon a grandmother arrived, having specially made phak kaat joh to send to the temple. "Stop! (Like in the boxing shows). What dish have you prepared?" She got nervous. She had never seen the novices holding clubs and had never been asked what dish she had made. She put the phak kaat joh on the ground and wailed, replying, "*Buu khieo hang dohk* [flowering phak kaat]." The monk thought she must mean chicken khieo hang dok, the kind of chicken with the white tail feathers. So he thought, "Ah, this must be chicken. . . ." The grandmother delivered her dish and scurried off home. The monk was all excited, he could finally eat chicken. He opened the lid. It was phak kaat joh again. . . .

There are people who are just good at making things sound good. There was a grandmother who felt sorry for the monks who were always having to eat phak kaat. One day she was heading to temple and she passed two children also on their way to temple. She asked them what they were bringing. The one said "phak kaat joh" and the other said "*kaeng phak kaat* [boiled greens]." "Oh dear, the poor monk. You're both bringing phak kaat. Why don't you think of bringing something else?" So they asked her what she was bringing. She replied, "*Nam phrik nam phak!*" [*Laughter.*] In other words, just another form of phak kaat. If you ask what it is made from, it is phak kaat, just condensed so the flavor is even more intense. [*Laughter.*]

So that's what they mean when they say, "Living the easy life of a monk [*sabaai yang tu*]." You don't have to buy rice or find a place to live. But just try it. Come and live like a monk. The abbot has nothing to give you, beyond just teaching you reading and writing. The monk teaches, *k kha ka kha nga* [northern alphabet]. The student copies him, *k kha kapka nga.* [*Laughter at the mistake.*] As they say:

Yuu kap tu kap phra	If you live with monks and novices
Dai kin im kin tem	You can eat until you're full
Kin kaeng ho kap khao yen	You can eat kaeng ho with cold rice
Bo jai khaa uu en	I'm not bragging
Tot dang bang bang.	With loud farts, bang, bang.
[*in a singing chant*]⁷⁰	

At another point, Luang Poh Bunthong told another story about a village abbot's efforts to teach some village boys a lesson:

> There was a group of children who kept gambling in the temple. The abbot told them to stop, but they wouldn't listen. So finally the abbot asked one of the temple boys to put *bakhang* [plant seeds known as a laxative] into a water pot [*nam ton*] and give it to the boys to drink. When it hit them, the group of children scattered, all looking for the bathroom. One bold boy was angry. He pointed his finger at the abbot and said, "You're evil." The abbot remained calm and said, "Why do you say I'm evil? Don't just stand there pointing your finger at me. Come over and sit down and let's talk it over calmly." The boy came over. But as he began to squat, he cried, "Oh no, I have to go again."[71]

Hidden Transcripts: Hints of Politics

Inverting the focus from Vessantara to Jujaka enables a very different reading of the *Vessantara Jataka*, resulting not in an idealized panegyric to virtuous royalty but a realistic engagement with villagers facing moral challenges in everyday village life. At this point in our analysis, we have learned of significant variations in the interpretations of the *Vessantara Jataka* in each of the three regions. We have traced Jujaka from his least comic role in the central region to his most fully elaborated role in the northern region. We can see humor gained from wordplay, from incongruous references to pop culture, and from bawdy, scatological, and sexual references.

While there is considerable humor to be found in these quotidian tensions, it is difficult to understand why the Bangkok court would have been upset by monks using humorous parables to teach moral principles. The northern versions are bawdy, but why would the court be so concerned? Had the Bangkok court developed Victorian prudishness to the degree that peasant humor shocked them? If the court was worried about European audiences, then why bother about bawdy humor in remote upcountry villages, spoken in dialects that few Europeans understood? The analysis of northern humor described in this chapter begins to provide some flesh to Charles Keyes's summary of the *Vessantara Jataka* as providing "moral models for the most important social relationships: those of father and child, husband and wife, mother and child, ruler and subject, world-renouncers and people who remain in the world" (1987, 181). But we have not considered one of these social relationships: the relationship between ruler and subjects. The politics is still missing.

Given the long-standing sensitivity of discussing politics, be it in the earlier times of absolute monarchy or in the more modern periods of military rule, it is

Table 1. A regional comparison of the *Vessantara Jataka*

	Central	Northeast	North
Frequency	Declining	Annual	Rare
Calendar	During Lent; often Wan Sart, or Wan Thewo. July–October	Not during Lent; always Bun Pha Wet (northeastern month 4). circa March	Not during Lent; often Dyan Yii Paeng (northern month 2). circa November
Duration of recitation	Several days/weeks	Within 24 hours	Within 24 hours
Number of monks	1–10 (average)	40–50	13
Individual chapter recitations	Novice ordination (former times)	No	Funerals Housewarmings
Lay sponsors	Reservations/Lots	Reservations/Lots	Birth years
Processions	Yes, in the past; chapter offerings	Yes; Upakut, Vessantara, thousand balls of rice, *kan lon*	No, except *tujok*; but developing now
Key symbols	Boat Sea of suffering	Scroll Trip from forest	Maze Trip to forest
Key chapters	Multiple, especially Kumarn	Nakornkan	Jujaka
Portrayal of Jujaka	Not humorous; frightening, though sometimes deified	Ambivalent; vaudevillian humor	Very humorous; beloved trickster

perhaps not surprising that we find less explicit engagement with the subject of peasant-court relations in either their ideal or actual forms. If discussions of royalty were salient but politically sensitive, we need to consider the extent to which performances were "hidden transcripts" (Scott 1990). Phrased in simplest terms, was the village reading non-royalist, pro-royalist or anti-royalist? To fully explore the possibility of implied resonances of the *Vessantara Jataka* for not merely a non-royalist interpretation but an anti-royalist reading, we need to consider more of the historical sociocultural context in which villagers listened to the jataka. As the next chapter will suggest, the court may have been concerned less with the scatological humor and more with the resonances of the ex-novice Jujaka with the trickster humor of the ex-novice Siang Miang.

Part II

The Politics of Diversity

4

Jujaka as Trickster
The Peasant Imaginaire

When the portrayals in central, northeastern, and northern Thailand are compared, Jujaka's importance as a comedic character emerges most clearly in the northern Thai performances of the *Vessantara Jataka*. The robust humor in these northern performances makes informed speculation about its historical political sensitivity possible. The northern portrayal of Jujaka bears much in common with the trickster, a well-known figure in Thai folklore. Mocking peasants, monks, and monarchs, the figure of the trickster opens up new possibilities for insight into the peasant imaginaire, into the political consciousness of villagers.[1] Although the court was unlikely to be upset if peasants mocked their own failings or those of local monks, it was likely to be worried about anti-royalist humor. Some scholars have portrayed the *Vessantara Jataka* as a pro-royalist text, but if we focus on the figure of Jujaka, the northern textual versions and performances emerge as potential vehicles for the covert expression of anti-royalist sentiments. Recognizing Jujaka as a type of trickster, understanding the peasantry's traditionally negative views toward the court, realizing the ever-present threat of revolt, and comprehending the widespread belief in the Maitreya Buddha—all help to explain why the court sought to suppress comedic recitations of the *Vessantara Jataka*.[2]

I divide this chapter into four sections. The first section draws parallels between Jujaka and other trickster figures and notes the cross-regional popularity of tricksters in Thailand. The second section describes the highly negative attitude villagers had toward ruling lords and officials. The third section highlights the importance of beliefs in Maitreya and the frequency of millenarian revolts in mainland Southeast Asia. The fourth section considers the evidence of the northern performances as "hidden transcripts" expressing anti-royalist

Figure 13. Jujaka in tree surrounded by Jetabutr's dogs. Temple mural scene of Chulaphon chapter, showing Jujaka up in the tree. Painted by Pramote Sriphrom in 2006. Wat Niramit, Amphur Dansai, Loei Province, July 2009. Photo by author.

sentiments (Scott 1992). When performances of the *Vessantara Jataka* are understood as implied critiques of earthly kings rather than homages, the court's desire to suppress comedic recitations becomes understandable. The court's reaction can be seen not merely as a show of deference to bourgeois morality but also as a response to perceived threats to its political security.

Tricksters as Moral Distance

Although tricksters are characterized in a variety of ways, the American Folklore website provides a good summary of the key elements. As can be seen, Jujaka shares these major characteristics: "A Trickster is a mischievous or roguish figure in myth or folklore who typically makes up for physical weakness with cunning and subversive humor. The Trickster alternates between cleverness and stupidity, kindness and cruelty, deceiver and deceived, breaker of taboos and creator of culture."[3]

Across all three regions, Jujaka is portrayed as old and ugly. While in central Thailand his ugliness is intended to evoke revulsion, in northern Thailand his homeliness is so exaggerated as to evoke a comic reaction. As Henri Bergson notes, while humor always depends on the comic figure having some resemblance to human characteristics, it also involves distancing in the form of physical caricaturing. Remarking that "laughter has no greater foe than emotion," Bergson suggests the comic is dependent on an "an absence of feeling" (2005, 2). As he explains: "I do not mean that we could not laugh at a person who inspires us with pity, for instance, or even with affection, but in such a case we must, for the moment, put our affection out of court and impose silence upon our pity.... To produce the whole of its effect, then, the comic demands something like a momentary anesthesia of the heart. Its appeal is to intelligence, pure and simple" ([1911] 2005, 2–3). Like other comic figures, Jujaka "is generally comic in proportion to his ignorance of himself. The comic person is unconscious. As though wearing the ring of Gyges with reverse effect, he becomes invisible to himself while remaining visible to all the world" (Bergson [1911] 2005, 8). However, despite comedy's focus on the physical, "it is the moral side that is concerned" (Bergson [1911] 2005, 25). This distancing made possible by the descriptions of Jujaka's physical form allows the audience to laugh at Jujaka's exploits, even while recognizing a common humanity in their shared desires for wealth and happiness.

Paul Radin describes the trickster as "an inchoate being of undetermined proportions" who mixes laughter with irony such that "it is difficult to say whether the audience is laughing at him, at the tricks he plays on others, or at the implications his behaviour and activities have for them" ([1956] 1972, xxiv). Similarly, Bergson suggests, "Laughter 'corrects men's manners.' It makes us at once endeavour to appear what we ought to be" ([1911] 2005, 9). By following Jujaka in his quest for wealth and happiness, the audience can contemplate the consequences of unfettered desires. As Bergson explains: "Look closely: you will find that the art of the comic poet consists in making us so well acquainted with the particular vice, in introducing us, the spectators, to such a degree of intimacy with it, that in the end we get hold of some of the strings of the marionette with which he is playing, and actually work them ourselves" ([1911] 2005, 8).

However, not only is Jujaka teaching the audience through his unconscious and uncontrolled greed; he is also making Vessantara's path to Buddhahood and the salvation of humanity possible. In this manner, the anthropological literature on the figure of the trickster provides helpful insights into the role Jujaka plays in the *Vessantara Jataka*. As Radin explains, "Trickster is at one and the same time creator and destroyer, giver and negator, he who dupes others and who is always duped himself. He wills nothing consciously. At all times he is constrained to behave as he does from impulses over which he has no control. He knows neither good nor evil yet he is responsible for both. He possesses no values, moral or social, is at the mercy of his passions and appetites, yet through his actions all values come into being" ([1956] 1972, xxiii).

In his discussion of tricksters, Lewis Hyde notes that "all tricksters are 'on the road.'" Similarly, through many of the chapters in the *Vessantara Jataka*, Jujaka is on the road, traveling through villages, towns, forests, and, finally, the palace. But he belongs in none of them. As Hyde explains:

> Tricksters are the lords of in-between. A trickster does not live near the hearth; he does not live in the halls of justice, the soldier's tent, the shaman's hut, the monastery. He passes through each of these when there is a moment of silence, and he enlivens each with mischief, but he is not their guiding spirit. . . . The road that trickster travels is a spirit road as well as a road in fact. He is the adept who can move between heaven and earth, and between the living and the dead. . . .
>
> In short, trickster is a boundary-crosser. Every group has its edge, its sense of in and out, and trickster is always there, at the gates of the city and the gates of life, making sure there is commerce. . . . Trickster is the mythic embodiment of ambiguity and ambivalence, doubleness and duplicity, contradiction and paradox. (1998, 6–7)

Hyde also notes that "tricksters are ridden by lust, but their hyperactive sexuality almost never results in any offspring, the implication being that the stories are above non-procreative creativity" (1998, 8). This is certainly true of Jujaka: he is ridden by lust for his beautiful young wife, but their marriage is childless. Yet in his quest to satisfy his wife, Jujaka enables Vessantara to complete his quest to reach enlightenment. As Hyde explains, "in spite of all their disruptive behavior, tricksters are regularly honored as the creators of culture" (1998, 8). The trickster is amoral, not immoral, and represents "the paradoxical category of sacred amorality" (Hyde 1998, 10). It is easy to see the parallels between Jujaka and Hyde's explanation of the role of Coyote in Navajo stories. Not only do both figures make people laugh, but "they teach people how to behave." In the vicarious pleasure people have in watching Coyote break rules lies also "a potentially fruitful fantasizing, too, for listeners are invited, if only in imagination, to scout the territory that lies beyond the local constraints" (Hyde 1998, 12).

Like other tricksters, Jujaka is not a normal person; he violates normal cultural expectations. He is a contradiction as both a beggar and a Brahmin. He is a poor beggar who has been able to acquire considerable wealth. He is an ugly old man, but he nonetheless is able to gain a beautiful young wife. Like other tricksters who are "on the road," Jujaka is a wandering beggar. To the extent he has a home, he has no living kin beyond Amitataa. His house with its four stilts and pillows made from chicken droppings is impoverished to the point of absurdity. In the course of his venture into the sacred forest, he is able to outwit two royal guardians and find his way to where Vessantara and his family are residing under the watchful eye of the god Indra. Jujaka's long journey ultimately leads him from his village home to the splendor of life within the palace walls, an area to which no villagers—let alone beggars— would normally gain access.

Like other tricksters, Jujaka is amoral rather than immoral. His desires for money, a beautiful wife, and delicious foods are human and understandable; however boundless his desires may be, they are not motivated by any malicious intent. To keep his one bond with a fellow human—his wife, Amitataa—he is willing to do all her domestic chores. His desire for Vessantara's two children is not for his own sake but in response to his wife's difficulties. Jujaka is at once clever and stupid. He is stupid enough to leave his gold with another person, yet clever enough to gain a young wife. He outwits royal guardians on his way into the forest. He even outwits Vessantara into giving him the children before Matsi returns, but he is too oblivious to know the angels are caring for the two children and too befuddled to find his way home, a hapless victim of divine intervention.

Jujaka provides a bridge between the village and the palace, between the earthly and heavenly worlds. The human village realm is ruled by desire, greed, jealousy, and anger; the sacred forest realm is characterized by self-restraint, generosity, and detachment. Jujaka bridges these two stylized extremes in a way that no normal person ever could. A normal person who is old and poor would not be likely to marry at all, let alone acquire a dutiful young wife; a normal person would not seek a prince's children to be his servants; a normal person would not be able to trick royal guardians, survive an attack by wild dogs, or gain entrance into the palace. A normal person would also not die from overeating. Jujaka's desire to please his young wife leads to his destruction; yet from his desire for Vessantara's children, all mankind gains the possibility of salvation. In the course of his journey, he teaches us all that the moderation of the Middle Path should guide us through our lives.

Tricksters as Anti-Monarchical Folk Heroes

Mainland Southeast Asian folklore is rife with trickster tales. Among the best-known tricksters are the so-called Siang Miang (also transliterated as Xieng Mieng) tales in northeastern and northern Thailand and the Sri Thanonchai stories in central Thailand.[4] In these sets of folktales, the primary tension lies in the relations between the trickster and a king, representing in a distanced form the relations between the peasantry and the court. Siang Miang is a peasant folk hero who conquers officialdom through wit, guile, and deceit; he thereby enables villagers to become "vicarious victors over their rulers" (Klausner 1993, 90). As William Klausner explains:

> The Siang Miang tales provide psychological release for the frustrations and antagonisms of a peasantry subject to the arbitrary power of the ruling aristocracy. Not only does Siang Miang challenge and ridicule authority, he emerges victorious in the battle of wits with the ruling establishment. He also proves to be indispensable to the rulers who must rely on his peasant cunning and genius to solve problems of state e.g. in administering outlying regions. Unable even to challenge their rulers, the villagers seek an understandable release in the accomplishments of the bold and artful Siang Miang. (1993, 90–91)

Trickster Tales in Northern and Northeastern Thailand

A few examples from the tales of Siang Miang will help to elucidate the manner in which the trickster figure provides vicarious pleasure and psychological release through humor. The trickster's name derives from the Lao word for a former novice, namely *siang*, and *miang* (mieng), a type of fermented tea particularly popular in northern Thailand. Although some storytellers begin before his earthly birth, others often begin with his escapades as a mischievous young novice. One day the novice tricks some merchants out of their stash of miang. When the king hears of these antics, he tells the novice that he must disrobe and gives him his new nickname, Siang Miang. Of course, his pranks only continue. As we have seen in both the northern and northeastern embellishments to the *Vessantara Jataka*, Jujaka is given a fabricated history as a novice who creates so many problems that the abbot expels him from the temple.

In one typical story, the king wished to gain revenge for all the tricks played on him by Siang Miang. So the king passed wind several times into a bamboo container and sealed it tightly shut. He ordered one of his officials to take the container to Siang Miang and have him unseal the gift and smell it. The king gave detailed instructions how to reach Siang Miang's home. After traveling for some time, the official approached Siang Miang's village and asked a villager, who happened to be Siang Miang himself, where he could find Siang Miang. Siang Miang asked the official why he was looking for this villager. The official replied that the king had passed wind into the bamboo container he held and that Siang Miang was going to be tricked into opening and smelling it. Siang Miang shook his head and remarked that the official had come a long way and surely the wind in the bamboo had evaporated and the smell was gone. The official worriedly opened the container and sniffed the full fragrance of his master's wind (Klausner 1993, 93).

In another story, the king and Siang Miang went for a picnic by a pond in the forest. After lunch, the king decided to issue a challenge to Siang Miang, saying that if Siang Miang could trick him into going into the pond, Siang Miang could ride his horse back. Siang Miang replied, "Your Majesty, you are much cleverer than I. You know that I cannot trick you into going into the pond. . . . But, Your Majesty, if you go into the pond I can trick you into getting out of the pond." The king accepted the challenge and walked into the pond. Siang Miang sat down by the pond. After eating all the mangoes, he took a nap:

> "Xieng Mieng! I am in the pond! Now trick me into coming out of the pond!"
>
> Xieng Mieng woke from his sleep. He yawned and stretched.
>
> "It is getting late, Your Majesty. I must go back now. I cannot trick you to come out of the pond. Since you will be staying in the pond, you will not have any need for your horse. So I know it won't be a problem if I ride it back."
>
> Xieng Mieng mounted the king's beautiful white horse.
>
> "Wait! You tricked me again! Wait!" said the king as he watched a laughing Xieng Mieng go galloping away. (Epstein 1995, 61–63)

In another story, titled "Siang Miang's Revenge," the king again seeks retribution. This story appears to have been particularly popular because it is painted on a temple mural at Wat Pathumwanaram, in Bangkok.[5] In this story, the king has invited Siang Miang to the palace. Complimenting Siang Miang on his cleverness, the king says to him, "I have invited you to the palace for a special dinner to celebrate your triumph. I have asked the royal cooks to prepare a special curry in your honor." The king's servants bring out the tray of food and Siang Miang eats away. The next morning Siang Miang returns to the palace. The king asks him how he enjoyed the meal and has him guess what the ingredients in the curry were. Laughing at his trick, he informs Siang Miang that he has just eaten vulture.

A few weeks later the populace was invited to the palace to discuss plans for civic improvement. There was a large blackboard in the front of the room:

> The king picked up a piece of chalk to draw on the blackboard.
> But, for some reason, the chalk would not write.
> "Lick the chalk, Your Majesty," suggested Xieng Mieng, "then the chalk will write."
> The king licked the chalk. He tried writing on the blackboard but it still did not write.
> "Lick it again, Your Majesty," said Xieng Mieng.
> The king licked the chalk again and tried to write on the blackboard but still it would not write.
> Xieng Mieng picked up the piece of chalk and examined it closely.
> "Oh, Your Majesty, there has been a terrible mistake. This is not chalk. This is a vulture dropping. Your Majesty, how did it taste?" (Epstein 1995, 53-56)

Trickster Tales in Central Thailand

Like the Siang Miang trickster stories that were widely known in northeastern and northern Thailand, the same genre of stories was told in central Thailand, with Sri Thanonchai as the trickster. Sri Thanonchai, believed to date from the Ayutthayan period (1350-1767), is the peasant-born trickster hero who employs guile, wordplay, and wit to best everyone he encounters, including the king. In addition to "a keen Thai appreciation of the ridiculous and absurd," Mechai Thongthep suggests that "common folk derived considerable vicarious pleasure from the ways the impudent hero irreverently challenged and bested officialdom, rich fools and foreigners with native intelligence, bluff and deception" (1991, 9). Sri Thanonchai was a prime example of someone neither cowed nor awed by authority or by seemingly towering intellect. Moreover, such anecdotes demonstrated how it was possible, employing lively wit, to talk oneself out of almost any threatening, oppressive, or inherently disadvantageous situation. As Mechai explains, in a society where heavy-handed authority was not uncommon, "failure to obey commands guaranteed, at least, subsequent rebuke, perhaps even physical abuse. On a personal level, little could be more immediately gratifying than literally obeying commands to the visible detriment of authorities issuing them" (1991, 11).

Like the Siang Miang tales, the Sri Thanonchai stories begin with the trickster's childhood. Following his parents' instructions to keep his brother clean, Sri Thanonchai kills his younger brother while cleaning him inside and out. He then ordains as a novice, has further misadventures, and is eventually expelled from the temple. After further escapades, he eventually becomes a courtier. A story from the Sri Thanonchai series will help to elucidate the parallels with the Siang Miang trickster tales. Shortly after Sri Thanonchai is presented to the court, he is able to build a house out of gold wood (*thong lang*). He begins to neglect his court duties. The king dispatches royal guards to bring him to court. Sri Thanonchai dons his courtly attire and goes to the palace:

> The King berated him, "Luang Sri, you've been absent for several days."
> "If it please Your Majesty, I did not miss work through laziness. I have just built myself a house of gold. I needed to guard it against thieves."
> The king was skeptical and said if he was lying, he would be beheaded. The king and his retinue arrive at Sri Thanonchai's house and saw no trace of gold. The king angrily exclaimed, "That's nothing but a house made from *Thong Lang* wood [wood from a goldwood tree]."

On uttering those words, the king realized he had been tricked. When the king returned to the palace, he immediately summoned the court ladies. He told them to go to Luang Sri's new house and befoul it with excrement to repay his impudence:

> The ladies immediately departed to Sri Thanonchai's 'golden' house. There Sri Thanonchai endured a symphony of sounds and stenches as the women squatted everywhere to defecate, fart, and urinate at will. The dwelling smelled foul, yet Sri Thanonchai dared not obstruct or oppose them, for they obeyed the King's orders.
> Unless...
> Suddenly, it seemed Sri Thanonchai had gone mad. He beat the squatting women, chasing them outside until they fled screaming, clothing in disarray, from his house back to the palace.
> The King immediately had guards fetch Sri Thanonchai.
> "How dare you, Luang Sri? We ordered these ladies to soil your house as punishment. Yet you dare inflict injury upon them without taking heed of our orders!"
> "Your Majesty, I acted because they disobeyed you."
> "What? Explain!"
> "They defecated, sire."
> "As they were ordered," [the king replied] testily.
> "And urinated. And farted. And befouled the air. Such disobedience could not go unpunished, no matter how minor or trivial the offence might seem."
> The King listened with a sinking heart.

"Otherwise, people would take such disobedience as an example. Your Majesty's words would no longer be law."

The King gritted his teeth and relented. "You are right. The ladies exceeded their instructions. You may go." (Mechai 1991, 36–38)

Like both Siang Miang and Sri Thanonchai, northern tujok monks invented adventures for Jujaka as a child and as a novice that appear to have drawn on these trickster stories. We saw echoes of this early life history in the northeastern portrayals of Jujaka as well. Kicked out of the temple, Jujaka sets off on his journey as a beggar, tricking royal guardians and ultimately being feted in grand style in the palace.

Historical Northern Village Attitudes toward Royalty

To understand the emotional resonance of these trickster tales among Thai villagers on a historical level, some background on the nineteenth- and twentieth-century political economy and peasant political consciousness is needed. If the nineteenth century saw isolated peasant revolts, the twentieth century saw the rise of a sustained, armed guerilla struggle led by the Communist Party of Thailand, which reached its peak in the 1960s and 1970s. Village surveys during this period revealed significant problems of debt, poverty, and landlessness. A 1968 survey of the National Statistical Office reported that 4 million out of 5 million farming families were in debt (Morell and Samudavanija 1981, 209). Figures from a 1971–73 survey provided by the National Statistical Office showed that 34.9 percent of rural households in the central plains; 45.2 percent of households in the south; 63.6 percent of households in the north; and 74.7 percent of households in the northeast were living below the poverty level, earning less than $300 per year (Turton 1978, 108). According to figures from the Land Development Department, 48 percent of Thailand's 5.5 million agricultural households owned 16 percent of the cultivated land (Turton 1978, 111). In the village where I lived, of a total of some 400 households surveyed in the 1970s, 40 percent were completely landless and worked as wage laborers.[6]

Of Poverty and Beggars

Peasant poverty has been a long-standing problem throughout Thailand. Carle Zimmerman undertook the first formal survey of rural landholdings in 1930; his survey found that 36 percent of villagers in the central plain were landless, 27 percent of villagers in the north, 18 percent in the northeast, and 14 percent in the south (1931, 18; see also Andrews 1935). Newspaper, consular, and missionary accounts for the northern region in the early twentieth century contain frequent reports of widespread famine. A report in 1907 indicates, "The scarcity of paddy would, at present, however, appear to be general in the North of Siam" (*BTWM*, September 18, 1907). In 1910 there are again reports of "a great deal of suffering throughout the country on account of the scarcity of rice" (*BTWM*, October 16, 1910). In Chiang Rai, a correspondent notes "misfortune in several recent harvests" and writes that "famine has become a reality," explaining, "[the people] do not have food to enable them to carry on till the harvest. Many were living on roots and green herbs, and others were going heavily into debt to provide food" (*BTWM*, November 7, 1910).[7] Poor harvest "estimated at one seventh of a good harvest" was reported again in Lampang in 1912, with a longtime resident noting that Lampang had been in a "semi-famine condition year after year" (*BTWM*, August 18, 1912; *BTWM*, September 17, 1912).[8] Also in Phrae, a reporter notes the "almost famine-like condition of the past two years due to lack of water" (*BTWM*, February 13, 1913). By April 1914, famine was widespread in Lampang; as the *Laos News* reports, "The famine in Lakawn [Lampang] this year is most distressing.... The people in many places are living only on roots, which they obtain in the forest. In their weakened condition they are victims of fever and many die" (quoted in *BTWM*, July 2, 1914).

Although the Chiang Mai Valley generally produced sufficient rice, the 1911 crop there was described as "a 66 per cent crop," and British Vice Consul Gorton notes "great scarcity" in Maehongsorn, Lampang, Phrae, and Nan as well (*BTWM*, October 2, 1912). A report from Lamphun in 1913 notes that "for several years past, the local rainfall has been exceedingly scanty, and the plain east of the city which is dependent upon that gives little prospect of a crop. Much of it has absolutely no water" (*BTWM*, September 4, 1913). In October 1915, east of Lamphun city "all the rice that is dependent on local rains is in bad shape. Much of it has not even been planted, and the same is true of some parts of the Me Ta valley" (*BTWM*, October 30, 1915). A subsequent account in September 1918 suggests continuing hardships in Lamphun, the correspondent having met a family en route to Chiang Rai "as there was not enough water down there to permit the ploughing of the fields" (*BTWM*, September 3, 1918).[9]

Accounts of the nineteenth-century rural economy are harder to find, but Hugh Taylor, a missionary working in Lampang, provides a moving account of 1892, when famine was widespread. The shortage of food was so severe that villagers were even begging for coconut husks to chop up and mix with whatever rice they had in order to fill their stomachs. As a stunning index of desperation, the price of coconut husks—in normal times used as kindling—rose to the price of four pounds of rice in ordinary times (Taylor Mss, 114). Hugh Taylor, who had organized some relief work, said, "We had to post a guard to keep the people from crowding in on us too hard . . . sifting the starving from the merely hungry" (Taylor Mss, 113). Taylor continues: "Yes, they were starving. More than three score starved to death in the next village down the river from us. . . . The Elders and Evangelists who were sent out to follow up those who had received help reported finding dead bodies in deserted houses. They set fire to the houses and cremated the bodies. They found village wells filled with starved bodies that the neighbors were too weak to bury" (Taylor Mss, 114).[10]

While famines of this severity were perhaps not the norm, evidence for the general extent of agrarian poverty is provided by oral histories. In the course of my interviews in 1984–86, I routinely asked elderly villagers throughout the Chiang Mai Valley if people in their villages had fallen short of rice in the past, and if so, for how many months out of the year. Of a total of 273 villages about which I have information, 96.7 percent of villages had at least some households who fell short of rice for at least two or three months each year. In nearly half (48.7 percent) of the villages, the *majority* of households fell short of rice at least two or three months each year. The significance of these figures is heightened when one considers the fact that relative to other regions of Thailand, the Chiang Mai Valley is one of the most fertile rice-producing areas in the country.

Repeated in numerous interviews was a sense of relentless poverty forcing villagers to unceasing industry. Villagers often traveled long distances to find work or food. Of life in the past, villagers often commented, "*Bo dai yuu, bo dai yang,*" "Couldn't rest, couldn't stop." As one woman (age seventy-nine in 1985) explained, "In the past no matter how tired or lazy one felt, one had no choice but to work." She continued, citing an old saying:

Bo ohk baan, ko bo dai kin	If one didn't leave the house, one didn't eat.
Bo soh, ko bo dai kin	If one didn't search, one didn't eat.
Bo luk, thohng ko hong	If one didn't get up, the stomach would soon cry out.[11]

In the context of village life, beggars are sympathetic figures. As I have noted elsewhere, in all my years in the countryside, I never heard a villager say anything derogatory about a rural beggar (see Bowie 1998). As one villager explained to Konrad Kingshill, "One priest told us that the Lord Buddha taught that we should present gifts to all living creatures, not only to priests, but also to other people who are in need, or even to animals. Thus merit can be made by giving gifts to anyone" (1976, 192). Whenever a beggar came to homes in the village where I lived, whoever was home would immediately get a bowl of unmilled rice from the kitchen. Before pouring rice into the beggar's bag, the villagers first removed their shoes. They then held the bowl above their heads briefly and then poured it into the beggar's bag, paralleling the way villagers make offerings to monks. Indeed, the word *bhikkhu*, a formal term for monks, is often translated as "beggar."

Of Northern Lords

In contrast with village sympathy for beggars, village attitudes toward lords were overwhelmingly negative. In the over five hundred interviews I conducted during the 1980s in northern Thailand, I did not encounter a single informant who spoke positively of the nineteenth-century ruling northern lords (*chao*). In response to my general question "What was life like in the old days, in the days of the lords?" villagers often responded with a narrative. The story usually was prefaced by the remark "In those days the lords had absolute power." The most frequently told stories generally centered on a fairly limited range of topics, all with a similar theme. These narratives, divided by theme, included the following: water dipper stories, the shooting oxen stories, confiscation stories, portering stories, and concubine stories.

WATER DIPPER STORIES

Many villagers told a variation on what I gloss as "the water dipper story."[12] Although the story varied, the basic structure of the story was as follows: There are two water dippers, a large one and a small one, placed next to a water jar at the edge of the lord's compound (clay water pots with coconut-shell water dippers are traditionally placed at the entryway to yards and homes as a gesture of hospitality to passing travelers or visiting guests). A villager passes by and helps himself to some water. The lord is sitting in his house, watching and waiting. If the villager takes water with the large dipper, drinks a mouthful, and throws the rest away, the lord punishes him. If, on the other hand, the villager takes the small dipper, drinks all the water and then helps himself to another dipperful, the lord also punishes him, since the villager should have used the large dipper!

The main variations in the story have to do with the form of punishment used. In most accounts the lord is sitting in wait with a slingshot; other accounts substitute a whip, and in one account the lord is described as using the second dipper to hit the thirsty villager over the head. Although I invariably pressed informants on the subject of whether they or anyone they knew had experienced such punishment, in no case did an informant give a specific example of someone to whom this actually happened. Unlike the other recurrent themes in village recollections of the "days of the lords," in which some villagers could cite specific incidents that actually occurred, the "water dipper story" appears to have operated at the level of myth.

Shooting Oxen Stories

Another common story that villagers told me involved accounts of lords or underlings of the lords shooting villagers' oxen or water buffaloes.[13] According to these accounts, the lord or his men had shotguns and rode on elephants through the countryside. In those days, villagers let their oxen and buffaloes graze freely in the paddy fields during the dry season. If a lord wanted to shoot an ox to eat, he did so, hoisting the carcass onto his elephant and riding off. If the owner saw his ox being shot or carried off, he could ask for compensation, but typically he would only be given a small token amount. If the owner found out too late, he was simply out of luck and received nothing. In some versions, villagers did not even ask for compensation because they were too afraid of the lords; instead villagers tried to avoid the problem in the first place by hiding their buffaloes and oxen at home or keeping constant watch over them in the fields.

When I pressed villagers as to whether they knew anyone whose ox or buffalo had been shot and carried off in this manner, they generally gave vague answers. However, one informant and his brother were adamant that this had happened in their village to three members of their community. The two brothers made a point about saying that these three individuals were among the village elite, that they were educated and the sort of people able to talk with *chaos* and other important people (*khon ithiphon, bo klua phai, khon mii lakthaan, khon bak dai, uu dai*). When one of the lord's underlings shot one of their oxen, they met up to go after him. The underling told the chao, and the chao sent a message written on palm leaf, summoning them to see him. They went, and when they arrived at the lord's home, he had them whipped until the flesh on their backs was a bloody pulp (*nya tua byyii*). They were sick for about a month afterward, but fortunately they did not die (S-163).

Confiscation Stories

Lords and their underlings also confiscated a range of other goods; these confiscated items included everything from fermented tea leaves (*miang*) to fermented fish sauce (*nam ha*), betel, serivine, coconuts, various fruits, chickens, ducks, and piglets. The predominant item taken was chickens. The second most commonly mentioned item was coconuts. In these accounts the lord or his underling is passing through the village and just helps himself to whatever he wants, with or without permission (*hyy ko ow, bo hyy, ko ow*): thus if the lord wanted coconuts, his underlings would pick enough to fill an elephant-howdah and ride off. The stories have an overtone of arbitrary greed, as in the case of the lord who wanted serivine leaf to chew with his betel: rather than just picking the ripe leaves, the lord slashed the entire vine and then picked the leaves he wanted.

One villager described her village's partial solution to royal demands for food. It seems that a lord's son was serving for a time as abbot in their temple. Whenever he got the urge, he would go into people's homes and demand that they prepare him a meal. So whenever they saw him coming, they would flee their houses: that way there was nobody home to receive his demands. When I asked whether there was any recourse to royal requisitions, most villagers replied that in those days royalty had "absolute power" (*atyaa chao*).

On this same theme, several villagers told me an amusing story about pig merchants who were passing by on the Ping River with a raft full of piglets. One of them saw the lord sitting by the river and asked if he wanted any piglets. The lord said, "Of course!" and took all the piglets the merchants had on their raft. Well, the merchants sat around all day waiting for the lord to return with their money. Finally one of them went to the lord and asked to be paid. The lord replied, "But you asked me if I wanted them!" (MR-382).

This quixotic story is much like the water dipper stories; the listener cannot help but think the pig merchant or passing thirsty villager is stupid to have any relations with the lords because he is in effect inviting trouble upon himself. The implied message is clear: all but the most stupid of villagers knew that they should not attempt to have normal dealings with lords. Even as basic an aspect of village life as petty trading or drinking plain water was risky if lords were involved.

Concubine Stories

Scores of villagers, when asked what they remembered about the days of the lords, volunteered some aspect of villagers' fears about their daughters being taken by the lord as "play-wives" (*mia len*), minor wives (*mia noi*), or concubines (*sanom*), as it was variously phrased.[14] Generally the theme of these "concubine" stories was that villagers hid their beautiful daughters away from the sight of the lords, lest the lord demand these daughters be given to him as mistresses. I quote from some of the interviews to give a sense of the range of these stories:

In those days the lords had absolute powers and were above the law. They could take anyone's life they wanted to. They could take someone's daughter to be a concubine [*nang sanom*]. So at the times of big festivals like Boi Luangs [a temple festival], villagers kept their beautiful daughters at home, lest they be seen and carried off by the lords" (HD-8; also S-174).

Those were the days of rule by the lords [*atyaa chao*]. In those days, when the royal boats were passing along the Ping River, anyone who had a beautiful daughter kept her hidden out of sight. Otherwise the lord might see her and demand her for a wife. If the parents refused, they would be punished, a wooden collar would be put around their necks and they would be whipped. (S-168)

In these accounts, village daughters are not safe, even from lords who are passing by in boats or who briefly attend temple festivals. Villagers who lived near the river commented that village girls had to be careful while they were catching fish in the rivers lest the lord see them (MR-398). In an effort to assess the extent to which these concubine stories were "real" as opposed to "mythological," I pressed for actual examples of village women who had had to flee the lords or who had become royal concubines. A surprising number of villagers responded with examples of women in their villages.[15] No less well-known a personage in Thailand than Kraisri Nimmanhaeminda told me about the experience of his own grandmother. She was apparently very beautiful, and one of the ruling lords wanted her for a wife; consequently, her father, who was Chinese, had her dressed in Chinese white robes of mourning to save her from the lord's requests.[16]

The tone of the stories varied. Some of the stories were funny — generally those of a more "mythological" character. One villager said that in those days, village girls, to make sure the lord would not find them attractive, covered themselves with rotted fish paste (*nam ha*) so that they would smell terrible! Several villagers commented that when the lord came courting village girls, he chased the village suitors out of the girls' houses. Some villagers portrayed funny scenes of village youths fleeing in all directions as soon as they heard the lord was coming courting; some village youths scattered so fast that they even fell into wells! Some youths fled because they were afraid the lord might hit them (*klua ton bup*) and others because they were afraid the lord would make them sing, dance, play musical instruments, or otherwise be in attendance throughout the night.

Other accounts were tragic and full of pathos. Generally the more tragic incidents were those involving specific village women known to the interviewees. The following are two examples:

Chao R. would take pretty girls that he saw to become dancers [*chang fon*] in the city, and eventually take them as his wives. One girl in this village was taken off to be one of his court dancing girls. There was nothing the girl's father could do because he was one of the lord's tenants. Only once in a long time would she be allowed to return to the village to visit her family. In time, she fell in love with one of the royal goldsmiths, and took him as her husband. The lord was furious, and had her whipped across her back. Right after that, the couple fled, stopping first in the village to give the young girl time to recuperate. (S-126, circa 1908).

In those days, lords just took wives at will. A village girl named Mae Kaew W. caught the eye of Chao S. He made her his play-wife [*mia len*]. He only slept with her once or twice, and thereafter essentially abandoned her. Once she had become a royal mistress, no one else dared to court her. By the time Chao S. died, she was also old and past the stage of such physical desires. Other than going into town on a few occasions and the 14 *rai* of land Chao S. gave her, she lived alone and without children until she died. (SS-478)

Specific examples fell into two broad patterns. In one pattern the village girl was able to escape the lord's demand. In a few cases the parents were of sufficient social standing, as in the case of Ajarn Kraisri, to allow them to circumvent a royal request. Yet other villagers had to resort to the more disruptive alternative of flight, the girl generally unable to return to her natal village. In the remaining accounts, she indeed became a royal mistress, against the wishes of both herself and her family. In cases in which the lord succeeded in forcing a village girl to marry him, the general pattern was that after a short time, he lost interest and abandoned the girl. Sometimes the mistress was given land or some form of compensation. In some cases there were children, some of whom became members of the royal household, providing both mother and child with some social security. In other cases, both mother and child were abandoned.[17] Once the lord had lost interest in a village girl, in some cases she was able to remarry and in other cases fellow villagers were reportedly afraid to become involved. The women were often, but not necessarily, slaves working in the royal household or the daughters of tenants.

To protect their daughters, villagers resorted to a variety of strategies and subterfuges. In addition to flight and avoidance in various forms, village responses ranged from the humorous to the violent. One villager (age 91 when I interviewed him in 1985) told of his village headman's response when the lord sent word to all the village headmen to bring two of their village's most beautiful girls to court to choose among for attendants. The headman, Puu Chan, picked the two homeliest girls, one who was cross-eyed and the other whose eyes bulged (although this story sounded to me like the beginning of a village folktale [*jia*], the villager assured me that he had personally seen both of these girls, but when they were already old ladies). They walked all the way to the court in Chiang Mai and then sat waiting all day at the royal residence. In this case it seems that Puu Chan's potentially risky maneuver went unnoticed as the lord failed to show up that day, and even the prettiest girls walked back home without event! (MR-422)

In another account, villagers took their revenge more violently. A lord who lived in their village was notorious for "using people" (*chai khon*) at will: "He was especially oppressive with his house slaves, even taking the woman who was his cook and forcing her to become his wife. In time however he got his just reward. A band of Shans [Ngio] plundered his home and murdered him" (SS-462). When I pressed this and other informants as to why the Shans had attacked him, they responded that the house servants had made arrangements with the Shans to help them into the compound. (The killing took place about 1915.)

PORTERING STORIES

Another common narrative centered on lords demanding that villagers carry them wherever they wanted to go, in some cases on litters and in other cases literally on their backs (*khii khob*).[18] Several villagers mentioned the specific name of a lord who had corvéed a villager in this way or a villager who had been corvéed in this way; one villager had himself carried a lord by litter (MR-389). According to these accounts, villagers fled when they heard the lord was coming, lest they be forced to carry the lord from place to place. The lord might want to be carried to see his lands, or to be taken courting, or to be taken home. Not only were villagers forced to carry the lord, but villagers had to make sure the ride was smooth or they would again be punished. According to another story told in various versions, the lord had conscripted four Karen to serve as his carriers. However, the four Karen were not all the same height. One of the four was much taller and as a result the lord was having a lop-sided and bumpy ride. He became irritated and angry. He demanded the carriers stop and ordered the tall fellow's leg be cut off. The tall Karen begged and cried for mercy, promising that he would stoop while carrying the lord the rest of the way to make sure that the lord experienced a smooth ride.[19]

It is interesting to note that the lords were often described as being carried piggy-back style.[20] It is hard to imagine that being carried in this manner was particularly comfortable to the lord, let alone the villager. In a certain sense the style of transportation itself communicates an arbitrariness of the peasant view of lordly power. One villager who had himself carried his landlord's daughter (a chao) on numerous occasions with a chair litter explicitly commented that he found the demand to carry her degrading. He found it particularly offensive since she was female and he was male (women are supposed to keep their heads below those of men). He commented that she did that just to show her power (*wang amnaat*). Yet another villager was also conscripted to carry a lord piggyback style. He was known to be pretty wild (*hai*). When the lord summoned him, he bent over so the lord could climb on his shoulders. Then, instead of getting up straight, he pushed the chao forward straight into the dirt![21]

ABUSE OF POWER

Thus through a range of stories, from the seemingly absurd "water dipper stories" to the "portering stories" describing the petty demands for piggy-back style rides, villagers demonstrated an overwhelmingly negative assessment of the northern Thai lords. The reality of village life mixed into their stories, some describing actual events and others reflecting their folklore. From ironic humor to tragic narratives, the accounts all indicate village resentment toward the abuse of power by the lords. I was amazed at the number of times I heard the "water dipper story," which initially seemed to me too trivial to be taken seriously. In retrospect I now see how its very triviality captures the essential attitude of villagers toward that period: the absolute and thoroughgoing exercise of arbitrary power over villagers' lives, even to the most commonplace and petty aspects of village life. Lords could not even be expected to extend a simple gesture of common courtesy such as providing drinking water for travelers without flaunting their power.

Villagers gave various anecdotes that in effect illustrated the all-pervasive and petty interference of lords in even the most insignificant aspects of village life. The following provide some of the flavor of the accounts:

> All power used to lie with the chaos. If a chao was dissatisfied with someone, he would call that person over and have him whistle until he was bored [*jon kai*]. Whatever the chaos wanted was done. (DS-320)

> In those days chaos had complete power. They even had people who would have to fan them all the time, and if that person fell asleep, the chao would splash water in their face to wake them up, so they would keep fanning. (S-177)

> A villager once had the audacity to send a message for the chao to come and visit him sometime. When the chao heard of this impertinence, he was furious. And visit he did—to give him a good whipping. (DS-354)

Villagers, in trying to summarize the difference between the past and the present, would explain that in the past *atyaa chao*, or "law by chao," was used. By *atyaa* (also *ai-yaa*) was meant the absolute power of the lord.²² They explained that the lords were above the law (*nya kotmai*), that whatever the lord said was the final word (*chao waa laeo, laeo han*). Villagers contrasted the past in which lords were above the law with the modern period, in which everyone is under the law (*tai kotmai*); villagers described lords following "the law of taking" (*kotmai ow*) — in effect, the lords being the law unto themselves and taking whatever they wanted at will.²³ Villagers also would criticize the behavior of fellow villagers, both in the past and today, as "acting like a lord" (*ia ayang pen chao*) or "behaving like a lord, like a master" (*ia pen chao pen nai*). Generally this criticism was intended for someone who was being arrogant, putting on airs, or ordering people around.

Another phrase frequently used in discussions of the character of royal power was *kham khon*, "to oppress or exploit people."²⁴ This phrase is the northern Thai equivalent of the central Thai words *khumhaeng, kotkhii, ow rat ow priab*. Another interesting phrase that was used frequently to characterize village relations with lords was *chai khon*, "to use people."²⁵ Even today the word in Thai for servant is *khonchai*, "a person to use." The negative connotations of this phrase can be seen in the following usages:

> The chaos owned a lot of land in the past in this area, but they have since gone to wrack and ruin [*chiiphai*]. How could they not have gone to wrack and ruin when they used people [*chai khon*]? (S-160)

> In those days people were afraid of the chaos, and the chaos could do whatever they wanted. They could use villagers for whatever work they wanted [*chao ow bai chai ngaan dai lyyii*]. (S-126)

To a remarkable extent the language villagers used to describe their feelings toward the lords was based on fear and avoidance. Repeatedly informants would use the phrase "to be afraid of the lords" (*klua chao*).²⁶ Villagers also described fellow villagers as "so honest they were stupid" (*syy jon sy*). In a story that echoes one told by Luang Poh Bunthong, one villager went on to tell a story as an illustration: "It seems that once the chao called a meeting and all the villagers were summoned into town. At the end of the meeting, the lord announced, 'Whoever stole the elephant ropes, stay put' [*ai tua lak chyak chang yaa pai nai na*]. Everyone fled the scene, except one fellow. The lord's underlings rushed up to the poor soul and clamped a wooden yoke about his neck [*khyy khaa*], and beat him to death" (S-163). I asked the informant if the villager in question was guilty. The informant replied that he may have been. However, as he explained, "villagers in those days were afraid of authority, honest and stupid. So maybe he did it and thought the lord already knew he was guilty." "Or maybe he was deaf," he added in a kind of whimsical way so characteristic of village humor (S-163).

War Captives and Slavery

These negative attitudes are also rooted in the long-standing practice of capturing slaves. One of the earliest mentions of war captives can be found in the famous thirteenth-century inscription of King Ramkhamhaeng in which the filial king records, "If I went to attack a village or a city and collected some elephants and ivory, men and women, silver and gold, I gave them to my father" (Benda and Larkin 1967, 40-41). Early chronicles record thousands of captives being taken at a time. For example, in 1462 King Tilok of Chiang Mai is reported to have conquered eleven Shan principalities and carried off 12,328 people, who were relocated in three towns and several frontier posts "where their descendants have lived until our days" (Notton 1926-32, 3:135, quoted in Turton 1980, 255). Dr. Richardson, in his diary of his journeys to Chiang Mai in the 1830s, noted that three-quarters of the northern kingdom's population were war captives (Richardson Mss, 143). William McLeod wrote of his trip to Chiang Mai in 1837 that war captives from regions north of Chiang Mai and Peguans (Talaings from southern Burma) "comprise more than two-thirds of the population of the country" (Grabowsky and Turton 2003, 304). John Freeman estimated that about half of the population of Lamphun province were descendants of war captives (1910, 100). Thus there is a remarkable consensus among several independent nineteenth-century observers that at least half of the northern population were war captives, with the lords "the principal slave-holders" (Hallett 1890, 202-3; Freeman 1910, 101).[27] Oral histories I collected confirm the presence of significant numbers of both war captives and slaves (Bowie 1988, 1996).

The famous quote "put vegetables into baskets and put slaves into kingdoms" (*kep phak sai saa, kep khaa sai muang*) has been used to characterize northern Thai kingdoms, but it holds true for all regions in Thailand as well (Kraisri 1965). In northeastern Thailand today at least 95 percent of the population are of Lao origin and have more in common with the inhabitants of Laos than the "Siamese" (Keyes 1967, 2). Many are descendants of Lao war captives relocated to the region in the wake of Bangkok's attack on Vientiane in 1778-79 and again in the wake of Chao Anu's unsuccessful revolt against Bangkok in 1828.

Although the topic is seldom discussed, in central Thailand war captives and debt slaves historically also comprised a significant portion of the population.

Figure 14. Villagers being taken as war captives. Temple mural at Wat Phrathat Duang Diaw, Amphur Lii, Lamphun, July 2011. Photo by author.

Writing of late seventeenth-century Ayutthaya, Simon de la Loubère observed that the Siamese "busie themselves only in making slaves" (1969, 90). H. G. Quaritch Wales described war expeditions as "the regular occupation of the dry season" (1934, 64). John Crawfurd observed, "The Siamese equally carry off the peasantry of the open country of both sexes" (Turton 1980, 255). Francis Garnier mentioned that after an uprising in Cambodia, the Siamese removed a large number of Annamite prisoners (1873, 147). John Bowring estimated that during the reign of Rama III (1824–51), there were 46,000 war slaves; he lists some 5,000 Malays, 10,000 Cochin Chinese, 10,000 Peguans, and 1,000 Burmese, in addition to 20,000 Laos ([1857] 1969, 190). The captured slaves became the property of the king, who either kept them or distributed them as rewards to favored underlings (Colquhoun 1885, 54; Hallett 1890, 203; Turton 1980, 256). Bowring suggests that "distinctly much more than a third of Siamese . . . are slaves" ([1857] 1969, 191; see also Colquhoun 1885, 189). Holt Hallett, citing Mr. Alabaster, a confidential adviser to the king, noted that "nine-tenths of the non-Chinese inhabitants of Bangkok were slaves" (1890, 447). Thus, describing central Thailand as a "heterogeneous melting pot," Barend Terweil concludes that "during the first fifty years of the nineteenth century, tens of thousands of

Mons and Laotians, and thousands of Khmers, Vietnamese, Malays and Burmese were distributed throughout the provinces" (1989, 253-54).

Evidence suggests that slaves were not well treated. Visiting Bangkok in 1822, Crawfurd writes, "At the Siamese capital we daily saw great numbers of these unfortunate persons [war captives] employed in sowing, ditching, and other severe labour" (Turton 1980, 256). Elsewhere I have described the trauma of war captives as they were force-marched to their new homes (Bowie 1996). Oral histories provide further evidence of hardships, the separation of family members, whippings, and other abuses of power (see Bowie 1988; see also Turton 1980, 256). One cannot but wonder how these war captives felt when they saw a slave being offered to a monk as part of the *Vessantara Jataka* performance, or heard that Vessantara gave away seven hundred male slaves and seven hundred female slaves.

Maitreya and Millenarianism

Eschatological belief in the future coming of the Maitreya Buddha was widespread throughout Thailand, and indeed throughout mainland Southeast Asia. As we have seen, in both northern and northeastern Thailand, the recitation of the *Vessantara Jataka* occurs in tandem with the recitation of the *Phra Malai Sutra*. In the northeast, the sutra is an important component of the scroll the villagers carry in a procession during Bun Pha Wet. The *Phra Malai Sutra* is the story of the monk named Phra Malai who travels to the various hells and heavens. As noted in the introduction, when in the Tusita heaven, Phra Malai meets Maitreya, who informs Phra Malai to tell people to listen to the *Vessantara Jataka* "in one night and one day" if they wish to be reborn during Maitreya's era (Brereton 1995, 64). Accordingly, villagers in the north and northeastern regions emphasize the importance of completing the recitation of the jataka within twenty-four hours. The admonition for the laity to listen to the *Vessantara Jataka* is given further impetus by the belief that Buddhism will fall into decline and that the *Vessantara Jataka* will be lost. The connection between Maitreya and the *Vessantara Jataka* is made clear in an early nineteenth-century northern Thai text of the *Phra Malai Sutra*: "When the teachings of the Buddha are destroyed at the time that the religion comes to an end, the Ten Jataka will disappear in reverse order; the *Vessantara Jataka* will disappear first. This is the reason that Metteyya Bodhisatta [Maitreya] exhorted the people to listen to the *Vessantara Jataka*" (Brereton 1995, 72).

Stories about the Maitreya Buddha were popularized by monks and troubadours whose sermons and ballads describe in apocalyptic terms the deterioration of Buddhism, the decrease in life expectancy, and the decline of social order prior to Maitreya's utopian reign (Brereton 1995, 10-11). But, as Bonnie Brereton notes, it was "primarily through the medium of the Phra Malai story that the common belief and hope in the coming of the future Buddha Metteyaa was disseminated in Thailand" (1995, 2). Intended to teach "the principles of right and wrong, merit and demerit, and reward and punishment," Maitreya is associated with generosity (*dana*), such as giving alms to beggars (Brereton 1995, 2, 10-11). Given a political economy characterized by considerable poverty and oppressive rule, it is not surprising that these messianic beliefs fueled millenarian movements throughout mainland Southeast Asia.[28]

Millennialism in Northern Thailand

Evidence of widespread belief in the Maitreya Buddha and the presence of millenarian leaders in northern Thailand is provided in archeological records, palm-leaf manuscripts, missionary accounts, and oral histories. As early as 1426 an inscription written by a king from Nan (now a province in northern Thailand) states that "he devoutly wishes to behold the Lord Sri Ariya [Maitreya]" (Griswold and Prasert 1969, 105). Brereton notes that "similar expressions of this belief frequently occur in dedicatory inscriptions on the bases of Buddha images and in the colophons of manuscripts presented to monasteries as acts of merit" (1995, 64; see also Hundius 1990). Hundreds of palm-leaf copies of the *Phra Malai Sutra* text exist in temples throughout northern Thailand, the oldest dating to 1516 (Brereton 1995, 17).[29] In 1728 in Lampang, Thep Singh proclaimed himself a saint or precursor of Maitreya (*tonbun*) and led a peasant revolt against repressive Burmese rule (Anan 1984, 40-41).

Belief in the Maitreya Buddha remained in northern Thailand throughout the nineteenth century. William Dodd, a Presbyterian missionary who lived in northern Thailand from 1886 to 1919, noted the presence of "many prophecies" that "cluster around The Coming One, Ariya Metteya" (1923, 334). According to these prophecies, forerunners of the Buddhist Messiah "shall level every mountain, exalt every valley, make crooked places straight, and rough places smooth" and "appear on the banks of the Meping" (Dodd 1923, 334). Another missionary in northern Thailand, Hugh Taylor, notes that "the devout Buddhist, when he bows before Buddha's image, prays the prayer, 'Oh, that I may live to see the face of Pra Allenyamathai [Ariya Maitreya] the Savior'" (Taylor Mss, 121). Taylor points to northern prophesies such as "In that day two men clothed in white raiment shall come from the West bringing a Sacred Book" and "In that day the slave will ride horseback down the street ahead of his master" (Taylor Mss, 121).

One old man was perplexed by a bread loaf on Taylor's breakfast table. When Taylor explained, "It is our rice," the man "humbly crawled to the table, keeping his head below the bread, and with his right hand supported at the wrist by the left hand, took the loaf from the plate and, holding it high above his head, reverently exclaimed, 'Great Buddha! Thy slave's eyes have seen it!'" Taylor continues, "He then told me one of the signs of Pra Allenyamathai's coming was that a grain of rice should be as large as a coconut" (Taylor Mss, 134–35). Ironically, several early Christian converts "worshipped Jesus under the name of their promised Buddha Metraya" (McGilvary 1912, 171; see also Dodd 1923, 334; Taylor Mss, 122–24, 132, 134).

As late as the 1980s, villagers in Chiang Mai still spoke to me in secretive, hushed tones about a hidden messianic text. As one elderly villager explained, in the past the government had forbidden people to discuss this subject. Although none of them had seen the text, they recalled predictions such as "there will be roads, but no one will walk on them"; "there will be rice, but no one will pound it"; "a red dust [*fun daeng*] will enter everyone's homes"; and "fire will burn . . . roofs, and . . . the religion will decline." In addition, one villager recalled, "if war comes from the easterly direction, there will be no way to stop it; the fighting will come up through Ayutthaya, Lampang, Lamphun, Chiang Mai and Fang and come down via Doi Kham to the area near the Chiang Mai airport. Then Phrayar Tham [Maitreya] will come" (HD-38).[30]

Subsequent dissertation research by Betty Nguyen has uncovered many of these texts, which she has called "calamity cosmologies" (2014). As Nguyen describes this genre of northern texts, "the Buddha or Indra prepare man for the catastrophic end of the world by relating the future events" (2011). She continues, "According to these texts, the future breakdown of the cosmo-social order will entail kings oppressing the populace, rampant unrestrained warfare, crop failure, natural disasters, famine, and the unleashing of evil spirits" (Nguyen 2011). These texts emphasize the importance of "the practice of giving of *dana*, keeping the moral precepts, listening to dhamma sermons, having loving-kindness (*metta*), and meditation (*phavana*)" to protect oneself from impending misfortunes. She notes that the authors exhort people to "to heed the prophecy and remain faithful for only the pure will be saved" (Nguyen 2011). According to one text:

> Beginning in the year *Sanga*, there is a great natural disaster. It is called '*chatue*' in the Ho language and in our Thai language 'earthquake.' Mountains will crumble, rain will fall in torrents, the sky will thunder. In the year *met*, countless numbers of people will die. So it will come to pass. In the year *san*, there will be

powerful storms causing flooding everywhere. . . . In the year *sed*, there will ominous events (*ubat*): tigers, not roaring, will come to live in the middle of the city, creating a troublesome situation. So it will be. In the year of *kay*, the city will be flooded. In the year of *cay*, chaos erupts (*kolahon*) causing enemies to arise. In the villages and cities, people stab one another to death. People will flee from the villages and cities. In the year *kot*, a *cao tonbun* [savior] will be born. (Tamnan Ho 1895 AD; translation by Nguyen 2011)

Gotama, the Cheating Buddha

Most scholarly attention has focused on the Gotama Buddha, with the assumption that he is universally respected by Buddhists. Remarkably, in northern Thailand I have come across various references to Gotama as the cheating Buddha and Maitreya as the legitimate Buddha. I was rather taken aback when during the course of an interview a villager asked me whether I knew which one was the older brother, Gotama or Ariya Maitreya, and how the poses of their respective Buddha images differed. Since I did not, he told me the following story:

> The god Phrayar Indra told both Gotama and Ariya to plant lotuses. Whosever lotus flowered first would be the first to be born on earth. Ariya's lotus opened first, but Gotama stole it and showed it to Indra. Consequently Gotama was born first. The people here on earth thought that Ariya was born, and so they made Buddha figures in his image, with both palms together. But when they realized this Buddha was not Ariya, they hid their images in the forest and caves. And that is why the Gotama image is in the incomplete meditation position; he is afraid of being caught out for his theft of the lotus. (HD-38)

Subsequently I learned that this remarkable story was familiar to other elderly villagers. This villager then explained to me that Gotama images are those with an incomplete meditation position—namely, one hand in the lap and the other resting on the knee; the Ariya Maitreya images are those with both hands folded on the lap, palms up, one hand on top of the other.[31]

Not only did this story about Maitreya and the cheating Gotama Buddha circulate in the Chiang Mai region, but I also came across it in an account by the missionary Hugh Taylor, who resided in Lampang. Evidently this subversive story was represented iconographically in lotus imagery as well as Buddha images. Taylor was told the story by a trader who sold him a lotus made in silver, gold, and rubies: "When lifted from its stand, it opens out into a full-blown lily. Placed back on the stand, it closes again to a bud" (Taylor Mss, 120). The trader's "legend of the lotus lily" was as follows:

Two brothers, Gotama and Allenyamathai (Al-e-nga-ma-thai [Ariya Maitreya]), learned that the one who had in his possession a certain lotus lily when it bloomed would become the next Buddha. Up to that time, there had been only three Buddhas. Allenyamathai found the lily; but Gotama his brother stole it from him. While the lily was in Gotama's possession, it bloomed, and Gotama became the Buddha. In compensation to Allenyamathai for his loss, it was decreed that he should be the next Buddha, and more than just a Buddha, he should be a real Savior from the penalties of sin. Buddha has taught how to save one's self. Pra Allenyamathai was to rescue the people from their fate. (Taylor Mss, 120-21; see also Landon 1939, 186)[32]

The story was also popular among the Karen followers of Khruubaa Khao Pi, who explained that because of Gotama's jealousy and deceit, society fell into moral decline and chaos (Kwanchewan 1998, 118; Cohen 2001, 232). Hallett notes that the wooden implements in several important temples were "for the use of expectant Buddhas" (1890, 322). This belief in the Maitreya Buddha fueled various millenarian movements. Elsewhere I have argued that such millenarian beliefs underlay the popular movement in support of the famous northern monk Khruubaa Srivichai, frequently called "the saint of Lanna" (*tonbun haeng laanaa*). Khruubaa Khao Pi was himself a disciple of Khruubaa Srivichai; both were considered by many to have been precursors of Maitreya (see Bowie 2014a, 2014b).

Millenarianism across Regions

As in the north, in the northeastern region belief in Maitreya was strong. Charles Keyes has documented the circulation of millenarian texts in northeastern Thailand in the late nineteenth century; these texts depict the *dhammik* "as a savior-ruler figure who will arrive to save the good and pure from the social chaos wrought in large part by the corruption and moral excesses of those in power" (1977, 295; see also Hansen 2007, 60). Northeastern Thailand has a long history of revolts led by "holy men." In 1820 a monk claiming such supernatural powers as the ability to "call up fire to burn towns, human beings and animals all over the world" led an uprising of more than six thousand people to attack the town of Champasak; a local chronicle records, "Our prince has now been born, our sufferings will be no more" (Chatthip 1984, 114-15). In 1850 a "shaman" fomented an uprising in Sisakhet (Gunn 1990, 110). An 1895 revolt in Khon Kaen province involved rituals to render its participants invulnerable (Chatthip 1984, 116). The most famous of the northeastern revolts are the "Holy Men Revolts" of 1901-2, led by Ong Man; his followers observed Buddhist precepts and dressed in white clothing (Chatthip 1984; see also Tej 1967;

Murdoch 1974; Keyes 1977; Gunn 1990, 112-14). In 1902 in Sakon Nakon province, a former monk reordained and declared himself to be an incarnation of Vishnu; he only ate one meal a day, "only ate vegetables, no meat; and he dressed in white" (Chatthip 1984, 118; see also Keyes 1977, 297-98). In 1924 three monks and a novice in Loei province predicted the birth of Maitreya in their village; villagers were asked to observe the precepts, pray constantly, give alms, respect their parents, and eat only fruit, sesame, beans, and rice (Chatthip 1984, 119). In 1936 and as late as 1959, revolts occurred based on the imminent arrival of Maitreya in Mahasarakham, Kalasin, and Ubon Ratchathani (Chatthip 1984, 120-21; for accounts in the 1970s, see Keyes 1977, 290).

Belief in Maitreya and associated messianic movements in central Thailand can be traced back to the late eighteenth century. After the fall of Ayutthaya in 1767, dissident monks, wearing reddish-brown robes symbolically associated with Maitreya, seized political power in Sawangburi and Uttaradit (Tambiah 1976, 184). Shortly after acceding to the throne in 1782, Rama I issued a decree against instigators of revolt who claimed to have supernatural powers (Tambiah 1976, 185).[33] Nonetheless, holy men still emerged in the central region; as late as 1909 a newspaper reports that a *phuu viset* monk was arrested in Petchaburi for providing invulnerability tattoos (*BTWM*, March 16, 1909).[34] The promise of the 1933 National Economic Policy plan to be "in fulfillment of the Buddhist prophecy to be found in the story of the religion of Araya Mettaya" indicates the widespread familiarity of the population with this utopian trope (Landon 1939, 292-93). Keyes notes that as recently as 1973 he came across several pamphlets describing a Maitreya cult in the Bangkok region (1977, 290).

Thus the Bangkok court had reason to be concerned with both the belief in Maitreya and its associated millenarian revolts. Indeed, these uprisings are explicitly mentioned as part of the justification for the Military Conscription Act of 1905. Although it is unclear if the court deliberately held recitations of the *Vessantara Jataka* during Buddhist Lent and without adhering necessarily to the twenty-four-hour rule as part of its efforts to undermine popular belief in the Maitreya Buddha, King Chulalongkorn did decree that monks should not begin the sermon with the prediction that Buddhism will disappear five thousand years after the Buddha's enlightenment. The court's concern about beliefs about Maitreya is suggested in an account of King Chulalongkorn's visit to Wat Mani Cholakhan in Phrommat subdistrict in Lopburi province in 1883, an area where evidently belief in the Maitreya Buddha was strong:

> Knowing that the king was coming to visit, they placed a statue upon the altar. When the king arrived he offered robes to the ten monks who held honorific

titles. After the monks put on the new robes and the king turned to the altar to light candles, he saw that the only image present was that of Maitreya.

The king immediately ordered an image of the Buddha to be brought to the altar so that he could perform his prostrations before the monks began chanting their blessing. According to the Record, the king said to the monks, "People should not take refuge in Metteyya. Metteyya is not part of the Triple Gem: The Buddha, Dhamma, and Sangha. The king donated money to restore this Metteyya statue and came to celebrate the festival with local people, but not because he shares their foolish belief in the coming of Metteyya." . . . The king turned to Phra Yanrakkhit, the monk with the highest title, and asked him, "So you prostrate yourself before the Metteyya image?" The Dhammayut [Thammayut] monk replied, "No, I do not." (Kamala 2003, 299)

The Trickster and the "Hidden Transcript"

Thus far in this chapter we have considered how the presence of irreverent trickster narratives, the political economy of villagers, and the prevalence of millenarianism linked to the Maitreya Buddha may have shaped the peasant imaginaire. We are now ready to explore whether following Jujaka into northern Thailand provides evidence of a more Bakhtinian reading, in which a "boundless world of humorous forms and manifestations opposed the official and serious tone of medieval ecclesiastical and feudal culture" (Bakhtin [1965] 1984, 4). We should not expect anti-royalist expressions to be overt, and certainly not in written texts or recordings taped for a wider public. As James C. Scott has argued, since public transcripts are shaped by prudence and fear, they are unlikely to reveal "the whole story about power relations"; indeed, "the more menacing the power, the thicker the mask" (1990, 2–3). Because, as Scott points out, "the theatrical imperatives that normally prevail in situations of domination produce a public transcript in close conformity with how the dominant group would wish to have things appear," we must search instead for the "hidden transcripts" (1990, 4).

Today charges of republicanism are tantamount to treason, with the courts handing down sentences of as long as sixty years for lèse majesté.[35] Lèse majesté, the crime of defaming, insulting, or threatening the king, queen, heir-apparent or regent, has been formally prohibited under Thai law since 1908; each charge can lead to imprisonment of three to fifteen years, with charges being cumulative.[36] At the time Luang Poh Bunthong was recording his performances of the *Vessantara Jataka* during the 1970s, Thailand had experienced decades of almost uninterrupted military dictatorships and was facing a growing internal communist guerrilla movement. Its neighboring countries of Laos, Cambodia, and Vietnam were battling insurgencies, now glossed as "the Vietnam War," which led to regime changes in each of these countries. The mantra of "King, Nation and Religion" was being brandished with ever-growing intensity. As the reach of the state expanded in the course of the 1960s and 1970s and as the government's anti-communist counterinsurgency campaigns to "win hearts and minds" grew, unfettered discussions of politics became increasingly fraught (on this period, see Thak 1979; Chai-anan and Morell 1981; Bowie 1997).

In such a sensitive political context, we would expect both written texts and tape-recorded performances to be highly circumspect in their engagements of the topic of ruler-subject relations. Luang Poh Bunthong suggests that the main points of the *Vessantara Jataka* are sevenfold: to believe in yourself, to be moral, to know shame (*khwaam la-ai nai jai*), to know respect (*krengklua*), to treasure knowledge, to be generous, and to be wise. When Luang Poh Bunthong's taped version of the *Vessantara Jataka* of the 1970s is compared with the performance Charles Keyes attended in the 1960s, in which the tujok monk was replicating the sounds of passing gas, one can already notice a certain degree of censorship. Thus we would expect that the explicit political message in Luang Poh Bunthong's taped version of the *Vessantara Jataka*, which has underlain much of this book, was to be fairly neutral and even apparently conservative. Albeit in bawdy fashion, Luang Poh Bunthong encouraged listeners not to listen to rumors and to focus on their own responsibilities. At the moment in the story when Vessantara was reluctant to leave his ascetic forest life to return to the palace, Luang Poh Bunthong explained, "We all have our work to do and we should just focus on doing that well." He went on to repeat a well-known adage with bawdy undertones:

Mii suan ia suan hia.	If you have gardens, work your gardens.
Mii naa ia naa hia	If you have paddy, work your paddy fields.
Mii mia ... ko liang duu hia.[37]	If you have a wife, take care of her.
Mii luuk ko liang duu luuk.	If you have children, take care of them.

Nonetheless, traces of hidden transcripts emerge. The more egalitarian underpinnings of Bunthong's interpretation can be found in his encouragement for people to treat each other with humanity. As he explained in his tape in a rare serious moment:

> It's like the crickets. Once there are enough on the stick, they get roasted on the fire. And then they are made into chili sauce [*nam phrik*]. The same with us.

When we stop breathing we are sent to the fire as well, just like the crickets. Even though the crickets are all on the stick, they still try to crawl over each other. They jump around and bang into each other. Why do they do that? They're all going to be made into nam phrik anyway. We all will die. So while we are alive, why do we get in each other's way, or try to take advantage of each other? We should love each other and help each other.[38]

In his various stories, one can see echoes of the stories that I have described earlier in this chapter. For example, using the scene in which the king asks if Jujaka has any surviving heirs, Luang Poh Bunthong comments about the honesty of people in the past, saying:

Can you imagine what would happen today? Nowadays, even before the parents have died, the children are wanting to get their inheritance. . . . People were honest in the old days.

Let me tell you a story. There was a novice who wanted to take a shit. He told a layperson that if anyone came, he should tell them. A grandmother came by and the layperson told her, "The novice is taking a shit." People were so honest they were stupid.

There was another fellow who stole a water buffalo and killed it and ate it. The headman called a village meeting and discussed various topics. As the meeting ended, the headman said, "Everyone can leave now, but will the person who stole the water buffalo please remain seated." Everyone left but this fellow remained seated. The headman asked him, "Did you steal the water buffalo?" "Yes, sir." Because he admitted his guilt, the headman set his punishment at repairing fifteen yards of road. "Excuse me, sir, does the fifteen yards also cover the buffalo I stole before?" [*Laughter.*] And so he was sentenced to repairing thirty yards. This is true honesty.[39]

A story Luang Poh Bunthong told about a government official has hints of the broader genre of political trickster stories, albeit in a modernized form, in which the outwitted king has been replaced with an outwitted government official. Luang Poh Bunthong sets it up by explaining that his next story is about getting in over one's head, about getting involved in matters about which one has insufficient knowledge. Whether it is gambling or another endeavor, he advises, "one should get informed first." He gives this example:

A long time ago there was a man who loved to gamble, so the story goes. Seems he was really good at it as well. In addition to gambling, he also drove a car. One time a *nai amphur* [district officer] advertised upcountry that he was inviting applications for a driver. So this man applied and ended up getting the job. So he drove the nai amphur around.

After about a month or so, the nai amphur had to attend a meeting in another province. This man drove the nai amphur. Once there the nai amphur booked a room in a swank, first-class hotel, so he decided to do the same and booked a room in the same hotel. He didn't want to have any less than the nai amphur. [*Laughs.*] In the morning the nai amphur ordered a fancy breakfast at this hotel, so the driver did the same.

The nai amphur began to worry. How was his driver going to be able to afford all of this since his salary was less than 2,000 baht per month? Sleeping in the same kind of hotel and eating the same kind of food, he was clearly going to be in over his head. So he called the driver over so he could explain matters to him. The nai amphur explained that you [*thyy*; familiar you] only earn a small salary and it is not possible for you to live the same lifestyle as if you were a nai amphur.

The driver replied to the nai amphur, "You don't have to be worried about me. There are some months that I might actually earn more money than you." The nai amphur was perplexed. "How can that be? You earn less than 2,000 baht per month even with a special travel per diem." "Oh no, sir, that is not my only income. I also gamble." The nai amphur explained that gambling was not a certain source of income, sometimes one won, but sometimes one lost.

The driver reassured the nai amphur that he always won. Since the nai amphur was skeptical, the driver asked if the nai amphur would like to place a bet with him. Two hundred baht said he would have a bump on his forehead by 9:00 a.m. in the morning. The nai amphur said no way, he had never had a bump on his forehead and would not by the next morning. The driver assured him he would and asked him if he would he like to make a wager. So they did. Two hundred baht said the nai amphur would have a bump; 200 baht said he would not.

The next morning the nai amphur felt all over his head, worried that there might be a bump and he would have to pay 200 baht. But everywhere he felt, there was no bump. Relieved, he summoned the driver and told him there was no bump. The driver said, "Really, that's not possible. There must be a bump." "No, there's no bump." "Yes, there is." Annoyed, the nai amphur said, "No, there is not. Check for yourself." The driver felt all over the nai amphur's head, rubbing his hands this way and that way for what seemed to be forever [given status hierarchy, a daring thing to do]. Sure enough there was no bump. "How about that, I must have made a mistake," the driver said, "so I owe you 200 baht." But the nai amphur felt bad taking the driver's money, so he said, "Never mind, take your money back. I don't want your 200 baht." But the driver insisted, "No, no, you keep it. I'm a good sport. And besides, I made more money than you did." "How can that be?" the nai amphur asked.

The driver explained that after he had left the nai amphur the night before, he had made a bet with people in the hotel that by 9:00 a.m. the next morning the nai amphur would summon him to feel his head. They hadn't believed him. How would it be possible that a lowly driver would ever be able to touch a nai amphur's head? Impossible. So they all eagerly took the bet. Four people, 100 baht per person for a total of 400 baht.

So in fact the driver was just splitting his bet with the nai amphur, 200 for the nai amphur and 200 baht for himself. After all, he had been able to touch the nai amphur's head. But he was someone who knew what he was doing. But not everyone knows what is going on. If you don't know what is going on, don't get involved. You will only lose. Always make sure you know what is happening, no matter what it is, if it is gambling, or business. If you don't understand the business, don't invest all your money at once. You will only lose it. [*Laughter.*][40]

Eschatological Hope in Scatological Humor

If today the comedy appears to center primarily on scatological humor and everyday tensions, placing the *Vessantara Jataka*'s portrayal of peasant-court relations becomes far more edgy in the broader historical context of poverty, oppression, and millenarian hopes. The contradiction that emerges from village recollections—between the image of the utopian moral ruler and the image of the oppressive earthly lords—could not be more dramatic. The northern Thai ruling lords were hardly viewed as generous, however generous individual lords may have been to individual followers on specific occasions. Instead they were glossed as "takers" rather than as "givers." Thus any given recitation of the *Vessantara Jataka* in northern Thailand may have been understood just as easily as an implicit indictment of the earthly administration of their ruling lords as an homage to their superior spiritual power.

To the extent that the *Vessantara Jataka*'s emphasis is on Vessantara's relentless generosity, one could argue that the text was a "weapon of the weak," an implicit critique of human kings who were unlikely to be generous. Unlike the earthly kings in the peasant imaginaire, Vessantara gave away everything to anyone who asked for assistance, from the drought-ridden villagers of a neighboring kingdom to the beggar who asked for his children as servants. The "ten duties of a righteous ruler" were a further admonition to earthly kings. Ideal kings were to have the following characteristics:

1. *Dana*: Liberality, generosity, charity, concern with the welfare of the people
2. *Sila*: High moral character, observing at least the Five Precepts
3. *Pariccaga*: Willingness to sacrifice everything for the people—comfort, fame, even one's own life
4. *Ajjava*: Honesty and integrity, not fearing some or favoring others
5. *Maddava*: Kindness and gentleness
6. *Tapa*: Austerity, contentment with the simple life
7. *Akkodha*: Freedom from hatred, ill-will, and anger
8. *Avihimsa*: Non-violence, a commitment to peace
9. *Khanti*: Patience, tolerance, and the ability to understand others' perspectives
10. *Avirodha*: Non-obstruction, ruling in harmony with the will of the people and in their best interests.[41]

Read against the background of village attitudes toward ruling authorities and the robust folk literature on tricksters, villagers were far more likely to identify with Jujaka, the beggar, rather than Vessantara, the future king. As a trickster-beggar, Jujaka crosses the thresholds between village and court, tricking royal guardians, tricking Vessantara to obtain royal children as his servants, and ultimately finding himself being feted by a grateful king. He represents human desires that exist in each of us and that wisdom must help us overcome. Other passages open up a discussion of kingship more directly, raising questions as to whether Vessantara had the right to give away the rain-making elephant, whether the benefits of helping drought-stricken citizens in a neighboring kingdom outweigh the loss of the elephant, or whether the king made the right decision in banishing his son Vessantara. Other passages encourage a debate about whether Vessantara had the right to give away his children, whether he was right to deliberately misinterpret his wife's dream, or whether he was being compassionate when he falsely accused Matsi of infidelity. If Vessantara is supposed to be a model of the ideal ruler, how could he misinterpret the arrival of the royal army; it is his wife who recognizes that the army is that of his own parents (Cone and Gombrich 1977, 87). I have no doubt that villagers in the past held similar debates to those held today. Indeed, I would suggest that the debate over whether the good of society should come before the good of one's own family is a central tension that has given the *Vessantara Jataka* its relevance over the centuries. As noted in the introduction, some monks such as Phra Thepwethi even suggest that the *Vessantara Jataka* provides an argument in support of peasant demonstrations.

A few moments in Luang Poh Bunthong's taped version provide hints of the jataka's potential for deeper political resonances. When Phusadi is about to be reborn on earth, attention often focuses on her request that her breasts not sag after breastfeeding, but her last request was to be able to free prisoners. In a society in which a significant portion of the population were debt slaves or war captives, the issue of the children's ransom may have been particularly significant to members of the earlier audiences. In Luang Poh Bunthong's interpretation of the jataka, he addresses Vessantara's decision to give his children to Jujaka, portraying it as an act of generosity motivated by his concern for the poor:

> The enemies of Phra Wesandorn were still around and were ready to criticize him. "Look at that, we send him into exile and he still gives away his children. No good person would do that."
>
> But Chalii said to his grandfather, "My father is a good person. He wanted Puu Phraam [Grandfather Brahmin, i.e. Jujaka] to live well because he saw that he was poor. He said that whoever redeemed us would make it possible for Puu Phraam to become wealthy and live well."[42]

The most explicit political moment occurs when Jujaka succeeds in tricking Jetabutr by portraying himself as a royal messenger. In Luang Poh Bunthong's version, one can still get a sense of how fraught peasant-court relations were in the past. His account is as follows:

> "Don't shoot. If you shoot me, you'll be sorry. I'm the ambassador of Phrayar Sonchai, the father of Phra Wesandorn. Phrayar Sonchai and Mae Phusadi have asked me to find their son to ask him to disrobe and return to their kingdom. They are crying every day because they are missing him."
> "Really?"
> "Really."
> "Do you have any evidence?"
> Listeners, this is very important, having evidence. So he asked, "What evidence do you have that you're a royal servant?" Puu Phraam didn't know what to do. He absent-mindedly felt around in his bag and came across his bamboo salt container. This is what we call quick thinking. So he grabbed the container and said, "The royal letter is in here. Go ahead and open it if you don't believe me."
> But who would dare to open a royal letter? Those were the days of absolute monarchy; you could be executed for something like that. Even nowadays, if you open an ordinary letter with a regular stamp, you can be fined 500 baht and imprisoned for two months. It's a secret. See, I even know the postal laws.
> Phraam Jetabutr saw the container and thought it was a royal missive. He was afraid he might go to jail or worse. So he put down the slingshot and bowed to Puu Phraam, twenty, thirty times, trembling.

"May I please invite you to descend from the tree? I will feed you well and make sure you want for nothing."

"I am happy to come down. I wanted to come down since this morning. But tie the dogs up."

So he forced Jetabutr to tie up the dogs. After all, it was a royal order. He called all thirty-two dogs. He couldn't tie them all up at the same place because they might get into fights with each other. He had to tie each of them up in a different place.[43]

Edginess of Humor

As the political satire of Bill Maher, Jon Stewart, Stephen Colbert, and their younger successors reminds us, humor is often on the edge of the socially acceptable and the socially outrageous. Similarly, tujok monks all had a consciousness of their humor as somehow "edgy." When I asked tujok monks how recitations of the *Vessantara Jataka* had changed over the decades and why, they all indicated that they had "toned down" their comedy in response to concerns about audience reactions. In the 1940s when a former tujok monk (now in his nineties) performed Jujaka, he explained that he was aware that there were some monks who felt comedy was inappropriate and they were afraid of incurring criticism (*bo klaa*). Proud of his ability to develop comic riffs, he added wryly, "And they lacked the ability." One can certainly imagine the shock of central Thai urbanites used to formal styles of chanting and a very different understanding of Jujaka upon hearing northern monks and laity enjoying bawdy tales.[44]

The tapes of Luang Poh Bunthong reveal his concern with how his audience would react to the bawdier moments. After his introductory remarks in which he prepares his modern audience to accept the legitimacy of using humor to teach the dharma, he begins by explaining his view of the role of monks in general. He remarks that many people associate preaching with criticism of their lifestyles and jokes about all the men who complain about the preaching their wives give them after they come home from a night of drinking or gambling (*mia haa thaet haem laeo*). He explained that in preaching the dharma his goal is "to take what is hard to understand and make it easy." He said that a monk is like a doctor administering medicine, but the doctor cannot force anyone to take the medicine. He explained that the goal is moderation—not outright prohibition, but an admonition to avoid harmful acts. He then launched into the first of several humorous examples of excess, beginning with the story of the three drunken old men lying by the ditch who could not even recognize the moon when they saw it:

These three men were all drunk and came from different provinces.⁴⁵ It was a full moon. The first fellow lies there and asks his companions, "Do you think that's the moon or is it the sun?"

The second man replies drunkenly, "I say it's the sun."

The first fellow is not convinced: "But how can the sun be out at night?"

The two drunks lay there arguing: "It's the moon." "It's the sun."

Finally the third companion tired of the arguing and asked, "What are you two arguing about?"

The first fellow said, "Up there, I say it's the moon. He says it's the sun. What do you think? Is it the sun or the moon?"

"How would I know? I'm not from this region [*bo chai chaobaan nii ro*]."

Luang Poh Bunthong concluded this story with the remark "They couldn't even recognize the moon because they couldn't teach themselves."⁴⁶

I did not ask Luang Poh Bunthong about his political views directly, but I did ask him if he thought comedic performances violated the monastic rules, given that one of the ten precepts states that monks and novices are to refrain from singing, dancing, playing music, or attending entertainment programs (Precept 7).⁴⁷ Luang Poh Bunthong was aware that he had come under criticism, but he took the criticism in stride, saying, "Yes, because they don't understand. Usually people criticize what they don't understand." He believed the good that came of reaching new audiences outweighed the negatives, adding with a chuckle that he was willing to accept any karmic retribution. He also noted that he had toned down his performances: he did not wear a tujok costume and no longer included many of the songs he had before. Luang Poh Bunthong explained his willingness to court criticism as follows:

> When I was a novice, there were already local regional differences. Some things were in violation of the monastic rules: to perform to earn money, to draw attention to oneself as a better performer than someone else. Criticizing Puu Phraam (Jujaka) as ugly is also against the vinaya. So Buddhism, if practiced in accord with local customs, can be considered against the monastic rules.
>
> But people aren't all the same. It's like the four lotus blossoms. One is a bud above the water and when the sun shines on it, it blossoms. Doesn't take much. Another is just below the surface, but once it reaches the surface it will bloom. And another is deeper and will take longer. The fourth is still in the mud, like the drug addicts and others. It may or may not reach the top and blossom. . . .
>
> People are like lotuses at different stages. We have to find a way to reach them. It's against the vinaya, but not a major violation. There are different

degrees of severity. This is not one that would get one arrested, more like probation! . . .

Preaching [*thaet*] so people have fun and laugh, all wrong. Who knows which hell I will end up in. [*Laughs.*] To entice people to be entranced in earthly carnal matters [*thaet hyy chakchuan khon hyy long laai nai kamalom*]. The five sensual pleasures [*kammakhun*] are form, sound, aroma, taste, and touch. So one uses all these to draw people in. So if there really is a hell, I'll be there since Jujaka involves all of these elements—joking, laughing. It violates Rule 7 that says that dancing, music, and other forms of entertainment are to be avoided. . . . So many things invite people into the sensual world. We have to find a way to remind people that life is suffering and death; nothing stays permanently. . . . Isn't it better to teach others than reach salvation alone? . . . People need a source of refuge [*thii phyng*]. They don't bow [*wai*] to their own parents, but bow to monks giving lottery numbers.[48]

A Weapon of the Weak

Our journey toward understanding the court's concern with comic performances of the *Vessantara Jataka* is nearing its end. The robust humor in the northern portrayal of Jujaka, the widespread familiarity of the trickster narratives across regions, the frequency of millenarian movements catalyzed by agrarian suffering, and the belief in the Maitreya Buddha all provide support for a political reading of the jataka that is more a critique of earthly royalty than a panegyric. Royalist interpretations have suggested that the narrative provided an opportunity for kings to present themselves as incipient Vessantaras and incipient Buddhas, their grand displays of offerings to the monks portrayed as physical evidence of royal generosity. The royalist interpretations of the *Vessantara Jataka* are based upon two questionable assumptions: (1) that villagers knew about or saw royal ceremonials at the court, and (2) that villagers were inclined to a positive view of their rulers. However much they may have respected kings who ruled in accordance with Buddhist morality (*dharmaraja*), the peasantry was more likely to have feared kings as one of the five evils.[49] Given the high percentage of war captives, the peasantry may not have viewed Vessantara's offerings of the seven hundred slave men and seven hundred slave women as a glorious gift. Given the high percentage of poor, villagers may also have found it easier to identify with Jujaka than Vessantara. Placing an emphasis on generosity may have been a "weapon of the weak," through which the poor sought to admonish the rich to be generous and perhaps to constrain the rapaciousness of representatives of the court.

Recognizing the potential role of the *Vessantara Jataka* in the peasant imaginaire helps to explain why the court sought to suppress its comedic recitations. To the extent that Jujaka can be read as a trickster, the *Vessantara Jataka* can be read as anti-royalist. One question remains: if the court sought to suppress the trickster Jujaka, why did he survive so robustly in the northern region, but not in the central or northeastern regions?

5

Jujaka as Threat
Consolidating Control

We have now reached the point in our journey where we have found the political Jujaka, a trickster figure who bridges not only the mythical village and the palace, but also the present earthly realm and the future Maitreyan utopia in the northern peasant imaginaire. Given that comic recitations of the *Vessantara Jataka* were once widespread across regions and given that the trickster motif was widely known, the evidence from northern Thailand suggests that Jujaka may have once been conceived as a trickster in other regions as well. To the extent that Jujaka was seen as a trickster, the *Vessantara Jataka* would have resonated more with its audiences across all three regions as an anti-royalist critique than as a pro-royalist panegyric. Furthermore, peasant discontent and Maitreyan millenarian movements were hardly limited to northern Thailand. The fact that the *Phra Malai Sutra* was closely associated with the *Vessantara Jataka* reinforces the performance's political resonances. Understanding these political resonances helps to explain the objections of the Bangkok court to comedic recitations.

But objections alone do not explain differences in the court's ability to shape Jujaka's escapades across these three regions. In the early twentieth century, Jujaka remained a beloved trickster in the northern region but had increasingly become a terrifying ghoul in the central region and a vaudevillian comic (and sometimes ghoul) in the northeastern region. If Jujaka as trickster was seen as a threat to state control, gaining control over the popular interpretation of the *Vessantara Jataka* would have been good politics. Wise rulers, even if they came to power through military force, also seek to establish legitimacy through cultural means.[1] Since monks were the primary performers of the *Vessantara Jataka* in Thailand, suppressing its humor would not be possible

Jujaka as Threat • 209

Figure 15. Jujaka surrounded at court. Jujaka (*center*) brings the royal grandchildren to court. Temple mural at Wat Suwannaram, Bangkok, July 2009. Photo by author.

without gaining control over the Buddhist monastic hierarchy (*sangha*). Dependent to varying degrees upon both royalty and commoners for support, the sangha provided a bridge between court and village. Given the historical pattern of ordination by village elites, most local leaders were either monks or former monks. Furthermore, given the frequency with which revolts were led by monks or former monks in the name of the future Buddha, gaining royal control of the sangha would have been an important strategy to establish political stability.

But why was the Bangkok court able to rein in Jujaka in the central and northeastern regions but not in the north? As this chapter will show, the degree of humor displayed in *Vessantara Jataka* performances in different regions inversely parallels the degree of control the court exercised over each respective region: the Bangkok court had the most control over the central region, a modicum of control over the northeastern region, and the least control over the northern region. The first two sections of this chapter describe how the growth of the Thammayut reform movement enabled the court to gain increasing control over the sangha in the central and northeastern regions, respectively.

As described in the third section, the Thammayut movement gained entry into northern Thailand much later than in either the central or northeastern region. The fourth section seeks to resolve an apparent paradox: that despite the relatively greater political independence of the north, *Vessantara Jataka* recitations have declined there, even as they have continued in the northeast.

Centralization of State Control over the Central Thai Sangha

Recognizing the origins of much of the population as war captives or as debt slaves sheds light on the challenges the Bangkok court faced in establishing its legitimacy and administrative control. At the time the Bangkok court came to power (in the wake of the fall of Ayutthaya, the former capital, to the Burmese in 1767), the region of central Thailand was in disarray. Authorship of the "standard" central Thai text of the *Vessantara Jataka*, with its frightening Jujaka character, was well underway in the early Bangkok period, but the available evidence suggests that comedic performances continued to be held among the populace at large. So how did the sober court version, with its emphasis on the Kumarn chapter and ghoulish portrayal of Jujaka, come to hold sway? The process involved in large measure royal patronage of monks and temples. This section describes the steps taken by the Bangkok kings to gain control over the sangha in the central Thai region, both through its secular administrative authority and through the rise of the royally supported Thammayut sect.

Early Efforts

Evidence from European travelers indicates that the *Vessantara Jataka* was well known among the Ayutthayan populace, presumably in both its bawdy and stately forms (e.g., Gervaise [1688] 1989, 129, 140–41; Tachard [1688] 1981, 291–92). Due to the paucity of historical records, it is difficult to know how the earlier Ayutthayan sangha was structured, but the sangha's political importance is intimated as Taksin (1734–82) sought to found his new capital at Thonburi in 1767. Facing at least two millenarian revolts, he moved quickly to establish control over the monkhood (Reynolds 1972, 31). In 1769 Taksin invited a monk from Nakhon Sithammarat to be supreme patriarch in his new capital at Thonburi. At the same time, he transported an edition of the Tripitaka from Nakhon Sithammarat to Bangkok, where it was copied (Reynolds 1972, 34; Heinze 1977, 20).[2] In the wake of the Phra Fang revolt, Taksin sent monks north to the Uttaradit-Phitsanulok region "to perform proper ordinations and to teach Dhamma" (Reynolds 1972, 35).[3] In 1777 the supreme patriarch and other high-ranking monks presented him with Pali texts on meditation. In 1778 he commissioned a revision of the important cosmological text *Traiphum* ("Three Worlds") (Reynolds 1972, 35; for translation, see Reynolds and Reynolds 1982). After Vientiane was overpowered in 1778, Taksin relocated the Emerald Buddha from Vientiane to Thonburi. Although Taksin sought to consolidate court control over the sangha, the end of his reign was marked by intense division. The supreme patriarch was replaced and the highest-ranking monks were demoted; more than five hundred monks were flogged and sentenced to menial labor at Wat Hong, the monastery of the new supreme patriarch (Reynolds 1972, 33). Increasingly viewed as insane, Taksin was deposed in a coup and executed.

Taksin's general, Chaophraya Chakri, ascended to the throne in 1782 as King Rama I. The founder of the current royal Chakri dynasty, Rama I (r. 1782–1809), decided to move the capital across the river to Bangkok (this event was celebrated in the state recitation of the *Vessantara Jataka* described in chapter 1). Characterized as a "subtle revolution," Rama I implemented a series of religious reforms to help establish his legitimacy (Wyatt 1994, 131). Shortly after assuming the throne, Rama I reinstated the former supreme patriarch and the other high-ranking monks who had refused to pay homage to Taksin (Reynolds 1972, 46). Although it would not be finished until nineteen years later, in 1783 he commissioned a new edition of the *Traiphum* (Reynolds 1972, 57; Reynolds and Reynolds 1982; Wyatt 1994, 150–54). He undertook the construction of several Buddhist temples, including Wat Phra Kaew. Upon its completion, he relocated the Emerald Buddha from Thonburi to the newly built Wat Phra Kaew, holding the consecration ceremony in 1784. Other important temples he built were Wat Suthat and Wat Pho, where fragments from the Buddha images from Ayutthaya's Wat Si Sanaphet, which had been destroyed by Burmese, were preserved.[4]

Rama I moved quickly to consolidate his control over the sangha, issuing seven sangha laws in his first two years on the throne (Reynolds 1972, 38).[5] In April 1783 two ex-monks from Nakhon Nayok instigated a revolt by claiming the power to make themselves invisible. A group of nobles and a number of palace women joined the ex-monks who succeeded in penetrating the Front Palace (Reynolds 1972, 42). As his introductory remarks to one of his first sangha laws reveal, Rama I was very concerned about the political threat from monks who claimed supernatural powers and sought to attract a mass following: "They travel about alone or in two's and three's hiding behind the pretense of keeping the precepts through meditation.... Clothing themselves in the reddish brown robes of Buddhism, they induce each other to scheme and deceive, extolling supernatural power to take the throne" (Reynolds 1972, 41).[6]

Decree 3, promulgated on May 8, 1783, was intended to limit the spread of revolts by identifying each monk with a specific monastery and a preceptor who would supervise his conduct. Each monk was required to obtain a certificate in *khom* script bearing his Pali name, his monastery of residence, his preceptor, his seniority in the sangha, and a seal of the ranking sangha officials in the principality where the monastery was located. When traveling outside their monasteries, monks had to carry their identifying certificates with them. According to the decree, no monk arriving at a monastery from another district was to be permitted to stay until his documents had been examined. Furthermore, all abbots had to forward a register of monks under their supervision for mobilization and control of manpower (Ishii 1986, 65; Taylor 1993, 24; see also Dhani Nivat 1955, 26; Reynolds 1972, 42–43; Tambiah 1976, 185; Heinze 1977, 22).

In Decree 6 he denounced monks who made a living by serving as masseurs, medicine sellers, and astrologers. Emphasizing scriptural scholarship and textual study, Rama I condemned monks who "had failed to maintain their discipline and their studies, and wandered about in the shops and markets, visited musical and dramatic performances, played chess and gambled and, in short, behaved like laypeople" (Wyatt 1994, 147–49). Decree 7 addressed the continuing factional disputes that were occurring in the sangha, decreeing that "all Mon and Lao [monks] heed the instructions of the Supreme Patriarch alone" and involve the king only as a last resort (Reynolds 1972, 46).[7] Seeking to end the disputes, the king demoted some monks, disrobed others, and even sentenced one to execution.[8] With his tenth edict, he expelled 128 monks who had been "guilty of all kinds of ignoble behavior, namely drinking, wandering about at night, rubbing shoulders with women, using improper language, [and] buying silly things from Chinese junks" (Wenk 1968, 39).

In addition to seeking to control the sangha itself, Rama I appeared to emphasize the primacy of a more philosophical form of Buddhism. In 1782, although allowing for the propitiation of various spirits, he ordered that his subjects revere no beliefs higher than Buddhism. He stated that he found no support for phallic worship in the Tripitaka and was concerned that foreign visitors found it offensive. He went so far as to forbid "the keeping of lingas, and ordered officials to gather and destroy them, on penalty of death" (Wyatt 1994, 157). Three years later, he required that officials participating in the annual oath-of-allegiance ceremony pay respect "to the Triple Gems of Buddhism, the Emerald Buddha and Buddhist relics before paying their respects to the guardian and tutelary deities or to the statues of previous rulers" (Wyatt 1994, 157). In 1788 Rama I donated large sums for copying the *Tripitaka* text and distributing it to all royal monasteries (Reynolds 1972, 50). Known as the Grand

Gilt Edition, these revisions were completed in April 1789 (Reynolds 1972, 53; Thiphakorawong 1978; Veidlinger 2006, 146-49).

Rama I died in 1809 and was succeeded by his son, who became Rama II (r. 1809-24). Another of Rama I's sons was Prince Paramanuchit. Also known for his literary skills, he was the author of five chapters of the "standard" version of the *Vessantara Jataka* and later became supreme patriarch (see the discussion in chapter 2). King Rama II was also known as a fine poet, and his reign was notably peaceful. Some of his contributions were reviving the celebrations of Visakha Bucha, revising the Buddhist Tripitaka by translating prayers from Pali into Thai so they would be comprehensible to those who were reciting them, and building and restoring Buddhist temples. He also sent a mission of monks to Sri Lanka to study Buddhism in that country; upon their return, these monks brought six bo sprigs to be planted at six temples (Reynolds 1972, 92).[9] John Crawfurd, who visited Bangkok in 1822, near the end of Rama II's reign, testified to the significant extent to which sangha affairs in the central region had been stabilized by that time. Remarking on the court's tight regulation of the sangha, Crawfurd notes, "religion was completely identified with the government" ([1828] 1987, 368). He continues: "The Sovereign himself is the real head of the religion of the country. The Talapoins depend upon him for subsistence and promotion. They have neither rank nor endowments independent of his will. They are not hereditary; they have no civil employments; and no tie which unites their interests with those of the people. They may therefore be considered as a kind of standing force, ready at all times with spiritual arms to enforce obedience to the will of the Sovereign, and to strengthen and aggravate his despotic authority" ([1828] 1967, 372).

While strengthening state control over the sangha, the court continued to promote an understanding of Buddhism that included the jatakas. In his edition of the Buddha's life, completed in 1845, Prince Paramanuchit still concluded with Buddhaghosa's famous prediction from the fifth century that Buddhism was destined to disappear in five thousand years.

The Rise of the Thammayut Order

If the reigns of Rama I and Rama II had made significant strides in unifying the sangha, the reign of King Rama III saw the expansion of the court administrative hierarchy and the emergence of a major division in the sangha. Rama III was known for his piety and lavish patronage of the sangha (Reynolds 1972, 158). Born in 1787 of a royal wife who came from a southern Muslim noble family, Rama III distinguished himself in his earlier position as minister of trade and foreign affairs. Trade flourished during his reign, the revenue enabling him to serve as a generous patron (Vella 1957, 19). Under Rama III the number of renovations and constructions of royal monastic complexes rose from fifteen in the first reign to forty (Worrasit 2006, 137). He also encouraged Chinese merchants and noblemen to build temples affiliated with the court (Worrasit 2006, 185).

During this reign, royal support for Buddhist education increased significantly. Examinations were standardized and held every three years, with rewards given to monks who passed. Elites and noblemen followed the king's example by hiring teachers to prepare monks throughout Bangkok for the Pali examination. Relatives of monks who passed their examination were exempted from royal obligations (Reynolds 1972, 160). Ex-monks with Pali knowledge were encouraged to enter the bureaucracy. These measures encouraged both commoners and noblemen to enter the monkhood and to continue studying in the hopes of receiving royal titles. Study of the Buddhist canon and Pali became a means of mobility in Thai society, while the social role of royal temples was strengthened when they became both educational centers and a point of entry into the bureaucracy (Worrasit 2006, 130-31).

However, his reign also saw the rise of a new order of monks called Thammayut. The older order came to be known as the Mahanikai, and this division "profoundly affected Sangha history in the second half of the 19th century" (Reynolds 1972, 125). The new order was founded by Rama III's younger half brother, Prince Mongkut, who ordained as a monk in 1824. During his twenty-seven years in the monkhood, Mongkut introduced a series of changes. Mongkut had the advantage of high royal birth as the son of King Rama II, his status as a legitimate heir to the throne, and the support of King Rama III (Reynolds 1972, 69). Put simply, "Without royal patronage the Thammayut nikai would not have survived" (Kamala 1997, 6). Because of its close connections with the court, it became highly influential.

Mongkut was impressed with Mon adherence to the *vinaya*, the monastic disciplinary code of conduct. Accordingly, he developed a small coterie of five to six other monks, including the future supreme patriarch Prince Pawaret.[10] In order to make monastic discipline stricter, Mongkut "insisted that laypeople ought to perform such necessary tasks as distributing monks' food, cleaning their living quarters, washing their robes, and caring for their communal property" (Kamala 1997, 6; see also Reynolds 1972, 90). The new sect was distinguished by "a new style of wearing robes (covering both shoulders, a Mon practice), new ordination rituals, a new pronunciation of the Pali scriptural language, new routines (including daily chanting), and new religious days to observe" (Kamala 1997, 6; see also Reynolds 1972, 90-91). The Thammayut order emphasized the life of the historical Buddha over the jatakas. As Kamala explains: "Mongkut also placed greater emphasis on the study of the Pali canon and commentaries than on the practice of meditation, which he considered mystical. He was convinced that true religion was a matter of rational doctrine and belief. Mongkut disdained all traditions in which folk stories and parables were used to teach the dharma and local culture was integrated with Buddhism. From his perspective, local stories full of demons, gods, miracles, magic, rituals, and exorcism were folklore; they had nothing to do with Buddhism" (1997, 6–7).

In 1837 Rama III invited Mongkut to serve as abbot at Wat Bowonniwet. This position brought Mongkut physically closer to Rama III while at the same time freeing him to introduce a number of innovations in monastic practice and legitimizing his following (Reynolds 1972, 87). Mongkut remained as abbot until he acceded to the throne in 1851 as Rama IV. By 1851, between 130 and 150 monks were spending the Lenten season at Wat Bowonniwet. Many of them "were princes and sons of nobles and all . . . were followers of Mongkut" (Reynolds 1972, 87; see also Bastian 1867, 95). At least three other branch chapters were established at other temples.[11] Because monks from his temple excelled in the examinations, Rama III put Mongkut in charge of all ecclesiastical examinations in the capital (Reynolds 1972, 89). Mongkut also sought new means of disseminating Buddhist teachings, setting up a printing press (Vella 1957, 42). Although the Thammayut sect was small, its influence was considerable. As founder of a new sect, Mongkut was treading a fine line. As Craig Reynolds notes, for some the new order was seen as rooted in an authentic tradition, but to others it had "the appearance of absolutism and arrogance" (1972, 97).

The growing strength of the Thammayut order was reflected in changes in the administrative structure of the sangha. The Siamese monastic order was previously comprised of three major regional patriarchs, each in charge of the northern, the southern, and the forest monasteries, respectively. The supreme patriarch was usually the head of the northern region and was seated at Wat Mahathat. Rama III revised this structure to four major regional groups: the northern, the southern, the forest, and the central monasteries (Heinze 1977, 24). He put his uncle, Prince Paramanuchit Chinorot at Wat Pho, in charge of all the monasteries of Bangkok and the central region. Wat Pho became the center of the administration of local Bangkok monasteries while Wat Mahathat remained the larger center encompassing the entire monastic order. The temples of the new Thammayut order were placed under the central control of Wat Pho. Rama III's appointment could be seen as shifting Wat Pho into the real center of the monastic order, thereby allowing the Thammayut order political space to expand (Worrasit 2006, 176).

Upon the death of Rama III in 1851, Mongkut became king. Seeking to balance his patronage between both orders, Mongkut appointed Prince Paramanuchit as supreme patriarch, marking the first time in Siamese history a member of the royal family was charged with the leadership of all monks in the kingdom (Reynolds 1972, 115). Since Prince Paramanuchit was at once a member of the Mahanikai order and the royal family, this deft appointment served to balance both Mahanikai and Thammayut interests. Safely under the authority of the royal supreme patriarch, the Thammayut order was able to develop. Mongkut appointed Prince Pawaret as abbot of Wat Bowonniwet and head of the Thammayut temples (Reynolds 1972, 120). Concerned that there might be a flood of candidates seeking to curry favor with the king, Prince Pawaret generally restricted ordinations to members of the royal family (Reynolds 1972, 106). Some senior Thammayut monks established chapters in other Mahanikai temples. In 1856 a Thammayut monk from Wat Samorai was made abbot of a new temple called Wat Samanatsawihan. In 1864 Mongkut built the first temple exclusively for his order (Wat Makutkasat); receiving considerable support from palace women, its first abbot was Sa, a monk from Wat Bowonniwet who later became supreme patriarch (Reynolds 1972, 107). As Craig Reynolds describes the expansion of the Thammayut, "Many young princes were ordained in the Thammayuttika during Mongkut's reign and an increasing number of monasteries, headed by Mongkut's followers, looked to Wat Bowonniwet and Wat Samanatsawihan for spiritual and administrative guidance. This growth had profound consequences for the Sangha, for the strength of Mongkut's nikai in terms of the talent it attracted" (Reynolds 1972, 114).

The Thammayut order provided a "new standard of orthodoxy" (Reynolds 1972, 125). There were growing numbers of educated Thai who were interested in science and believed "rain fell not because the rain-making deities dared to emerge from their abode or because a great serpent thrashed its tail, but because of winds which suck water out of the clouds" (Reynolds 1972, 130; see also Alabaster 1870, 7-11). This growing rationalism is reflected in this criticism of Thai literature by Chaophraya Thiphakorawong (Kham Bunnag): "Our Siamese literature is not only scanty but nonsensical, full of stories of genii stealing women, and men fighting with genii, and extraordinary persons who could fly through the air, and bring dead people to life" (Alabaster 1870, 7). In his book *Kitchanukit*, Thiphakorawong challenges the mythical explanations of diseases, earthquakes, comets, eclipses, and other such natural events, providing scientific explanations in their place. Instead of stories from previous lives, he draws upon incidents from the Buddha's life. During his visit, Bastian records Thiphakorawong describing "the new Buddhist sect that the king was trying to found in an attempt to reform the religion, banning all that was fantastic and improbable from the Pali scriptures, and retaining only their moral essence" ([1867] 2005, 58). The influence of the Thammayut order expanded beyond its own temples since "Mahanikai monasteries also experimented with Thammayuttika practice" and these new perspectives were shared "by increasing numbers of Mahanikai monks as well" (Reynolds 1972, 111,137). Nonetheless, the tight organization and discipline enabled the Thammayut to become "an elite corps which transmitted the energy of Mongkut's reform to the entire sangha" (Reynolds 1972, 137).

Centralizing Administrative Control

After King Mongkut's death, his son Chulalongkorn developed a national system of administration in which the sangha came to play an important role (see Tej 1977). Chulalongkorn appointed Prince Pawaret head of the sangha in January 1874; his appointment showed "the degree to which the Thammayut had been absorbed into the Sangha" (Reynolds 1972, 121).[12] In 1882 a half brother of Chulalongkorn, Prince Vajiranana (Wachirayan), was appointed as deputy head of the Thammayut order. With two princes holding formal status in the monastic hierarchy, the Thammayut order was becoming increasingly influential (Reynolds 1972, 123). When Prince Pawaret died in 1892, Prince Vajiranana assumed the position of abbot of Wat Bowonniwet and was made head of the Thammayut order. Later, when Rama VI came into power in 1910, Prince Vajiranana was appointed the supreme patriarch of the Thai monkhood.

During Rama V's reign three major developments are of significance for our understanding of the *Vessantara Jataka*: (1) the establishment of religious academic institutions, (2) the institution of public education, and (3) the enactment of the Sangha Act of 1902. Under Prince Vajiranana the Thammayut order became closely integrated with the newly centralizing bureaucracy.[13] Shortly after becoming abbot, Prince Vajiranana proceeded to establish the Thammayut's Mahamakut Buddhist University at Wat Bowonniwet in 1893. Named in commemoration of his father's death, Mahamakut was the first formal Buddhist college for monks and novices. To counterbalance the Thammayut university, King Chulalongkorn also established Mahachulalongkorn University at the Mahanikai temple of Wat Mahathat in 1896 (see Reynolds 1972, 169-93). The graduates of these universities were to play an important role in the development of public education through the country's temple schools.

Called "the first modern law pertaining to the sangha," the purpose of the 1902 Sangha Act was to integrate the country's sangha under a single administrative organization. The act was initially implemented in fourteen of the seventeen monthons (Ishii 1986, 71).[14] The 1902 Sangha Act created a national administrative hierarchy that paralleled the provincial administrative hierarchy established by Prince Damrong in the 1897 Local Administration Act. The sangha was to be ruled by a Council of Elders, under which came the heads of *monthons, muangs, khwaengs*, and individual temples, respectively (for a diagram, see Ishii 1986, 71). The Council of Elders was comprised of eight members, two from each of the four major divisions: the Thammayut, northern region, southern region, and central region. The act also described three major types of temples: royal temples, commoner temples, and monastic residences.[15] Although the act stated that Mahanikai monks could govern Thammayut monks, in practice Mahanikai monks were invariably governed by Thammayut monks. As Peter Jackson notes, "the 1902 Act provided a legal framework for, and legitimised, the Thammayut Order's administrative control of the entire Thai sangha" (1989, 69).

The implementation of the 1902 Sangha Act also led to the establishment of a "centrally controlled doctrinal orthodoxy with regard to the interpretation of Buddhist teachings" (Jackson 1989, 69). Prince Vajiranana wrote almost all the textbooks used in the new national monastic education system based on his interpretation of Pali canonical works, commentaries, and vinaya texts (Kamala 1997, 8–9; Jory 2000). As Kamala explains, the act created a monastic system, still in use today, that rested on degrees, examinations, and ranks in the sangha hierarchy and defined "the ideal Buddhist monk as one who observes strict monastic rules, has mastered Vajiranana's texts, teaches in Bangkok Thai, carries out administrative duties, observes holy days, and performs religious ceremonies based on Bangkok customs" (1997, 8–9). "With the act's passage, a modern nation-state with a centralized, urban-based bureaucracy began to control local communities distinguished by diverse ethnic traditions. Formerly autonomous Buddhist monks belonging to diverse lineages became part of the Siamese religious hierarchy with its standard texts and practices, whereas previously no single tradition had predominated" (Kamala 1997, 8–9).

Thus, over the course of the nineteenth century, the court was able to insert itself into a religio-educational system with ever-expanding influence. In contrast to the Ayutthayan period, when only four sons of kings made the monkhood their careers over the course of four hundred years, six royal sons became influential monks in the nineteenth century (Reynolds 1972, 66).[16] The number of royal temples supported by the king grew. The king acquired many royal monasteries from pious noblemen who made merit by building a monastery and then made additional merit by presenting it to the king. In the mid-nineteenth century there were some fifty-four royal monasteries with some eight thousand monks of the total ten thousand monks in the city (Pallegoix 1854, 312, cited in Reynolds 1972, 21). By 1914 there were seventy-two royal temples in Bangkok and thirty-eight in the nearby countryside (Reynolds 1972, 21). As Reynolds notes, "The Sangha was acutely aware of its dependency on the crown, especially when social and economic conditions limited the flow of support from the laity" (1972, 24).

Court control over the sangha was reinforced through its establishment of a separate secular government department, called the Krom Thammakan, or Department of Religious Affairs. Dating back to at least the reign of King Rama I, this department "managed finances, supervised monastery construction and restoration, and recommended appointments to the king" (Reynolds 1972, 16). Initially, only royal temples fell under the supervision of the Krom Thammakan; these were primarily located in Bangkok. In 1888–89 the krom became part of the new Ministry of Public Instruction (Reynolds 1972, 21). In 1893 the department comprised four subdivisions: royal ceremonies, monastic registers, monasteries (overseeing monastic lands and rents), and a subdivision to investigate legal cases (Reynolds 1972, 22–23). Today, under the Ministry of Culture, its jurisdiction has expanded such that it now oversees temples throughout Thailand.

Thus, over the course of the nineteenth century, the court was increasingly in a position to shape performances of the *Vessantara Jataka* in central Thailand. Although its influence initially would have been limited to royal temples, the court came to exert greater control over the sangha with the rise of the Thammayut order, the promulgation of various laws, and the existence of a Department of Religious Affairs. How did the court succeed in gaining access to monks in northeastern Thailand?

Bangkok Expansion into the Northeast

Although Thai control over northeastern Thailand had been minimal during the Ayutthayan period, it became tighter over the course of the nineteenth century. From its inception, the Chakri dynasty was more concerned to establish its direct jurisdiction over the northeastern and southern regions of Thailand than the north. As Constance Wilson explains the geopolitical position, "Control of the northeast by another state would be more of a threat to central Thailand than control of any other area. An army coming down from Nakhon Ratchasima could descend more quickly on the capital than one from either the north or the south" (1970, 120–23). While other regions were characterized by "fairly compact areas of settlement in clearly defined geographic regions," the northeast is "an extensive interior plateau which does not contain many natural internal regional units" (Wilson 1970, 120). She explains the resulting problem: "In the nineteenth century, the Korat Plateau contained a number of *muang* [city-states] which appear to have been of approximately equal size and status. No single *muang* in the area was dominant. Instead of a relatively stable hierarchy of *muang* and *huamuang* similar to that found in the south . . . the *huamuang* of the northeast were almost constantly at each other's throats. . . . The Chao Muang of the northeast, unable to settle their own internal conflicts, were forever seeking outside help" (Wilson 1970, 120-23).

Adding to the volatility of the northeastern region was the existence of competing kingdoms to the east. With the demise of the Lao kingdom of Lan Chang after the death of its king in 1695, the region had split into three kingdoms of Luang Prabang, Vientiane, and Champasak.[17] As Wilson explains: "The Korat Plateau was an area of competition between the Thai and the Lao. This meant that one family faction could look to the Thai for help, while another turned toward the Lao kingdoms. The presence of three external centers of power encouraged internal dissension in the Korat Plateau" (1970, 120-23).

Thus the process of establishing control over the northeast was continually fraught. In 1804 Chao Anu was appointed ruler of Vientiane by Bangkok. In 1827, following the death of Bangkok's King Rama II, Chao Anu and his son launched a military attack on Bangkok. Although ultimately the attack failed, the Bangkok court responded by destroying Vientiane and forcibly relocating the population into the region known today as northeastern Thailand (see Wyatt 1994, 185-209). As Wilson summarizes, "Few family groups survived the events of 1826-1827 intact" (1970, 128). Furthermore, the population continued to be disrupted by Thai demands on the northeast to supply officials, conscripts, and provisions for Thai attacks on Vietnam in 1833-34, 1840-41, and 1845 (Wilson 1970, 128).

Bangkok took measures to ensure that local power in the northeast remained dispersed. As Wilson explains, "Instead of permitting a *huamuang* to exercise jurisdiction over a large number of lesser *muangs*, the Thai sought to make lesser *muangs* direct dependencies of Bangkok" (1970, 125). Between 1767 and 1882, in the Lao areas 145 huamuang were created, of which about 95-100 were located on the Khorat plateau (Keyes 1967, 15). These huamuang were later consolidated to 42 major huamuang.

Concerned with growing colonial expansion by the British in Burma and the French in Indochina, the Thai government instituted a system of royal commissioners for the Lao areas. In 1882 a royal commissioner in charge of the Lao huamuang was stationed at Champasak (Vella 1955, 344; Keyes 1967, 16). In 1890 the Lao huamuang were grouped into four monthons, each with its own royal commissioner (Keyes 1967, 16). The purpose of these monthons was "to tighten central control over the provinces by sending out a Royal Commissioner to coordinate the administration of several provinces and report directly to the Ministry of Interior" (Vickery 1970, 875). With the establishment of the new Ministry of the Interior in 1892, the monthons were administered by ministry officials (see Tej 1977, 101). Gradually the major huamuang became districts (*amphur*) and the chao muang became "governors" whose salaries came from the central government rather than from tribute money, as had been the case before. As Keyes explains: "As a *cao muang* passed away in one of the northeastern or other 'outer provinces,' he was replaced not in accordance with the traditional method whereby provincial officials chose the new ruler (usually from among the close relatives of the old ruler), but instead through an appointment made by the Ministry of Interior" (1967, 17).

As Michael Vickery's review of eleven provinces or districts of northeastern Thailand shows, "the elites of the Northeast are conspicuous by their apparently total exclusion from high office under the reformed system" (1970, 878). None of the northeastern elites was appointed a monthon royal commissioner; a few of the old hereditary governors were maintained in office for a certain number of years after the introduction of the reformed administrative system; and many others were either given lower-level posts or virtually demoted to the status of district officers or unsalaried positions called *krom kan phiset* (Vickery 1970; Tambiah 1976, 196).[18]

The Bangkok court had good reason to be worried about the growing French presence. In 1893 Bangkok was forced to cede all the Lao area on the left bank of the Mekong River; in addition, two areas on the right bank, Sayaboury and Champasak, passed to French control in 1904 (Keyes 1967, 12).[19] That Bangkok chose not to appoint local hereditary rulers to administrative positions indicates (1) its considerable concern over the administration of this region, and (2) its misgivings regarding the "loyalty of the northeastern regions precisely because of their strong Laotian connections and their linguistic and cultural variations from central Thai" (Tambiah 1976, 197). Central Thai administration of the northeast was based on a semi-feudal principle whereby villagers were subject to indigenous elites and the elites were in turn subject to Bangkok (Keyes 1967, 15). As Vickery remarks, "the system encouraged local particularism and the attachment of the population to local leaders rather than to the capital" (1970, 873).

Thammayut Expansion into the Northeast

The challenge facing the Bangkok court in domesticating northeastern religious practices is quickly made visible by their ever-prevalent lingas. As I have described in chapter 2, anyone traveling to villages in northeastern Thailand can see ample evidence of the continuing use of phalluses, not only during the Rocket Festival but even on the elephant that Vessantara and Matsi ride in the village processions. As noted earlier in this chapter, the court's efforts to destroy all lingas and reform local practices began as early as 1782 under Rama I, but they have clearly met with only a modicum of success.

Given the long-standing tradition of monks traveling from temple to temple in the past, it is likely that northeastern monks would have traveled to Bangkok and familiarized themselves with the developing trends in Bangkok-based practices of Buddhism. Since Rama I had led military campaigns in Vientiane and Champasak, it is entirely possible that he developed a network of personal contacts through which to begin to influence the sangha hierarchy throughout the northeastern region.[20] Certainly by the time of Rama III, there is clear evidence of Bangkok's growing interest in establishing a presence in the northeastern sangha. While Rama IV was still a monk, he had sent Ajarn Sui to become head of the early Thammayut sect in Ubon; Ajarn Sui is credited with introducing formal Pali and Thai studies in Ubon, which he had learned at Wat Saket in Bangkok (Taylor 1993, 36, 46). Ajarn Sui initially resided at Wat Paa Noi in Ubon, a Mahanikai temple. Ubon temples were considered to be in the Vientiane or Lao tradition; Ajarn Sui's disciples became known as the "Thai order."

In 1851 the Bangkok-supported Chao Muang of Ubon asked two monks, Than Phanthulo "Dii" and his disciple Than Thewathammii "Maao," to set up the first Thammayut temple. Called Wat Supat, this temple was affiliated with Wat Bowonniwet in Bangkok; Dii became its first abbot. According to the official history of Wat Supat, Mongkut himself ordered the construction of Wat Supat in Ubon in 1850, personally contributing 800 baht for its construction and giving a stipend of 8 baht per month to the abbot. The temple was also allocated sixty corvée laborers to help with its upkeep. Phra Ubalii, the fourth abbot of Wat Bowonniwet in Bangkok, became the fourth abbot of Wat Supat (Taylor 1993, 35, 48; for more on Ubalii, see Anake 2007).

Ubon's local *uparaat* (viceroy) subsequently established Wat Sii Thong (now Wat Sii Ubon) in 1855, with Maao as its first abbot (he died in 1890) (Taylor 1993, 46). The Thammayut monks in Ubon became known as the Mon order. Thereafter, a number of reform monasteries were established within a short time of each other both in Ubon and in two muang that were vassals of Ubon (see Taylor 1993, 46, for list). Each of these monasteries was supported by the local aristocratic rulers (the Chao Muang, Uparaat, Ratchawong, and Ratchabut) (see Taylor 1993, 48). As Taylor notes, "Dii could not have succeeded in promoting the Thammayut Khana had it not been for the enthusiasm of Mongkut, then king, and the support of local-based elites, especially the local lord (Jao Meuang) of Ubon" (1993, 46). Mongkut knew both Dii and Maao personally (Taylor 1993, 46).

Another monk who illustrates the growing connections between Bangkok and the northeast was Phra Ariyakawii Orn, who was appointed *chaokhana yai* (sangha governor) for the Thammayut of the northeastern region's Monthon Isan. He was born in Ubon in 1845 and ordained in the Thammayut order under Maao when he was twenty-one. In 1869 he was sent to Bangkok to pursue Pali studies. For a time he was an abbot of a temple in Nonthaburi.[21] He then returned to Ubon, residing at the Thammayut Wat Supat. In addition to teaching, Orn was responsible for sending many northeastern pupils to Bangkok for advanced Pali studies and established a number of provincial *pariyat* schools (Taylor 1993, 51). Orn worked closely with King Chulalongkorn's younger half brother, Krom Luang Phichit Priichaakorn, the *khaaluang thaen phra-ong* (special envoy) in Ubon.[22] Phichit gave one baht of his own allowance for each Thammayut monk in Ubon toward food (Taylor 1993, 51).[23] As ecclesiastical head in Ubon, Orn enforced strict standards of behavior with monks under his control, "such as forbidding participation in indigenous rituals such as the 'rocket festival' (*bun bangfai*), boat-racing, drum-beating competitions, and horse raising" (Taylor 1993, 51-52). His prohibitions likely included bawdy performances of the *Vessantara Jataka*.

Phra Ubalii (1856-1932) succeeded Orn as sangha governor in Ubon.[24] One of the most famous monks of the northeast, Ubalii was born in a village outside Ubon; he was a childhood friend of a famous forest monk, Ajarn Man. He went to Wat Sii Thong in Ubon to study as a novice. He had to disrobe in 1874 to help his family farm, but he re-ordained in 1877 with Maao as his preceptor; he resided at Wat Chaiyamongkhon, a Thammayut temple in Ubon. For a time he studied with Maao but then went to further his education in Bangkok. In 1885 he and seven or eight other northeastern monks and novices returned to Ubon with the intention of establishing their own temple for meditation. In 1888, when the Chao Muang of Champasak heard of Ubalii's abilities, he invited Ubalii to establish the first Thammayut temple in Champasak. After coming into conflict with a local monk in Champasak, Ubalii moved to Bangkok (to Wat Pichaiyaattikaraam in Thonburi), bringing many pupils with him. In

1890 he was promoted to sangha governor of Champasak and returned to Champasak to establish a school for Pali and Thai studies. In 1893, after Champasak was ceded to France, Ubalii returned to Ubon where he stayed at Wat Supat. In 1894 he went to Bangkok, again bringing promising pariyat students with him. Ubalii was appointed to the committee of Mahamakut Buddhist University at Wat Bowonniwet. He continued to alternate teaching in Bangkok and in the northeast, returning to Ubon again in 1896. In 1898 Prince Vajiranana asked him to become one of the monthon education directors of Monthon Isan. In 1903 Ubalii replaced Orn as preceptor for the Thammayut sect in Ubon. At that point he had traveled back and forth from the northeast to Bangkok ten times. In 1904 he was appointed abbot at Wat Bowonniwet in Bangkok. He received several subsequent promotions and in 1910 became Chaokhana Monthon Hua Muang Krungthep.[25]

In addition to strong links between Ubon and Bangkok, Thammayut links also expanded to other regions in the northeast. A monk named Saeng, who had ordained with Maao at Wat Sii Thong in Ubon, established a Thammayut temple in Udon called Wat Mahachai. At the request of the Chao Muang in Udon, he became the head of Wat Mahachai and later the *chaokhana khwaeng*. Wat Mahachai was a branch of Wat Somanat in Bangkok and became an important center for the dissemination of Thammayut ideas in Udon (Taylor 1993, 50). As Taylor explains, "From its successful missionary ventures in Udorn, the Thammayut spreads to Khorn Kaen, then to the more distant provinces of Nakhorn Phanom and Loei" (1993, 62).

Ajarn Man Phurithatto, a childhood friend of Ubalii, became an even more famous Thammayut monk. Widely believed to have reached arahantship while meditating in the mountains in Chiang Mai province, Man is considered to be the founder of the modern Thammayut forest meditation tradition. He was born in 1870 in a village in Ubon and first ordained at age fifteen in his home village. After having disrobed, he was re-ordained as a monk in 1892 at Wat Sii Thong in Ubon; his preceptor was Orn (Taylor 1993, 75–77).

The Thammayut temples were always significantly fewer in number than the Mahanikai temples, but their links to the court in Bangkok and the elite — both Siamese administrators and local aristocrats — in their local regions gave them significant influence.[26] Indeed, Taylor suggests that "in fact the efforts of the Thammayut's missionary scholar-monks would not have been possible, given local resentment, without the backing of the Bangkok-appointed civil officials in northeastern monthon" (1993, 66).[27] Local Mahanikai monks "were understandably upset by this inequitable situation." Taylor describes hostilities between monks in Ubon at Wat Supat and those of Mahanikai's Wat Paa Noi:

"When the two lines of monks passed each other on morning alms, after the front senior monks had passed, the rest of the line consisting of junior monks and novices would sometimes brawl" (1993, 69).

However, another factor facilitating the growth of Thammayut influence was the fact that many of the monks were themselves northeasterners. Taylor summarizes the process this way: "Because educational and administrative reforms involved both the Thammayut and the civil administrators, reform monks were seen as part of the same hegemonic process of domestication over Lao-speaking lands. Yet these particular reform monks, in contrast to the new civil administrators, were themselves northeasterners, educated in the Siamese capital. . . . For the ambitious provincial boys, the sangha was the most accessible means to attain social mobility in the new Siamese bureaucracy" (1993, 67).

Although the northeastern Thammayut monks do not seem to have participated in recitations of the *Vessantara Jataka*, they do not seem to have been necessarily hostile to the tradition. Thus, Ubalii, in his report for Monthon Isan, finds that the preferred popular religious practices did not conform to doctrinal traditions, explicitly noting that villagers still preferred to spend their time listening to the Mahachat. Nonetheless, Ajarn Man evidently considered that the *Vessantara Jataka* supported basic human ideals worthy of emulation—namely, giving, maintaining precepts, and developing the mind (Taylor 1993, 74). Although Man appears to have shared the Thammayut disdain for many indigenous religious practices, it is interesting that his sparse biography does mention that in his youth, Man enjoyed the verbal repartee of *morlam*. Apparently, Ubalii even came to Man's rescue when he was losing a verbal exchange with a local girl. As Taylor explains, "*Morlam* is a context in improvised rhyming, frequently enacting male-female conflicts in which a battle of wits can become quite febrile and excitable. In *Morlam* much use is made of word play, riddles, puns, innuendoes, and the use of metaphors" (1993, 76). The rhetorical style that Man developed in morlam apparently carried over to his mode of teaching. As Taylor writes, Man "would often instruct his pupils in extemporaneous puns and rhymes, an old Thai-Lao discursive style rarely heard today and indicative of a sharp and subtle mind" (1993, 76).

Expansion of Provincial Education

Although plans for public education can be traced to 1875 (Wyatt 1969, 116), the Ministry of Education was first formed in 1887 (Wyatt 1969, 114). Prince Damrong, then minister of education, sought to establish government-supported schools, but there was little initial interest beyond Bangkok. Upon his return from Europe in 1897, Chulalongkorn was intent on developing public education. He was extremely frustrated with the slow pace of the Education Department (Wyatt 1969, 205-15). Of the 30,000 boys of school age in Bangkok alone, only 3,468 were enrolled in the modernized government and religious schools of Prince Vajiranana (Wyatt 1969, 209). Outside of Bangkok, out of a male school age population of some 450,000 boys, 28,000 boys were receiving a traditional-style education in the monasteries and only 1,364 were attending modern-style schools (Wyatt 1969, 210-11). The government faced dual challenges: a lack of financial resources and a lack of trained teachers. The latter problem could be solved by encouraging monks to be the teachers of the villages in the outer provinces. At the instigation of King Chulalongkorn, Prince Damrong and Prince Vajiranana presented a proposal to "get rid of the idea that monasteries have only a religious function, and consider all monasteries as schools" (Wyatt 1969, 221).

The decree on the organization of provincial education was promulgated in 1898. Prince Damrong, who was then minister of the interior, and Prince Vajiranana, then abbot of Wat Bowonniwet and head of the Thammayut sect, worked together to expand public education in the provinces by setting up schools in the some 12,000 monasteries that existed throughout the kingdom (Wyatt 1969, 233-35). Although all monasteries were to be made places of study, at least one school supported by government funds would be established in every province (Wyatt 1969, 237). Local monks who were interested would be sent to Mahamakut Academy in Bangkok for further training (Wyatt 1969, 237). Funds were to be provided to Mahamakut Academy for the compilation and publication of textbooks, for the training of teacher-monks, and for administrative expenses. Furthermore, a corps of high-ranking monks was established whose duties were to serve as education and religion directors (*phuuamnuaikaan*) in each monthon; they were to travel each dry season in their provinces and meet annually in Bangkok (Wyatt 1969, 237).

Recognizing that much of the success of this plan would depend on the quality of these educational directors, Prince Vajiranana sought to nominate monks with local knowledge and family connections in the provinces to which they were sent. Wyatt describes their instructions as follows:

> The directors were enjoined to travel in their provinces with local ecclesiastical dignitaries, where these had been appointed, so as not to appear to be ignoring established hierarchical relationships. They were to inspect all monasteries for consideration as sites for government schools, assessing the strength and weaknesses of each in terms of its location, relative popularity, and availability to draw upon local support, and the availability of monks teaching or capable of

teaching to modern standards.... To monks and monasteries they were to distribute the Rapid Readers and religious books.... Finally, the provincial directors were to select young monks in the provinces for training as teachers in Bangkok, so that they might "become teachers who will work to follow the plans which have been made to support the extension of religion in the provinces in the future." (1967, 239)

These directors left Bangkok in January 1899, surveying eleven monthons in the central region (Wyatt 1967, 242-43). Their efforts resulted in the establishment of 177 new schools in provincial temples by the end of the first year, having successfully persuaded 177 provincial abbots to agree to "using government textbooks and submitting to regular examinations and inspection by the director and his designated local subordinates" (Wyatt 1967, 246).

The next year (1899-1900) it was decided to send education directors to four additional monthons. In addition to Phuket in the south, the other three monthons were in the northeast, namely, Isan (Ubon), Nakhon Ratchasima (Khorat), and Burapha (western Cambodia) (Wyatt 1967, 249). The Monthon Isan director (Ubalii) had already established a flourishing Pali school in Ubon in 1897 with two Pali teachers and three Thai teachers that had attracted 205 students in its first year; consequently, in 1899 Ubon was designated as a special center for Pali and religious studies (Wyatt 1967, 248). In 1899/1900 the annual Mahamakut Academy examination was held in four central provinces and taken by 988 students; examinations were taken by an additional seventy-one students in Ubon (Wyatt 1967, 254).[28] The directors also chose thirty-eight provincial monks and novices who were sent to Bangkok for teacher training, four of whom came from Monthon Isan and the remainder of whom were from the central region (Wyatt 1967, 253).[29] Some sense of this overall impact can be gained from the rapid explosion in the number of students attending these new schools. In 1898 there were 790 students; by 1900/1901 there were 12,062.

The effort to establish provincial education was facilitated by the 1902 Sangha Act. As David Wyatt noted, the 1898 educational reform was a "double-edged revolutionary sword," one "bringing the monkhood under government control along with the schools in which they taught" (1969, 238). The 1902 Sangha law required that the abbot of every monastery be responsible for making certain that all boys committed to his charge be instructed. Furthermore, it specified that it was the duty of the ecclesiastical hierarchy at each level "to inspect and support religious and secular instruction in the monasteries under his jurisdiction" (Wyatt 1967, 304, 330). However, this educational initiative did not include the northern Monthon Phayab or the northeastern Monthon

228 • *Part II: The Politics of Diversity*

Udon, "where special problems of language and ecclesiastical control prevented rapid action" (Wyatt 1967, 249, 305). The Sangha law was not applied to Monthon Udon until 1908 and to the north until 1924 (Wyatt 1967, 329).

Bangkok's Efforts to Penetrate the North

The Bangkok court was able to exert growing control over the sangha and the populace in the central and northeastern regions, both through the growth of the Thammayut order and by the establishment of public schooling within

Figure 16. Statue of Khruubaa Srivichai. Wat Huarin, Tambon Tungsatok, Amphur Sanpatong, Chiang Mai, July, 2011. Photo by author.

temples. But unlike in the central and northeastern regions, the Thammayut order had little initial influence in the north. Consequently, northern monks maintained their own Buddhist practices longer. In this section, I will provide evidence suggesting that the northern sangha maintained a much greater degree of independence from the Lanna courts, being oriented more toward the peasantry than toward the ruling elites. Although the Bangkok court sought to establish a presence in the northern sangha in the early twentieth century, its efforts failed, instead provoking a strong northern irredentist movement centered on Khruubaa Srivichai.

The Practice of Northern Thai Buddhism

Unlike northeastern Thailand, the Lanna kingdoms of northern Thailand were classified as self-governing tributaries of the Bangkok court and maintained much of their independence until the late nineteenth century. The history of the Lanna kingdoms was more closely entwined with kingdoms in Burma than those of Siam. With brief exceptions, from 1558, when Chiang Mai was first conquered by King Bayinnaung (1551–81), to the final revolt in 1774, the Lanna kingdoms came primarily under Burmese rule.[30] Very little has been written speculating on Burmese influence on Lanna practices of Buddhism; however, Colquhoun writes of his visit to Chiang Mai, "Their religion is the Buddhism of Ava, and almost all the *zedi*, or pagodas, both in and out of the town, were erected by the Burmese while they held the place" (1885, 138). For whatever reasons, Buddhism appeared to be flourishing in the northern region during the nineteenth century. As Colquhoun writes, the city "is a perfect nest of *poongyees*, or Buddhist monks: I should think there must be at least five hundred of them inhabiting the seventy-five monasteries in the town" (1885, 138).

In addition to its own sangharaja (supreme patriarch), the Lanna sangha appears to have had a senior council of monks. Certainly by the later nineteenth century, the Chiang Mai sangha was governed by a Council of Seven, comprised of seven senior monks and headed by a sangharaja (Pranii [1964] 1995, 180). Senior monastic officials in the court cities likely had strong links to monks in the countryside. Many ceremonies involved the participation of monks from more than one temple, as is evidenced in the *Chiang Mai Chronicle* (Wyatt and Aroonrut 1995) and in the practice that continued into the twentieth century of village networks working together for large ceremonial occasions such as *boi luang*. Also, literacy was high and temples were the primary source of education. As Dr. Richardson writes of the Lanna population in the early nineteenth century, "they can nearly all read and write" (Farrington 2004, 43; see also Bock [1884] 1986, 187; Colquhoun 1885, 232). The longtime missionary Daniel

McGilvary clearly held northern monks and former monks in high regard, describing them as "among the best educated men in the country" (1912, 414).

Evidence suggests that the Lanna sangha maintained a certain degree of independence from secular power. Whereas in Siam the selection of the sangharaja appears to have been primarily at the discretion of the king, in the Lanna kingdoms the sangha itself appears to have determined the choice. Richardson writes of his visit in 1834 that the sangharaja "has been raised by the votes of his priests for his piety and strict observance of the precepts of the Boodh" (Farrington 2004, 75). The balance of power between court and sangha in the Lanna kingdoms was made explicit during the investiture of the sangharaja. Richardson provides a description of the investiture of the sangharaja in 1834: "The Chow before investing him with the high office asks him if he will obey his lawful orders, which being answered in the affirmative, he makes over to him all authority over all ranks of the priesthood. The high priest then asks the Tsoboa if he will listen to his intercession in favor of criminals condemned to death when it shall appear to him the punishment is too severe for the offence, to which he assents" (Farrington 2004, 75; see also Colquhoun 1885, 151–52).

The right to intervene on behalf of the population does not seem to have been limited to the sangharaja alone but was a right utilized by all monks. Various villagers that I talked to in northern Thailand had heard of the custom of *binthabatr chiwit*, the request to spare a person's life phrased as a form of almsgiving. Although I and many others whom I have asked have never heard of this monastic right to intervene in executions in Siam, the practice was evidently known in Burma (Spiro 1970, 380; for related examples in Chieng Tung and Monay, see Grabowsky and Turton 2003, 401, 506–7).[31] Relevant for our consideration of the *Vessantara Jataka*, Lanna *tamnan* tell of great rewards for properly performed donations; they also tell of tragedy and death befalling kings who disobeyed monks. As Angela Chiu concludes from her analysis, these texts were important ways that monks were able to assert their power and control their relationship to the monarchy and to Buddhism (Chiu 2012).

Beholden to Populace

Rather than the court controlling the sangha, in the Lanna region it was the monks who exercised their moral authority to assert their influence on the court. The region's political independence went so far that monks were leading revolts and deposing kings. The *Chiang Mai Chronicle* suggests the role of several monks in resisting the Burmese (e.g., Wyatt and Aroonrut 1995, 132–39). McCarthy even mentioned a man in Muang Fang who was starting a new religion, "the chief tenet of which was that the people should not respect the princes" (1900, 127). Also contributing to the independence of the Lanna monkhood from state authority was the widespread practice that parents "select the monk by whom they wish their son to be taught" (Hallett 1890, 304; see also Bock [1884] 1986, 204).[32] The separation between state and monastic order is also reflected in the fact that monks and novices could not be conscripted to perform corvée labor or serve in the military, an issue that would take on growing importance when Bangkok tried to introduce military conscription in the north (Bowie 2014a).

The central Thai court gained its foothold into the Lanna kingdoms when King Taksin provided military assistance to the Lanna rulers in their effort to oust the Burmese. From the perspective of Bangkok, the Lanna leaders were rulers of tributary states; however, the Lanna rulers regarded themselves as independent. Geographically the northern regions were relatively inaccessible to Bangkok, the trip between Chiang Mai and Bangkok by boat or elephant taking anywhere from six weeks to three months (Schomburgk 1863, 387; McGilvary 1912, 63, 71, 77). Well into the twentieth century the prevailing currency of northern Thailand was not the Thai baht but the rupee, reflecting the region's close relations with Burma. Linguistic barriers further impeded communication: the northern Thai kingdoms had their own distinctive dialect and written script (e.g., Schomburgk 1863, 392).

Over the course of the nineteenth century, following the British victories in Burma, Bangkok felt increasing pressure to bring the Lanna region under direct control. With conflicts over teak concessions mounting, Bangkok negotiated a treaty with the British in 1873 setting up an international court in Chiang Mai. Siam then appointed a royal commissioner, together with about seventy soldiers, clerks, lawyers, and interpreters, to oversee the court. However, relations between the Siamese commissioners and the Lanna rulers remained fraught. During Inthawarorot's reign (r. 1901–9), Bangkok began the process of undermining the independent power base of the northern rulers, putting them on salary and implementing increasingly direct administrative control (Sarassawadee 2005, 142). The central Thai initiative to gain control of the northern sangha took two intertwined forms: one was to establish a Thammayut presence and the second was to gain control of the Lanna monastic hierarchy. Neither effort went smoothly.

Chiang Mai:
Khruubaa Sophaa versus Tu Ping

Bangkok's first steps toward gaining control over the Lanna sangha met with near disaster. In 1884 Prince Phichit Prichakorn, while serving as Siamese commissioner to Chiang Mai, sent a young novice to study at Wat Bowonniwet, the Thammayut temple in Bangkok, under the tutelage of Prince Vajiranana. The novice, later known as Tu Ping, was born in Tambon Luang Nya in Doi Saket district and had been studying as a novice at Wat Hua Khuang in Chiang Mai. Supported by Phichit Prichakorn, Ping excelled at his studies and passed the Parien 5 level; he was given his formal title Phra Naphisiphisanukhun. He returned to the north circa 1895, with the assignment to organize the Lanna sangha.[33] Upon his return, he resided at Wat Jedi Luang (also called Wat Hoh Tham), a very important temple in the center of Chiang Mai, under the patronage of Chiang Mai's aristocracy.[34] As William Dodd notes, "the Siamese officials through him attempted to institute a reform in Chiengmai" (1923, 319).

However, Tu Ping met with considerable resistance, led by Chiang Mai's sangharaja. The sangharaja at the time was the abbot of Wat Fai Hin in Chiang Mai, Khruubaa Sophaa (1832-1915). Sophaa was widely respected for his preaching abilities and was also believed to be able to predict the future; he was often consulted by the ruling lords of Chiang Mai for advice (Pranii [1964] 1995, 182). He became sangharaja circa 1895.[35] According to Pranii Sirithorn na Pathalung's account, the conflict was less about doctrine than it was about etiquette. It seems that Tu Ping never bothered to visit Sophaa; he was similarly disrespectful of the other senior monks in the Council of Seven, each of whom had large followings among both monks and laity. Wanting to convene a meeting of senior monks to invite them to join the Thammayut order, Tu Ping summoned them to his temple. This action was seen as arrogant, and none of the senior monks attended. As one monk I interviewed summarized the story, the king in Bangkok invited all the temples to convert to Thammayut, but while monks in Ubon and Udon agreed, Sophaa and all the other northern monks refused (SKP-231).

Tu Ping's possible breach of etiquette aside, the question remains what underlying issue aroused such opposition in the northern sangha. It may have been that Sophaa was concerned less about the specifics of Thammayut practice and more about Bangkok's encroachment on the political independence of the northern sangha. By all accounts, Sophaa was extremely resistant to Siamese pressure. Sophaa refused to preach in central Thai and viewed becoming Thammayut as submitting to the authority of Bangkok. As Khruubaa Laa phrased it, "Why become their slaves?" (*ben khaa khao thammai*) (SKP-231; see also Pranii [1964] 1995; Ratanaporn 2010). Sophaa's name came up often among villagers I interviewed in the 1980s. He was known for being strict in his practice of Buddhism and for not being afraid to stand up to secular authorities.

He was particularly remembered for his stance on military conscription. As one villager, himself a former monk, in San Sai explained, "If one wanted to avoid the draft, one became a novice and fled to be with the abbot of Wat Fai Hin. He wouldn't let his novices be drafted. He would accuse the draft officials of having no respect for the religion. Monks had more freedom and more power then. They were more respected" (SS-521). Sophaa's outrage at Siamese efforts to draft monks and novices into the military was manifested in a famous vignette in which he stormed over to the residence of the Siamese commissioner and, in a booming voice, did not hesitate to voice his anger (for details, see Pranii [1964] 1995, 187; Bowie 2014b).[36] A similar Thammayut reform initiative was no more successful in Chiang Rai (see Dodd 1923, 318).

A consideration of the sheer number of monks and novices in the north compared to the northeast helps to shed light on the difference in the amount of control Bangkok was able to exercise in the northeast versus the north at the turn of the twentieth century. Of the 13,164 temples listed in Thailand in 1908, Udon had 1,322 and Isan (Ubon) had 2,630 under ever-closer Bangkok control; by contrast, Phayab had 2,614 temples that remained relatively independent of Bangkok control (Wyatt 1967, 335). Of Thailand's total population of 94,854 monks listed in 1908, Isan had 13,668 monks and Udon had 5,311 monks who were under ever-closer control; by contrast Phayab had 12,039 monks who remained relatively independent. Of a combined total of 155,726 novices and temple boys listed in 1908, by far the greatest number were to be found in Monthon Phayab, 32,445. By comparison, Isan had 19,706. Monthon Phayab had an average of approximately 4.61 monks per temple and 12.41 novices and temple boys. Monthon Isan had approximately 5.20 monks per temple and 7.49 novices and temple boys. The national average was 7.21 monks per temple and 11 novices and temple boys per temple. Bangkok had 14.46 monks per temple and 17.88 novices or temple boys per temple. Thus Phayab had a significantly larger number of novices per monk, which might further explain the importance of using humor as a way to teach the novices and temple boys (and the many funny stories about problems in the relationships between monks and novices). Unlike today, individual temples would not have had much difficulty in finding enough monks and novices to recite texts. However, Bangkok would have had little influence on the 12,039 monks and the 32,445 novices and temple boys in Monthon Phayab, whereas it would have been in a position to influence the monks, novices, and temple boys in Monthon Isan (Ubon), and after 1908, also in Monthon Udon (see Wyatt 1967, 335, for table; see also Tambiah 1976 for figures for 1968).

Increasing Control

Although the Bangkok court failed to change Lanna sangha practices, these early efforts did succeed in gaining a modicum of increased administrative control. After his failed overture in Chiang Mai, Tu Ping wrote a letter to Prince Vajiranana in Bangkok, complaining that Sophaa was obstructing his efforts. As a result, in 1905 Sophaa was summoned to Bangkok. Although this news caused great consternation throughout Chiang Mai, Sophaa decided to make the trip. Traveling by boat with his entourage, he stayed at Wat Pho in Bangkok after his arrival. Chao Dara, the daughter of Chiang Mai's ruler and one of King Chulalongkorn's senior wives, visited Sophaa there and learned of Tu Ping's disrespectful behavior. The king and the head of the Siamese sangha, Prince Vajiranana, were informed of the problems. Sophaa and the Lanna monks met with both the king and Prince Vajiranana. King Chulalongkorn expressed his pleasure at being able to meet Sophaa, even holding Sophaa's hand as he escorted him to his seat (Pranii [1964] 1995, 186). At this meeting, King Chulalongkorn asked Sophaa for his assistance in developing the country. Sophaa was promoted to a new title of Phra Aphaisaratha Sangkhapamok, head of the Chiang Mai provincial sangha (*chaokhana cangwat*). The crisis was averted, but it succeeded in bringing the existing Lanna monastic order nominally under Bangkok's jurisdiction by issuing, in effect, dual titles.

In consultation with Sophaa, Prince Vajiranana decided to send Phra Thamworodom (Chai; he later became Phra Wanarat), the abbot of Wat Benchamabophit, to help organize the Lanna sangha. In 1924 the 1902 Sangha Act went into effect in the north, thereby formally bringing the northern sangha into the national sangha hierarchy (Wyatt 1969, 329). In 1928 another attempt to establish a Thammayut presence took place when Phra Ubalii was sent to become the abbot of Wat Jedi Luang (Taylor 1993, 85). Phra Ubalii then invited the famous northeastern Thammayut meditation monk, Ajarn Man, to come to Chiang Mai "to teach meditation and monastic discipline to Chiang Mai monks" (Taylor 1993, 86). However, this initiative also met with little success. In 1932 Ubalii became ill and returned to Wat Bowonniwet (he died shortly after his return). Ajarn Man then became abbot of Wat Jedi Luang, with the prince of Chiang Mai as his official patron (Taylor 1993, 86). However, Ajarn Man's preference for wandering and his dislike for administrative duties led to a very short tenure as abbot (Taylor 1993, 87). Although Ajarn Man remained in northern Thailand for a total of eleven years from 1929 to 1940, he had little impact. He was described contemptuously as "the old 'vagabond' monk" (Taylor 1993, 87). He ordained one monk at Wat Jedi Luang, who was "far from impressive" (*mai dai ryang*) (Taylor 1993, 107n13).³⁷ No more successful was an initiative in Lamphun where a former abbot had apparently been impressed by the wandering Thammayut monks and invited Thet Thetsarangsii, a one-time disciple of Man, to serve as abbot. But Thet only remained for one Lent and then returned to the northeast. To this day, the Thammayut order has only a minimal presence in the north. However, the reality was more complex.

Bangkok imposed two major policy changes that had serious consequences for the everyday lives of villagers: the capitation tax and military conscription.³⁸ Whereas villagers in the past had owed tribute and corvée labor to the ruling northern lords, the Capitation Act stipulated that adult males between the ages of eighteen and sixty were to pay 4 baht annually. Instituted after 1900, the capitation tax provided dramatic increases in revenue for the central Thai court.³⁹ This revenue enabled the central Thai administration to place members of the northern ruling families on monthly retainers, thereby deftly depriving them of their former powers (*BTWM*, May 10, 1902; Sarassawadee 2005, 228). Each village headman was "to keep a correct list of all males in his district" (*BTWM*, January 28, 1902). Monks, novices, village headmen, government officials, and "all of royal descent" were among those who were exempt (*BTWM*, January 28, 1902). Villagers who were unable to pay the annual head tax were expected to contribute labor for state projects for up to one month.⁴⁰

The imposition of the head tax provoked profound resentment among villagers, and this in turn contributed to the Shan uprising in 1902 (*BTWM*, October 14, 1902). Men who failed to pay their taxes or perform state labor were subject to arrest. Newspaper accounts in Bangkok report police making "hundreds of arrests" in a single day (*BTWM*, August 2, 1911; also August 5, 1911; August 3, 1912; August 7, 1912). The impact of this policy in northern Thailand was likely even more dramatic because Monthon Phayab "had more people conscripted for public works than any other monthon in Siam" (Sarassawadee 2005, 230). Elderly villagers I interviewed in the 1980s regularly mentioned being arrested and ordered to perform public labor, many of them working on road construction and the train tunnel near Lampang. Although the head tax was supposed to replace the former corvée labor and tribute paid to the northern lords, in many cases it was simply an addition. Labor in lieu of the head tax, traditional corvée labor, and "voluntary" labor for the benefit of the community were easily conflated. Thus a district officer in Phrae is reported as "pursuing the rather ancient custom of requiring of the people labour, timber, thatch, rattan, rice, etc., without remuneration" (*BTWM*, August 24, 1918).⁴¹ Noting that such labor was a "great source of discontent" in the north, an editorial adds, "the actual work is the unpaid labour of people who have already done more than the amount of Government work required by Siamese law" (*BTWM*, May 10, 1902). One account of a "cleaning bee" in Chiang Rai in 1917 describes "an average of 400 to 500 workmen" who were "working daily on streets, ditches, culverts, etc." (*BTWM*, September 25, 1917). The extraction of labor would likely have intensified over the decade as officials sought to press the "development" of their jurisdictions with the construction of various new government buildings and roads.

Rather than bring the Lanna sangha and populace under Siamese control, Siamese efforts had the opposite effect, generating intense resistance. Not only did the Lanna sangha resist the incursions of the Siamese Thammayut order; it resisted the encroachments of the secular state. The widespread resentment being catalyzed by Siamese administrative changes became centered on a monk called Khruubaa Srivichai (1878-1939). Known today as a "Buddhist saint," he remains the most famous monk in northern Thailand, but during his lifetime, Srivichai provoked tremendous controversy.[42] He was detained under multiple protracted temple arrests in Lamphun, Chiang Mai, and Bangkok; forced to surrender his administrative positions as abbot and subdistrict head; and sent under police guard to Bangkok for investigation in 1920 and 1935-36.

Elsewhere I have argued that Srivichai's conflict originated with secular authorities as a result of the implementation of two new interrelated regulations, namely the Ordination Act of 1913 and the Military Conscription Act of 1905, which went into effect in Monthon Phayab in April 1914.[43] The Ordination Act increased state supervision of not only who could conduct ordinations but also who could be ordained. The Military Conscription Act affected the exemptions of the monastic community. Each act increased state control over the monastic community and therefore over access to manpower, thus marking a dramatic shift in the former balance between state, sangha, and laity in northern Thailand. In his refusal to recognize secular authority to conscript monks and otherwise regulate the sangha, Srivichai was simultaneously defending the traditional independence of the northern sangha and de facto protecting the right of the population to ordain. Srivichai generated impassioned support among the populace. A 1920 newspaper correspondent avowed that Srivichai had the support of "80 per cent of the people" (*BTWM*, June 7, 1920). The Bangkok ecclesiastical officials assigned to investigate the charges against Srivichai basically absolved Srivichai of further punishment, even finding in his favor on some of the charges.[44] Upon his return to the north, Srivichai went on to build or restore well over one hundred temples throughout the region, developing a wide network of followers among the monks and laity alike.

However, for reasons that remain unclear, Srivichai again came into conflict with Siamese authorities and was again summoned for investigation in Bangkok. By the time of his second trip to Bangkok in November 1935, conflicts in the north had become so intense that "the independent monks of the north had openly severed connections with their ecclesiastical superiors and declared Phra Sri Vijaya to be their leader" (Thompson [1941] 1967, 642). Pressured by fear over Srivichai's safety, over four hundred monks and novices residing in some sixty northern temples left the order, some disrobing "voluntarily" in protest and some forced to disrobe by police (e.g., Sangaa 1956, 260–82; Faa 1976–77; Sommai 2002, 40). The overt crisis was resolved in May 1936 when Srivichai signed an agreement to abide by the national sangha regulations. Only then was he allowed to return to the north, where a crowd of "more than eight thousand people" welcomed him back (Thompson [1941] 1967, 643).

In the context of the earlier northern sangha, which had a history of political and economic independence from court control, it is not surprising that monks were primarily oriented toward the peasantry who provided its foundation of support. Considering the negative attitudes villagers had toward the lords (as discussed in chapter 4), it is also not surprising that village monks would have shared many of the attitudes of their fellow villagers and lived in the relative freedom that village temples would have provided them. However, the moment when Srivichai signed this statement marks the end of the independence of the northern sangha.

The Demise of the *Vessantara Jataka* in Northern Thailand

The later half of the twentieth century appears to have seen major changes in the frequency of recitations of the *Vessantara Jataka*, with major declines in both the central and northern regions. In chapter 1, I suggested that the decline in the central region was likely due to two major factors: the decline of humor and the impact of 1932, when many members of the aristocracy found themselves in exile or otherwise facing financial difficulties. Humor survived most intact in the north, but performances today are rare. According to Manee Phayomyong (1986, 2, 26–27), some fifty years ago the Tang Tham Luang was the most important ceremony among the northern Thai. Davis suggests that as late as the 1960s every temple performed the *Vessantara Jataka* in the course of the Full Moon Festival (Dyan Yii Paeng) in November (Davis 1984, 218); his view is supported by Konrad Kingshill (1976, 274). However, John Ferguson and Shalardchai Ramitanondh suggest that the full Tang Tham Luang recitations of the *Vessantara Jataka* "reached the peak of its popularity before the last World War" (1976, 131). Sommai Premchit and Amphay Dore also note its decline, writing "the *tang tham luang* in Northern Thailand as performed today is not as popular as in the past" (1992, 85).[45] Bonnie Brereton also notes, "The importance of this festival in the north has declined dramatically in the past three decades. The recitation of the Maha Chat at the Tang Tham Luang festival now is held at only a handful of wats in the north" (1995, 83; see also Swearer 1978, 3). Interviews I conducted confirmed this pattern.

If the independence of the northern sangha allowed the trickster Jujaka to continue his comic escapades well into the twentieth century, why then did recitations decline in the north but remain vibrant in the northeast? Northern Thai monks and villagers pointed to four main issues in explaining the overall decline of *Vessantara Jataka* recitations in their region: the financial expenses involved, the labor commitment, the impact of secular education, and competition from the secular world. However, I do not find these arguments particularly compelling since the same arguments can be made for the northeast.

Although monetary costs related to these recitations vary, some insight can be gained from a look at the budget of a northern tambon council in 2009. The council members anticipated expenses totaling 100,000 baht, which included 20,000 baht for offerings of 1,000 baht per monk to recite a total of twenty chapters; 8,000 baht for the khao wongkot maze; 25,000 baht for five meals for an anticipated audience of five hundred people; 10,000 for sound system rental; and 10,000 baht for the rental of a wooden elephant and other parade expenses. The remainder was budgeted for decorating the temple (22,000 baht) and advertising (5,000 baht). The development of a parade in which members of the royal family ride on either actual or wooden elephants is a new addition that appears likely to have been copied from northeastern Thailand (monks and villagers had no recollections of such parades in earlier decades). The wood or bamboo for the mazes now must be bought. The parade, sound system, and advertising expenses are new. However, expenses in the northeast are similar, historically raised by contributions from individual households.

The labor involved in preparations for a Tang Tham Luang were significant. Historically the wood or bamboo for the maze had to be collected from the forest, but today designing and building the maze remains time-consuming. Also particularly time-consuming is the production of myriad lengths of string, particularly given that the string is supposed to be hand spun. Nowadays with so many villagers no longer farming but instead working in construction, factories, the service sector, and also a range of other jobs, it is difficult to find people with free time on their hands. Already so many of the village festivals are finding hosts hiring caterers to provide food that in the past would have been prepared by villagers themselves. However, the preparations in the northeast are similarly time-consuming.

A third factor northerners mentioned is the radical impact of secular education on the monastic community. In the past, village youth were educated in the temples.[46] Today, nearly all children receive a secular education in public schools. With fewer youth spending their childhoods in the temples, the wonderful stories of the foibles of monks and novices no longer resonate with most of the population. Furthermore, with fewer northern boys entering the monastery for an education, there are fewer monks and novices to learn, let alone perform, the traditional texts such as the *Vessantara Jataka*. In the past, monks and novices were educated in the northern Thai script, but the central Thai government banned the script's use. Consequently very few monks and novices can read text written in the northern Thai script. Recent years have seen a resurgence of interest in learning the Lanna script, but that is not the same as wanting to apprentice to a tujok monk to learn how to perform the key chapters of the *Vessantara Jataka*. The northern dialect has undergone significant changes with the growing influence of central Thai, which is taught in schools and spoken on television. Many of the northern Thai words have become archaic and many in the younger generation can no longer understand their meanings. Monks involved in the *Vessantara Jataka* recitations would frequently substitute modern words into the original text, but the rhyming patterns suffered. The original texts came to be viewed as increasingly archaic. Fewer and fewer people understood the words; the text became increasingly less funny.[47] The fourth factor is that with television, movie theaters, malls, and the Internet increasingly occupying leisure time, fewer young people are seeking to spend time in the temples listening to monks. However, each of these reasons also holds for northeastern Thailand.

Two more compelling factors are the growing official condemnation of humor and the devastating impact of the forced disrobings of hundreds of monks and novices in 1936. Both Luang Poh Bunthong and Manee pointed to the role of the central sangha administration and its condemnation of humor. As Manee explained, "the National Ecclesiastical Council (*Mahatherasamakhom*) in Bangkok forbad this practice all over the country, in about BE 2480 [1937], when they issued various monastic reforms. They felt monks should be well behaved [*riaprooj*] and that it was not appropriate for monks to be performing comedic roles."[48] In 1937 the Ecclesiastical Council issued a regulation that specifically forbad additions and humor in recitations of the *Vessantara Jataka*:

Lately the thet maha chat has become a comic affair because the reciter brings in new material which is not part of the original text, and changes the *thamnorng* into a racy tune (*lot phon*). Sometimes the reciter only starts with a little of the text from the maha chat and then just sings various kinds of *lae*. The reciter behaves comically which is damaging to monastic dignity.... The monastic council therefore unanimously decrees that reciting lae outside the maha chat which are raucous (*samrak*), obscene (*yap lon*), and which have a racy tune, as well as comic behaviour which is damaging to monastic dignity, is forbidden. (Jory 1996, 40)

The mass disrobings of hundreds of northern monks must have also been very traumatic. Although Srivichai himself was not known for reciting the *Vessantara Jataka*, many of the monks in his network were known for their skill in various chapters.[49] After Khruubaa Srivichai signed the statement in 1936 agreeing to abide by the regulations of the national sangha, northern monks either had to agree to submit to the national sangha or be forcibly disrobed. When the 1937 ruling condemning humor in performances of the *Vessantara Jataka* was issued, the remaining monks in the northern sangha were likely dispirited and disinclined to go against the national sangha.[50]

In contrast to the demoralized northern sangha, the northeastern sangha appears to have reached a detente with Bangkok much earlier, at least with regard to the Jujaka chapter. Northeasterners, given their shared experience as migrant workers, came to place more emphasis on the family reunion theme of the Nakornkan rather than the trickster comedy of the northern Jujaka chapter. As resistance to Bangkok was collapsing in the north, the communist guerrilla movement, facilitated by the strength of the Free Thai movement during World War II, was growing in the northeast.[51] Furthermore, northeasterners had a sense of greater ethnic cohesion than villagers in the northern region, who were more likely to have been war captives from different regions or from different ethnic groups (e.g., Keyes 1967, 12). Even when northeasterners were relocated, they appear to have maintained their own cultural traditions as a matter of ethnic pride or as political resistance. Lao war captives, relocated to a village in the Tron district of Uttaradit province, even named a street after Matsi and another after Jujaka. They named their temple Wat Kalingkaraat; they have also named a nearby mountain Matsi and another Khao Wongkot in the neighboring Thongsaenkhan District.[52] Thus it seems the northeast, be it out of defiance or pride in tradition, maintained its annual custom of Bun Phrawet. Frustrations with Bangkok were strong in each region, but the ability of northerners to organize resistance had been significantly weakened by the forcible disrobings of the northern sangha.

Further contributing to the decline of comedic jataka performances in the north was the growth of an urban middle class and a growing number of non-northerners in the region. Modern audiences evidently find the traditional humor too bawdy and risqué. Temples today are increasingly considered as serious sacred spaces and no longer as spaces where the sacral comic is engaged. As one tujok commented, "Chiang Mai has many non-locals from other provinces and foreigners. When they hear the Lanna monks, they may misunderstand us, dismissing us by saying, 'Oh the Lanna monks just sing *joi joi soh soh*, but they are not really preaching.' Since they may criticize [*tamni*] it, I have changed my preaching style. Outsiders don't understand the northern style. They might think Lanna monks are crazy [*phii baa*]."[53] This tujok monk stopped using the *joi joi soh soh* format over twenty years ago after he had encountered criticism from someone who had heard him performing. Even though many enjoyed the comic style exemplified in this witty courtship repartee, he felt that if one or two listeners had a bad reaction, he should reflect on this and change his style. As this tujok monk explained, "the point of this form is to reach listeners, not turn them off." A few years ago, he was invited to Bangkok to "chant in the northern style." He included some of the humorous verses he and other tujok recited about Jujaka's exploits but cut out the joi and soh of Jujaka's wedding to Amitataa for fear listeners from the other three regions would misunderstand. He explained, "One has to be careful when one does Chuchok; it is like a double-edged sword. Some words, if misunderstood, could result in criticism."[54]

The jataka still emerges in passing comments by older villagers. A villager who wants to criticize a boy's uncouth eating habits might say, "He eats like the brahmin" (*Ai nii kin yang phraam*) or point out that a protruding stomach "is just like the brahmin's" (*khiipum phraam tae, pum laam myan phraam thao*). Someone who is greedy might be accused of acting like the old Brahmin (*khiilop myan puu phraam*), referring to Jujaka. Alternatively, villagers might refer to someone as being "as kind-hearted or generous as Prince Vessantara" (*jaidii myan Phrayaa Wesantara*) (Manee 1976, 251; see also Prakong 1983, 5).[55]

However beloved tujok recitations may have been among previous generations of northerners, few among the younger generation have firsthand knowledge of the jataka or the tujok. When a close friend of mine died in November 2014, I offered to host a tujok performance at his funeral, both because this friend had taken me to meet the first tujok monk I ever interviewed and because his oldest brother had himself been a tujok monk. The lay leader of the temple, a man in his seventies, had heard of tujok but did not know how to contact one. With my assistance, he was able to arrange for a tujok to come. However, even before beginning to perform, the tujok offered an extended apology if the idea of a monk telling jokes offended anyone in the audience. He explained that he was doing this performance in response to a request from a foreign university professor.[56]

The rise of secular education, the growing presence of central Thais throughout the country, and a growing acceptance of Thammayut interpretations among the urban populations have contributed to a more formal practice of Buddhism. However, the changes may go even beyond disdain for the bawdy sexual and scatological humor. The political context has undergone a significant transformation following the establishment of a constitutional monarchy in 1932. As the Lanna aristocracy and the Siamese court were replaced by elected members of parliament and an ever-growing bureaucracy of government officials, the targets of political satire would have become more dissipated. Somehow a story mocking a district officer does not have the same edginess as one mocking a king. Increasingly over the course of the twentieth century, the political rhetoric—the dramatic surge in lèse majesté charges notwithstanding—shifted from one of serving the king to serving the people (see Bowie 2008b for an overview of changes in local administrative law). This radical political shift raises the question of whether the *Vessantara Jataka* is losing its relevance for the twenty-first century. Will Jujaka survive the transition from the era of feudalism to the era of global capitalism?

6

Jujaka as Deity
Rebirths under Global Capitalism

With its bawdy humor disdained and its political resonances buried, is the *Vessantara Jataka* doomed to fade into Thailand's feudal history, as evidently occurred in India, its country of origin? As this book has shown, performances have been declining in the central and northern regions. Even in northeastern villages, its performances have been abridged. However, lest we be overcome with nostalgia for feudal phantasmagoria, there are signs of its contemporary rebirths. Instead of receding onto temple walls as a passive backdrop for modern life, Jujaka is now becoming a growing presence in urban shops, temples, and homes—now not as ghoul, comedian, or trickster but as a money-making deity who can help the middle classes with the serious business of getting rich. The meaning of Jujaka is transmogrifying from the beggar embedded in a feudal story about generosity to a patron saint of capitalist acquisitiveness, from cruel villain to compassionate hero, from reviled ghost to revered deity, from devil to future Buddha. He is even following the routes taken by Thais and other Theravada Buddhists as they travel globally. Thus the twenty-first century is witnessing yet another series of Jujaka rebirths, with capitalism and the global political economy serving as midwives.[1] These transformations lend further substance to how in the context of a growing capitalist economy and proliferating mass media, "the processes of deification, mediation and commodification run riot, constantly creating new forms of religious practice" (Pattana 2012, 149).

In this chapter, divided into four sections, I summarize the ongoing patterns of change in performances and interpretations of the *Vessantara Jataka*. In the first three sections, I discuss the transformation of the story from its former roles (promoting dharma instruction, temple construction, village cooperation, and even national unity) into its new roles (serving the promotion of personal wealth, tourism, and cultural heritage, both locally and globally). In the final section, I will reflect on the jataka's appeal for women because they have long been its primary audience. Because the jataka's future may well lie with women, their responses to it warrant particular attention. With this discussion of female reception, I complete the alliterations with which I began this book, adding mothers to the list of the jataka's essential audiences: monarchs, monks, and masses.

Promotion of Personal Wealth

One sign of the *Vessantara Jataka*'s modern resurrection is the growing popularity of Jujaka worship, in the form of amulets, yantra cloths, and statues. The worship of Jujaka is particularly popular among people hoping to get rich, be it through business or the lottery. Amulets have long been hugely popular in Thailand. Although many amulets are intended for protection, others are believed to hold special powers. Arthid Sheravanichkul notes, "[the] popularity

Figure 17. Jujaka statues. Some of the more than four thousand figures of Jujaka at Jujaka House in Bangkok, July 2013. Photo by author.

of Jujaka amulets was phenomenal in Thailand in 2009-10" (2012b). Indeed, I first stumbled across these Jujaka amulets at the cattle market held weekly in Sanpatong district in Chiang Mai province in 2009. The vendors explained that because Jujaka was able to gain the Buddha's own children, a beautiful young wife, and everything else he wanted, his power would encourage money to flow toward the owner of this amulet. I acquired two, one about one inch in height made from dark wood (*mai duu dam*, which the vendor assured me was a scarce type of wood) for 400 baht and a bronze version for 100 baht.[2] My friends with shops in the district town told me that these amulets were not common among ordinary northern villagers but were becoming very popular with store owners who bought them to help with their businesses. Some men I talked with at a temple in Lampang in 2009 were also familiar with Jujaka amulets, even naming Wat Mai Pinkriaw, a central Thai temple in Nakhon Pathom, as a place that produces them. I also found them for sale together with magical penises (*palad khik*) in a religious store in Khon Kaen in northeastern Thailand and in the amulet stalls in Thaprachan market, adjoining Thammasat University in Bangkok.

Jujaka Amulets

The Jujaka amulet cult appears to have its origins and be most widespread in the central region. Although the nineteenth-century court text portrayed Jujaka as a frightening and evil figure, this cult provides evidence of popular counter-narratives in the region that portrayed Jujaka as a beneficent and even kind-hearted deity. Contributing to the argument that the worship of Jujaka is long-standing in the central region is the discovery of "old" wooden images of Jujaka and Amitataa at Wat Songtham, a Mon Temple in Phra Pradaeng district, Samutprakarn (Arthid 2012a). It is hard to date the origin of Jujaka amulet production. According to an amulet seller Tambiah interviewed, "since the old brahman was an evil person, monks will never sacralize his amulet by chanting. This is left to a lay expert" (1984, 226). However, other sources indicate that central Thai monks have long been involved in the sacralization of Jujaka amulets.

According to knowledgeable amulet dealers, the first monk believed to produce Jujaka amulets was Luang Puu Roht from Samut Sakorn, a province in central Thailand.[3] Of Mon heritage, he lived from 1863 to 1945. Believed to have mystical powers evidenced ultimately in his alleged ability to predict the day of his death, his Jujaka amulets sell for over 100,000 baht. His amulets were made using wood from the jackfruit tree; the Thai word for jackfruit is *mai khanun*, *nun* meaning "supportive." Jujaka amulets attributed to him include at least one carved wooden version portraying Jujaka and the two children. Luang Puu Thim Isariko (1879–1975) is another monk famous for his Jujaka amulets.[4] Thim resided at Wat Lahaanrai, Amphur Baan Khaai, in the central Thai province of Rayong. Thim was known for his invulnerability magic; many other central Thai monks establish their credentials by publicizing their links to him.[5] Ceremonies sacralizing the amulets today are drawing large crowds (see photos in Thosaphol 2010).

Advertised variously as helping with making money in business, winning the lottery, enjoying success at gambling, protecting travelers, or attracting romantic partners, Jujaka amulets are also marketed in the ever-popular amulet magazines and online. The credentials of the amulets are established either by advertising the lineage of the monk or by attesting to the "ancient" way the amulet was made. Magazines I viewed were selling amulets ranging from a few hundred baht to several thousand baht. Remarkably, these amulets are marketed not only in Thailand but also globally on English-language websites.

Most amulets are simply representations of an old man, bare-chested and hunched over, walking with a cane and a bag. Made variously of wood or metal, some are encased in transparent plastic cases so they can be worn around their owners' necks. One surprising amulet shows Jujaka copulating with a female deity. Described as being made from red magical powders ground from the bones of ninety-nine ghosts, the *payawan dokthong* flower (which only blooms once a year), *kumarn* (a fetus), earth from seven cemeteries, and seven giant termite nests, this amulet is advertised as "a wondrous thing, for indeed, even though Choo Chok [Jujaka] is Ugly, he can still ask for a pretty wife and get one when he asks." This amulet is also considered useful as a love charm and for gambling.[6] In addition to amulets, there are also Jujaka *yantra* cloths (cloths typically with a painting of Jujaka surrounded by magical formulas) of varying sizes and cloth money bags bearing yantras with Jujaka's image that have been sacralized in ceremonies performed by monks. One store's website includes a link to a YouTube video of monks chanting the mantra called "Choo Chok for Riches," with the moderator explaining that Jujaka is a "symbol of successful attainment of all possessions which one attempts."

The logic tying Jujaka to riches varies. One English-language advertisement explains that Jujaka is the "deity for accumulating Riches and good business sales" who can be worshiped at work or home, or "even folded in your pocket for travelling salesmen." Jujaka "functions as a bridge" to Vessantara: "Through Choo Chok we can call upon Prince Vessantara for his generosity and ask for things." The ad goes on to explain that the "lucky aura of Choo Chok enabled him to be able to ask for and obtain anything he wanted, even able to convince others to give away their own children. So Choo Chok can even ask to sit on the Throne of a King if he wants."[7] Other ads suggest that Jujaka became rich because he "looked after [the Buddha's] children for him."[8] Excerpts from the $126 Jujaka with Nine Wishes will serve as an illustration of the basic pattern:

> Choo Chok is a wealth attractor for both Businessmen, Merchants and especially good for travelling salesmen. . . . The fact that Choo Chok was able to even ask for somebody's children and get them, shows the immense attraction and power of Metta Mahaniyom [great compassion] which the beggar Choo Chok possesses. This is the reason why the Choo Chok Deity is such a powerful attractor of riches, because Choo Chok has a special Baramee [charisma] that allows even the least likely gifts to be given with the greatest of ease. Sales are made so easily with Choo Chok to help.[9]

In addition to Jujaka amulets, there are also amulets of Vessantara's two children, Kanhaa and Chalii. As Tambiah describes them, "these figures are joined together and are shown in a kneeling position showing obedience to their father. The implication is that the amulet owner will have control over servants and young subordinates" (1984, 226). These amulets are not as well known and are much harder to find, but they are believed to have power similar to that of Jujaka's as charms and good luck tokens. Because the two children helped their father become the Buddha in his next life, they can help with anything. According to one amulet dealer, the Kanhaa-Chalii amulet is believed to be stronger than the Jujaka amulets, and the two types cannot be kept together. If, for example, someone places a Jujaka amulet on the table with a Kanhaa-Chalii, the next morning Jujaka will have fallen from the table. Similarly, if both amulets are placed in the same bag, the Jujaka amulet will disappear. The most famous Kanhaa-Chalii amulets are from Wat Bangkhrai Nok in Nonthaburi; made by its abbot, Luang Poh Kloi, they date back to 1948.[10]

Jujaka House and Coyote Dancing

Another intriguing recent development is Jujaka House in Bangkok, widely known through media accounts as a place where coyote dancers perform erotic dance routines for several thousand Jujaka figures. Jujaka House is owned and run by a woman named Kemika na Songkla, now in her midforties. It began circa 2002, when Kemika was suffering from advanced kidney failure and was on dialysis. No longer able to walk and on death's doorstep, Kemika recalled a tiny figure of Jujaka (one centimeter tall) her maternal grandmother had given her when she was a child. Her grandmother had told her that if she ever had any problems, she should pray to Jujaka. So Kemika prayed to Jujaka for the impossible: a kidney transplant. She promised him that if he found her a donor, she would make him so famous he would end up in the Guinness Book of World Records. Out of the blue, her long-lost brother called her asking for a loan. When he learned how ill she was, he offered her one of his kidneys. After some six months on dialysis, she was able to have the much-needed operation.

Kemika views Jujaka as a father figure who takes care of her. Interestingly, she has nicknamed him "Jujaka with Large Testicles." Kemika is a former model whose primary business occupation is a type of massage to enhance women's breast size. She subsequently performed various additional tests of her amulet's power, asking him to help her attract more customers and win the lottery. All of her wishes came true. When Kemika won 50 million baht in the lottery, she gave Jujaka a million baht Rolex watch. When she had his image tattooed on the base of her neck, her neck pains disappeared. When she won the lottery again, she had her amulet carried in a procession through the streets from her house all the way to the National Lottery Office. She began acquiring more and more Jujaka amulets and figurines. She now has a collection of over four thousand Jujaka figurines, some coming from temples all over Thailand and others that she has commissioned. She has Jujaka statues representing days of the week, countries around the world, television and newspaper outlets that have visited her, and the like.

Word of her good fortune spread among her clientele. Coyote dancing for Jujaka came about after a customer won the lottery five times in a row. Typically when requesting a favor from a deity, many will make a vow of a return favor if their wish is granted (*kae bon*) (e.g., see Grow 1991). To repay Jujaka for making her wishes come true, and believing Jujaka to be an old man who likes young women, the customer had promised to arrange for some coyote dancers to perform for the old Brahmin. Based on the movie *Coyote Ugly*, which is in turn based upon a restaurant in New York called the Coyote Ugly Saloon, coyote dancing is a provocative dance with sexually explicit moves.[11] According to the rumors, when the dancers were first performing, a camera recorded the eyes of one of the Jujaka images widening. Coyote dancing has now become a regular feature. Kemika herself does not perform coyote dancing but instead takes Jujaka with her when she goes to make merit at Buddhist temples. When I visited Jujaka House, attendants told me that coyote dancers performed at least twice a month to this day; the attendants there keep several photo albums full of pictures of these various performances.

Figure 18. Coyote dancers at Jujaka House. Coyote dancers pay their respects to Jujaka before their performance. From photo album at Jujaka House in Bangkok, July 2013. Photo by author.

Jujaka Statuaries

Paralleling the growing popularity of Jujaka amulets is the increase in large statues of Jujaka in temples, often with placards providing the Pali words to be recited by his worshippers. In northern Thailand, the Mae Rim temple of Luang Poh Bunthong has nearly life-size statues of Jujaka holding Amitataa's hand, but the practice seems more common in the central region. Located in the central Thai province of Angthong, Wat Muang advertises itself as home not only to the reportedly tallest Buddha image in Thailand but also a series of colorful scenes of hell and a series of events in Jujaka's journey. Made out of concrete and painted in bright colors, the scenes include Jujaka holding Amitataa's hand, Jujaka stuck up a tree surrounded by barking dogs with Jetabutr ready to shoot his arrow, and Jujaka asking directions from Ajuta (Thosaphol 2010, 10-12). In Bangkok, a statue of Jujaka is worshipped at Wat Laksi.[12] Images are also found at Wat Bangphra (Nakhonchaisri district) in Nakhon Pathom, Wat Phanomyong in Ayutthaya, and Wat Amphawan (Bang Yai district) of Nonthaburi province (see Thosaphol 2010).

The most famous image of Jujaka is likely the life-size wood figure at Wat Mai Pinkriaw (in the city of Nakhon Pathom), now covered with gold leaf and garlands of flowers from its throngs of worshippers. The temple, founded over 150 years ago, appears to have a long-standing reputation for occult practices since it is reputed to have twin *kumarnthongs* (corpses of fetuses) that protect the temple and the abbot.[13] The image, called "Grandfather Jujaka Who Increases Wealth" (*Poh Puu Chuchok Phyymphuun Sap*), is on the Buddha's left. Next to the large Jujaka figure is a sign explaining how to worship Jujaka; it says worshippers should light five sticks of incense and repeat the following Pali mantra five times: "*ithi sukhato chanaasupho Chuchako sukhato iti.*"

The temple's abbot, Luang Poh Somphong Thirathammo, deputy head of the provincial sangha, is now probably the most famous of the monks currently sacralizing Jujaka amulets and yantra; his name came up repeatedly in interviews I conducted in the north and the northeast when I asked about Jujaka amulets. As part of the temple's modern publicity efforts, the abbot's grandson has produced a YouTube video describing the abbot and the temple's history, announcing the bank to which contributions should be sent and including an interview with the temple's abbot. As the video explains, Somphong was born in 1936 in Chainat province. Even as a child he was interested in magical formulas (*khaathaa*). Today he is known as a monk who is knowledgeable in Pali (having passed level 3 of the Pali examinations), in meditation, in astrology, and in magic formulas. In his interview, Somphong explains that he had a vision in which he saw Jujaka floating in the sky. Jujaka was beckoning with his hand (*kwak myy*) and then said to Somphong, "Tell me [*kuu*] what you want. Just give me three lengths of *khaolaam* [slightly sweet sticky rice steamed in bamboo, a specialty of Nakhon Pathom] and some liquor." Shortly thereafter a northeasterner passed by the temple with a carving of Jujaka that he believed was carved from the jackfruit tree (*mai khanun*).

The abbot then had the large carving of Jujaka made in wood with black lacquer. Thereafter Somphong began making Jujaka figurines, beginning about 1993. Initially there was little interest. When another temple in the province was having a sema stone consecration ceremony (*luuk nimit*) in 2004 during Chinese New Year, Somphong had his Jujaka carving carried to the festivities. On the second night of the nine-day ceremony, Jujaka appeared to Somphong in a dream, informing him that he was hungry, asking that he be given traditional offerings, including various fruits, desserts, sugarcane, and honey; he particularly wanted *khaolaam* because it is good for traveling. When the laity brought the offerings Jujaka had requested, they found their various wishes coming true.

As word spread, more and more people began coming to his temple. Nowadays on the weekends and holidays hundreds of people come, making offerings to Jujaka, seeking to be blessed by Somphong, and purchasing Jujaka figurines, amulets, and yantra cloths at the temple store. In the past Somphong would sacralize the amulets in a ceremony with other monks, but now he is unable to travel and so sacralizes them himself. Somphong's Jujaka amulets are believed to help creditors retrieve their outstanding debts, to help business owners succeed in their businesses, to help travelers reach their destinations, and to help in a range of other similar worldly desires. Described as being "like gold hidden in rags" (*phaa khiiriaw hoh thohng*), Jujaka is considered particularly appropriate for people who are, like Jujaka, mild-mannered, calm in speech, calm in temperament, and thrifty. In his blessing to his listeners, Somphong informs his audience that Jujaka poses no danger to people but only seeks to protect them from harm. Jujaka is compassionate. When he walks in the forests, animals always follow him. In response to my question about whether Jujaka was an incarnation of Devadatta, the Buddha's enemy, Somphong agreed he was. However, he explained that Jujaka was destined to become a Pacceka Buddha of the future.[14]

Promotion of Tourism

The *Vessantara Jataka* lives on in contemporary culture, not only in Jujaka worship for private gain but also in performances for the promotion of tourism. Tourism plays a major role in the Thai economy and is promoted globally through the Tourism Authority of Thailand. Since the jataka is performed with the greatest regularity in the northeast, these efforts are primarily concentrated in that region's provincial capitals.[15] The general trend in recent decades has been toward a decline in the number of recitations at many northeastern urban temples; this development parallels the lack of interest nationwide in these performances among the urban middle classes. Growing numbers of northeastern villages have also been deciding not to hold their own recitations each year but instead to join in celebrations held at neighboring villages. Even village recitations have shifted to the abbreviated Hok Kasat form. Nevertheless, the performance has maintained its overall importance as an occasion for family members to return home, much like Thanksgiving in the United States. The possibilities emerging through tourism are encouraging more provincial capitals to promote full recitations. Further supporting their revival is the development of a Preaching Institute in Khon Kaen. This institute is seeking to standardize the text and also the manner in which the text is performed, to ensure that future generations of monks will be able to maintain this operatic religious art form.[16]

As part of tourism promotion, organizers in provincial capitals are expanding the procession celebrating Vessantara and Matsi's return to the court. This procession is already a major component of the northeastern village celebration. In addition to growing retinues of gaily clad royal attendants, the processions are increasingly incorporating the bawdy phiitaakhon. The religious logic of their incorporation is that there is so much rejoicing at Vessantara's return that it arouses these spirits and they follow in the procession. However, several monks stated an explicit practical logic—namely, that they are a way to promote public interest and attract larger crowds to their celebration. At present, two provinces have developed their processions into significant national tourist attractions: Roi Et and Loei. Phiitaakhon have recently been added to processions in the cities of Ubon and Korat.

Roi Et's effort to garner national attention for its parade dates back to 1991. The annual event is now being promoted as part of the "Amazing Thailand" campaign of the Tourism Authority of Thailand, advertising local hotels and other businesses in Roi Et. The festival is called the Rice Noodle Bun Phrawet (Kin Khao Pun Bun Phawet) and features food, including free rice noodles (*khao pun*) for participants. Arranged by various public and private organizations, the event includes a procession for Upakut, a huge parade comprised of thirteen floats corresponding to the number of chapters in the story, and theatrical performances recounting the story, in addition to the actual recitation by the monks. In March 2011 the Roi Et parade included two live elephants, hundreds of beautifully clad dancers, and scores of phiitaakhon, represented by men wearing raggedy burlap costumes with eyes painted in white on their masks.[17] The phiitaakhon received far more notice than Jujaka.

In Loei, the bacchanalian phiitaakhon festival described in chapter 2 has long been a major component of the Bun Pha Wet in Dansai district. However, it was in decline until recently. According to the abbot I interviewed at Wat Phonchai, the phiitaakhon festival was once much more widespread, celebrated by at least ten villages in addition to the amphur town. However, more and more of the younger generation were working and it was getting hard for them to find the time to contribute their time for the common good (*suan ruam*); participation had dwindled to four other villages.[18] But at Dansai itself, the custom survived with government support, garnering increasing media attention and turning this otherwise sleepy remote mountain town in northeastern Thailand into a major tourist attraction each year. The parade is growing, adding to its procession of monks, semi-naked wild men and phiitaakhon, people dressed in royal costumes representing Vessantara, Matsi and the two royal children; the royal family walks in the procession with umbrellas held over them and are followed by beautifully dressed attendants (see photos in Jetjaras 2009).

At Wat Phonchai, where the procession concludes and the jataka is recited, a permanent, year-round museum with a small gift shop exhibits some of the costumes. In the past the phiitaakhon masks and costumes were supposed to be thrown into the river; nowadays only the ancestral figures are thrown into the river. The other masks are saved and used as decorations in local guesthouses and stores. Stores along the main street in the town now sell T-shirts, CDs of songs newly created for the parade, phiitaakhon masks, figurines, and other knick-knacks. The production of phiitaakhon masks has become a government-supported OTOP handicraft industry.[19] Even the nearby hilltop temple, Wat Niramit Vipassana—which does not perform the jataka—has a recently commissioned set of mural paintings of the *Vessantara Jataka* on its walls. The last scene, showing the return of the royal family to the palace, not only has the usual royal retinue but also includes the phiitaakhon and, perhaps even more anachronistically, the ghost of Jujaka.[20]

Another variation on this mix of tourism and cultural preservation comprises the efforts to preserve public knowledge of the jataka in museums. In addition to the museum in Dansai, Loei province, Roi Et's Provincial Administrative Organization invested over 28 million baht to build a *Vessantara Jataka* Park (located at Ban Noi Hua Fai, Tambon Rohb Muang subdistrict) in 2002 "to encourage interest in Thai folklore" and support economic development; the park presents a drive-through variation where the jataka chapters are staged with the help of large white figures placed along the roadside.[21] In 2006 the Siam Cultural Park in Ratburi province opened the Jujaka Light and Sound Cave, "reflecting Thai culture and ways of life from the past until the present for the next generations to learn about the uniqueness of Thai culture." Various dioramas tell the story of Vessantara, with Jujaka featured prominently. The park is intended as a destination for educational tourism. Supaporn Siripornlert, the park's managing director, explains, "Our target groups are youngsters or anyone who wants to understand Thai values and customs." According to Supaporn, she chose to show this particular story because it teaches us to be self-content and rid ourselves of all worldly attachments.[22] In this interpretation, the earlier theme of generosity for others appears to have been altered to self-contentment for the individual.

Promotion of Cultural Heritage

With growing national interest in preserving cultural heritage (e.g., Baker 2013), the *Vessantara Jataka* is increasingly being resurrected in the central and northern regions through varying combinations of royal, state, and local support. The performances receiving these forms of governmental and community support are generally more formal than the ones intended to appeal to tourists, and they may or may not involve processions.

As we saw in chapter 1, members of the royal family continue to support performances of the jataka. In addition to their attendance at Wat Phra Kaew on the occasion of the changing of the Emerald Buddha's robes, members of the royal family, most notably Princess Sirindhorn, have played an important role in re-energizing annual recitations at Phutthamonthon. Other formal recitations are held in the name of members of the royal family. The recitation held in July 2011 to raise funds for Siriraj Hospital was sponsored in honor of the king's eighty-fourth birthday and the queen's seventy-ninth birthday; the king was staying at the hospital at the time. The staging was stunningly beautiful, but very formal. At the front of the hall where each monk sat as he recited his respective chapter a pavilion had been built, surrounded with pond lily stalks, bunches of bananas, mounds of coconuts, flowers, and various kinds of greenery—all there to reconstruct the forest exile. Around the hall were gorgeous floral arrangements and money trees. Outside the hall were flat-screen TVs broadcasting the chanting monks to those outside the main hall. The audience at the time I was there was overwhelmingly female. Even though the monk was chanting the Maharaat chapter at the time, which included a variety of operatic special effects and comic moments as Jujaka stuffed himself, no one in the audience even smiled. That same year, the National Buddhist Youth Society also held a *Vessantara Jataka* recitation (on July 31), also in honor of the king's eighty-fourth (seventh cycle) birthday. Other recitations are increasingly being held to mark other important royal life-cycle events.[23]

State Support

A concerted effort to preserve recitations of the *Vessantara Jataka* also appears to be emerging within the state-supported sangha. Monks at some of the royal temples in the Mahanikai lineage such as Wat Mahathat, Wat Suthat, Wat Chetuphon (Wat Pho), and Wat Laksi have long been involved in recitations, be they at their own temples or at other ones (as noted earlier in this chapter, Wat Laksi houses a popular large wooden carving of Jujaka). These also tend to be formal recitations.

In July 2013 I visited Wat Samien Nari and saw that they were about to host a *Vessantara Jataka* recitation, on the weekend just before the beginning of Buddhist Lent. Upon making further inquiries, a monk informed me that this performance was the first in a long time and was being held in response to a special request from Bangkok's monastic head. Concerned that future generations would not know the story, the Bangkok monastic head asked the heads of each monastic subdivision (*chaokhana khet*) in Bangkok to hold a performance at their temple. The recitation was being held over a three-day period, with the first five chapters to be performed on Friday, three on Saturday, and the final five on Sunday.[24] Two monks were invited on each of the three days, with one monk coming twice. The monks on Friday came from Wat Chetuphon and Wat Laksi; on Saturday they came from Wat Saam Phrayaa and Wat Laksi; and on Sunday they came from Wat Saam Phrayaa, Wat Laksi, and Wat Samien Nari.

I attended the Friday performance since I was particularly interested in hearing the Jujaka chapter. Once again the staging was stunningly beautiful. Two raised pulpits, each inlaid with mother-of-pearl, were set up for the two monks to sit on, at the base of which were flowers and fruits. In the front was a huge metal bowl with sacral water, surrounded by pineapples, coconuts, and other fruits. In the back were two large, artificial waterfalls about five feet high, banana tree fronds, candles, money trees, and colored flags. A variety of fruits were placed at the bases of the pillars of the open-air temple pavilion. Once again, the audience was overwhelmingly female, with the exception of rows of school children in uniform sitting in the back. Even though one of the monks was nationally known for his comic performance of Jujaka, and he was doing a wonderful job, the schoolchildren were inattentive and the adults were remarkably stony-faced. Surrounding the seated area were numerous venues for making monetary donations to the temple.

A jataka performance in Lampang in December 2008 provides another example. Wat Bunyawat in Lampang had not held recitations for years, but has just revived the tradition in the past decade. The revival is part of a project of the Mahachulalongkorn Buddhist University of Wat Mahathat, in Bangkok, which has a branch at this Lampang temple. Their purpose was twofold: to preserve Lanna cultural traditions and to bring in money for the university. Promoting its goal of educational outreach, the recitation was preceded by a lengthy parade involving hundreds of students and laity who walked through the city of Lampang en route to the temple. Different area schools and villages (not organized by birth years) served as the sponsors of the thirteen chapters of the jataka, the *Phra Malai Sutra*, and the *Khathaphan*. Each subgroup of the parade carried a placard announcing the chapter they were sponsoring and the name of their school or village. There were also school bands playing and groups playing traditional instruments, such as flutes, gongs, and cymbals. Some carried flags representing Thailand, the Buddhist sangha, or their respective schools; others carried traditional long decorative woven banners. Other participants carried offerings ranging from brooms and dishes to betel, candles, flowers, and other ceremonial items. Several men carried a large lacquer box borne on a litter, presumably containing the sacred texts. Schoolchildren wore their school or scout uniforms; the representatives of the various village housewives' groups also wore matching traditional dress. Spearheading the Matsi chapter was a young woman dressed in white. One of the banners announced that the ceremony was for the "communal preservation of our customs" (*ruam syybsaan praphaenii*).

In support of its fund-raising goal, the temple had various stalls set up inside where participants could make additional donations. Some stalls had 108 small begging bowls into which donors could deposit coins; one stall had seven poses of the Buddha, one for each day of the week (donors could deposit money according to the day of the week on which they or family members were born); another stall allowed participants to test their luck to win a small gift; and still another featured a set of money trees, one for each of the chapters, with small tags noting the number of verses in each chapter and the associated birth year. Unlike the donations made to the monks directly at the end of each recitation, these temple stalls raised money for the use of the hosting temple.

Viewing the VCD of the 2008 recitation reveals a very formal recitation, with high-ranking government officials and spouses occupying seats of honor in the front rows. Hanging on the ceiling was a grid of strings to transport the sacral flow from the monk's recitations to the heads of audience members. Also hanging from the ceiling were fruits such as oranges and vegetables such as chilis, long green beans, carrots, and the like. By the pulpit were banana trees and coconuts, as well as other plants and flowers. In one corner was a bowl of sacral water with small candles burning, one for each of the verses in each chapter. There was little in the audience reaction to suggest they were paying much attention to the monks at all. The audience seemed more dutiful than rapt.[25]

Local Council Funds

With increasing local control over tambon (subdistrict) and municipal council funds resulting from national decentralization policies begun in earnest after the Thai Rak Thai government took office in 2001, local communities had more say in how their local budgets would be used. Tambons and municipalities

Figure 19. "Grandfather" Jujaka at parade. Now supported with local municipal council funds, this tradition was begun circa the mid-twentieth century by local abbot Luang Poh Pii (1902–74) and woodcarver Lung Loi Duangkaew (1911–92) to encourage involvement by the younger generation. Masks are considered sacred and kept at the local temple. Photo courtesy of Daan Laan Hoi Municipal Council, Amphur Daan Laan Hoi, Sukhothai, January 2006.

throughout the country began allocating a portion of their local budgets for such activities as repairing the archaeological remains of deserted temples or creating local museums. Some local councils are beginning to sponsor *Vessantara Jataka* recitations. Thus in a northern district with fifteen tambons in Chiang Mai province, three have organized full Tang Tham Luang in the past decade. In 2008 one tambon administrative organization decided to hold annual recitations, rotating the host temple through the thirteen villages in the tambon each year. Even though not previously considered a typical part of northern recitations, the villagers decided to include a real elephant "in order to draw greater interest." Some one thousand people attended the 2008 recitation, drawing primarily from all thirteen villages in the tambon as well as from elsewhere. This local level interest in promoting cultural heritage is leading some villages to become specialized in ritual paraphernalia. Thus one village in this district is becoming known as the source for actors and wooden elephants for hire for the Vessantara procession. An abbot in another village has hired seamstresses to sew costumes and stores them for rental for various processions.

Fund-raising is a frequent motivation for sponsoring contemporary *Vessantara Jataka* recitations. I observed one such recitation held in Hang Dong in 2009 to raise money to build a temple.[26] However, if in the past recitations were a way to encourage village unification, today the decision is often highly contentious. In one subdistrict, a village abbot proposed using tambon development funds to underwrite the costs of a *Vessantara Jataka* recitation at his temple. However, the abbot was widely disliked in the village since he had ordained after a questionable lay life of drinking, drugs, and criminal behavior. Even though these funds were initially approved, the villagers refused to cooperate with the abbot because they felt such a large gathering of monks and laity from outside their village would serve to enhance his reputation. Guised in language suggesting that everyone was too busy, the funds were reallocated.

In another village, controversy arose following a recitation. An abbot from a neighboring village temple had offered to organize a *Vessantara Jataka* recitation in order to raise money to build a temple in this village. Villagers were pleased to accept the offer, but problems arose in generating support outside the village. This abbot was also widely disliked because of his reputation for promiscuity as well as corruption in handling temple funds at his own temple. Villagers in the abbot's own village and elsewhere refused to cooperate because they did not want to do anything to expand the abbot's reputation; they felt that the abbot's offer was motivated by a desire to become more influential. The recitation was held nonetheless, but it apparently lost money. The villagers were then upset both because of the loss and because of a controversy over the accounting; the abbot would not reveal the actual amounts of money donated during the recitation, and many believed that he had siphoned off monies. The village is still without its own temple.

Global Nostalgia

Performances of the *Vessantara Jataka* are now occurring on a global stage. With ties between Thailand and the United States growing, more and more Thais have relocated to America to seek educational and economic opportunities.[27] In the wake of the Vietnam War, refugees from Laos and Cambodia were resettled around the world, particularly in the United States, Canada, Australia, France, Germany, the United Kingdom, and Japan. Theravada Buddhist temples are now springing up in all of these countries.[28] In addition, large numbers of Thai women, particularly from northeastern villages, have married

European men and settled in Europe (Patcharin 2013). Monks who were known for their preaching abilities are now making recordings to send overseas. Today, recitations are available for sale on DVD and performances are being posted on the Internet, thereby allowing a global audience to access in-country sermons and merit-makings.

In addition, Theravada Buddhist temples are increasingly beginning to hold recitations of the *Vessantara Jataka* globally, motivated by a combination of nostalgia, heritage preservation, and fund-raising. Advertised as teaching "the ability to give and to forgive in all circumstances," the Thai Buddhapadipa Temple in London, England, held a recitation inviting thirteen monks and included a version in English in September 2013. Bodhikaram Temple, in Ottawa, Canada, posted a YouTube video of a Khmer monk reading the jataka.[29] Wat Phrayortkeo Dhammayanaram, a Lao Buddhist Temple in Sydney, Australia, also holds recitations. Wat Lao Samakhitham, in Castle Creek, New York, has posted highlights of its Bun Pha Wet set poignantly to the song "Heart of a Lion," by Tommy C; the festival was held in June 2012, replete with scrolls and money trees laden with dollars.[30] YouTube videos are posted of the Bun Pha Wet at Wat Lao Buddharam at Elgin, Illinois, in 2011 and of a Lao temple in north Philadelphia on June 2013. The Lao Temple at Vipassana Center in Forest Lake, Minnesota, held its first Bun Pha Wet ceremony in June 2013.[31] In some cases, monks are flown in from Thailand, Laos, or Cambodia; one of the monks I interviewed in Ubon travels regularly in June to the Thai wat in Switzerland, where there are many northeastern women married to Swiss men. Increasingly these temples have their own resident monks who are conducting the recitations. Thus Kamala describes the efforts of Luang Ta Chi, abbot of Wat Thai, in Washington, DC, to hold a *Vessantara Jataka* recitation; he held his first recitation in March 2005, inviting monks from Arizona and Texas, and was able to raise significant funds for the construction of a new building (2009, 27). Although some full recitations are held, most are in the abridged form.

Although recitations of the *Vessantara Jataka* are being revivified in Thailand and are even expanding globally, the recitations are drawing audiences with different motivations. The frustrations leading to the desire to be reborn in the days of the Maitreya Buddha are no longer primary factors. As the social and political context shifts, the recitations are becoming more formal and their former comic elements are gradually disappearing. The trickster Jujaka is being absorbed into the cults of his amulets and lost in the processions of villagers beautifully attired in "traditional" dress and riding rented elephants. Northern Thailand still has tujok monks, most of whom were students of (or were influenced by) Luang Poh Bunthong, but they are increasingly less risqué.[32] Chapters are still being recited at northern funerals, albeit with less frequency than in the 1970s, and increasingly the Matsi rather than the Jujaka chapter is chosen. In sum, today recitations are taking new forms as they are appropriated for the promotion of tourism, the preservation of cultural heritage, the expression of nostalgia for the past, and fund-raising.

The Future: Of Mothers and Other Women

Given the major transformations in its meanings already underway, how likely is the *Vessantara Jataka* to remain relevant in the future? Any consideration of the jataka's future prospects must include the attitudes of its female audiences. In all the jataka performances I have observed in central, northeastern, and northern Thailand, women comprise the majority of the listening audience.[33] That this pattern is long-standing is suggested by Tachard's remark of seventeenth-century Ayutthaya: "The Women are the most solicitous to go to those meetings of Piety" ([1688] 1981, 306–7). However, the contemporary feminist interpretation of the jataka as a plot to subordinate women does not bode well for the jataka's survival into the future. Kornvipa Boonsue roundly denounces the *Vessantara Jataka* for its portrayal of women as only good for "two things— procreation and cooking," with Matsi collecting roots and fruits for the family to eat so that Vessantara had more time to meditate (1989, 36–38). In this interpretation, if women accept Matsi as their ideal image, they then accept an image of themselves "as being the passive victims of patriarchal power" (Kornvipa 1989, 38). As Kornvipa writes:

> Maddi played a big role in Vessantara's achievement but she did not receive any credit for her contribution. All appreciation and honour was given to Vessantara, even for what he achieved via Maddi's painful sacrifices, faithfulness, and virtue, as well as the physical and mental pain inflicted on his children. . . .
>
> From a feminist perspective, how could one consider this kind of merit accumulation as the ultimate step? It is in fact very inhumane and the way in which Vessantara wanted to prove his detachment from worldly things is very selfish. He thought only of himself and of the benefit to himself alone. (1989, 37–38)

The Burmese feminist Khin Thitsa has made a similar argument, writing that the story of Vessantara and Matsi is a paradigmatic example of the jatakas where the wise, pure male is "assisted in following his spiritual goal by the services of a devoted female, usually mother or wife. The other portrayal of woman is again as seductive and avaricious, an evil force which is duly chastised" (1980, 20; see also the discussion in Gabaude 2016). Clearly feminists with this perspective would happily see the jataka's demise.

Given the jataka's seemingly misogynist perspective, it is surprising that so little attention has been given to why women comprise the majority of its audience. Some scholars have tried to justify Vessantara's gift of his wife and children as merely representing the cultural values of Indian society millennia ago. Thus, Cone and Gombrich suggested ancient India was "a rigid patriarchy," "a world where it is the man's unquestioned right to dispose of his family as he thinks fit," a world in which widows have no legal rights and "sons are the only security in old age" (1977, xxii). Some Thai monks also offer this explanation. The implication of this argument is that Vessantara would not make such a decision today—hardly a strong justification for the jataka's relevance in the modern era. After all, jataka performances largely died out in South Asia.

Perhaps such appeals to ancient patriarchy are intended to encourage Southeast Asian women to feel grateful that their generation was born under better circumstances. Indeed, in comparison with this portrayal of ancient South Asia, women in mainland Southeast Asia hold a stronger position. As noted in the introduction, in Theravada Buddhist mainland Southeast Asia, women have long been recognized as influential in all aspects of village life (e.g., Bowie 2008a). Villagers have historically practiced primarily uxorilocal post-marriage residence patterns. Furthermore, because daughters were more likely to take care of parents in their old age, village life in Thailand has a tendency toward female ultimogeniture. Gascoigne's summary of the condition of Burmese women holds elsewhere on the mainland: "The Burmese are all 'new women,' and take a very forward and active part in all matters pertaining to business. Few husbands would dare to enter into any mercantile arrangements without the aid or advice of their wives; at least the probability is that should any poor deluded man be so unwise he would hear a good deal more about the matter than he quite desired" (1896, 43).

The primary female characters are Phusadi, Matsi, Amitataa, and Kanhaa. Phusadi and Matsi are invariably described in positive terms. In their previous lives, Phusadi and her sister made merit to a previous Buddha; her sister requested to reach enlightenment, but Phusadi requested, "May I in the future become the mother of a Buddha!" (Cone and Gombrich 1977, 5). She is reborn as the queen of the god Indra. When her time in the heavens has lapsed, she requests that she be granted the boon of giving birth to "a son who will be open-handed in granting requests, and without avarice, who will have fame and good repute, and be honoured by rival kings" (Cone and Gombrich 1977,

7). In addition to her desire for breasts that remain firm, she also requests to be able to "have the condemned set free," suggesting she is compassionate in her own right. She is born to the chief queen of the king of the Maddas and at age sixteen is married to King Sonchai. The god Indra notes that all her wishes have been granted except one. So he goes to the future Buddha and tells him that it is time for him to be reborn on earth as the son of Phusadi. From the time of her conception, she gives alms. She requests that six almshouses be built and that 600,000 gold coins be given away. When Vessantara is born, he wants to give gifts, and Phusadi places "a purse of one thousand gold coins in his outstretched hands" (Cone and Gombrich 1977, 9). Thus Phusadi can be interpreted as a strong, virtuous woman who makes Vessantara's earthly birth possible. In the performance I observed in northeast Thailand, Phusadi's grief at the loss of not only her son but also her grandchildren served to heighten the emotions leading up to the eventual joy at the family's reunification. One can easily imagine women sharing not only Phusadi's dream of unchanging physical perfection but also her pain as her earthly family goes into exile.

Portrayals of Matsi are more diverse, ranging from conservative to progressive interpretations. The conservative interpretation portrays Matsi as dutiful, supporting her husband no matter what her personal hardship might be, even to the extent of being willing to be given away to a stranger. The progressive interpretation highlights Matsi as an equal and even wiser partner. In this reading, Matsi chose to leave her life of comfort in the palace and have the children accompany them. When King Sonchai and Queen Phusadi come to the forest, Vessantara is afraid an enemy army is approaching; it is Matsi who reassures him that in fact the army belongs to his own parents. Although some monks viewed Matsi as submitting out of wifely duty to Vessantara's decision to give her away, other monks insisted that Matsi was fully aware that humanity would only be saved through her sacrifice as well.[34]

Similarly, opinions differed as to whether the children were vulnerable, obedient victims forced to go with Jujaka or whether the children made conscious decisions to go with Jujaka because they agreed with their father's mission. Part of the debate centers on whether one sees Vessantara's goal as personal enlightenment or as a quest for enlightenment in order to be able to save humanity. If Vessantara had a personal goal, then his children are more likely to be seen as victims. However, if Vessantara's quest was to help humanity, the children can be portrayed as having understood its importance. Many people I interviewed noted that Chalii was born as the Buddha's son in his next life, but that Kanhaa was angry with her father. As a consequence, Kanhaa was not reborn as the Buddha's daughter but instead as the nun Uppalavanna (Ubonwanna), one of the two most eminent female apostles of Gautama. As Gerini explains, "upon being given over to Jujaka she conceived a moral hatred of her father and solemnly swore that she would never again be reborn a child to such an inhuman parent" ([1892] 1976, 31). Uppalavanna was born as the beautiful daughter of a wealthy merchant. Accounts differ as to whether or not she married, but they converge again about her decision to become a bhikkhuni. Upon reaching enlightenment, the Buddha declared her to be the foremost in supernormal powers among the nuns and she was able to withstand an assault by the devil Mara. In some accounts, Uppalavanna was raped. One monk I interviewed in Hua Hin said that because Kanhaa was upset with her father, she was reborn as "Ubonwanna, a bhikkhuni who was raped and then swallowed up by the earth."[35] Interestingly, in the Pali version no mention is made of Kanhaa's special anger, and in fact, Vessantara sets her ransom higher than Chalii's, evidently to ensure that she will only be ransomed by royalty. Yet another version has the brother and sister marrying each other. A villager in Uttaradit province told me that in the past his village would parade Chalii and Kanhaa to the village temple, replete with the ceremonial *khan maak*, and stage the wedding at the temple.[36]

As we have seen in the course of this book, the portrayal of Amitataa varied. The Pali text tells us that Amitataa was reborn as the wicked nun Ciñcamānavikā. Monks who were aware of the Pali text coda tended to view Amitataa in a negative light. Ciñcamānavikā tried to destroy the Buddha's reputation by claiming that the Buddha had impregnated her. At a public hearing, a snake came along and bit the string holding up her fake belly and the truth became known.[37] And at that moment, the earth opened and swallowed her up. Despite this Pali coda, the majority of monks and villagers I interviewed portrayed Amitataa in a positive light, emphasizing her role as the perfect daughter (with Matsi exemplifying the perfect wife).

All versions presented Amitataa as a young girl, but interpretations varied as to whether Amitataa was a victim or a shrew. In central Thailand, Amitataa appeared to be a tragic victim: her impoverished parents had no choice but to give their beloved daughter to Jujaka. This version buttressed a portrayal of Jujaka as horrible, uncaring, and selfish. In other versions, also compatible with negative portrayals of Jujaka, she is a heroic daughter who volunteers herself to help her parents protect their honor. In a version found in southern Thailand, Jujaka essentially forces himself on Amitataa in an act of rape; in other versions he is said to have loved magic such that Amitataa willingly surrenders herself.

Yet another interpretation, seemingly more common in the north, portrays Amitataa as no less conniving than Jujaka. In this portrayal, Amitataa sees that the old man has been able to accumulate a considerable amount of gold and probably has an enormous amount of gold and property squirreled away. Since he is not likely to live long and since she is still young, she is likely to inherit everything Jujaka has and lead a comfortable life. So she decides to marry Jujaka.[38] An overwhelming majority of monks and laity in all regions of Thailand that I interviewed told me that Amitataa was basically a good daughter and a good wife; however, in her previous life she had made a mistake in her offerings to monks. Instead of offering beautiful flowers, she had placed an old wilted flower on the tray; consequently, when she was born as Amitataa she got a wrinkled old man as her husband. While some may see Amitataa's misfortunes as caused by her actions in a previous life, the role of the cruel, jealous village women can also be blamed.

The emotional resonances the jataka had for its female audiences would have varied according to its interpretation. Observers have noted that audiences were often in tears during recitations of the Kumarn and Matsi chapters. Perhaps the Kumarn chapter encourages audience members to relive the hardships of their own lives, particularly if they had ever found themselves in any form of servitude. That the Matsi chapter has been chosen to be recited at many northern funerals parallels the pain impermanence causes. Matsi coming to peace with the loss of her children must have resonated profoundly with earlier generations, who would have lost children in childbirth or to childhood diseases. Vessantara's convoluted and awkward handling of his wife's grief provides listeners with an avenue to work through their mixed feelings toward the death or departure of a loved one. To minimize the agony of these chapters is to ignore much of the jataka's emotional power in the face of life's sufferings.

Furthermore, the jataka allows an exploration of problems in daily life, as we have particularly seen in the northern interpretation. Amitataa's problems with the villagers would resonate with anyone familiar with the gossiping and petty jealousies that can emerge in village life. Given how many village girls from northern and northeastern Thailand found themselves working as domestic servants in Bangkok in the 1940s and 1950s, as prostitutes during the 1960s and 1970s, and as factory workers up to the present day, one can imagine that many identified with Amitataa's plight at being separated from her family and thrown into unfriendly environments. Men in the audience may well have vicariously enjoyed Jujaka's good fortune in acquiring such a wonderful young wife. But after witnessing Jujaka's difficult quest to make his wife happy, they may then have come to see the matter in a different light. Giving the story a modern twist, some people laughed as they pointed out that nowadays many younger village women are marrying older foreign men in the hope that these men have money and will give them comfortable lives.

Both Matsi and Amitataa allow explorations into husband-wife relations. As we have seen, audiences debate Vessantara's decisions. As Julia Gengenbach notes, Vessantara was not a perfect husband: after all, he lied to his wife about the meaning of her dream because he knew that if she were present when Jujaka asked for the children, he would not be able to give them away (2009; see also Collins 1998, 528). However, for villagers, Vessantara's actions are also a topic of debate; on the one hand he was lying, and on the other hand he was being compassionate and trying to find a way to allow Matsi to come to terms with her loss. For many listeners the overwrought account of Vessantara's extreme decision may have helped ease them back into the reality of their daily lives. No matter how impossible their spouses might be, they were hopefully not as bad as Vessantara. No matter how difficult the situations they confronted, hopefully they were not as bad as Matsi's fate, living in the forest without the support of an extended family network. I can imagine many a village woman going home to her family, grateful she still had her children, a husband who was not as extreme as Vessantara, and an extended village community.

If some modern feminists denounce the conservatism of the *Vessantara Jataka*, other feminists suggest a more positive feminist reading. Suwanna Sathaanand has written an essay titled "Madsi: A Female Bodhisattva Denied?" in which she suggests that Matsi should also be considered a bodhisattva. Arguing that Matsi was a life partner of Vessantara who made her own decisions, Suwanna argues, "It is time we opened up the possibility of giving credit to Madsi and to women in general" (1997, 251). She concludes, "It is about time we introduced new elements into our classical heritage, so that it belongs to the people and becomes more relevant" (1997, 251).[39] Northern Thai monks such as Luang Poh Bunthong were already encouraging a positive reading, noting that Matsi's knowledge even surpassed that of Vessantara's at certain moments. A similar argument can easily be made for Phusadi; she had the opportunity to reach enlightenment with her sister in her previous life but relinquished it to give birth to a Buddha and save humanity.

If the *Vessantara Jataka* is to survive into the future, it must continue to resonate emotionally with its audiences. With women comprising the majority of its listeners, their interpretations will be important. That changes in the interpretations of the appropriate role of women in Theravada Buddhism are occurring can be seen in the growing number of representations of Chao Mae Kuan Im in temples, the growing number of women involved in lay meditation movements, and the growing number of women ordaining both as *mae chii* and as bhikkhuni. Without positive readings of its major female figures, the future of the jataka will increasingly be in jeopardy.

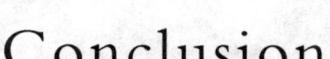

Conclusion
The Journey's End

Poised at the edge of new vistas, our journey has come to an end. We have followed Jujaka on his travels over the course of nearly two centuries as he disappeared behind the glitter of formal state ceremonials of Bangkok, as he pursued Amitataa alongside the scrolls escorting the royal family in the processions through the villages of the northeast, and as he found his way through the mazes of northern Thailand. We followed Jujaka because we were curious as to why the Thai kings of the nineteenth century supported sober recitations but sought to suppress comic performances of the *Vessantara Jataka*. When we reached northern Thailand, we encountered the anti-authoritarian trickster Jujaka, who in his connection with the utopian Maitreya Buddha and the associated millenarian uprisings gave us a plausible reason for royal concern. Assuming comic performances were once widespread, we have watched as the state brought the trickster under control in each of the three regions over the course of the twentieth century. Ironically, the politics of the absolute monarchy shaped both the humor of the jataka in the nineteenth century and its demise over the course of the twentieth century.

This book has focused on Thailand, but I hope that it gives further impetus to a newly emerging awareness of vernacular variations across time and space (e.g., Collins 2016). The humor of the northern trickster provides insight not only into a peasant critique of the social order but also into the prevailing paradigm of scholarship. In revealing the extent of variation in three regions of Thailand, this book helps to illuminate six interrelated biases. First, the prevailing paradigm has prioritized texts over performances. Second, the approach has prioritized the Pali recension over vernacular recensions, viewing the Pali version as the most "authentic." Third, it is decontextualized, collapsing

Figure 20. Temple mural of Nakornkan chapter. Scene of the final chapter, showing the royal family returning to the palace with royal guards, phiitaakhon, ghosts of the dead, and Jujaka in the royal procession. Painted by Pramote Sriphrom in 2006. Wat Niramit, Amphur Dan Sai, Loei Province, July 2009. Photo by author.

significant cultural differences across Asia. Fourth, it has denied the importance of local variation. Fifth, it is ahistorical, ignoring the importance of considering social changes over some two millennia of history. And last, it is apolitical, denying the creative agency of its myriad participants.

In his inquiry into historiography, Paul Ricoeur suggests that historical theory should be linked to a theory of action—in other words, "that history articulates the plot of action by coordinating intentions, causes and accidents" (1994, 22). As he explains, "history has for its subject people like you and me, who act and suffer within circumstances that they themselves did not create, and with results both desired and undesired" (1994, 22). As one reflects on the three main social groupings in nineteenth-century Thailand—monarchs, monks, and masses—one can see how their respective interests converged in the ambiguity of the *Vessantara Jataka*. Monarchs could hope to gain legitimacy for their rule. Monks could hope to vouchsafe generous alms for themselves and offerings of youth for the well-being of the order. The masses could hope to convince their rulers of the importance of generosity and affirm a vision of social justice symbolized by the coming Maitreya Buddha, while also gaining immediate practical benefits such as good rains, good health, and a moral village economy. The jataka served pro-royalist, non-royalist, and anti-royalist agendas simultaneously. As this book has shown, the regional differences in the *Vessantara Jataka* emerged from the interplay of the varying interests and actions within each regional context.

Charles Hallisey, in his review of the current state of Theravada Buddhist studies, notes that "texts fade in their significance as social change occurs." He suggests that once we ask what conditions are necessary for the preservation of a text, "a range of other historical questions immediately opens out" (1995, 51). In addition to an understanding of "the technology, practices and institutions which made their survival possible," he writes, "discovering answers to such questions will require investigations about the extent to which the production and survival of a text is both dependent and independent of the audiences which receive it" (1995, 51). Monarchs, monks, and the masses have all undergone significant transformations in the Theravada Buddhist countries of Southeast Asia. Thailand is no longer an absolute monarchy, having become a constitutional monarchy after 1932. With the expansion of the secular public education system, monks no longer provide the primary avenue for educational advancement and village prestige. New technologies in agriculture and medicine have contributed to the immediate economic and physical health of village communities. With recourse to electoral politics, mass demonstrations, and social media, villagers no longer need to wait for Maitreya for redress of their political and economic grievances. Thus the context in which the *Vessantara Jataka* once flourished has changed dramatically, and it is now possible to imagine the jataka fading into obscurity. After all, the story originated in India but is no longer celebrated in its birthplace.

The jataka's future remains uncertain. Although evidence suggests that emotional comic performances were once widespread, our travels have made it clear that these are giving way to emotionless formal recitations. The beloved trickster of villagers in the past has transmogrified to become the revered god of sectors of the urban middle classes, a Jujaka who helps provide not the intangible benefits of laughter in the face of feudal authority but the tangible benefits of money in the face of global capitalism. Unlike the earlier Jujaka, who made our baser desires laughable, the capitalist era Jujaka now appears to celebrate them. Increasingly, the jataka no longer champions charity but glorifies gain, and the earlier village story about giving is being inverted into an urban story about getting. Even among those for whom the jataka is not about the personal accumulation of wealth, the jataka is transforming from a reminder of the importance of generosity in a moral economy into a symbol promoting cultural heritage, local tourism, and diasporic nostalgia in a global economy. That an increasing number of women, historically the jataka's primary audience, view the text as misogynistic does not bode well for its future. Furthermore, without the laughter and tears that were an integral part of recitations in the past, these performances are becoming increasingly devoid of the emotional content that constituted an important part of their meaning for their audiences.

Nonetheless, the *Vessantara Jataka* has shown itself to be remarkable both in its malleability and its resiliency. I find it disconcerting to realize that a story I had once found appalling and best relegated to the dustbin of history has now beguiled me. Since I began working on this book, there have been many times that I have found the sacro-magical world of the jataka infiltrating the earthly reality of my own everyday life. As a mother, I have thought of Vessantara giving up his children at various moments in recent years, such as when my sons drove the car without me for the first time, each time they flew off to college, and now as they face life journeys along paths beyond my control. After all, my sons do not have the god Indra watching out to ensure they reach the palaces in their dreams. Thinking of Vessantara's agony at giving up his wife and children is making it easier for me to part with earthly valuables through monetary contributions to charities and gifts of treasured heirlooms to family and friends. The story was particularly helpful when I had to return my mother's cat to her after she moved into a retirement community that allowed pets.

Charity and gift-giving comprise the foundation of moral economies across societies as an integral mechanism to counter the forces of primitive accumulation.[1] Many in the Christian tradition are familiar with the moment when Jesus told the rich man that if he wanted to gain eternal life, he should sell his possessions and give the proceeds to the poor, for "it is easier for a camel to go through the eye of a needle than for someone who is rich to enter the kingdom of God" (Matthew 19:24). Max Mueller was a founding figure in the study of comparative religions. Critiquing the "absurd wealth" and the "hideous, hopeless penury" of England in the late nineteenth century, Mueller presents the Buddha's more radical remedy:

He turned to the rich and said, "Give! Give not only one tithe: give not only what you do not want; but give all that is wanted to feed the hungry, to clothe the naked, to teach the ignorant, to nurse the sick, to save the sinner. Give, because nothing belongs to you, nothing can belong to you, neither land nor treasure, not even your own body. Give, because life is a fleeting shadow, which will soon pass away from you with that you now call your own. Give, because what you leave to your own children, and not to all, is more often a curse than a blessing to them." (1885, 235-36)

While many modern readers may sympathize with the virtue of generosity as they reflect on the growing class divides around the globe, many are shocked by Vessantara's decision to sacrifice his family for the greater good of enlightenment. I also continue to grapple with this decision. Yet, although the *Vessantara Jataka* may seem bizarre or extreme, one can find the theme of giving up one's family for a greater cause throughout world history. Indeed, in the very same chapter in which Jesus exhorted the rich to give up their possessions we find another, commonly overlooked passage in which Jesus assures his disciples: "And everyone who has left houses or brothers or sisters or father or mother or wife or children or fields for my sake will receive a hundred times as much and will inherit eternal life" (Matthew 19:29).[2]

If one reviews the biographies of many of the world's great leaders whose lives have shaped their societies for the better, one reads about the personal sacrifices their decisions entailed. If one looks at the family lives of Nelson Mandela, Aung San Suu Kyi, or any other number of major political leaders, one sees immense costs to their spouses and children. I have interviewed many Thais who were involved in the pro-democracy movements of the 1960s and 1970s; their political activism often entailed personal sacrifices and often came at the expense of their families, even in cases when they had their families' full support. The same can be said of the modern generation of activists working for social justice.

Understood as the story of someone seeking to help the suffering, the *Vessantara Jataka* becomes an inspirational tale about the personal sacrifices one makes in the struggle for social justice for all. In such a telling, Matsi and her children can be seen not as victims but as willing participants who contributed no less than Vessantara to the cause of easing humanity's suffering; Phusadi gave birth not only to Vessantara but to a discussion of the ideals of modern society.

The *Vessantara Jataka* appears to have flourished in the days of absolute monarchy, messaging both overt royal quests for legitimacy and covert peasant resistance. However, the jataka can resonate even when kings have been displaced. Thus, although Burma no longer has a monarchy, Aung San Suu Kyi (1991) still finds value in the *Vessantara Jataka* as political critique. She highlights Buddhism's compatibility with democracy by echoing the *Aggana Sutra*, suggesting that the agreement by which the first monarch undertakes to rule righteously in return for a portion of the rice crop represents the Buddhist version of government by social contract (see also Tambiah 1976, 9–18). Furthermore, the Ten Duties of rulers are "liberality, morality, self-sacrifice, integrity, kindness, austerity, non-anger, non-violence, forbearance and non-opposition (to the will of the people)"; these, she points out, "could be applied just as well to modern government as to the first monarch of the world" (Aung San 1991, 170). Suggesting that Vessantara was exiled for giving away the white elephant without the consent of the people, Aung San argues, "the legitimacy of government is founded on the consent of the people, who may withdraw their mandate at any time if they lose confidence in the ability of the ruler to serve their best interests" (1991, 173).

If the *Vessantara Jataka* and other stories have long been a way of teaching Buddhist values, Charles Hallisey and Anne Hansen raise the question, "What did Buddhists learn from their stories?" (1996, 310). As they point out, the "story literature" has often been denigrated as not representative of "real" Buddhist thought but a means "to communicate doctrines that the Buddhist *lumpen* could not otherwise understand" (1996, 309). Gananath Obeyesekere has commented on the contradiction behind the fact that these stories have been "relegated as unimportant folktales that have little to do with the profoundly philosophical corpus" even though they were "how we learned to be Buddhists" (1991, 231; see also R. Obeyesekere 1991, x). In considering how stories might prefigure, configure, and refigure moral life, Hallisey and Hansen suggest that the mythical realms of the jatakas "enable us to appreciate the ethical significance of our coexistence with other humans, even as they portray a world that is quite dissimilar to our ordinary experience" (1996, 312). Through the jataka, when "we leave aside our own social location . . . and enter imaginatively into the experience of a character in a narrative, we cultivate capabilities that are necessary to all moral agency" (Hallisey and Hansen 1996, 314). We are then "better able to perceive universal obligations and rights in a world characterized by social diversity" and develop sympathy for others. Similarly, the *Vessantara Jataka* becomes provocative because the story can be told in ways that one can develop sympathy for the complex positions of each of the characters. From rulers' quests for political legitimacy to peasant critiques of political injustice, the jataka can serve as an imaginative moral exercise for both rich and poor.

At its heart, politics is always about the dynamics of ever-shifting moral tensions. Increasingly over the course of the twentieth century, the political rhetoric shifted from one of subjects serving their rulers to one of governments serving their citizenry (e.g., Bowie 2008b). As I write this conclusion, Thailand is in the midst of political uncertainty. I for one may still find humor in the everyday foibles of human life, but I cannot find any humor in the modern challenges the country is facing. But then I am no political satirist with the skills of John Winyu, Note Udom, or other Thai avatars of a modern Jujaka.[3]

In this book, I have sought to show that the *Vessantara Jataka*, like the Ramayana and other major folk stories, also has had "many tellings." The prevailing academic text-based narrative that has portrayed the jataka as a pro-royalist panegyric is at once ahistorical and misleading. In a region in which military conquests led to war captives and slavery, it beggars belief to think that the relocated war captives would have associated Vessantara with their immediate captors. Following Jujaka into northern Thailand has opened new avenues for interpretation, providing insight into non-royalist and anti-royalist readings of the jataka. Exploring the politics of humor helps shed light on the historical vicissitudes of the *Vessantara Jataka* in Thailand. Whether Jujaka survives his millennia-long journey into the next century remains in the hands of Indra and charitable humans.

Notes

Introduction

1. The class was on Buddhism and taught by Frank Reynolds, then at Stanford University on sabbatical from the University of Chicago.

2. The jataka stories are found in the *Suttapitaka*, the tenth book of the *Khuddakanikaya* in the *Tripitaka* or Buddhist Canon. The theme of generosity runs through many jataka (see Shaw 2006, xxxii). Vessantara's name may have come from the street where he was born—namely, the street where the vessas, or merchants, live, and not the palace. Cone and Gombrich believe the name has no significance (1977, xxxiii, 9).

3. Of the 547 jataka included in the Theravada Buddhist canon, emphasis is placed on the final ten jatakas in which the future Buddha perfects the virtues of renunciation, courage, loving-kindness, resolution, wisdom, perseverance, forbearance, equanimity, truthfulness, and generosity, respectively (Wray, Rosenfield, and Bailey 1972, 16). They are collectively called *dasajati* in Pali or *thotsachaat* in Thai. The future Buddha is not always virtuous (e.g., Appleton 2010). Indeed, Collins suggests that some jataka may even be "meant to be offensive" (1998, 46, 498).

4. As Sarah Shaw points out, "Jatakas are unique: they are the only collection of stories in the world in which the development of one central character is tested not just through the events of one lifetime but of hundreds" (2006, xx). Considered by many scholars to have been precursors of Aesop's fables, the famous Pali scholar T. W. Rhys Davids suggests that the jatakas are "the oldest, most complete and most important collection of folklore extant" ([1880] 1925, iii–iv). Jataka are found in the eighth-century Persian stories of Kalilag and Damnag, in Aesop's fables, in Christian folklore through the adventures of Barlaam and Josaphat (i.e., boddhisatva), and later in the works of Giovanni Boccaccio, Poggio Bracciolini, Jean de La Fontaine, Geoffrey Chaucer, and William Shakespeare (Rhys Davids [1880] 2000, xxix-l; Shaw 2006, lv).

5. The earliest known carving of the story, discovered at Bharhut in Madhya Pradesh, India, dates back to the second century bce. Carvings and paintings of the jataka have also been found across the continent of Asia, in India, Pakistan, Afghanistan, Tibet, China, and Indonesia (e.g., Cunningham 1962; Marshall and Foucher 1982; Schlingloff 1988; Dehejia 1990; Murray 1995). Jataka are particularly important in the Theravada Buddhist tradition but can also be found in Chinese, Khotanese, Sogdian, Tibetan, and Tocharian traditions (Shaw 2006, lv; see also Cone and Gombrich 1977, 109–11). Christoph Emmrich (2016) describes a variant in Nepal.

6. This performance was by Bruce Gaston.

7. Swearer notes that preaching was "gradually dying out" (1978, 3). Baker and Pasuk suggest that "royal patronage of the Mahachat ceased in the Fifth Reign, and the importance of the recitation festival declined steeply after the centralizing reform of the Sangha in 1902" (Nidhi [1982] 2005, 200; see also Pattaratorn 2009, 33).

8. On its growing popularity in temple murals, see Ferguson and Johannsen 1976. A special Vessantara stamp edition was issued in Thailand in 1998, in Laos in 2001, and in Sri Lanka in 1973 and in 2006 in honor of the 2,550th anniversary of the Buddha's enlightenment (Deegalle 2012, 127–46; see also Stamp Wench 2015).

9. In the nineteenth century it sparked a vigorous debate between Buddhists and Christian missionaries in Sri Lanka (see Deegalle 2012, 141–44).

10. Not only were women crying, but Forbes records, "[Matsi's] agonised appeals are beautiful in their simple pathos, and I have seen men moved to tears by a good representation of this play" (1878, 150).

11. E.g., Weiner 1976; S. H. Potter 1977; Van Esterik 1982; Gailey 1987; Atkinson and Errington 1990; Linnekin 1990; Lepowsky 1993; Ong and Peletz 1995; Peletz 1996; Carsten 1997; Brenner 1998; Andaya 2000, 2006; Blackwood 2000; Bowie 2008a, 2010; Hadler 2008; Jacobsen 2008.

12. The senator was Rabiabrat Pongpanich. For further discussion, see Bowie 2011.

13. One of my village friends said that as a child she first thought the word "tujok" denoted a monk who liked to grab people (*jok pyan*) since the monks often chased children.

14. The gift of the seven hundreds is often mentioned when the Buddha reaches enlightenment, rather than his other significant gifts as Vessantara, for example the rain-making elephants, his children, or his wife (Cone and Gombrich 1977, xix).

15. The Pali version merely states that "Jujaka ate too much and could not digest it, so he died on the spot. The king arranged for his funeral" (Cowell [1895] 1957, 299). Ferguson and Johannsen comment that Brahmins are typically portrayed as "reluctant converts or even protagonists" (1976, 656). Gombrich suggests the possibility that the jataka is "a satire on brahminical greed" (1985, 436; see also Pierce 1969, 247–48).

16. All the chapters in a northeastern temple mural of the jataka had sponsors, with the exception of the Jujaka chapter. When Thomas Kaiser asked why this was so, the monk laughingly replied that no one wanted to sponsor that panel, so the artist had to paint it for free—after all, it was part of the story! Thomas Kaiser, personal communication, July 13, 2015.

17. Sarah Shaw writes, "It is remarkable how little Jatakas changed over a long period. There are certainly differences between details described in the verses, the early layer of the text, and the narrative, an indicator of some sort of evolution, but given the centuries involved in their development these are surprisingly minimal" (2006, lii).

18. The Buddha's former life as Vessantara is mentioned in consecration rituals for new Buddha images in northern Thailand. The northern text appears to highlight not Vessantara's gifts of the seven hundreds but rather "the generous sacrifice of my wife and children" (Swearer 1995, 277).

19. This earlier generation of Pali scholars merely focused on these discrepancies in order to establish which version was likely to be the oldest and therefore the most "authentic." Thus M. Winternitz does not suggest that an exploration of these differences might provide insight into different social processes. Winternitz also mentions a new edition of the jataka in Siamese issued by their Majesties Queen Aunt and Queen Suddhasinninath in 1925 (1928, 4).

20. Harald Hundius suggests there are more than 230 non-canonical jatakas (1995, 46). The non-canonical jatakas include the *Padipadana Jataka*, which speaks of a time when Gotama was female (Jaini 1989, 27–28). Pali recensions of these stories have been found in Burma, Cambodia, Laos, and Siam, but while each consists of fifty stories, not all the stories were identical (see Feer [1865] 1963; Terral 1956; Prakong 1983, 6; Horner and Jaini 1985; Jaini 1989; McDaniel 2000; Skilling 2006; Veidlinger 2006, 186; see Finot 1917 on Laos).

21. Not all traditions agree on when enlightenment took place. In Burmese Buddhist tradition, it was May 13, 544 BCE; in Thailand, it was March 11, 545 BCE. For further details, see Eade 1995, 15, 140.

22. Griswold and Prasert note that the 1357 inscription reverses the order of the second and third disappearances as listed by Buddhaghosa, which begins with the Abhidharma "continuing retrogressively with the other six, then the Vinaya, then the Suttas, and finally even the Jatakas will be forgotten." During the fourth one thousand years, "the monks will forget the proper way to carry the almsbowl or wear the yellow robe," and during the final one thousand years the relics will no longer be honored (1973, 98–99).

23. These prophecies have their own historical trajectories. Thus Steven Collins notes that in early post-canonical texts Maitreya (Mettreya) is only mentioned once but becomes more frequent in later literature (1998, 355–56).

24. Lillian Handlin's work on the *Vessantara Jataka* in Burma reveals "the story's transmutations over the centuries" (2016, 180). Catherine Raymond notes differences in Burmese emphases, with Vessantara even struggling with the urge to attack Jujaka (2012, 133, 141; see also Green 2012). Common sense suggests that the political upheavals in Cambodia, Laos, and Sri Lanka also impacted the story's tellings in these countries, but this research awaits. As Rajini Obeyesekere suggests in the case of Sri Lanka, "The rich ritual dramas of the peasant tradition have become moribund in most parts of the nation today" (1991, 234). In a Cambodian variation, Kanhaa and Chalii marry (Roveda and Sothon 2010, 108).

25. Spiro goes on to suggest that "the monastery is a perfect institutionalized solution for the personality whose narcissistic needs permit—perhaps motivate—abandonment of wife and children" (1970, 346, 348).

26. Village definitions of merit-making include charity to beggars and a broader range of generosity than simply offerings to monks. See Bowie 1998.

27. Nidhi's translators also suggest that with the "shift to a stricter, canonical interpretation of Buddhism in the court, royal patronage of the Mahachat ceased in the Fifth

Reign, and the importance of their recitation festival declined steeply after the centralizing reform of the Sangha in 1902" ([1982] 2005, 200).

28. Jory recognizes the contradiction in his argument but suggests that the reason for Mongkut's continued involvement was because "Mongkut's political enemies, the conservative faction at the court (the so-called 'old Siam' party), were still influential enough to insist that such royal ceremonial as the *thet maha chat* . . . be retained" (1996, 117).

29. Gerini's text is based on the *Bangkok Recorder*, vol. 1, no. 18 (November 18, 1865). Anne Hansen notes that a Khmer biography of Mongkut records Mongkut's view that preaching the Mahachat as "verse-lakhon with musical accompaniment" was contrary to the Dhamma-vinay (the Khmer term for *Tripitaka*) (2007, 90).

30. Even as late as 1886, when King Chulalongkorn traveled to Chanthaburi incognito, he expressed shock upon realizing that local sermons were primarily jataka stories (Jory 2002a, 910).

31. On Korean humor, see Chun Shin-Yong 1977; on Tamil humor, see Eichinger Ferro-Luzzi 1992; on middle-class humor, see Gay 1999; on Russian humor, see Milne 2004; on humor in the Spanish Netherlands, see Verberckmoes 1999; on American cowboy humor, see West 1990; on religious humor, see Hyers 1969; on women's humor, see Sheppard 1986; Pailer 2009; see also Wickberg 1998.

32. In addition to their well-known popularity in the north and northeast, Kamala notes that the Phra Malai texts could be found in practically every wat in central and southern Siam (2003, 305).

33. Similarly, Paritta Chalermpow-Koanantakool, who noted that southern puppet performances often included comments on local and national issues, observes that in these performances some part of the clown's body, usually his forefinger, "is cut out in the shape of the male sexual organ figure," and that "their jokes play on sex, both implicitly and explicitly" (1989, 43,46).

34. For discussion of my use of "peasant imaginaire," see chapter 4, note 1.

35. Manee does include excerpts from southern recensions in his analysis (1976).

36. My thanks to Justin McDaniel for giving me a Thai cartoon version.

Chapter 1. Central Thailand

1. In the northern and northeastern regions, performances are typically not held during Buddhist Lent. The difference between the performance by lay officials as opposed to monks is marked linguistically in the difference between *suat* (to chant) and *thet* (to preach). I thank Arthid Sheravanichkul for bringing these formal lay recitations to my attention.

2. According to Khun Somchai, historically the *Vessantara Jataka* was chanted three times each year for a total of nine days during Lent: (1) beginning of Lent for three days (14-15 kham and wan raem 1 kham dyan 8); (2) middle of Lent for three days (13-14 kham dyan 9 and wan khyn 1 kham dyan 10); (3) end of Lent for three days (wan khyn

13–14 kham and wan raem 1 kham of dyan 11). See also Gerini (1891) 1976, 23; Notton 1933.

3. My thanks to Ajarn Arthid Sheravanichkul for facilitating this interview. Khun Somchai was ordained at age seventeen in Kanchanburi. When he disrobed, he became an official in the Religious Affairs Department (Krom Kaan Saasanaa). Taught by Ajarn Prayong Sornwong, Somchai has been chanting for over thirty years now. According to Khun Somchai, in the Ayutthayan period, there were four people chanting at a time in three groups for a total of twelve people; the king was in attendance for all nine days. However, Rama IV felt it wasted officials' time, and today only four people chant. For further details, see Nidhi 1982, 203–6.

4. For an account of the image's earlier history, see Notton 1933.

5. See "History of the Emerald Buddha," *Bangkok Magazine*, http://www.bangkokmag.infothai.com/emeraldhistory.htm, accessed August 22, 2016.

6. Phone interview with Lung Kriangkrai, March 3, 2010.

7. Phone interview with Phra Racha Thammawaathii, Wat Prayoon, Bangkok, March 3, 2010.

8. For details, see "The Second Lineage of Rajineekul Sai Chao Khun Nual," Bunnag Lineage Club, http://www.bunnag.in.th/english/history_12.html, accessed August 22, 2016.

9. For more on the Chulasakarat calendar, see Eade 1995, 17.

10. The location was the Busabok Mala Maha Chakraphaddi Phiman throne hall. The three head monks were Phra Phimonlatham, Phra Thamma-warodom (Udom), and Phra Phutta Khosachan. Wenk mentions that Phra Phimonlatham was in charge of one of the four committees to revise the Tripitaka (1968, 41).

11. Mary Cort provides additional descriptions of krajaat, writing that the king "commands the princes of the royal family to make the large baskets for him, and they must buy useful things to furnish them and make them more beautiful" (1886, 61). A schoolboy provided her with the following description: "One was made in the shape of a cart, with two buffaloes, which were covered with tobacco instead of hair, to draw it, and the eyes of the buffaloes were made of brass dippers that were painted black and white. The owner had put many useful things in the cart. Also, there was the figure of a man that was covered with dried peppers, and wore spectacles on his nose, sitting in front of the cart" (1886, 61). Another krajaat was a tree with lamps, augers, saws, knives, handkerchiefs, cigars and matches hanging from its branches. Another had birds that had "silver and copper coins instead of feathers" (Cort 1886, 61).

Cort said these royal krajaat ceremonies were an annual occurrence. The recitation lasted for seven days. Near the end of the week the king invited monks to come and cast lots for the baskets. She mentions one that began on August 15, 1883, as being especially interesting since they marked "precisely the number of years, months, and days" that the king had reigned as long as his grandfather. Thirty baskets, eight feet wide and more than sixteen feet long, were prepared. Five hundred monks participated on one day and thirty sermons were read. She adds that the "Krachat [krajaat] festival is usually held in the seventh Siamese month, and the people observe it in a much more simple way than obtains within the palace walls" (1886, 63). (For further details, see Cort 1886, 60–63.)

12. The eldest son, Prince Isara Sunthon, was then front palace vice king (*wang naa*) and later became Rama II. The second son was Prince Senanurak, later appointed as front palace vice king by Rama II.

13. See Gerini (1892) 1976, 37, for further details.

14. Prince Vajiranana (the future sangharaja) mentions that he met with Rama V in 1881 and learned that the king had planned "that I would preach from the *Vessantara Jataka*, the very same chapter that he had offered as merit for our father" in the ceremonies for the Bangkok centennial (Reynolds 1979, 53). The Bangkok Centennial mentions Buddhistic religious ceremonies as part of the celebrations, but is not explicit about which texts were recited. I believe Vajiranana likely chanted Sakabap.

15. Several monks noted the role of Princess Sirindhorn in reviving this royal tradition, one monk adding how the palace and the temples (*wat* and *wang*) were intertwined in the past. An official at Phutthamonthon I interviewed in August 2013 said they had been holding Mahachat recitations for twenty-four years. In 2012 Princess Sirindhorn sponsored the Matsi chapter for a recitation held to raise money for Chitrlada School. The event took place in the palace in honor of her mother's eightieth birthday and the sixtieth birthday of her brother, the crown prince (my thanks to Sujittra Chanthakawanich for this information). Recently Princess Chulabhorn has been coming and has hosted the Jujaka chapter, chanted by Dr. Manop. Prathep has hosted the Kumarn and often the Maharaat chapters (interview with Dr. Manop, August 4, 2013).

16. Despite my repeated inquiries in northern and northeastern Thailand, I have found no evidence that novice recitation was practiced outside of the central region. In central Thailand, the occasions in which the *Vessantara Jataka* was performed outside a temple setting and in a private home were primarily for novice ordinations and secondarily for private recitations by wealthy families (e.g., in Hua Hin; see also Pattaratorn 2009, 32). Conversely, central Thais were not familiar with the northern custom of performing chapters at funerals. That this custom may have been more widespread in the central region is suggested by Kamala's interview with Phrakhruu Wanna at Wat Lak Hok in Ratburi province. Phrakhruu Wanna recalled, "During a wake monks used to deliver long chants or recite a story in verse that lasted until late at night. People were afraid of ghosts, and they liked to have the monks around for company. By the time the monks paddled back to their monastery, it might be close to midnight. Today laypeople don't want the monks to deliver long chants at a funeral. They prefer short chants so they can play cards or gamble after the monks leave" (Kamala 2003, 240). Claus-Bachmann mentions performances of the jataka at funerals "or other sad occasions" in Sri Lanka (2002, 115, 118).

17. Fournereau provides a description and photographs of the Thet Maha Xat (Mahachat) he attended in 1891, noting that "it had not been celebrated for a quarter of a century" and adding that "this ceremony only takes place at the occasion of the novitiate

of the king or the crown prince in a Buddhist temple" ([1894] 1998, 123). Lyons suggests that paintings of the jataka were borrowed from the novice's temple to illustrate his recitation (1960, 168).

18. A monk I interviewed in the city of Hua Hin had never heard of novice recitations, but he said rich lay people often invite monks to recite all thirteen chapters at their homes. A wealthy family near his temple hosts a recitation every year.

19. Mongkut was a novice at Wat Mahathat. Crown Princes Chulalongkorn and Vajirunhis were both novices at Wat Bowonniwet (Gerini [1892] 1976, 35–36).

20. Crown Prince Maha Vajirunhis (1878–95) was the eldest son of King Chulalongkorn and Queen Savang Vadhana. After the death of the last vice king, King Chulalongkorn chose not to appoint a new vice king, but instead, on January 14, 1886, appointed Vajirunhis as crown prince. Upon Vajirunhis's tragic death from typhoid in 1895, Prince Vajiravudh was named crown prince. Both Vajiravudh (Rama VI) and his younger brother (Rama VII) were sent to England for schooling. Although both ordained as monks upon their returns, neither were novices. For photos of Vajirunhis's "great sermon recitation," see "Siam: Days of Glory," *Bangkok 101*, December 2010, 44–53, http://issuu.com/talismanmedia/docs/bangkok-101---december-2010, accessed August 22, 2016.

21. Sulak suggested that the custom has died out because few novices today ordain long enough to study any of the chapters.

22. According to a monk I interviewed, Wat Raatbamrung, a Thammayut temple located in Nong Khaem, Bangkok, does perform the jataka.

23. David Wyatt describes Chaophraya Phrakhlang (Hon) as "a lavish patron of the literature, with a taste for translations from Chinese and the foreign languages, and . . . an accomplished poet himself" (1969, 24).

24. Prince Paramanuchit (1790–1853), abbot of Wat Pho, was appointed supreme patriarch in 1851. Other versions of various chapters were written by other members of the court or high-ranking monks (including from Wat Prayoon). See Gerini (1892) 1976, 54; Manee 1976, 24; Nidhi (1982) 2005, 211–14.

25. In the Lanna version, the text is short, paralleling the Pali (see Prakong 1983, 82). With the exception of the Kumarn chapter, Nidhi suggests that the changes made to other central Thai chapters were minor. Nidhi notes that unlike Prince Paramanuchit, "who attempted to preserve older literary traditions," Phrakhlang Hon was an innovator ([1982] 2005, 216, 218). For more on boat imagery in Pali literature, see Shaw 2012.

26. A donjon is the keep, or fortified main tower, of a castle.

27. A figure of Vessantara with his two children at his feet is also kept at Wat Yannawa but is accessible to the public only on special occasions.

28. When Crown Princess Sirindhorn sponsored the Kumarn chapter in 1972, she also used boat replicas for her offerings. (For this information I thank Dr. Manop, Wat Pho.)

29. Interview with Ajarn Sulak Sivaraksa, Bangkok, March 3, 2010.

30. Waen (Khamwaen) was the daughter of the King of Vientiane and the Princess of Nongbualamphuu, and the sister of Chao Anuwong. I thank Prakirati Satasut and Sujittra (Nion) Chanthakawanich for help with this research.

31. Rama I's chief queen was Queen Amarindra (1737-1826). The daughter of a wealthy Mon from Bang Chang, Samut Songkhram province, she bore three sons and seven daughters. Her sister was married to the founder of the Bunnag family. After the fight with Rama I, she fled to live with her daughter, a consort of the former King Taksin. Although she and Rama I never reconciled, her son became Rama II.

32. A *piiphaat* is a musical ensemble with wind and percussion instruments. It is associated with sacred and "high-class" compositions of the Thai classical repertoire. See Wong 2001, 109, 263-65.

33. But the central Thai amulets I discuss in chapter 6 suggest court control was not complete.

34. Nidhi makes a very interesting argument that Ayutthayan court literature was sexually "absolutely explicit," and only during the Bangkok period did court literature begin to incorporate the robust metaphors from folk literature ([1982] 2005, 29-32).

35. Scenes portraying ordinary people are called *phap kak*, or "the dregs," and are typically located at the bottom of the temple murals. In response to Boisselier's remarks that Thai art and literature only bring up issues dealing with sexuality in a most discreet manner, Napat and Gordon drolly comment, "We wonder where he has been looking" (1999, 11; see also Boisselier 1976, 66-67,114).

36. Also called "Day of the Ghosts" (*wan ching pret*). Wan Sart is also celebrated in Nakhon Sri Thammarat and elsewhere in the southern region.

37. Wan Thewo parallels the Thadingyut Festival in Burma.

38. Wat Pho holds their recitation on khyyn 8 kham, dyan 11.

39. Interview with Phra Racha Vijitphatiphaan, Deputy Abbot, Wat Suthat Thepwaraaraam, Bangkok, January 15, 2008.

40. Gerini was aware of the belief that the jataka "was to be delivered in a single day" ([1892] 1976, 25). Furthermore, Kamala has observed that the Phra Malai texts "could be found in practically every wat in central and southern Siam" (2003, 305; see also 301-16; see also Priyawat 1995). King Chulalongkorn expressed dismay when he traveled to Lopburi and found people worshipped Maitreya (Kamala 2003, 299). It is thus possible that the shift in timing represented court influence in the central region.

41. He added that monks used to practice their recitations underwater or under rain jars in order to get a fuller sound.

42. One person in Samut Sakorn said that the temple was decorated to look like heaven, not a forest.

43. My thanks to Ajarn Paritta Chalermpow Koanantakool for taking me to see a *wai khruu* ceremony in Ayutthaya province. For more on pigs' heads at wai khruu ceremonies, see Paritta 1980; Grow 1991, 169; Wong 2001, 22. Northern friends have assured me they have never seen this in the northern performances. Leedom Lefferts confirms

that he has never seen a pig's head as part of any of the numerous jataka recitations he has observed in the northeast (personal communication, 2013).

44. Brahmins were also involved in the Giant Swing Ceremony, until it was discontinued in 1935.

45. Specialized food offerings for Jujaka appear to have been expanding more recently. At Wat Mai Pinkriaw, Jujaka is said to like *khaw laam*, a dessert specialty of Nakhon Pathom, where the temple is located. For more, see chapter 6.

46. Many villages in the northeast and north will have jars with fish and lily pads to represent this pond.

47. Interview with Phra Racha Vijitphatiphaan, Deputy Abbot, Wat Suthat Thepwaraaraam, Bangkok, January 15, 2008.

48. Wat Chaichanasongkram is a temple of Mon heritage. To maintain their heritage they perform a special reading of the Wanaprawet chapter in Mon.

49. Phone interview with Phra Racha Thammawaathii, Wat Prayoon, Bangkok, March 3, 2010.

50. Interview with Phrakhruu Winaithorn Dr. Manop Paalaphan, Deputy Abbot at Wat Pho (also called Wat Chetuphon), March 4, 2010.

51. Maha Fai was so named because his skin was white like cotton and he wanted to be a farang. He later moved to the Wat Thai in North Hollywood and eventually died.

52. He told the story of the smart city crow. Crows are considered to be thieving birds because they fly from the nest in the morning and steal food all day (hence the phrase *khayan yang ka*, to be industrious like a crow). The village crow saw the Chinaman in the boat selling lots of food from his boat; he tried to swoop down to steal the food but was caught and turned into food by the Chinaman. But the city crow landed on the Chinaman's hat unnoticed and was able to steal the food.

53. He uses the Himaphan chapter (2) to talk about Vessantara and being a good husband.

54. A taxi driver from Chachoengsao thought Amitataa was not a good person; she was envious of others and wanted servants. He said that Amitataa in her previous life had offered wilted old flowers and so in the next life ended up with an old man. He went on to talk about Thai women who married foreign men but were not happy overseas because the food and customs were so different from what they had grown up with in Thailand. Sombat (1981) suggests that she was an exemplar of a bad wife since she forced Jujaka to undertake the journey that eventually killed him.

55. The total may have been more since people were continuing to donate when I was there. Reflecting a somewhat similar pattern were the sums for another performance in honor of the king's birthday at Wat Yannawa in 2009, in which the Maharaat chapter brought in 1,244,058 baht, followed by Himaphan at 391,900 baht; bringing in over 300,000 baht each were, in order, Thotsaphon, Thanakan, Chohkasat, Wanaprawet, and Matsi. Jujaka brought in 252,780 baht, followed by Mahaphon, Kumarn, and

Chulaphon, each of which brought in over 200,000 baht. Sakabap brought in 85,500 baht and Nakornkan raised only 69,430 baht.

56. Frank Vincent also mentions theatrical entertainment, which he described as "gross and obscene throughout" ([1873] 1988, 127).

57. State ritual performances themselves underwent change; thus Gerini notes that "the custom of the uparaja or viceroy going to collect lotus flowers from the people has long become a mere reminiscence" ([1892] 1976, 37).

58. Sharp and Hanks suggest that Vessantara's generosity parallels the act of parents "giving their sons to the temple" (1978, 143). Ironically, their footnote describes a conflict over an ordination that caused a rift in a family.

59. Based primarily on his fieldwork conducted in 1967, Terweil has several mentions of Phra Malai ([1975] 2012, 210, 238, 251, 259–60). Interestingly, he adds that in the past, monks chanted the story, drinking alcohol and dancing through the night at the home of a person who had recently died, "practices that are now forbidden" (251, 259–60).

60. Nonetheless, she provides translations of excerpts of the *Vessantara Jataka* in her discussion of village folklore (1967, 527–34). Kingkeo does mention that Loi Krathong is not celebrated in Napa but that Napa villagers may join in the celebrations held in the municipality of Cholburi (1967, 71).

61. Anuman is not wholly reliable since he presents a composite description without consideration of the geographical variation (e.g., including the maze as if that were a universal element). However, he would have been a firsthand witness to changes in Bangkok and the central region. He continues, "Many of the younger generation whose attitude of mind tends to subordinate the traditional to the novel, view the performance of the Thet Maha Chat unappreciatively. Certainly, they are right in a sense. To hear such recitations takes too long a time and the droning sounds are too monotonous for them to appreciate." He notes that "in order to save this old tradition from being lost altogether, a novel way is introduced in Bangkok today when a theatrical performance of each episode of the story is given just before the recitation takes place of each kan" (1988, 196).

Chapter 2. Northeastern Thailand

1. Some villages celebrate the Bun Pha Wet less often and some perform the recitation "in association with other major wat rites—e.g., the consecration of a Buddha image and Songkhran, the Thai-Lao New Year" (Cate and Lefferts 2012, 168).

2. Calendrical cycles differ. For the northern cycle, see Sommai and Dore 1992, 42–43; for the central Thai cycle, see Wales (1931) 1992; Wells 1939; Terweil (1975) 2012, 215.

3. Among the Phu Thai, Bun Pha Wet and Bun Bangfai, intended for rain, are celebrated simultaneously (Kirsch 1967, 298, 300).

4. While 83 percent ranked Bun Pha Wet within the top three annual rituals, only 6.5 percent ranked New Year's (Songkran) among the top three (Hayashi 2003, 121). In

northern Thailand, Songkran would undoubtedly rank among the most important. I cannot imagine any northern or central Thai villager today even mentioning the *Vessantara Jataka* in response to Hayashi's question.

5. Phu Thai live primarily in Sakon Nakhon, Kalasin, and Nakhon Phanom.
6. My thanks to Leedom Lefferts for facilitating this meeting.
7. My thanks to Sandra Cate for drawing my attention to this festival.
8. The celebration can also draw outsiders seeking to make local connections. At the recitation I attended, a hospital administrator came who was interested in buying land in the area.
9. Hayashi does note that the monks should have "a melodious voice" and are expected to "have mastered the art of speaking" (2003, 134).
10. No northeasterner I interviewed had heard of the northern pattern of chapter sponsorship by birth year.
11. At the Bun Pha Wet I observed, the extra offering arrived after the Hok Kasat monks had already departed; the additional money was given to the local abbot and temple committee.
12. Tambiah does not mention the Vessantara procession but does discuss the invitation of Upakut (1970, 161–62). Klausner mentions a flower and elephant parade, but not Upakut; instead he notes a novice or monk ordination ([1981] 1993, 46–48). Nonetheless, based on interviews with various monks and laity, and with Leedom Lefferts, processions of the Upakut, Vessantara, and the thousand balls of rice are quite typical.
13. According to Tambiah, Upakut is not invited for any other northeastern ceremony (1970, 170; see also Sommai and Dore 1992, 93–94). However, Lefferts has observed Upakut in other northeastern ceremonies (personal communication, June 1, 2013).
14. Tambiah suggests these items represent Buddha's victorious battle with Mara (1970, 163). See Tambiah 1970 for text of the rite of invitation.
15. Sommai and Dore observed a ceremony at about 4:00 a.m. (1992, 94). Manee observed an invitation to Phra Upakut at 3:00 p.m. followed by the invitation to Vessantara and Matsi to enter the city at about 4:00 p.m. Led by spirit-ghosts (*phii khon*), Vessantara and Matsi rode in on elephants. The procession, a raucous group with drums, cymbals, and firecrackers, danced through the streets, going from house to house. Home owners were expected to offer liquor and food, in exchange for which they received blessings. There was a drumming competition at night, replete with drinking, dancing, and general merriment (Manee 1976, 51–53).
16. Some villages hang the scroll without a procession. Neither Klausner nor Tambiah mentions a scroll procession, but Klausner refers to the scroll hanging in the temple (1993, 47), and Tambiah's photograph shows it hanging there (1970, 160; see also Cate and Lefferts 2012, 168). Scrolls are fairly expensive by village standards. I saw a scroll for sale at a Buddhist bookstore in Khon Kaen for 3,900 baht in 2010. For further discussion of scrolls, see Lefferts 2006/7; Lefferts and Cate 2012.

17. Before only the scroll was processed, but the procession was expanded a few years ago to appeal more to the younger generation (Lefferts, personal communication, March 2010).

18. In contrast to the Upakut procession, in this case no specific space in the temple was designated for Vessantara and Matsi once the procession arrived.

19. My thanks to Leedom Lefferts for this insight (personal communication, June 8, 2013).

20. Tambiah's account mentions four such flag poles and suggests that these may represent *kalpavrksa* trees, associated with the coming of Maitreya (1970, 165).

21. In Tambiah's account, this procession took place at 2:30 a.m. when the village fair was in full swing. Instead of a big display, the rice balls were carried in bowls (1970, 165).

22. After the Siamese capture of Vientiane in 1826, some six thousand families were removed to Thailand (Turton 1980, 255).

23. Red Shirts are aware of the *Forbes* article on the royal family's wealth. Tatiana Serafin Cristina von Zeppelin, "In Pictures: The World's Richest Royals," July 7, 2010, http://www.forbes.com/2010/07/07/richest-royals-wealth-monarch-wedding-divorce-billionaire_slide_2.html.

24. Lefferts and Cate note a 1995 scroll depicting an array of policemen, soldiers, merchants, and citizens "in near-contemporary dress" (2012, 92).

25. Interview with Phra Uthai, Petchabun, March 7, 2010.

26. Brereton and Somroay suggest that northeastern "villains and demons are not entirely intimidating," but instead are presented as "symbols of craving and desire to be pitied rather than feared" (2010, 21). Thus the emotional tone Jujaka evoked among northeasterners may have reflected a modicum of compassion or pity rather than sheer horror or terror.

27. None of the northeastern monks or laity had ever heard of individual chapters being performed for funerals, ordinations, housewarmings, or any other occasion.

28. A version of the Buddha's life by Supreme Patriarch Somdet Phra Ariyawongsakhatayana (Sa) (1813–99) omits many mythological episodes included in earlier versions and does not conclude with Buddhaghosa's prediction, instead emphasizing the Buddha's teachings as motivation for behavior in this world rather than fear of its disappearance (Reynolds 1973, 136; Swearer 1996, 325).

29. Akin notes how the festival came to be a factor in vote-getting in local elections, becoming "an instrument which serves the political ambitions of the business group" and providing "an opportunity for the relatively poor urbanites to gain access to public funds and support from private businesses" (1992, 22–23).

30. "Loei, Thailand," http://www.triposo.com/loc/Loei/sightseeing/background, accessed August 22, 2016.

31. Manee suggests that the northeastern processions typically include "*phii khon*" (1976, 52). Processions in Roi Et have phiitaakhon, and Ubon has recently added them.

32. See further discussion in chapter 6.

33. Such ancestral figures are reminiscent of Puu Sae Yaa Sae, celebrated in the New Year's festival in Luang Prabang and elsewhere in Laos. See Archaimbault 1971.

34. The actual date is chosen by spirit mediums. The timing corresponds more with the Rocket Festival, which occurs typically at the beginning of the rainy season circa June.

35. Although Thailand has white-robed nuns (*mae chii*), it does not provide formal recognition for fully ordained nuns (*bhikkhuni*). For more on this controversy, see Chartsumarn 1991; Falk 2008; Koret 2012.

36. In Daan Laan Hoi in Sukhothai province, a woodcarver named Lung Loi Duangkaew (1911–92) and the local abbot, Luang Poh Pii (1902–74), began holding processions to gain the interest of the younger generation. Lung Loi carved scary masks of Jujaka. The masks are considered sacred and kept at the local temple. I thank Davisakd Puaksom for helping me with this series of interviews.

37. When Amitataa returns home crying after being teased, Jujaka asks her why. In the northeastern versions, Amitataa does not say much more than that the village women were mean and she will no longer go there to fetch water for him.

38. In fact, nineteenth-century central Thai paintings also show village women mooning Amitataa. See McGill 2009, 61, 157,169. My thanks to Forrest McGill for drawing my attention to these images.

39. Upakut is known in northern Thailand but is not given particular emphasis in the recitations of the *Vessantara Jataka*. Monks and laity I interviewed in Chiang Mai and Lampang did not mention any special invitation of Upakut (see also Manee 1976, 91). Upakut is mentioned in association with Dyan Yii Paeng (Davis 1984, 223–30, illustration plate 17–18; see Davis for translation of an 1808 text titled "Dhamma Maha Upagrutta." See also Rhum 1994, 149–50). To the extent that northern Thailand performed *Vessantara Jataka* recitations in association with Dyan Yii Paeng, it is possible that Upakut and *Vessantara Jataka* were once linked in northern Thailand as well. On the other hand, Nan may have incorporated more practices similar to the Lao of Laos or northeastern Thailand due to its proximity to them.

John Strong has conducted an extensive study of Upakut. He concludes that the belief in Upakut was strong in the Shan States regions of Burma, northern Thailand, northeastern Thailand, and Laos (1992, 14). He differentiates between an iconic tradition centered in Burma, in which Upakut is depicted as a monk, and an aniconic tradition centered between the Menam and Mekong Rivers, in which Upakut is represented in the form of stone taken from a riverbed or a swamp (1992, 171–72). Unlike in northeastern Thailand, where Upakut is particularly associated with Bun Pha Wet, in the north, "Upakut is not necessarily connected with the Vessantara tradition; he can be invited anytime for any festival at all" (Strong 1992, 17). Interestingly Strong notes that in a Shan monastery in Mae Hong Son he saw four images of Upakut in storage. These "are used once a year in a rite called Khao Wong Kot," which "involves proceeding through a large and elaborate labyrinth.... Devotees try to get to the Buddha by finding their way through the maze; when they fail, they must make a donation to the monastery by paying a helper who will assist them on their way. The four Upakut images are installed on four smaller platforms at the four corners of the labyrinth, where they appear to play a guardian role" (Strong 1992, 243-44, 341n38). Upakut is mentioned in various sources on Burma (e.g., Forbes 1878, 194-95; Shway Yoe [1882] 1963, 228; Ferrars and Ferrars 1900, 185-87; Htin Aung 1962, 132).

40. McDaniel has noted significant cultural connections between the Lao and Lanna regions manifest in religious texts (2008). Dhawat also remarks on similarities in northern and northeastern literature and suggests that central Thai literature was more oriented toward extolling the monarchy than either northern or northeastern literatures (1995, 256, 260).

41. In the central and southern versions, Jujaka has Jetabutr bow down to his case, which he says contains the royal letter; this scenario is not in the northern or northeastern versions. In the southern version, Jujaka shows off his status as a powerful ambassador, claiming that if he is killed, the king will come after Jetabutr and punish him. At first Jetabutr does not believe Jujaka and sees how old he is; a royal messenger should be young and strong. But Jujaka replies that the young people were the ones who chased Vessantara out of the city, so the king only put his faith in him since he was old and a trusted adviser (*ammaat*) (Manee 1976, 233).

42. Manee suggests that both the northern and northeastern versions are making fun of monks who do not know how to perform the religious chants; these monks might have become ordained only to flee the military, to escape suffering, or to have fun with friends (*buat nii tahaan, buat phon ayasuk, buat sanuk taam phyan*) (Manee 1976, 261). In northern versions, the monk is typically a *phra chiidok*, someone who has been ordained for a long time but has gained no knowledge; the monk is described as having *miang* (fermented tea leaves, a favorite northern delicacy) still in his mouth and a cigarette burnt to ashes in his hand. The monk stands by the funeral pyre but does not know what to say, hits a pile of wood, chants nonsensical Pali words, and tells Jujaka's spirit to go to hell instead of heaven, as he should. In some northern versions Jujaka is told to go to the hell where Devathat is. Manee is critical of this passage because Devathat was not yet born (1976, 261-62).

43. On the other hand, Cate and Lefferts note that Thai monarchs attempted to suppress the messianic readings of the *Vessantara Jataka* that were taking place in the late 1800s and early 1900s. Cate and Lefferts, drawing upon Jory's argument, suggest that these attempts to displace the centrality of the *Vessantara Jataka* were intended in part to mute direct associations of the monarchy with the future Maitreya Buddha and keep attitudes toward state authority centralized upon the King rather than local rulers (2012, 179).

Chapter 3. Northern Thailand

An earlier version of this chapter was published as "Jūjaka as Trickster: The Comedic Monks of Northern Thailand," in *Readings of the "Vessantara Jātaka,"* edited by Steven

Collins, copyright © 2016 Columbia University Press, reprinted with permission of the publisher.

1. A Pali version in Lampang dates to 1714 (Veidlinger 2006, 138). Manee provides a list of some sixty-one Lanna versions (1976, 45, 75–77; see also Brereton 1995, 62).

2. This monk was almost certainly Luang Poh Bunthong.

3. Interview with Ajarn Manee Phayomyong, Mae Rim, Chiang Mai, August 1, 2005.

4. Indeed, a former tujok monk I interviewed founded a well-known traveling theatrical troupe (likay) after he disrobed.

5. Luang Poh Bunthong is known variously as Tu Lung Thong, Phrakhruu Bunthong Suwanno, and Phrakhruu Soponbunyaporn. Bunthong was born in Baan Dong Makhoi, Tambon Sanphiisya, A. Muang. The family later moved to Mae Rim. Over time, they were able to buy three rai of land, but the land has since been sold. Bunthong had not planned to spend his life as a monk. His brother had ordained at the same temple. After feeding the water buffaloes there was not much to do, so his mother had Bunthong bring food to his brother at night. Bunthong became a novice in 1945 and ordained as a monk in 1954. Because he had studied naktham and there were few monks who were able to teach it, he became a naktham teacher. More and more children began attending his classes. His age-mates were disrobing, but his mother told him not to. Her view was that of her six children, he was her best hope (*phyng baramii luuk khon diaw*). As Bunthong explained, "Whenever she died, she said I could disrobe. When my mother died I was over forty, and what could I do? I didn't have any worldly knowledge. I became the abbot and was being invited to *thet* more and more places. Pretty soon there was no time left to think about disrobing." Wat Sophanaram (also called Wat Pa Tyng) has a website with a link to a recording of his Jujaka chapter (http://www.watsopanaram.com/?page_id=165, accessed February 1, 2016). The temple also continues to sell tapes and CDs of his recordings.

6. Sources in English are Keyes 1975; Kingshill 1976, 152–53; Davis 1984; and Sommai and Dore 1991.

7. Manee was a respected Pali scholar, having passed the level six examinations; he ordained as a novice in 1943 and disrobed from the monkhood in 1962. In his interview with me, Manee explained that while he was a monk, he decided to make a radical change in preaching style to respond to the growing inability of modern audiences to understand the *Vessantara Jataka* and their growing time constraints. He decided to tell an abridged version of the story, combining chanted excerpts from the northern Thai and Pali texts, but explaining them in a normal voice to his audiences so they could understand (*thaet*, then *banyai*). His abridged version took approximately three hours. Manee dated the change to about 2500 BE, or about 1957. He first tried this format in Lampang (in Hang Chat) and found it to be very successful. As he commented to me, "I had a bigger audience than the likay performance. Every one was amazed that a monk could beat out a likay performance. It was something new" (interview with Ajarn Manee Phayomyong, Mae Rim, Chiang Mai, August 1, 2005). For details on his life, see

"Honorary Professor Dr. Manee Phayomyong," Northern Thai Information Center, http://library.cmu.ac.th/ntic/en_lannatradition/expertdetail.php?id=12, accessed August 24, 2016.

Although Manee was not known as a tujok, Luang Poh Bunthong was influenced by Manee's innovations. Bunthong and Manee agreed their styles were very different: Manee's was more based in his knowledge of Pali while Bunthong's was based more in his knowledge of village folklore. Bunthong had always enjoyed the Jujaka chapter. As he explained, "Chuchok [Jujaka] has always been funny and I always enjoyed it in particular. So I took Chuchok as a technique to help teach people. Manee didn't *thaet* Chuchok; he would speak (*phuut bai*) and include certain parts which were humorous. But he was an important scholar. He studied Pali. I didn't study Pali. But I studied psychology to see what people were interested in. I never studied it formally. I just read books about it."

Bunthong studied with Ajarn Manee and Ajarn Insom at Doi Saket District (Baan San Pong, Tambon Samranraat). Poh Naan Insom had been a monk but later disrobed; when later the temple needed an abbot, he re-ordained and remained a monk until his death. Insom did not perform the Jujaka chapter but was famous for his performance of the Nakornkan chapter. Bunthong commented, "Just getting the *namo thasa* . . . right took three days. It's like learning a song; one had to learn the melody. Now there are tapes one can practice with, but before one had to learn directly from the teacher. Just learning the Nakornkan chapter took easily a month. [*He demonstrates a section.*] One did a whole section in one breath, not like I just did now, with breaths in between" (interview with Luang Poh [Phrakhruu] Bunthong Suwanno, Wat Sothannaraam, Tambon Don Kaew, Amphur Mae Rim, Chiang Mai, August 1, 2005).

8. This recitation was somewhat anomalous because it was an out-of-season fundraiser sponsored by a central Thai.

9. Although the famous thirteenth-century Ramkhamhaeng inscription does not mention the jataka explicitly, it does mention the importance of generosity, noting that "the inhabitants of this city of Sukhothai are fond of almsgiving, charity and the maintenance of the precepts" (Benda and Larkin 1967, 42).

10. Wray 1972, 116-17; Brereton 1976; Gosling 1984; Pattaratorn 2008, 38; Skilling 2008.

11. Harold Hundius suggests that there are more than 230 non-canonical jatakas in the Lanna region (1995, 46).

12. They are sometimes called the apocryphal or extra-canonical jatakas. See also Feer (1865) 1963; Finot 1917; Terral 1956; Prakong 1983, 6; McDaniel 2000; Veidlinger 2006, 63, 186.

13. Chapter titles in central and northern Thai differ, with Kumarn becoming Kumaarabaan, Matsi becoming Matthi, and Chohkasat becoming Sakkhati (Manee 1976, 47).

14. Bangkok authorities subsequently banned these raised pulpit booths, evidently hoping "to put an end to this kind of dramatic preaching" (Kamala 1997, 32). Raised

about a meter and a half above the floor, the Lanna pulpit had "walls of carved wood on three sides, while the fourth was left wide open for entry by means of a ladder" (Kamala 1997, 32). Monks now recite while seated on an open preaching chair, chanting behind fans.

15. Famous tujok included Tu Luang Som at Wat Long Than in Tambon Baan Klang, Sanpatong district, Chiang Mai province (who brought dogs along); Luang Poh Bonsong at Wat Chang Taem (in Lampang city); Luang Poh Laan at Wat Pangtru, Tambon Baan Kho, Amphur Chae Hom, Lampang (who wore the brown robes of a forest monk [*aranyawasi*]); and Phrakhruu Danuphol at Wat Mae Suk in Amphur Chae Hom, who apparently had apprenticed under Luang Poh Bunthong in Mae Rim.

16. Interview with Luang Poh (Phrakhruu) Bunthong Suwanno, Wat Sothannaraam, Tambon Don Kaew, Amphur Mae Rim, Chiang Mai, August 1, 2005.

17. Mazes are not constructed in northeast or central Thailand (Anuman mentions mazes, but I believe this is because his account is a composite). I asked at least a dozen people in the central region if they had ever heard of mazes, and they had not. Although neither Richard Davis nor Kingshill notes the presence of mazes, mazes are mentioned by Swearer (2009, 36), and Kenneth Wells mentions that during the Loi Krathong celebrations of November 17-19, 1937, in Chiang Mai "temple yards are adorned with paper flags, Chinese lanterns, and sometimes with scenery representing the mountain which figures in the tale of Vessantara" (1939, 104). Mazes (*wingaba*) are found in Burma (e.g., Bird 1897, 260; Ferrars and Ferrars 1900, 186).

18. For further details on the decorations, see Sommai and Dore 1991, 35-36; 1992, 79; see also Manee 1976, 50; "Yipeng Festival," Northern Thai Information Center, http://library.cmu.ac.th/ntic/en_lannatradition/yeepeng-thongtom.php, accessed August 24, 2016. Some suggest that it is the ransom for the daughter even more than for the son. The Pali version reads, "None but a king can give all things by the hundred; therefore if your sister would be free let her pay the brahmin a hundred male and a hundred female slaves, with elephants, horses, bulls, and gold pieces, all a hundred each." The son's ransom was a thousand pieces of gold (Cowell [1895] 1957, 283).

19. Prakong says it was performed in Lanna during months 7-8 (i.e., in April and May; 1983, 4); Manee states that it was performed during months 5-6 (February-March; 1976, 50).

20. His temple recited the chapter that corresponded to his personal birth year.

21. I consistently asked monks and laity in northeastern and central Thailand if they had ever heard of *Vessantara Jataka* chapters being recited at funerals. None had.

22. Interview with Phrakhruu Athong Visutikhul, Abbot, Wat Nong Tong, Tambon Nong Tong, Amphur Hang Dong, Chiang Mai, July 13, 2005.

23. Today many northern temples have not hosted a Tang Tham Luang in decades. In the past it appears to have been held as often as every two to three years (Manee 1976, 48-49).

24. The *Anisong* (blessings) and the *Khaiwibaak* (hardship) of Vessantara describe the merit to be gained from listening to the story and the previous lives of the main

characters. One translation of a northern *Anisong* is: "It is said that any person having listened to the sermon of Maha Vessandon Jataka will become a ruler of the human realm and will receive a high and noble rank and possess an abundance of elephants and horses as well as sweet musical playing of all kinds of drums and lyres whether in his sleep or awake. He will be surrounded by servants to accommodate him in whichever way he wishes. He will continually acquire great wealth of clothing, silver, gold, as well as precious stones. His storage houses will be filled with rice and grain to the point of overflowing. Whatever he wishes will be granted. He will be prosperous. In the time of the incarnation of Ariyamettai [Maitreya] or the next Buddha, he will have the chance to hear and appreciate his wisdom and be granted with the great opportunity of meeting him in person and, because of his merit gained from listening to the recitation of the Vessandon Jataka sermon, to be presented hereby, he will surely attain the most desirable nirvana." See "Yipeng Festival," Northern Thai Information Center, http://library.cmu.ac.th/ntic/en_lannatradition/yeepeng-thongtom.php, accessed August 24, 2016.

25. The belief that the recitation must be completed within twenty-four hours in order to meet Ariya Maitreya in next life is widely known and was often articulated to me in interviews. Interestingly Manee also notes offerings being made to the forty-nine Buddhas "like those Nang Suchada gave to Buddha before his enlightenment." He adds that many villagers also brought Buddha images with them to be consecrated (*buat prachao*), replete with cooked rice, bananas, sugarcane, betel, and sweets (Manee 1976, 49).

26. According to Kingshill, one donates the chapter bearing the same number as one's month of birth, except for the seventh month, "which requires the donation of both chapters 7 and 13" (2000, 20). I have not found this pattern corroborated elsewhere.

27. The Lanna twelve-year cycle differs slightly from the Chinese cycle—e.g., elephant versus pig and great and little serpent versus dragon and snake.

28. In addition to the offerings made to each of the thirteen monks, one will usually find twelve money trees arranged according to one's animal birth year; these money trees are offerings made in support of the host temple. The money tree is usually made from tamarind (*makkham*) tree because it has many branches. (A common element in many village ceremonies, the trees are often dedicated in memory of someone who has died, so even though monks have no hair, they may include combs, mirrors, and face powder.)

29. Interview with Phrakhruu Athong Visutikhul, Abbot, Wat Nong Tong, Tambon Nong Tong, Amphur Hang Dong, Chiang Mai, July 13, 2005.

30. Although the specifics vary, throughout Thailand, Jujaka is widely described as having eighteen characteristics. A sample list includes: (1) big, deformed feet; (2) stubby finger and toes; (3) huge calves on his legs; (4) his upper lip is longer than his lower lip; (5) dribbles saliva; (6) cuspid teeth sticking out of his mouth as long as a pig's; (7) broken nose, curling like an elephant's trunk; (8) belly is round like a pot; (9) humped back; (10) squinty eyes; (11) red beard; (12) thin hair; (13) visible tendons; (14) flecks all over his skin; (15) eyes as yellow as a cat's; (16) both foot are split; (17) crooked neck, bended back; (18) body hair coarse like a pig's. In the northern text, Jujaka's mouth has a harelip

and sucked-in cheeks; he has no teeth, his jaw is long, and he has a protruding belly. I thank Chaiyaporn Singdee for his assistance with this list.

31. Luang Poh Bunthong, TE 066, tape 3, side B.

32. Luang Poh Bunthong, TE 066, tape 3, side B.

33. This addition is also found in northeastern versions. Thus one scroll records, "There [in Benares] was a vile Brahmin. His house was burnt down because of his bad deeds. So he fled to live in Kalingarat city" (Lefferts and Cate 2012, 118).

34. On courtship poetry in northeastern Thailand, see Compton 1979.

35. Luang Poh Bunthong, TE 066, tape 3, side B.

36. Villagers believe the "soul" or life-force has thirty-two aspects. If a villager has an accident or meets with other misfortune, villagers will often hold a ceremony to "call" (*hong*) back the soul's thirty-two aspects.

37. Interview with Phrakhruu Athong Visutikhul, Abbot, Wat Nong Tong, Tambon Nong Tong, Amphur Hang Dong, Chiang Mai, July 13, 2005. See Prakong 1983, 60, for two other similar variations.

38. *Mai bao* is apparently used as an herbal medicine for pregnant women and as a cure for wrinkles. I thank Narong Mahakhom for this information.

39. In the Pali version, when Jujaka asks why Amitataa is crying after she returns home, Amitataa merely says, "I cannot fetch the water home, the women mock me so: Because my husband is so old they mock me when I go" (Cowell [1895] 1957, 271). In central Thai versions, which are only slightly longer than the Pali version, she says, "Old brahmin, I will no longer go to the pier [*thaa nam*], I will no longer collect plants, I will no longer touch any cooking pots, no longer pound rice, I won't fetch water, I won't steam rice or roast fish, I won't fetch firewood" (Prakong 1983, 17).

40. Interview with Phrakhruu Athong Visutikhul, Abbot, Wat Nong Tong, Tambon Nong Tong, Amphur Hang Dong, Chiang Mai, July 13, 2005.

41. I remember the shocked silence of some younger villagers when an elderly village woman who had known me for many years once called me "Ii Kat." There was a sigh of relief when I smiled.

42. *Kulawaa* is an Indian or other foreigner.

43. Jujaka also lists normal men's chores that he does not know how to perform, such as making coconut ladles, water dippers, cooking pots, knives, and fingernail clippers—or raising cattle or water buffaloes. Some northern versions mention he did not know how to sign checks, do the sword dance, or engage in other such activities that would not be expected of village men either (Prakong 1983, 21, 46).

44. Interview with Phrakhruu Athong Visutikhul, Abbot, Wat Nong Tong, Tambon Nong Tong, Amphur Hang Dong, Chiang Mai, July 13, 2005. One of my village friends recalls that she and others in her family also used to defecate through a hole in the floor. In the morning they would cover it with dirt and eventually move the mound elsewhere.

45. In the Pali version, the dogs are only mentioned. One northern version has seven dogs, each of a different nationality, namely a Thai, Burmese, Hot, Yuan, Shan,

farang (Kullawa), and Thai Lyy dog (see the text included in Prakong 1983, 38). Other Lanna versions have twenty-two dogs, twenty-four dogs, forty-two dogs, and one even has eighty-two dogs. However, the most common number seems to be thirty-two, which allows for linkage with the thirty-two *khwan* (soul-substances) or thirty-two elements of our bodies (e.g., heart, lungs, kidney, saliva, etc.; see Prakong 1983, 65–66).

46. Here is an example of Luang Poh Bunthong describing Jujaka falling on different kinds of trees, done in the rhyme pattern we have seen earlier. The basic pattern has the branch of one kind of tree bending or falling onto the branch of another kind of tree (mai pao, mai sisiat, mai bodiimii, etc., all types of trees). It begins with Jujaka scrambling up a mai san tree; its branch bends so Jujaka lands on a mai pao tree, and so on. I have highlighted the rhyming pattern: "*Khing mai kaan yua sai mai pao / Pao wao bai haa mai sisiat / Biat bai haa mai bodiimii / Nii bai haa lamyai / Bai haa phak la / Yua bai maa bo-oo (som-oo) / Jolo bai haa mai hua / Luat bai haa mai yohm / Ngom bai haa mai chamchaa / Bhawaa bai haa mai sisiat / Biat bai haa mai bodiimii / Nii bai haa balomraeng.*" He brings the sequence to an end by breaking the rhyming pattern with the final lines, "*Khing haeng mii, man bo ko / Bai ko khing daai*" (There was a dry branch, but he didn't grab it. He grabbed a dead branch).

47. Luang Poh Bunthong, TE 066, tape 4, side A.

48. In the Pali version, the Chulaphon chapter is only thirty-five verses.

49. See the list in Prakong 1983, 23–24.

50. In several northern temples, I saw mural paintings of Jujaka vomiting and having diarrhea. In two temples the painting included dogs coming to lap up the diarrhea.

51. Lomphong is an ancient word that no one I asked could translate.

52. Luang Poh Bunthong, TE 066, tape 5, side A.

53. Luang Poh Bunthong, TE 066, tape 5, side B. See Prakong 1983, 51, for another variation based on the same principles.

54. In part the reason for the laughter is because northerners view central Thais as arrogant. See Prakong 1983, 52, and Manee 1976, 260, for similar variations.

55. It is customary to tap the coffin to make sure the spirit of the deceased is paying attention.

56. Luang Poh Bunthong, TE 066, tape 5, side B. See Prakong 1983, 53, for a similar variation.

57. He then says this is true of all of us, including himself, but jokes that he has slightly less *kilesa* because he is the one giving the sermon. Interview with Phrakhruu Athong Visutikhul, Abbot, Wat Nong Tong, Tambon Nong Tong, Amphur Hang Dong, Chiang Mai, July 13, 2005.

58. Prakong observes that overall the Lanna version is more interested in emotions (*arom*) than mellifluousness (*khwaam phairoh*) (1983, 72).

59. Bunthong prefaced his remarks by saying, "Excuse me, Goddesses, Gods, Buddha, Dharma, Sangha, Elders, Teachers [*thewadaa, thewaabutr, phrachao, phratham, phrasong, khon thao, khon kae, kruubaa ajarn*] listening, please forgive me. But it is in the texts, you can read it for yourself. I don't want to say this. But it's not right if I say it and

it's not right if I don't. So let me just get it over with. She wanted to breastfeed her children with her own breasts, but she didn't want her breasts to stretch out. So now you see why I didn't want to say it [*Waa bo yaak waa, tae ca tong waa, bo waa, ko waa, waa ko waa, bo waa ko waa*]."

60. Luang Poh Bunthong, TE 066, tape 2, side B.
61. Luang Poh Bunthong, TE 066, tape 2, side B.
62. Luang Poh Bunthong, TE 066, tape 4, side A.
63. Sticky rice needs to be soaked overnight.
64. Luang Poh Bunthong, TE 066, tape 3, side B.
65. Luang Poh Bunthong, TE 066, tape 5, side B.
66. Luang Poh Bunthong, TE 006, side A.
67. Luang Poh Bunthong, TE 066, tape 3, side B.
68. Luang Poh Bunthong, TE 066, tape 5, side B.
69. Luang Poh Bunthong was corpulent and as a monk already had a shaved head.
70. Luang Poh Bunthong, TE 066, tape 3, side B.
71. Luang Poh Bunthong, TE 066, tape 2, side B.

Chapter 4. Jujaka as Trickster

1. Due largely to the work of Steven Collins, the phrase "Pali imaginaire" has become increasingly popular among scholars of Theravada Buddhism. Tracing his use of the term back to Émile Durkheim, Jacques LeGoff, and others, Collins is seeking to relate the Pali texts he studies to the social world in which they were interpreted. Rejecting as "the other extreme" the idea that "there is no ideological domination of the peasantry by the elite in an agrarian society" (1998, 75), Collins sympathizes more with Fernand Braudel's description of "ways of thought," a concept that Braudel explains as follows: "In every period, a certain view of the world, a collective mentality, dominates the whole mass of society. . . . These basic values, these psychological structures, are assuredly the features that civilizations can least immediately communicate to each other. . . . Here religion is the strongest feature of civilizations, at the heart of both their present and their past" (quoted in Collins 1998, 75; for fuller discussion, see Collins 1998, 72–89).

My use of "peasant imaginaire" is an anthropological continuation both of Durkheim's interest in collective consciousness and Collins's interest in placing texts in their sociohistorical context. However, my usage is intended to problematize the extent to which a given text, such as the *Vessantara Jataka*, can be understood as part of a shared worldview. Here I am suggesting that the cultural worldview, and particularly the political consciousness, of the peasantry was not necessarily the same as the elites in the same society. Focusing on the character of Jujaka reveals differing political interpretations of the *Vessantara Jataka*, hopefully enlivening our understanding of the dynamics of texts in the historical process.

2. There is a growing awareness of the role of tricksters in Buddhism, from Monkey to Jigong (Wu Ch'Eng-En 1958; DeBernardi 2006). Sara McClintock (2011) even suggests considering the Buddha as a trickster figure.

3. S. E. Schlosser, "Tricksters," http://www.americanfolklore.net/tricksters.html, accessed August 25, 2016.

4. Also popular in Laos, Epstein notes that Siang Miang "represents the common man and his struggle against the bourgeoisie and the monarchy" (1995, vii). According to Steven Epstein, these tales were also used by the Pathet Lao "in their struggle to defeat the wealthier and better-armed royalist troops" (1995, vii-viii). In Thailand, Phya Anuman Rajadhon also mentions similar tales about a monk named Theen Thaung (1958, 13-16). Reginald LeMay tells a tale of "Lazybones" ([1926] 1986, 223-28). Fleeson includes folktales about the foibles of villagers and monks in her collection (1899). Trickster stories were also popular in Burma (e.g., Maung Htin Aung 1976).

5. Wat Pathumwanaram's laity is largely of northeastern heritage (Hartmann 2013).

6. While national statistics give a general indication of economic hardship overall, the accounts of anthropologists working in various regions of the country provide evidence of landlessness. Writing of northern Thailand, John De Young "found 27.7 per cent of the farmers in the region to be tenants" (1955, 28). Kingshill noted that 14 percent of the inhabitants in his village were landless (1976, 30). Jack Potter determined that 32.5 percent in the village he conducted his fieldwork owned no land at all and 71 percent owned *less* than 5 rai, the minimum for subsistence (1976, 56). A survey conducted in 1974 in Chiang Mai province found 36 percent of village households were landless (Turton 1978, 112). Numerous other studies also detail stratification in other northern Thai villages (e.g., Moerman 1968, 84, 105; Anan 1984, 388; Chayan 1984, 235). Similar patterns of internal village stratification were found in the other main regions of Thailand. For an overview of anthropological literature on this subject, see Potter 1976; see also Turton 1978; Cohen 1983; Witayakorn 1983; Haberkorn 2011.

7. Interest rates were high. The report continues, "The present rate is one rupee for every rupee lent, and a bucket of rice as interest on each rupee. The end of the rice harvest is the final date. In case the crop fails of course the lender takes the field. This amounts to practically one hundred percent interest for seven to eight months" (*BTWM*, August 18, 1912).

8. Such shortages also affected Buddhist clergy. A report from Lampang in 1913 noted the nai amphur organizing rice collection to stop monks and novices leaving (*BTWM*, September 16, 1913).

9. Chiang Mai, Lamphun, Chiang Rai, Lampang, Phrae, Nan, and Maehongsorn are all provinces in northern Thailand.

10. See McGilvary (1912, 351) for another account of this famine. Sir Ernest Satow writes of an earlier serious drought in the area in 1885, which also affected thousands of villagers (Satow Mss 20/1, 200).

11. For other such village sayings, see Bowie 1988. For further details on poverty, see Bowie 1988, 1992, 1998, 2014.

12. Interviews included HD-14, SPT-62, S-147, S-151, S-155, S-163, S-168, SKP-245, SKP-254, SKP-257, SKP-286, DS-298, DS-339, DS-353, SS-523, M-546.

13. Interviews included HD-11, HD-14, HD-36, S-127, S-155, S-163, SKP-247, SKP-253, SKP-258, SKP-264, SKP-286, DS-352, MR-370, MR-422, MR-438, SS-478, SS-512.

14. Interviews included HD-8, HD-14, HD-19, HD-36, CT-59, SPT-62, S-114, S-126, S-127, S-147, S-156, S-163, S-168, S-174, S-177, SKP-225, SKP-247, SKP-253, SKP-257, SKP-258, S-260, SKP-273, SKP-285, DS-298, DS-305, 343, DS-352, MR-386, MR-398, MR-422, SS-462, SS-476, SS-478. One went on to add that it would be terrible if the new laws had not come into force in 1932 and things were still as they had been in the past (SS-515).

15. Interviews included HD-19, CT-59, S-126, SKP-253, SKP-273, DS-305, DS-352, MR-386, MR-422, SS-462, SS-478, SS-515.

16. Interview with Kraisri Nimmanahaeminda, April 2, 1985.

17. One villager specifically added with regard to a tenant's daughter, who had been made into a mistress, "fortunately she didn't get pregnant" (S-126, SKP-253).

18. Interviews included HD-8, SPT-62, CT-101, S-146, S-147, S-173, 174, SKP-257, SKP-285, DS-307, DS-330, DS-352, DS-354, MR-389.

19. In another common version, one of the corvéed villagers starts to bark like a dog, and the other corvéed villagers meow like cats and all run away, leaving the lord standing there!

20. I recall seeing senior government officials being carried piggy-back across rivers in the 1970s.

21. Anecdotes portray villagers on a spectrum from helpless to impish and clever. Stories in which villagers dare to stand up to royal authority still meet with laughter today. One villager told a story of when villagers were called up to dig the foundations of a house. A fellow named Lung Noi Pan, whom the villager knew personally, was rather lazy and was just wandering about while everyone else was working. So the chao saw this and called him over. He then assigned him a posthole to dig all by himself—usually two people would dig together. Finally, everyone finished digging the foundations for the day. The lord provided refreshments for everyone—including liquid palm sugar (*namtaan*), which Lung Noi Pan really liked. So Lung Noi Pan helped himself to two scoopfuls of sugar—after all, he had done the work of two! (SS-505).

22. Interviews included HD-8, S-113, S-114, S-127, S-162, S-168, S-173, SKP-225, SKP-232, DS-298, MR-438, SS-445.

23. Interviews included HD-14, CT-59, SPT-62, S-113, S-114, S-126, S-127, S-147, S-168, S-177, S-187, SKP-232, SKP-253, SKP-267, SKP-286, DS-298, DS-322, DS-335, SS-448.

24. Interviews included HD-11, HD-14, HD-36, CT-105, S-116, S-155, S-156, S-166, S-168, SKP-253, DS-322, MR-367, MR-392, MR-438, SS-462, MR-527.

25. Interviews included S-126, S-160, M-194, SKP-231, DS-335, DS-343, M-534, M-542.

26. Interviews included HD-14, HD-30, HD-53, S-124, S-126, S-145, S-163, S-174, S-175, S-177, S-187, SKP-285, SS-460, SS-490.

27. See further discussion in Grabowsky and Turton 2003, 188–91.

28. Various revolts were led by "saints" or "holy men" who were seen as incarnations of the future Maitreya Buddha (called variously *tonbun* in northern Thailand; *phuu mii bun* or *phuu viset* in northeastern Thailand and Laos; *setkya-min* in Burma; and *qanak man puny* or *nak sel* in Cambodia. Messianic revolts also took place in Laos (e.g., Baird 2007; see Gunn 1990, 102, for a fuller listing); Cambodia (Tai 1983, 27–33; Chandler 1996, 64–75; Harris 2005, 131–35; Hansen 2007, 56–59, 113); and Burma (Cady 1958, 309–21; Sarkisyanz 1965, 160–65; Spiro 1970, 172–79; Mendelson 1975, 208). In the course of his fieldwork in 1961–62, Melford Spiro noted that many Burmese peasants "firmly believed in the coming of a Future King"; he added that "indeed most of my informants believed he would appear in their own lifetime" (1970, 172–73). Despite regional variation, the overall themes of Maitreya's precursors were remarkably similar. These movements were typified by a "belief in imminent catastrophes to be followed by a new society of material abundance" and an appeal to followers "to observe the moral precepts strictly, to meditate, and to chant Buddhist texts" in order to be saved (Chatthip 1984, 123; see also Murdoch 1974; Hansen 2007, 59). As exemplified in surviving nineteenth-century Khmer texts, "natural" disasters were harbingers of the impending millennium, signs of supernatural discontent with earthly immorality. Although some scholars view these holy men as consistent with a royalist ideology, others see them as founders of "a new society of village 'socialism' free from state power" (Chatthip 1984, 123; see also the discussions in Sarkisyanz 1965, 106; Cohen 2001; Hansen 2007, 59–60).

29. A Burmese version, dating to 1201 CE, evidently also was paired with the recitation of the *Vessantara Jataka* (in the month of Tazaugmon, circa October to November). Some scholars believe the Phra Malai legend originated in Chiang Rai (Brereton 1995, 39).

30. Villagers commented about how all of these predictions were coming true. Now people do not walk on roads because there are cars; now they do not pound rice with a mortar and pestle anymore because there are rice mills; and now there is so much traffic that red dust settles everywhere in their homes.

31. Contemporary Thai Buddhists will describe this classic pose as the Buddha calling the earth (in the form of the goddess of the earth, Mae Thoranii) to witness his generosity from his life as Prince Vessantara at the moment of his enlightenment. Instead, LeMay describes this pose as "Buddha Frightened by the Burmans" (Phra Sadung Man) ([1926] 1986, 119). Carl Bock provides yet another interpretation ([1884] 1986, 282–83). I heard another variation of the Buddha image story in an interview in Sankhamphaeng district (SKP-205); this villager explained the difference in the two images by saying that the Lord Indra had built a pulpit (*ten kaew*) for the Buddha. While the Buddha was meditating, Phrayar Man tried to steal it. Mae Thoranii helped the Buddha by making a flood, which swept Phrayar Man away. But in the course of these events, the Buddha was surprised or lost his balance, and hence the one hand on one leg.

32. Kenneth Landon's interpretation of the lotus story is less derogatory to Gotama (1939, 186).

33. Even Taksin (1734–82), the founder of the Bangkok dynasty, appears to have laid claim to a form of sainthood (see Tambiah 1976, 184).

34. In southern Thailand a *phuu viset* was reported as causing "trouble in Patani" (*BTWM*, November 21, 1911).

35. Historically the law was rarely applied; however, recent years have seen a dramatic increase in lèse majesté cases, with 478 coming to trial in 2010 alone (for more, see Streckfuss 1995, 2011; Johnston 2011; Thongchai 2012). A factory worker alleged to have made a sarcastic Internet post about the king's dog found himself facing charges of sedition and lèse majesté, with a possible thirty-seven-year jail sentence (Fuller 2015).

36. All constitutions since 1932 have contained the clause "The King shall be enthroned in a position of revered worship and shall not be violated."

37. Luang Poh Bunthong, TE 066, tape 5, side B. The phrase implied by the pause (indicated here with ellipses) and readily understood by villagers is "*mii mia, ko ia hii hia,* "if you have a wife, work her vagina."

38. Luang Poh Bunthong, TE 066, tape 3, side A.

39. Luang Poh Bunthong, TE 066, tape 5, side B.

40. Luang Poh Bunthong, TE 006, side A.

41. See C. George Boeree, "Buddhist Morality," http://webspace.ship.edu/cgboer/buddhamorals.html, accessed August 27, 2016.

42. Luang Poh Bunthong, TE 066, tape 5, side A.

43. Luang Poh Bunthong, TE 066, tape 4, side A. In another northern version, Jujaka is also terrified. With tears falling and saliva drooling, he raises both hands (*wai*) and then he bows down (*kraab*) to Jetabutr, saying: "Royal nephew [*chao laan*], I [*khaa*] am afraid. Please listen to me. The royal grandfather [*prachao puu*] in the city court wants me [*khaa*] to invite [*kraabthuun*] his son to return to ascend the throne to rule again. Why do you say I am a bad person and you will kill me? Listen to me, nephew, don't act hastily. I am a royal ambassador, not someone who takes advantage of others, who exploits or kills others. The royal grandfather has sent me [uncle] as his ambassador. Nephew should not hit or harm me. It would violate ancient customs and tradition [*jaariit praphaenii*]. Don't speak with such recklessness, nephew" (Manee 1976, 231–32).

44. Their shock perhaps parallels mine when I attended a black inner city church and the woman next to me went into trance.

45. Luang Poh Bunthong used a different regional accent for each fellow.

46. Luang Poh Bunthong, TE 066, tape 1, side B. Bunthong also used his long introduction to teach about the virtue of patience, commenting that he realized they were wondering when he would ever get round to preaching the Vessantara story. But he said that people who were impatient often ended up in unfortunate situations, like people who went into debt because they could not wait for their paycheck or the woman who ends up marrying an alcoholic because she couldn't wait and was too worried that she wouldn't get a husband. He explained that preaching was like watering a tree; the

water must reach the roots of the tree to be effective: "If the earth around the roots is too hard, the water runs off in other directions and never reaches the roots. People who are conceited or stubborn are like hard earth. They are like some ex-monks or ex-novices—some who had even been abbots of their temples—who drink liquor until the saliva is dribbling down their cheeks and get into fights around the village. They know all the precepts, but can't follow them. They are like hard earth. They know what they are doing is wrong, but they are arrogant about it at the same time. Ask them why they don't enter the temple. 'Oh, I disrobed already. Why would I want to go to temple? I was sick of the temple. That's why I disrobed.' They should be the ones encouraging others to go to temple, but instead they avoid going anywhere near it. 'Why should I go?' they ask. 'Well to hear the preaching of the Dharma.' 'I know it already. I used to preach it myself. I know all the texts.' The saliva is dribbling down his cheek. His wife gets mad at him and he calls her stupid.

"That's the way it is with arrogant people who think they know better. There's no one like that here, this happened somewhere else. But for the dharma to be effective the water must reach the roots of the trees. You have to take the hoe and prepare the soil around the tree before the water can soak in. So first one has to lower one's arrogance [*thithi mana*]. It doesn't matter how much money one has, however many millions, or how much education, however many degrees, however many honors; they often don't want to hear the dharma. There are even monks who try to find something else to do rather than listen to the dharma; they should be the example to others. They are also like hard earth. The soil has to be prepared first."

47. I do know he supported the education of village students, often gave villagers water buffaloes, and favored the ordination of women.

48. Interview with Luang Poh (Phrakhruu) Bunthong Suwanno, Wat Sothannaraam, Tambon Don Kaew, Amphur Mae Rim, Chiang Mai, August 1, 2005.

49. The other evils are floods, fires, thieves, and enemies (Spiro 1970, 210).

Chapter 5. Jujaka as Threat

1. The founder of the Han dynasty (206 BC-221 AD) is said to have balked when advised that the time had come to consult books on Confucian ethics and ritual. "All I possess I have won on horseback," he exclaimed. "Why should I now bother with those musty old texts?" "Your Majesty may have won it on horseback," retorted his chief counselor, "but can you rule it on horseback?" (Bell 1992, 193).

2. It was later returned to the south.

3. One of these monks was the high-ranking Phra Thammaratmuni (Chun), who later under Rama I was assigned responsibility for overseeing the Abhidhamma in the *Tripitaka* revisions (Reynolds 1972, 47).

4. For more on this period, see Dhani Nivat 1955; Wenk 1968; Wyatt 1994, 141–74.

5. He issued ten sangha laws in all, ending with the tenth in 1801. According to Reynolds, the king became interested in sangha matters when a woman rebel punished

by death left her possessions to a monk of Wat Bang Wa Yai (Wat Rakhang) instead of to the crown itself (1972, 39).

6. The reddish-brown robes were emblematic of the Maitreya Buddha (Reynolds 1972, 42).

7. Noting frequent mentions of Mon and Lao, Reynolds suggests that "the removal of conquered populations to the capital area may have introduced non-Siamese strains of Buddhist practice" (1972, 50).

8. The disrobed monks were given positions in the civil service, and the monk sentenced to execution was pardoned. For more, see Reynolds (1972, 43-49). The supreme patriarch resided at Wat Rakhang.

9. These temples were Wat Suthat, Wat Mahathat, Wat Saket in Bangkok, a temple in Kelantan, and two temples in Nakhon Sri Thammarat (Reynolds 1972, 92). For more on Siamese-Sri Lankan exchanges, see Blackburn 2010.

10. As a young man, Mongkut had been sent by his father to help settle Mon refugees fleeing unrest in Burma (Reynolds 1972, 79-80).

11. In the early 1830s Wat Samorai and Wat Boromniwat housed chapters of his followers. The additional three temples were Wat Khruawan, Wat Phichaiyat, and Wat Buppharam (Reynolds 1972, 87).

12. Nonetheless, Pawaret was never made prince-patriarch, intimating "the delicacy of the assimilation process" (Reynolds 1972, 121).

13. For his very interesting autobiography, see Reynolds 1979.

14. The 14 monthons formed between 1893 and 1899 were: Prachinburi and Nakhon Ratchasima (1893); Pitsanulok (1894); Nakhon Chaisi, Nakhon Sawan, and Ratburi (1895); Ayutthaya, Burapha (Cambodia), Chumpon, Nakhon Si Thammarat (1896); Kedah (1897); Phuket (1898); Petchaburi and Udonthani (1899). Each monthon was under *a chaokhana monthon* and, on the provincial level, a *chaokhana muang* (Reynolds 1972, 237-47; Heinze 1977, 27).

15. Monastic residences lack *sima* stones, which mark the sacred space for ordinations. For more on sima, see Irwin 2011.

16. The royal sangharajas or supreme patriarchs during this period were Prince Paramanuchit (1851-53), Prince Pawaret (1853-92), Prince Vajiranana (1910-21), and Prince Chinaworn (1921-37).

17. Vientiane included the regions of present-day Loei, Nong Khai, and Nakhon Phanom provinces, while Champasak included Ubon and Roi Et provinces (Keyes 1967, 9). This split mirrors the difference in *Vessantara Jataka* recitation styles between northern isan (Nong Khai) and southern isan (Ubon) to this day.

18. Vickery writes that Ubon was placed under a royal commissioner for defense even before the Damrong reforms. Surin's line of local governors terminated in 1907; Nakhon Phanom's ended in 1903 (when a Bangkok appointee took over). Sakhon Nakhon in the nineteenth century was ruled by a family of trans-Mekhong origin until probably 1892, when a royal commissioner was transferred there. Mahasarakham's ruling family was related to that of Roi Et; the last of the line died in 1913 and was replaced by

a member of Bangkok royalty. After the Chao Anu rebellion (1826-28), Nakhon Ratchasima was promoted to first-class status, ruled by members of the Singhaseni family (descendants of Chaophraya Bodin, who defeated Chao Anu and destroyed Vientiane) (Vickery 1970; Tambiah 1976, 195).

19. See Strate 2015 for discussion of the continuing significance of these events.

20. Rama I's favorite concubine, Chaochom Waen, the daughter of a Lao king, appears to have played an important role in shaping the Jujaka chapter (see chapter 1) and may have had other political roles.

21. Wat Khemmapirataram in Nonthaburi (Taylor 1993, 51).

22. Two other special envoys were sent to Nong Khai and Korat (Taylor 1993, 51).

23. Phichit's replacement was another member of the Bangkok royal family, Luang Sanphasitthiprasong (1893-1910); he was similarly supportive of the Thammayut monks. In 1910 Ubon was integrated into the monthon system, following Korat and Udon (Tej 1977, 268-9; Taylor 1993, 51).

24. His name is variously Ubaalii Khunuupamaajaan Sirichantho (Chan), also Phra Yaanarakhit. See Anake 2007.

25. Although in 1914 he was promoted to the title of Phra Thepmoli, he was demoted in 1915 because of a controversial publication in which he criticized Siam's intended involvement in World War I. Ubalii was kept under temple arrest at Wat Bowonniwet. While under temple arrest, Ubalii hung a bag of tubers (*man*) outside his room as a sign of his continuing defiance. He was released after a few months and in 1922 traveled to northern Thailand, where we shall meet him again in this chapter. (For further details of Ubalii's life, see Taylor 1993, 53-58; Anake 2007).

26. Even as late as the 1960s, Keyes suggests there was an average of one Thammayut monastery for each province (1967b; see also Taylor 1993, 64).

27. In 1902, of the fourteen monthon heads, only five were Mahanikai (Taylor 1993, 68).

28. The central Thai monthons were Krungthep, Krung Kao (Ayutthaya), Nakhon Sawan, and Chanthaburi (Wyatt 1967, 254).

29. The breakdown was Monthon Chumphon (10), Chanthaburi (4), Ratburi (2), Phitsanulok (8), Krung Kao (4), and Isan (4) (Wyatt 1967, 253).

30. After Bayinnaung's death in 1581, his vast kingdom collapsed. In 1596 Lanna was able to declare brief independence from Burma, coming under Ayutthayan control from 1602 to 1605. However, King Anaukpetlun (r. 1606-28) regained control of Chiang Mai in 1614. Chiang Mai did become a tributary of Ayutthaya in 1660 but switched allegiances back to Ava in 1664 (Lieberman 1984, 200-202).

31. A case of binthabatr chiwit occurred during the reign of the Ayutthayan King Naresuan (r. 1590-1605). When the king was fighting the Burmese prince in 1592, he drove his elephant ahead so quickly that the soldiers in charge of protecting the royal elephant's legs could not keep up. After his famous victory, Naresuan wanted to behead those soldiers. On hearing the news, the sangharaja of Wat Pa Kaew (Wat Yai Chaiyamongkhon), together with twenty-five other senior monks, asked to spare their

lives, suggesting that precisely because the soldiers could not keep up, his victory was all the more glorious. The sangharaja, a Mon monk who was King Naresuan's mentor, is known variously as Somdet Phra Wanarat, Heng Khemajaari, and Phra Mahaathera Khanchong. My thanks to Apinya Fuengfusakul for this information (personal communication).

32. Bangkok sought to end this practice by only allowing certain authorized monks to ordain monks and novices. This effort caused considerable resentment in northern Thailand, contributing to the irredentist movement against Bangkok, which centered on Khruubaa Srivichai in the early twentieth century (see Bowie 2014a, 2014b).

33. Khaimuk 1999; Ratanaporn Sethakul, e-mail communication, July 13, 2010.

34. This temple is home to the city pillar.

35. Ratanaporn Sethakul, e-mail communication, July 19, 2010.

36. The commissioner was Chao Phrayar Surasihwisitsak (Choei Kanlayanamit), *thesaphiban* 1902-15 (Sarassawadee 2005, 209-13).

37. Ajarn Man did have some disciples at northern temples including Waen Sujinno (Wat Doi Mae Pang, Phrao district), Luang Katapunyo (Wat Samraaniwaat, Lampang), Sim Phuttahaajaaro (Wat Tham Phra-sabaai, Lampang), each of whom came originally from northeastern Thailand (see Taylor 1993, 83).

38. Other important acts were the land tax and an act regulating the slaughter of bullocks, buffaloes, and pigs, which went into effect in Phayap in 1902 (*BTWM*, June 19, 1902).

39. Income increased from 15,378,114 ticals in 1892 to 60,859,508 ticals in 1908 (*BTWM*, November 29, 1910).

40. If villagers provided their own food, they worked up to fifteen days; if the government provided food, they were to work for not more than thirty days (*BTWM*, January 28, 1902). This act was revised in 1917 (see Sarassawadee 2005, 229).

41. Villagers also protested land tax abuse "in the form of inflating the actual number of rai in their paddy fields to twice the number" (*BTWM*, August 24, 1918).

42. On his life, see Sangaa 1956; Faa 1976-77; Sophaa 1991; Sommai 2002; Singkha 2010. In English, see Keyes 1982, Cohen 2001. Srivichai's name is variously transliterated as Siwichai and Srivijaya; Srivichai seems to be most common, so I have used this form.

43. Scholarly explanations have attributed the 1920 detention to misunderstandings over ordination caused by the implementation of the 1902 Sangha Act. However, the Sangha Act did not go into effect in Monthon Phayab until 1924. Furthermore, the Act makes no mention of ordination. This prevailing interpretation does not accord well with the available evidence. For details, see Bowie 2014a.

44. Srivichai faced eight charges in 1920, including a charge of treason. For further discussion, see Bowie 2014a, 2014b.

45. Of their survey in 1990, Sommai and Dore conclude, "only a few monasteries such as Wat Chang Taem, Wat Suan Dok and Wat That Kham in Chiang Mai and in other provinces were still found performing *tang tham luang*." Other monasteries such

as Wat Chomphu, Wat Usaikham, and Wat Phra Singh preached the *Anisong Patit* and flew paper balloons (1992, 85).

46. Having ordained as a novice or monk was a mark of prestige that carried over into one's life after one disrobed, with the permanent addition of the honorific "Noi" or "Naan" to one's name; not to have such an honorific was to be literally called a "raw person" (*khon dip*). Today these titles survive only among the older generation of villagers.

47. Luang Poh Bunthong gave several examples of tonal changes and linguistic changes. The central Thai "whose" is *khong krai* (midtone), but in northern Thai it is *khong phai* (rising tone). Now the younger generation uses *khong khrai* (combining the central Thai word with the northern tone). The phrase "I did not see it," in central Thai is *maj hen* and in northern is *bo han*, but it is now becoming *bo hen* among the younger northerners. In other cases the words are significantly different: e.g., "to open the window" is *byyt naatang* in central Thai versus *khai pong* in dialect.

48. Interview with Ajarn Manee Phayomyong, Mae Rim, Chiang Mai, August 1, 2005.

49. Villagers told me that he had scores of people coming to see him each day, so he had time for little else.

50. Bunthong also traced the change in the northern custom of laity bringing food to the temple at night to the same period, adding that Chiang Mai was no longer a separate monthon but had become part of the national sangha after about 1932.

51. For more on the Free Thai, see Haseman 1978; Wimon 1997; Sorasak 2005.

52. Interview with Lung Waai Ryangdej, Baan Den Samrong, Tambon Haat Song Khwae, Amphur Tron, Uttaradit, August 24, 2015; see also Wongthet 1989. Lung Waai also mentioned a village named Nang Khamnyng (because Matsi is missing Phrayar Sonchai) and a now deserted village called Taa Jujaka. Although both Jujaka and Amitataa were portrayed as evil (*naakliat*), Waai's village used to celebrate a wedding ceremony for Kanhaa and Chalii, parading them around the village. My thanks to Davisakd Puaksom to traveling with me to Uttaradit.

53. Interview with Phrakhruu Athong Visutikhul, Abbot, Wat Nong Tong, Tambon Nong Tong, Amphur Hang Dong, Chiang Mai, July 13, 2005.

54. Interview with Phrakhruu Athong Visutikhul, Abbot, Wat Nong Tong, Tambon Nong Tong, Amphur Hang Dong, Chiang Mai, July 13, 2005. He went on to say that, although no formal meeting had been held, he and other tujok monks had agreed in private conversations among themselves to tone down their performances lest modern audiences take offense.

55. The influence of this jataka can also be found in other northern literature such as "Khlong Chao Withuun Sorn Laan," a poem intended to teach officials, royalty, and commoners about proper behavior; it suggests that queens (*mahesi*) should care for their husbands, other minor wives, and slaves as Matsi cared for her royal husband. Similarly, "Khlong Phra Lor Sorn Lok" (Phra Lor teaches the world) praises Matsi as an ideal wife who treated her husband as her lord (*ao phua pen chao*) (Prakong 1983, 5–6).

56. The performance was so successful that an audience member invited a tujok to perform for a funeral at her village shortly thereafter.

Chapter 6. Jujaka as Deity

1. For a provocative discussion of the role of merchants in early Buddhism, see Gokhale 1977; see also F. Reynolds 1990.

2. One does not "buy" amulets but rather requests to worship them (*buchaa*). For more on the role of magic and amulets, see especially Tambiah 1984; Pattana 2012; McDaniel 2014.

3. My thanks to Chaiyaporn Singdee for this research. On Luang Puu Roht (Wat Bangnamwon), see "Khui fyang ryang phra Luang Puu Roht," October 30, 2013, http://www.youtube.com/watch?v=QEnbS19l5l4. See also Thosaphol 1994.

4. Luang Puu Thim had a *khaathaa* for easy childbirth. He is also mentioned by Khun Khemika of Jujaka House. For more on him, see Thosaphol 1994.

5. Amulet magazines also mention the Jujaka amulets of Luang Puu Khui at Wat Saptakhien in Petchabun province, Luang Poh Daeng of Wat Huay Chalong in Uttaradit province, and others. See also Thosaphol (1994, 2010) for fuller discussion.

6. The amulet is called Choo Chok Khor Dai (Jujaka who gets what he asks for).

7. See http://www.lersi.net/amulets/#!/Pha-Yant-Choo-Chok-Riak-Sap-Por-Tao-Nang-Ballangk-Luang-Por-Phan-Wat-Dong-Mae-Sri-Mueang/p/4181827, accessed August 18, 2016.

8. See http://www.lersi.net/amulets/#!/Choo-Chok-Haa-Kin-Millionaire-Lucky-Jujaka-Beggar-Nuea-Tong-Tip-Divine-Brass-Luang-Por-Daeng-Wat-Huay-Chalong-2552-BE/p/3698018, accessed August 18, 2016.

9. See http://www.mitmor.com/#!/~/product/id=10045199, accessed August 18, 2016.

10. I thank Chaiyaporn Singdee for his help with this research.

11. On coyote dancing, see "Payback Time," *Bangkok Post*, July 5, 2012, http://www.bangkokpost.com/vdo/thailand/301082/payback-time, accessed August 18, 2016. For Jujaka House's website, see http://www.chuchok.com/, accessed August 18, 2016.

12. I thank Chaiyaporn Singdee and Wiriyaporn Ekphon for this information.

13. The temple was apparently built by Chaophraya Thiphakorawong (Kham Bunnag, 1813–70) in honor of his wife, Nuu, and was originally called Wat Mai Musikaram. On *kumarnthongs*, see Sinnott 2014.

14. I thank Neeranooch Malangpoo for being my intermediary. According to Stephen Collins, this linkage is not in Pali texts (e-mail, July 6, 2014). Nonetheless, various Buddhist accounts of Devadatta do say that he will become enlightened as the Pacceka Buddha named Atthissara. See "Life of the Buddha," Buddha Dharma Education Association & BuddhaNet, http://www.buddhanet.net/e-learning/buddhism/lifebuddha/2_5lbud.htm, accessed August 18, 2016.

15. Tourist authorities also promote the celebration in Nakhon Sri Thammarat (Wan Sart) and Uthai Thani (Wan Tak Bat Thevo).

16. Some monks I interviewed in northern Thailand and in Loei province informed me that they used texts printed at this institute in Khon Kaen for their recitations.

17. See "Boon Phawade Festival 2001," https://sites.google.com/site/putsarsporn top/naeana-cang-hwad-ry-xed/10-prapheni-buy-pha-hew-d-canghwad-rxyxed/1-ngan-prapheni-kin-kha-wpu-nbuy-pha-hew-d, accessed August 18, 2016. I thank Sandra Cate for drawing my attention to this festival.

18. Villages involved included Naa Wieng, Nam Thaeng, and Naa Hoh.

19. One Tambon One Product (OTOP) is a stimulus program designed during Thaksin Shinawatra's 2001–6 Thai Rak Thai government. The program sought to support the locally made and marketed products of each Thai tambon (subdistrict).

20. The mural was painted by Pramote Sriphrom, a local artist.

21. See "Wetsandon Chadok Park Roi-Et, Northeast Thailand," *Isaan Life* (blog), May 20, 2012, http://isaan-life.blogspot.com/2012/05/wetsandon-chadok-park-roi-et-northeast.html, accessed February 23, 2016.

22. See "Travel News—Attractions in Thailand," http://www.thailandtraveltours.com/news/5-siam-cultural-park-bang-phae-ratchaburi.htm, accessed August 18, 2016.

23. On March 9, 2015, Wat Pho, together with the Department of Religious Affairs and the Ministry of Culture, held a recitation in honor of the sixtieth birthday of Princess Maha Chakri Sirindhorn. See "Vessantara Sermon at Wat Pho," http://www.watpho.com/news_detail.php?id=386&lang=en, accessed August 18, 2016.

24. On Friday Dr. Manop Kaanthasilo (Wat Chetuphon) and Phra Maha Som Sutthipaphaasoo (Wat Laksi) recited the first five chapters. On Saturday Chulaphon, Mahaphon, and Kumarn were recited by Phra Rachawisutthidilok (Wat Saam Phrayaa) and Phra Mahaa Sin Titamaetho (Wat Laksi). On Sunday the last five chapters were performed by Phra Rachiwisutthidilok, Phrakhruu Wiphat-aathawaathi (Wat Samien-Nari), and Phra Mahaa Som Suthipaphaasoo.

25. Some of the texts the monks preached came from Khon Kaen.

26. Its main organizer was a central Thai. The event occurred during Lent because the organizer said it was convenient.

27. See Patcharin (2013) for discussion of transnational marriages in the northeast.

28. On temples in the United States, see Numrich 1996; Smith-Hefner 1999; Yamada 2004. On temples in England, see Cate 2003; and in France, see Kalab 1994.

29. See "Vessantara Jataka 15/15," November 11, 2012, http://www.youtube.com/watch?v=ZOvdnPqJN-k, accessed August 18, 2016.

30. See "Wat Lao Samakhitham Boun Pravet June 2012," July 10, 2012, https://www.youtube.com/watch?v=yNspiI8zTwQ, accessed August 18, 2016.

31. "The Revival of Minnesota's Boun Phra Vet Celebration," *Little Laos on the Prairie* (blog), June 30, 2013, littlelaosontheprairie.wordpress.com/2013/06/30/the-revival-of-minnesotas-boun-phra-vet-celebration/ Minnesota Vessantara Jataka, accessed August 18, 2016.

32. Monks mentioned included Phrakhruu Sophon Withayaphorn in Mae Rim, Phrakhruu Athong in Hang Dong, Phrakhruu Khammuul in Bangkok, and Luang Poh Pankaew in Phrae.

33. The same was true more broadly. In Cambodia, Leclère quaintly remarked, "The women, even the children, are able to explain them and enumerate the details almost without omitting a single one" (1899, 119-20). Writing of nineteenth-century Sri Lanka, Hardy comments that "a great number of the Jatakas are familiar even to the women" ([1853] 1967, 101). Holt notes that "most of the audience (approximately three-fourths) were very elderly women" (2009, 219).

34. Luang Poh Bunthong is an example of one monk who saw Matsi and her children as making informed decisions for the good of society; in the emerging controversy over whether women should have the right to be ordained as full bhikkuni, he supported female ordination. Similarly, the Hok Kasat recitation I attended in northeastern Thailand also emphasized Matsi's own decision-making.

35. For one version of Uppalavanna's life, see Radhika Abeysekera, "The Nun Uppalavanna," *Wisdom Quarterly American Buddhist Journal*, October 2008, http://wisdomquarterly.blogspot.com/2008/10/female-chief-disciple-uppalavanna.html, accessed August 18, 2016.

36. Interview with Lung Waaj Ryangdej, Baan Den Samrong, T. Haat Song Khwae, A. Tron, Uttaradit, August 24, 2015. The marriage of the two children is also found in Cambodia, their marriage thereby founding a royal dynasty that can be traced down to the present. In one version, the *Satra of King Chea-Ly* (Chalii), the king becomes infatuated with a servant girl and the couple live apart; other versions have happier endings. See Leclère 1895; Hansen 2007, 34; Roveda and Yem 2010, 108, 116-17.

37. In the Pali version gods disguised as mice bit the string. Steven Collins, e-mail communication, July 6, 2014.

38. Likely drawing on a northern recension, Swearer describes Amitataa as "young and selfish" (1978, 3).

39. See Ruenruthai 1995 for a broader discussion of female characters in Thai historical literature.

Conclusion

1. For a literature review, see Bowie 1998.

2. Matthew 19:16-30, New International Version (NIV). I thank Hugh Wilson for these references.

3. Winyu (John) Wongsurawat is a young Thai political satirist who hosts an online news show, *Shallow News in Depth*, together with his sister, Janya Wongsurawat, and co-presenter, Nattapong Tiendee; the show is often compared to John Stewart's *The Daily Show*. Udom (Note) Taepanich is another familiar Thai comedian, known most recently for his satire on General Prayut's curt responses to journalists.

Bibliography

Archival Sources

BTWM: *Bangkok Times Weekly Mail.*
Dansai Mss. "Prawat khwaampenmaa kaanlalen Phiitaakhon." Dansai Folk Museum, Wat Phonchai, Dansai district, Loei, Thailand, ca. 2009.
Richardson Mss. Journal of Dr. Richardson. Manuscript Division, British Museum, London, England, 1830–36.
Satow Mss. Journal of Sir Ernest Satow. PRO30/33(21/1). Public Records Office, London, England, 1885–86.
Taylor Mss. Autobiography of Hugh Taylor. Manuscript, Phayab College Library, Chiang Mai, Thailand, 1888–1930.

Oral Histories

The following interviews are numbered according to the appendix in Bowie 1988. Abbreviations indicate the following districts: Chom Thong (CT), Doi Saket (DS), Hang Dong (HD), Muang (M), Mae Rim (MR), Saraphi (S), Sankamphaeng (SKP), Sanpatong (SPT), San Sai (SS).

HD-8. Mae Chin (age 54). #5, Baan Nong Khwaaj, Tambon Nong Khwaaj, Amphur Hang Dong. Interviewed November 20, 1984.
HD-11. Poh Luang Waen, ex-village headman (age 88). #7, Baan Myang Kung, Tambon Nong Khwaaj, Amphur Hang Dong. Interviewed November 23, 1984.
HD-14. Lung Bunyyyn Thaabunsom (age 70). Baan San Phak Waan, Tambon San Phak Waan, Amphur Hang Dong. Interviewed November 23, 1984.
HD-19. Mae Ui Buathip (age 84) and daughter Baa Chanthip Thaakhamthip (age 53). #3, Baan Thawbunryang, Tambon Baan Waen, Amphur Hang Dong. Interviewed November 27, 1984.
HD-30. Naaj Bunsong Wannaphii (age 53); Mae Ui Bundii Khantha (age 83); and Baa Yohthyan (age 52). #2, Baan Buak Khrok, Tambon Nong Tong, Amphur Hang Dong. Interviewed December 11, 1984.
HD-36. Lung Saen Khambaa (age 77) and relatives. #6, Baan Khuan, Tambon Hankaew, Amphur Hang Dong. Interviewed December 25, 1984.
HD-38. Lung Pan Thong In (age 60-plus). #1, Baan San Pa Sak, Tambon Hankaew, Amphur Hang Dong. Interviewed December 28, 1984.

HD-53. Abbot Uthaa (age 60). #13, Wat Arambarahu, Baan Pae Kwang, Tambon Hang Dong, Amphur Hang Dong. Interviewed January 21, 1985.

CT-59. Abbot Phraakhruu Kantha Khanto (Luang Poh Phintha) (age 86). #5, Wat, Tambon Sop Tia, Amphur Chom Thong. Interviewed February 6, 1985.

SPT-62. Poh Noi Ton Suriyamon (age 88). Baan Thawangphraw, Tambon Thawangphraw, Amphur San Patong. Interviewed 18, 1985.

CT-101. Poh Luang Pan Phomcamcaj, village headman (age 48). #1, Baan Mae Klang Baan Boh, Tambon Doi Kaew, Amphur Chom Thong. Interviewed May 8, 1985.

CT-105. Poh Ui Paeng Phynthana (age 88). #3, Baan Mae Soi, Tambon Mae Soi, Amphur Chom Thong. Interviewed May 10, 1985.

S-113. Lung Maa Srichan (age 81). #6, Baan Hua Dong, Tambon Khua Mung, Amphur Saraphi. Interviewed May 13, 1985.

S-114. Ui Naan Luang Thii (Damrii Maethalaat), ex-village headman (age 91). #7, Baan Hua Dong, Tambon Khua Mung, Amphur Saraphi. Interviewed May 13, 1985.

S-116. Poh Naan Saw (age 83). #10, Baan Dya Ngok, Tambon Khua Mung, Amphur Saraphi. Interviewed May 13, 1985.

S-124. Mae Ui Thaa Wongaa (age 90). #6, Baan Thaa Kwang, Tambon Thaa Kwang, Amphur Saraphi. Interviewed May 14, 1985.

S-126. Mae Ui Khiewkham Panyarsailert (age 89). #7, Baan Bakhetthii, Tambon Nong Phyng, Amphur Saraphi. Interviewed May 16, 1985.

S-127. Duangthip Suksawaen, ex-kamnan (age 80). #6, Baan Kong Saaj, Tambon Nong Phyng, Amphur Saraphi. Interviewed May 16, 1985.

S-145. Poh Luang Pan Yamwong (age 68). #1, Baan Nong Sri Chaeng, Tambon Nong Faek, Amphur Saraphi. Interviewed May 21, 1985.

S-146. Poh Naan Nuan Wongwalii (age 83). #7, Baan Chieng Khang, Tambon Chajsataan, Amphur Saraphi. Interviewed May 24, 1985.

S-147. Poh Luang Duanglaa (age 78). #6, Baan Kalapo, Tambon Chajsataan, Amphur Saraphi. Interviewed May 24, 1985.

S-151. Poh Daeng Narin (age 93). #3, Baan Sribunryang, Tambon Chajsataan, Amphur Saraphi. Interviewed May 24, 1985.

S-155. Poh Luang Taan Kham Rungrit (age 61). #6, Baan Bak Kong, Tambon Saraphi, Amphur Saraphi. Interviewed May 26, 1985.

S-156. Mae Ui Tun Chuandii (age 90). #7, Baan San Kap Tong, Tambon Saraphi, Amphur Saraphi. Interviewed May 26, 1985.

S-160. Mae Ui Dii Myangcaj (age 94). #2, Baan Phrayar Chomphuu, Tambon Chomphuu, Amphur Saraphi. Interviewed May 28, 1985.

S-162. Poh Ui Som Khanya (age 83). #5, Baan Khii Sya, Tambon Chomphuu, Amphur Saraphi. Interviewed May 28, 1985.

S-163. Poh Naan In Saengbun (age 77); Baa Buakhiew, his wife; and his younger brother. #4, Baan Thaa, Tambon Chomphuu, Amphur Saraphi. Interviewed May 28, 1985.

S-166. Mae Ui Kaew Thast (age 89). #1, Baan San Sai, Tambon San Sai, Amphur Saraphi. Interviewed May 31, 1985.

S-168. Mae Ui Khaaj Yawannaa (age 84). #5, Baan Thaa Makkham, Tambon San Sai, Amphur Saraphi. Interviewed May 31, 1985.
S-173. Chaw Noi Chanthawong Utama (age 88). #4, Baan Ba Bong, Tambon Ba Bong, Amphur Saraphi. Interviewed June 4, 1985.
S-174. Poh Khwaen Caj Inworn (age 82). #3, Baan Sri Kham Chomphuu, Tambon Ba Bong, Amphur Saraphi. Interviewed June 4, 1985.
S-175. Mae Ui Pan Bunpaeng (age 83). #4, Baan Pong, Tambon Thaawangtaan, Amphur Saraphi. Interviewed June 6, 1985.
S-177. Poh Ui Aj (age 84). #8, Baan San Nu Nya/Baan Buak Khrok Nya, Tambon Thaawangtaan, Amphur Saraphi. Interviewed June 6, 1985.
S-187. Poh Naan Dii Sunket (age 78). #4, Baan Yang Nyng, Tambon Yang Nyng, Amphur Saraphi. Interviewed June 9, 1985.
M-195. Abbot, Baan Pa Pao Nok. #2, Tambon Badaet, Amphur Myang. Interviewed June 12, 1985.
SKP-205. Poh Ui Kaew Thongkhambaj (age 86). #4, Baan Mae Thaw Din, Tambon Huaj Kaew, Amphur San Khampaeng. Interviewed July 5, 1985.
SKP-225. Ajarn Chyyn Wongsuwan (age 60-plus). #7, Tambon Chae Chang, Amphur San Khampaeng. Interviewed July 11, 1985.
SKP-231. Kruubaa La (Luang Buu La Thaathip) (age 88). #7, Wat Ba Tyng, Baan Ba Tyng, Tambon Ohn Tai, Amphur San Khampaeng. July 10 and July 18, 1985.
SKP-232. Poh Naan Tyy Chanthadaa (age 88). #7, Tambon Rong Wua Daeng, Amphur San Khampaeng. Interviewed July 18, 1985.
SKP-245. Mae Ui Aem Naanpoh (age 84). #2, Baan Nong Sae, Tambon Huaj Saaj, Amphur San Khampaeng. Interviewed July 19, 1985.
SKP-247. Poh Ui Muun Chajsaan (age 78-79). #7, Baan Hua Faaj, Tambon Phuukhaa, Amphur San Khampaeng. Interviewed July 19, 1985.
SKP-253. Mae Ui Kaew Panyarryang (age 88). #14, Baan Mae Laen, Tambon Ohn Nya, Amphur San Khampaeng. Interviewed July 25, 1985.
SKP-254. Mae Ui Muu Khamuun (age 93). #5, Baan San Khampaeng, Tambon San Khampaeng, Amphur San Khampaeng. Interviewed July 26, 1985.
SKP-257. Mae Ui Wan Namwongphrom (age 90). #14, Baan Ohn, Tambon San Khampaeng, Amphur San Khampaeng. Interviewed July 26, 1985.
SKP-258. Poh Naan Myangcaj Chanta (age 84). #9, Baan San Tai, Tambon San Khampaeng, Amphur San Khampaeng. Interviewed July 26, 1985.
SKP-260. Kamnan Sawang Fongsaa (age 65). #6, Baan Rooj Phrom, Tambon Buak Khang, Amphur San Khampaeng. Interviewed July 30, 1985.
SKP-264. Poh Ui Caj Ngenkhamchan (age 86). #11, Tambon Buak Khang, Amphur San Khampaeng. Interviewed July 30, 1985.
SKP-267. Poh Ui Noi Kham Raat-uun (age 92). #1, Baan Mohn, Tambon San Klang, Amphur San Khampaeng. Interviewed August 4, 1985.
SKP-273. Mae Ui Yohthyan Phiiwong (age 84). #3, Baan San Klang Nya, Tambon San Klang, Amphur San Khampaeng. Interviewed August 4, 1985.

SKP-285. Poh Ui Noi Saen Cajbu (age 85) and Poh Ui Sii Kaewkham (age 80). #3, Wat Bo Sang, Baan Bo Sang, Tambon Ohn Pao, Amphur San Khampaeng. Interviewed August 8 1985.

SKP-286. Poh Luang Hyan Wongthip, ex-village headman (age 70) and others. #1, Wat Don Pau, Tambon Don Pao, Amphur San Khampaeng. Interviewed August 8, 1985.

DS-298. Poh Ui Thaa Thalaabun (age 76) and others in temple. #6-7, Baan Huaj Ang/ Tong Phyng, Tambon Mae Bong, Amphur Doi Saket. Interviewed August 15, 1985.

DS-305. Mae Ui Tut Bajsukhan (age 99). #5, Baan Luang Nya, Tambon Luang Nya, Amphur Doi Saket. Interviewed August 20, 1985.

DS-307. Poh Naan Taa (Thaworn) Buabyyt (age 81). #3, Baan Myang Wa, Tambon Luang Nya, Amphur Doi Saket. Interviewed August 20, 1985.

DS-322. Poh Ui Suk Chajket (age 92). #11, Baan Yang Phrathat, Tambon Sanbulyaj, Amphur Doi Saket. Interviewed September 4, 1985.

DS-330. Poh Noi Hyang Taaphuuyoi (age 91) and Mae Ui Noi Taaphuuyoi (age 83). #2, Baan Mae Roi Ngen, Tambon Mae Roi Ngen, Amphur Doi Saket. Interviewed September 3, 1985.

DS-335. Lung Mii Kaewwiengchan (age 63). #4, Tambon Palan, Amphur Doi Saket. Interviewed August 21, 1985.

DS-339. Mae Ui Caa Kanthamang (age 84). #2, Baan Nam Phrae, Tambon Talaat Khwan, Amphur Doi Saket. Interviewed August 22, 1985.

DS-343. Khruu Bunsom Kanthawang (age 72). #4, Baan Phrayaak Luang (Bo Hin), Tambon Talaat Khwan, Amphur Doi Saket. Interviewed August 22, 1985.

DS-352. Poh Ui Kham Chajkaen (age 84). #4, Baan Phanlang, Tambon Samranraat, Amphur Doi Saket. Interviewed September 11, 1985.

DS-353. Poh Ui Cajmaa Chakkaew (age 88). #5, Baan Ba Myy-at, Tambon Samranraat, Amphur Doi Saket. Interviewed September 11, 1985.

DS-354. Poh Ui Noi Puk Caajkaew (age 95) (kradaaj). #4, Baan San Ton Myang, Tambon Samranraat, Amphur Doi Saket. Interviewed September 11, 1985.

MR-367. Poh Ui Mo Chantaa (age 89). #3, Baan Mae Saa Luang, Tambon Mae Saa, Amphur Mae Rim. Interviewed October 2, 1985.

MR-370. Poh Naan Kaew Khanthamanii (age 83). #1, Baan Sribunryang, Tambon Mae Saa, Amphur Mae Rim. Interviewed October 2, 1985.

MR-386. Poh Ui Maa Phakphorn (age 78). #4, Baan Ba Ngae, Tambon Don Kaew, Amphur Mae Rim. Interviewed October 9, 1985.

MR-389. Poh Ui Kaew Khemphet (age 83). #5, Baan Ba Huak, Tambon Don Kaew, Amphur Mae Rim. Interviewed October 9, 1985.

MR-392. Poh Naan Kaew Phyakphon (age 83). #4, Baan Wang Muun, Tambon San Pong, Amphur Mae Rim. Interviewed October 10, 1985.

MR-398. Poh Ui Maa Wongsuaj (age 84). #3, Baan San Pong, Tambon San Pong, Amphur Mae Rim. Interviewed October 10, 1985.

MR-422. Poh Noi Ai Myangmaa (age 91). Baan Thung Pong, Tambon Mae Laem, Amphur Mae Rim. Interviewed October 22, 1985.

MR-438. Poh Noi Hohm Siripin (age 84). #2, Baan Ton Phyng, Tambon Myang Kaew, Amphur Mae Rim. Interviewed October 26, 1985.
SS-445. Poh Naan Kam Ratchakit (age 66). #1, Baan Mae Yoi, Tambon San Sai Noi, Amphur San Sai. Interviewed October 26, 1985.
SS-448. Poh Ui Muun Asaakhit (age 92). #3. Baan Saimuun, Tambon San Sai Noi, Amphur San Sai. Interviewed October 26, 1985.
SS-460. Mae Ui Kaew Chomduang (age 85) and Mae Ui Daeng Kongngen (age 82). #2, Baan Ba Bong, Tambon Mae Faek, Amphur San Sai. Interviewed October 30, 1985.
SS-462. Poh Ui Thip Bunyyyn (age 84). #4, Baan Rom Luang, Tambon Mae Faek, Amphur San Sai. Interviewed October 30, 1985.
SS-476. Poh Ui Thaa Issara (age 75). #2, Baan Sup Faek, Tambon Mae Faek Mai, Amphur San Sai. Interviewed November 8, 1985.
SS-478. Poh Naan Kong Thongvilaat (age 76). #1, Baan Mae Faek Luang, Tambon Mae Faek Mai, Amphur San Sai. Interviewed November 8, 1985.
SS-490. Mae Ui Kaew Borilak (age 89). #4, Baan Thung Faa Tok, Tambon Nong Yaeng, Amphur San Sai. Interviewed November 13, 1985.
SS-512. Poh Ui Noi Buk Phongsiri (age 92). #1, Baan Mae Yoi, Tambon San Sai Noi, Amphur San Sai. Interviewed November 17, 1985.
SS-515. Mae Ui Uun Inthaa (age 94). #5, Baan T, Tambon San Sai Luang, Amphur San Sai. Interviewed November 18, 1985.
SS-521. Poh Ui Naan Singhkham Kaehang (age 86). #2, Baan Ba Tong, Tambon San Sai Luang, Amphur San Sai. Interviewed November 18, 1985.
SS-523. Mae Ui Kaew Nanthakham (age 87). #5, Tambon San Sai Luang, Amphur San Sai. Interviewed November 18, 1985.
SS-527. Poh Luang Naan Phet Prichaaraa (age 59). #4, Baan Ba Myat, Tambon Phaphai, Amphur San Sai. Interviewed November 19, 1985.
M-534. Mae Ui Khiew Arunsit (age 76). Behind Wat Jetawan, Tambon Chang Moi, Amphur Myang. Interviewed November 28, 1985.
M-542. Nen Khaw Waan Sathaanmuun (age 140?!) (phyng wua). #8, Tambon Suthep, Amphur Myang. Interviewed December 3, 1985.
M-542a. Monks, Wat Khuang Singh. #3, Tambon Chang Phyak, Amphur Myang. Interviewed December 3, 1985.
M-546. Mae Ui Khiew na Chiang Mai (age 95); Baa Dii Chatkaew, daughter; and Sipek Sri, son (age 63). #5, Baan Myang Sat, Tambon Nong Hooj, Amphur Myang. Interviewed December 4, 1985.

Recent Interviews

Ajarn Manee Phayomyong. Mae Rim, Chiang Mai. August 1, 2005.
Ajarn Sulak Sivaraksa. Bangkok. March 3, 2010.
Luang Poh (Phrakhruu) Bunthong Suwanno. Wat Sothannaraam, Tambon Don Kaew, Amphur Mae Rim, Chiang Mai. August 1, 2005.

Lung Kriangkrai. Grand Palace official. Bangkok. March 3, 2010.
Lung Naan Saengmuang Ryansin. Baan Kilenoi, Tambon Baan Mae, Amphur Sanpatong, Chiang Mai. July 30, 2005.
Lung Waai Ryangdej. Baan Den Samrong, Tambon Haat Song Khwae, Amphur Tron, Uttaradit. August 24, 2015.
Phrakhruu Athong Visutikhul. Abbot, Wat Nong Tong, Tambon Nong Tong, Amphur Hang Dong, Chiang Mai. July 13, 2005.
Phrakhruu Prachotipacharothai (Uthai Chutmanuto). Wat Pothiyen, Baan Thaa Phuaa, Tambon Hinhao, Amphur Lommkao, Petchabun. March 7, 2010.
Phrakhruu Winaithorn Dr. Manop Paalaphan. Deputy Abbot at Wat Pho (Wat Chetuphon), Bangkok. March 4, 2010.
Phra Racha Thammawaathii. Deputy Abbot, Wat Prayoon (Wat Prayurawongsawat), Bangkok. Interview by phone, March 3, 2010.
Phra Racha Vijitphatiphaan. Deputy Abbot, Wat Suthat Thepwaraaraam, Bangkok. January 15, 2008.

Tapes

Luang Poh Bunthong. TE 006. Tu Lung Thong [Luang Poh (Phrakhruu) Bunthong Suwanno]. n.d. (circa 1970s). *Lao Jia Muang Nya* [Telling humorous northern tales]. Distributor: Thippanetr Enterprise, Tambon Haiya, Amphur Muang, Chiang Mai.
———. TE 050. Tu Lung Thong [Luang Poh (Phrakhruu) Bunthong Suwanno]. n.d. (circa 1970s). *Lao Jia Muang Nya* [Telling humorous northern tales]. Distributor: Thippanetr Enterprise, Tambon Haiya, Amphur Muang, Chiang Mai.
———. TE 066. Tu Lung Thong [Luang Poh (Phrakhruu) Bunthong Suwanno]. n.d. (circa 1970s). *Mahachaat 13 Kan* [Mahachat in 13 chapters]. 5 tapes. November 23, 1990.
———. TE 011. Tu Lung Thong [Luang Poh (Phrakhruu) Bunthong Suwanno]. n.d. (circa 1970s). *Thet Mahachaat Prayuk (baep muang nya): Kan Chuchok* [Preaching the Mahachat in modern northern style: The Jujaka chapter].

Published Sources

Akin Rabibhadana. 1992. *Tourism and Culture: Bang-Fai Festival in Esan*. Bangkok: Thailand Development Research Institute Foundation.
Alabaster, Henry, trans. 1870. *The Modern Buddhist; Being the Views of a Siamese Minister of State on His Own and Other Religions*. By Chaophraya Thiphakonwongmahakosathibodi (Kham Bunnag). London: Trubner.
Anake Nawigamune. 2007. *Phra Ubaali khunuupamaajaarn Sirijanutho (Chan): Nakpraat jaak daen isaan* (Phra Upali: Scholar from the Northeast). Bangkok: Saengdao.
Anan Ganjanapan. 1984. "The Partial Commercialization of Rice Production in Northern Thailand, 1900–1981." PhD diss., Cornell University.

Andaya, Barbara Watson, ed. 2000. *Other Pasts: Women, Gender and History in Early Modern Southeast Asia*. Manoa: Center for Southeast Asian Studies, University of Hawai'i.

———. 2002. "Women, Motherhood and the Appeal of Early Theravada Buddhism." *Journal of Southeast Asian Studies* 33 (1): 1–30.

———. 2006. *The Flaming Womb: Repositioning Women in Early Modern Southeast Asia*. Honolulu: University of Hawai'i Press.

Andrew, James M. 1935. *Siam: Second Rural Economic Survey, 1934–35*. Bangkok: Bangkok Times Press.

Anonymous. 1895. *An Englishman's Siamese Journals, 1890–1893*. Bangkok: Siam Media International Books.

———. 1982. *Wat Chong Nonsi*. Mural Paintings of Thailand Series. Bangkok: Muang Boran Publishing House.

———. 1991. *Tales of Sri Thanonchai, Thailand's Artful Trickster*. Bangkok: NAGA Books.

Anuman Rajadhon, Phya. 1958. *Five Papers on Thai Custom*. Southeast Asia Program Data Paper 28. Ithaca, NY: Southeast Asia Program, Cornell University.

———. 1961. *Life and Ritual in Old Siam: Three Studies of Thai Life and Customs*. Translated and edited by William J. Gedney. New Haven, CT: HRAF Press.

———. 1963. *Thai Literature in Relation to the Diffusion of Her Cultures*. 2nd ed. Thai Culture, New Series 9. Bangkok: Fine Arts Department.

———. 1986. *Popular Buddhism in Siam and Other Essays on Thai Studies*. Bangkok: Thai Inter-Religious Commission for Development and Sathirakoses Nagapradipa Foundation.

———. 1988. "Thet Maha Chat." In *Essays on Thai Folklore*, 186–200. Bangkok: Thai Inter-Religious Commission for Development and Sathirakoses Nagapradipa Foundation.

———. 1990. *Essays on Cultural Thailand*. Bangkok: Office of the National Culture Commission.

Appleton, Naomi. 2010. *Jataka Stories in Theravada Buddhism: Narrating the Bodhisatta Path*. Farnham, Surrey: Ashgate.

Apte, Mahadev L. 1985. *Humor and Laughter: An Anthropological Approach*. Ithaca, NY: Cornell University Press.

Archaimbault, Charles. 1971. *The New Year Ceremony at Basak (South Laos)*. Cornell Southeast Asia Data Paper 78. Ithaca, NY: Cornell University.

———. 1972. *La course de pirogues au Laos: Un complexe culturel*. Artibus Asiae Supplementum XXIX. Ascona, Switzerland: Artibus Asiae.

Aroonrut Wichienkeeo and Volker Grabowsky. 1996. "Ethnic Groups in Chiang Mai by the Turn of the Twentieth Century: A Study Based on Names of Old Monasteries." Paper presented at 14th Conference of International Association of Historians of Asia, Chulalongkorn University, Bangkok, May 20–24.

Aroonrut Wichienkhiew and Gehan Wijewardene, eds. and trans. 1987. *The Laws of King Mangrai*. Canberra: R. Davis Fund.

Arthid Sheravanichkul. 2008. "Self-Sacrifice of the Bodhisatta in the Paññāsa Jātaka." *Religion Compass* 2 (5): 769–87.

———. 2012a. "Narrative and Gift-Giving in Thai Anisamsa Texts." In *Buddhist Narrative in Asia and Beyond*, edited by Peter Skilling and Justin McDaniel, 37–46. Bangkok: Institute of Thai Studies, Chulalongkorn University.

———. 2012b. "To Compensate Bad Karma, to Help Those Who Suffer: A Mon Manuscript and 'Narratives' on Jujaka Amulets." Paper presented at the European Association of Southeast Asian Archaeologists 14th International Conference, Dublin, Ireland, September 18–21.

Atkinson, Jane Monnig, and Shelly Errington, eds. 1990. *Power and Difference: Gender in Island Southeast Asia*. Stanford: Stanford University Press.

Aung San Suu Kyi. 1991. *Freedom from Fear and Other Writings*. New York: Penguin.

Aung Thwin, Michael. 1979. "The Role of Sasana Reform in Burmese History: Economic Dimensions of a Religious Purification." *Journal of Asian Studies* 38 (4): 671–88.

Baird, Ian G. 2007. "Contested History, Ethnicity and Remembering the Past: The Case of the Ay Sa Rebellion in Southern Laos." *Crossroads* 18 (2): 119–59.

Baker, Chris, ed. 2013. *Protecting Siam's Heritage*. Bangkok: Siam Society; Chiang Mai: Silkworm Books.

Baker, Chris, and Pasuk Phongpaichit, eds. and trans. 2010. *The Tale of Khun Chang Khun Phaen*. Chiang Mai: Silkworm Books.

Baker, Chris, Dhiravat na Pomberja, Alfons van der Kraan, and David K. Wyatt, eds. 2005. *Van Vliet's Siam*. Chiang Mai: Silkworm Books.

Bakhtin, Mikhail. (1965) 1984. *Rabelais and His World*. Translated by Helene Iswolsky. Bloomington: Indiana University Press.

Bastian, Adolf. (1867) 2005. *A Journey in Siam, 1863*. Translated by Walter E. J. Tips. Bangkok: White Lotus Press.

Bechert, Heinz, and Richard Gombrich. 1991. *The World of Buddhism: Buddhist Monks and Nuns in Society and Culture*. New York: Thames and Hudson.

Bell, Catherine. 1992. *Ritual Theory, Ritual Practice*. New York: Oxford University Press.

Benda, Harry J., and John A. Larkin, eds. 1967. *The World of Southeast Asia: Selected Historical Readings*. New York: Harper & Row.

Bergson, Henri. (1911) 2005. *Laughter: An Essay on the Meaning of the Comic*. Translated by Cloudesley Brereton and Fred Rothwell. Mineola, NY: Dover.

Bhasit Chitrabhasa. 1990. "Thet Mahaachaat thii sombuunbaeb ja haa fang dai thiinai?" [Where can you hear a Recitation of the *Vessantara Jataka*?]. *Silapawathanatham* 7 (1): 16–18.

Bird, George W. 1897. *Wanderings in Burma*. Bournemouth: F. J. Bright & Son.

Blackburn, Anne M. 2010. *Locations of Buddhism: Colonialism and Modernity in Sri Lanka*. University of Chicago Press.

Blackwood, Evelyn. 2000. *Webs of Power: Women, Kin and Community in a Sumatran Village*. Lanham, MD: Rowman and Littlefield.

Bock, Carl. (1884) 1986. *Temples and Elephants: Travels in Siam in 1881–1882*. Singapore: Oxford University Press.
Boisselier, Jean. 1976. *Thai Painting*. Translated by Janet Seligman. Tokyo: Kodansha International.
Bokenkamp, Stephen R. 2006. "The Visvantara-Jataka in Buddhist and Daoist Translation." In *Daoism in History: Essays in Honour of Liu Ts'un-yan*, edited by Benjamin Penny, 56–73. New York: Routledge.
Boskin, Joseph. 1997. *Rebellious Laughter: People's Humor in American Culture*. Syracuse: Syracuse University Press.
Bowers, Amy. 2011. "Pha Lak Pha Lam in Popular Practice: How the Ramayana Is Lived in Laos." BA Honors Thesis, University of Wisconsin–Madison.
Bowie, Katherine. 1988. "Peasant Perspectives on the Political Economy of the Northern Thai Kingdom of Chiang Mai in the Nineteenth Century: Implications for the Understanding of Peasant Political Expression." PhD diss., University of Chicago.
———. 1992. "Unraveling the Myth of the Subsistence Economy: The Case of Textile Production in Nineteenth-Century Northern Thailand." *Journal of Asian Studies* 51 (4): 797–823.
———. 1993. "Cloth and the Fabric of Northern Thai Society in the Nineteenth Century: From Peasants in Cotton to Lords in Silks." *American Ethnologist* 20 (1): 138–58.
———. 1996. "Slavery in Nineteenth-Century Northern Thailand: Archival Anecdotes and Village Voices." In *State Power and Culture in Thailand*, edited by E. Paul Durrenberger, 100–138. Yale University Southeast Asia Monograph 44. New Haven, CT: Yale University Southeast Asia Studies.
———. 1998. "The Alchemy of Charity: Of Class and Buddhism in Northern Thailand." *American Anthropologist* 100 (2): 469–81.
———. 2000. "Ethnic Heterogeneity and Elephants in Nineteenth-Century Lanna Statecraft." In *Civility and Savagery: Social Identity in Tai States*, edited by Andrew Turton, 330–48. London: Curzon.
———. 2006. "Of Corvée and Slavery: Historical Intricacies of the Division of Labor and State Power in Northern Thailand." In *Labor in Cross-Cultural Perspective*, edited by E. Paul Durrenberger and Judith E. Marti, 245–64. Society for Economic Anthropology Monographs 23. Lanham, MD: AltaMira Press.
———. 2008a. "Standing in the Shadows: Of Matrilocality and the Role of Women in a Village Election in Northern Thailand." *American Ethnologist* 35 (1): 136–53.
———. 2008b. "Vote Buying and Village Outrage in an Election in Northern Thailand: Recent Legal Reforms in Historical Context." *Journal of Asian Studies* 67 (2): 469–511.
———. 2010. "Women's Suffrage in Thailand: A Southeast Asian Historiographical Challenge." *Comparative Studies in Society and History* 52 (4): 708–41.
———. 2011. "Polluted Identities: Ethnic Diversity and the Constitution of Northern Thai Beliefs on Gender." In *Southeast Asian Historiography Unravelling the Myths: Essays in Honour of Barend Jan Terweil*, edited by Volker Grabowsky, 112–27. Bangkok: River Books.

———. 2014a. "Buddhism and Militarism in Northern Thailand: Solving the Puzzle of the Saint Khruubaa Srivichai." *Journal of Asian Studies* 73 (3): 711–32.

———. 2014b. "The Saint with Indra's Sword: Kruubaa Srivichai and Buddhist Millenarianism in Northern Thailand." *Comparative Studies in Society and History* 56 (3): 681–713.

Bowring, Sir John. (1857) 1969. *The Kingdom and People of Siam*. 2 vols. New York: Oxford University Press.

Brac de la Perrière, Bénédicte. 1992. "La fête de Taunbyon: Le grand rituel du culte des naq de Birmanie (Myanmar)." *Bulletin de l'Ecole française d'Extrême-Orient* 79 (2): 201–31.

Braudel, Fernand. (1979) 1981. *The Structures of Everyday Life: Civilization and Capitalism, 15th–18th Century*. Translated by Sian Reynolds. New York: Harper & Row.

Brennan, Jonathan, ed. 2003. *When Brer Rabbit Meets Coyote*. Urbana: University of Illinois Press.

Brenner, Suzanne. 1998. *The Domestication of Desire: Women, Wealth, and Modernity in Java*. Princeton, NJ: Princeton University Press.

Brereton, Bonnie Pacala. 1978. "The Wat Si Chum Engravings and Their Place within the Art of Sukhothai." MA thesis, University of Michigan.

———. 1995. *Thai Tellings of Phra Malai: Texts and Rituals Concerning a Popular Buddhist Saint*. Tempe: Arizona State University.

Brereton, Bonnie Pacala, and Somroay Yencheuy. 2010. *Buddhist Murals of Northeast Thailand: Reflections of the Isan Heartland*. Chiang Mai: Mekong Press.

Bunnag, Jane. 1973. *Buddhist Monk, Buddhist Layman: A Study of Urban Monastic Organization in Central Thailand*. Cambridge: Cambridge University Press.

Cady, John F. 1958. *A History of Modern Burma*. Ithaca, NY: Cornell University Press.

Calavan, Kay Mitchell. 1974. "Aristocrats and Commoners in Rural Northern Thailand." PhD diss., University of Illinois at Urbana-Champaign.

Carsten, Janet. 1997. *The Heat of the Hearth: The Process of Kinship in a Malay Fishing Community*. Oxford: Clarendon Press.

Cate, Sandra. 2003. *Making Merit, Making Art: A Thai Temple in Wimbledon*. Honolulu: University of Hawai'i Press.

Cate, Sandra, and Leedom Lefferts. 2012. "Becoming Active/Active Becoming: Prince Vessantara Scrolls and the Creation of a Moral Community." In *The Spirit of Things: Materiality and Religious Diversity in Southeast Asia*, edited by Julius Bautista, 165–81. Studies on Southeast Asia 58. Ithaca, NY: Southeast Asia Program, Cornell University.

Chandler, David. 1996. *Facing the Cambodian Past: Selected Essays, 1971–1994*. Chiang Mai: Silkworm Books.

Chartsumarn Kabilsingh. 1991. *Thai Women in Buddhism*. Berkeley: Parallax Press.

Chatthip Nartsupha. 1984. "The Ideology of Holy Men Revolts in North East Thailand." In *History and Peasant Consciousness in Southeast Asia*, edited by A. Turton and S. Tanabe, 111–134. Osaka, Japan: National Museum of Ethnology.

Chayan Vaddhanaphuti. 1984. "Cultural and Ideological Reproduction in Rural Northern Thai Society." PhD diss., Stanford University.
Chiu, Angela Shih Chih. 2012. "The Social and Religious World of Northern Thai Buddha Images: Art, Lineage, Power and Place in Lan Na Monastic Chronicles (Tamnan)." PhD diss., School of Oriental and African Studies, University of London.
Chula Chakrabongse, Prince. 1982. *Lords of Life: A History of the Kings of Thailand.* Bangkok: DD Books.
Chun Shin-Yong, ed. 1977. *Humour in Korean Literature.* Seoul, Korea: International Cultural Foundation.
Claus-Bachmann, Martina. 2002. "Jataka Narrations as Multimedial Reconstructive Embodiments of the Mental System Buddha Shakyamuni." *World of Music* 44 (2): 115–34.
Coedes, George. 1956. "The Twenty-Five-Hundredth Anniversary of the Buddha." *Diogenes* 15:95–111.
Cohen, Paul T. 1981. "The Politics of Economic Development in Northern Thailand, 1967–1978." PhD diss., London School of Economics and Political Science, University of London.
———. 1983. "A Bodhisattva on Horseback: Buddhist Ethics and Pragmatism in Northern Thailand." *Mankind* 14 (2): 101–11.
———. 2001. "Buddhism Unshackled: The Yuan 'Holy Man' Tradition and the Nation-State in the Tai World." *Journal of Southeast Asian Studies* 32 (2): 227–47.
Collins, Steven. 1993. "The Story of the Elder Maleyyadeva." *Journal of the Pali Text Society* 28:65–96.
———. 1998. *Nirvana and other Buddhist Felicities.* New York: Cambridge University Press.
———, ed. 2016. *Readings of the "Vessantara Jātaka."* New York: Columbia University Press.
Colquhoun, Archibald R. 1885. *Amongst the Shans.* With illustrations and "An Historical Sketch of the Shans" by Holt S. Hallett. Introduction by Terrien de Lacouperie. London: Field & Tuer; Simpkin, Marshall & Co; Hamilton, Adams & Co.
Compton, Carol. 1979. *Courting Poetry in Laos: A Textual and Linguistic Analysis.* Special Report 18. DeKalb: Northern Illinois University, Center for Southeast Asian Studies.
Compton, Carol, John F. Hartmann, and Vinya Sysamouth, eds. 2009. *Contemporary Lao Studies: Research on Development, Language and Culture, and Traditional Medicine.* San Francisco: Center for Lao Studies; DeKalb: Northern Illinois University, Center for Southeast Asian Studies.
Condominas, Georges. 1968. "Notes sur le bouddhisme populaire en milieu rural Lao." *Archives de sociologie des religions* 25:81–110.
Cone, Margaret, and Richard F. Gombrich. 1977. *The Perfect Generosity of Prince Vessantara: A Buddhist Epic.* Oxford: Clarendon Press.

———, eds. 2011. *The Perfect Generosity of Prince Vessantara*. Bristol: Pali Text Society.
Copeland, Matthew. 1993. "Contested Nationalism and the 1932 Overthrow of the Absolute Monarchy in Siam." PhD diss., Australian National University.
Cort, Mary Lovina. 1886. *Siam, or the Heart of Farther India*. New York: Anson D. F. Randolph and Co.
Cowell, E. B., ed. (1895) 1957. *The Jataka or the Stories of the Buddha's Former Births*. London: Luzac & Co Ltd. 5 vols. For the Pali Text Society.
Crawfurd, John. (1828) 1987. *Journal of an Embassy to the Courts of Siam and Cochin China*. Introduction by David Wyatt. Singapore: Oxford University Press.
Cunningham, Alexander. 1962. *The Stūpa of Bharhut: A Buddhist Monument Ornamented with Numerous Sculptures, Illustrative of Buddhist Legend and History in the Third Century BC*. Varanasi, India: Indological Book House.
Da Matta, Roberto. 1991. *Carnivals, Rogues, and Heroes: An Interpretation of the Brazilian Dilemma*. Notre Dame: University of Notre Dame Press.
Damrong Rajanubhab, HRH Prince, ed. 1918. *Thet Chuchok Khwaamkao*. First printed for the funeral of Ammaat Ek Phrayaanakhonphraraam (M.R.W. Lek Phakhomsenaa na Krungthep). Bangkok: Sophonphiphatthanakon Press. Introduction by Prince Damrong Rachanuphab. Wat Sangkajaai version.
———. 1919. Preface to *Mahaaphon kham chieng kap Mahaaphon khwaam Phra Thepmoli Klin*. Printed for funeral of Khun Rachaphichitr (Jui Krisnaamara). Bangkok: Sophonphiphattanakon Press.
Davis, Erik W. 2009. "Treasures of the Buddha: Imagining Death and Life in Contemporary Cambodia." PhD diss., University of Chicago.
Davis, Richard. 1984. *Muang Metaphysics: A Study of Northern Thai Myth and Ritual*. Bangkok: Pandora.
DeBernardi, Jean. 2006. *The Way That Lives in the Heart: Chinese Popular Religion and Spirit Mediums in Penang, Malaysia*. Stanford: Stanford University Press.
Deegalle, Mahinda. 2012. "Jataka Narratives in Buddhist Preaching and their Contested Popular Imagination in Sri Lanka." In *Buddhist Narrative in Asia and Beyond*, edited by Peter Skilling and Justin McDaniel, 1:127-46. Bangkok: Institute of Thai Studies, Chulalongkorn University.
Dehejia, Vidya. 1990. "On Modes of Visual Narration in Early Buddhist Art." *The Art Bulletin* 72 (3): 374-92.
Dembicki, Matt. 2010. *Trickster: Native American Tales*. Golden, CO: Fulcrum.
De Young, John E. 1955. *Village Life in Modern Thailand*. Berkeley: University of California Press.
Dhani Niwat, Prince. 1955. "The Reconstruction of Rama I of the Chakri Dynasty." *Journal of the Siam Society* 43 (1): 21-47.
Dhawat Poonotoke. 1995. "A Comparative Study of Isan and Lanna Thai Literature." In *Thai Literary Traditions*, edited by Manas Chitakasem, 248-64. Bangkok: Chulalongkorn University Press.

Dodd, William Clifton. 1923. *The Tai Race, Elder Brother of the Chinese*. Cedar Rapids, IA: Torch Press.
D'Oldenburg, Serge. 1893. "On the Buddhist Jatakas." *Journal of the Royal Asiatic Society of Great Britain and Ireland* 25 (2): 301-56.
Dolias, Jacques. 1990. "Visvakarman: Un exemple d'adaptation des mythes indiens en pays khmer." *Cahiers de l'Asie du Sud-Est* 28:109-46.
Doniger, Wendy. 2000. *The Bedtrick: Tales of Sex and Masquerade*. Chicago: University of Chicago Press.
Dorje, Rinjing. 1997. *Tales of Uncle Tompa: The Legendary Rascal of Tibet*. Barrytown, NY: Station Hill Arts.
Eade, J. C. 1995. *The Calendrical Systems of Mainland South-East Asia*. New York: Brill.
Ebihara, May. 1968. "Svay, a Khmer Village in Cambodia." PhD diss., Columbia University.
Edwards, Penny. 2007. *Cambodge: The Cultivation of a Nation, 1860-1945*. Honolulu: University of Hawai'i Press.
Eichinger Ferro-Luzzi, Gabriella. 1992. *The Taste of Laughter: Aspects of Tamil Humour*. Wiesbaden: Harrassowitz Verlag.
Emmrich, Christoph. 2016. "Vessantara Opts Out: Newer Versions of the Tale of the Generous Prince." In *Readings of the "Vessantara Jātaka,"* edited by Steven Collins, 183-209. New York: Columbia University Press.
Epstein, Steven Jay. (1995) 2005. *Lao Folktales*. Chiang Mai: Silkworm Books.
Evans, Grant. 1998. *The Politics of Ritual and Remembrance: Laos since 1975*. Honolulu: University of Hawai'i Press.
Faa Wongmahaa. 1976-77. "Khruubaa Srivichai." Serialized in *Thaan Tawan* (Bangkok). Vols. 170-203 (July 30, 1976-March 28, 1977).
Falk, Monica Lindberg. 2008. *Making Fields of Merit: Buddhist Female Ascetics and Gendered Orders in Thailand*. Seattle: University of Washington Press; Copenhagen: Nordic Institute of Asian Studies Press.
Farrington, Anthony, ed. 2004. *Dr. Richardson's Missions to Siam, 1829-1839*. Bangkok: White Lotus Press.
Faure, Marie-Daniel. 1959. "The 'Boun' Pha-Vet (4th Month Festival)." In *Kingdom of Laos: The Land of the Million Elephants and of the White Parasol*, edited by René de Berval, 294-97. Saigon: France-Asie.
———. 1937. "Trois fêtes laotiennes." *Bulletin des "Amis du Laos."* 1:21-43.
Feer, M. L. (1865) 1963. *A Study of the Jatakas: Analytical and Critical*. Translated by G. M. Foulkes. Calcutta: Susil Gupta Private Ltd. Originally published as *Études bouddhiques: Les Jātakas* (Paris: Imprimerie Nationale, 1865).
Feinberg, Leonard, ed. 1971. *Asian Laughter: An Anthology of Oriental Satire and Humor*. New York: Weatherhill.
Ferguson, John Palmer. 1975. "The Symbolic Dimensions of the Burmese Sangha." PhD diss., Cornell University.

Ferguson, John P., and Christina B. Johannsen. 1976. "Modern Buddhist Murals in Northern Thailand: A Study of Religious Symbols and Meaning." *American Ethnologist* 3 (4): 645–69.

Ferguson, John P., and Shalardchai Ramitanondh. 1976. "Monks and Hierarchy in Northern Thailand." *Journal of the Siam Society* 64 (1): 104–50.

Ferrars, Max, and Bertha Ferrars. 1900. *Burma*. London: Sampson Low, Marston and Co.

Finot, Louis. 1917. "Recherches sur la littérature Laotienne." *Bulletin de l'Ecole française d'Extrême-Orient* 17:1–219.

Fleeson, Katherine Neville. 1899. *Laos Folk-Lore of Farther India*. New York: Fleming H. Revell.

Flueckiger, Joyce Burkhalter. 1996. *Gender and Genre in the Folklore of Middle India*. Ithaca, NY: Cornell University Press.

Forbes, Captain Charles James F. S. 1878. *British Burma and its People, Being Sketches of Native Manners, Customs and Religion*. London: John Murray.

Ford, Ryan. 2011. "Memories of Chao Anu: New History and Post-Socialist Ideology." *Journal of Lao Studies* 2 (2): 104–26.

Formoso, Bernard. 1992. "Le Bun Pha Wet des Lao du Nord-est de la Thaïlande." *Bulletin de l'Ecole française d'Extrême-Orient* 79:233–60.

Foucher, Alfred. 1955. *Les vies antérieures du Bouddha: D'après les textes et les monuments de l'Inde*. Paris: Presses Universitaires de France.

———. 1963. *The Life of the Buddha, According to the Ancient Texts and Monuments of India*. Abridged translation by Simone Brangier Boas. Middletown, CT: Wesleyan University Press.

Fournereau, Lucien. (1894) 1998. *Bangkok in 1892*. Translated and with an introduction by Walter E. J. Tips. Bangkok: White Lotus Press.

Freeman, John H. 1910. *An Oriental Land of the Free*. Philadelphia: Westminster Press.

Freud, Sigmund. (1960) 1989. *Jokes and Their Relation to the Unconscious*. New York: W. W. Norton.

Fuller, Thomas. 2015. "Thai Man May Go to Prison for Insulting King's Dog." *New York Times*, December 14.

Gabaude, Louis. 1991. "Controverses modernes autour du Vessantara Jātaka." *Cahiers de l'Asie du Sud-Est* 29–30:51–72.

———. 2016. "Readers in the Maze: Modern Debates about the Vessantara Story in Thailand." In *Readings of the "Vessantara Jātaka,"* edited by Steven Collins, 37–52. New York: Columbia University Press.

Gailey, Christine Ward. 1987. *Kinship to Kingship: Gender Hierarchy and State Formation in the Tongan Islands*. Austin: University of Texas Press.

Garnier, Francis. 1873. *Voyage d'exploration en Indo-chine effectué pendant les années 1866, 1867 et 1868*. 2 vols. Paris: Librairie Hachette et Cie.

Gascoigne, Gwendolen Trench. 1896. *Among Pagodas and Fair Ladies: An Account of a Tour through Burma*. London: A. D. Innes & Co.

Gay, Bernard. 2002. "Millenarian Movements in Laos, 1895-1936." In *Breaking New Ground in Lao History: Essays on the Seventh to Twentieth Centuries*, edited by Mayoury Ngaosrivathana and Kennon Breazeale, 281-96. Chiang Mai: Silkworm Books.

Gay, Peter. 1999. "The Bite of Wit." In *The Bourgeois Experience: Victoria to Freud*, vol. 3, *The Cultivation of Hatred*, 368-423. New York: W. W. Norton.

Gengenbach, Julia. 2009. "Give Away Your Wife and Children—Find Inner Peace. (Some Restrictions Apply): How Narratives Can Be Used in the Formation of Moral Persons in Buddhism. With Special Focus on the Vessantara Jataka." MA thesis, University of Wisconsin-Madison.

Gerini, G. E. (1892) 1976. *A Retrospective View and Account of the Origin of the Thet Maha Ch'at Ceremony*. Bangkok: Sathirakoses-Nagapradipa Foundation.

Gervaise, Nicholas. (1688) 1989. *The Natural and Political History of the Kingdom of Siam*. Bangkok: White Lotus Co.

Gluckman, Max. 1954. *Rituals of Rebellion in South-East Africa*. Manchester: Manchester University Press.

Gokhale, Balkrishna Govind. 1977. "The Merchant in Ancient India." *Journal of the American Oriental Society* 97 (2): 125-30.

Goldstein, Donna M. 2003. *Laughter Out of Place: Race, Class, Violence and Sexuality in a Rio Shantytown*. Berkeley: University of California Press.

Gombrich, Richard F. 1971. *Precept and Practice: Traditional Buddhism in the Rural Highlands of Ceylon*. Oxford: Oxford University Press.

———. 1985. "The Vessantara Jātaka, the Rāmāyaṇa and the Dasaratha Jātaka: A Comparison of Buddhist and Hindu Ethics." *Journal of the American Oriental Society* 105 (3): 427-37.

Goscha, Christopher E., and Soren Ivarsson, eds. 2003. *Contesting Visions of the Lao Past: Lao Historiography at the Crossroads*. Copenhagen: Nordic Institute of Asian Studies.

Gosling, Betty. 1984. "Why Were the Jatakas 'Hidden Away' at Wat Sichum?" *Journal of the Siam Society* 72:14-18.

Goss, L. Allan. 1895. *The Story of We-than-da-ya: A Buddhist Legend, Sketched from the Burmese Version of the Pali Text*. 2nd ed. Rangoon: American Baptist Mission Press.

Grabowsky, Volker, ed. 1995. *Regions and National Integration in Thailand, 1892-1992*. Wiesbaden: Harrassowitz Verlag.

———. 1999. "Forced Resettlement Campaigns in Northern Thailand during the Early Bangkok Period." *Journal of the Siam Society* 87 (Parts 1 and 2): 45-86.

———. 2001. "Note on Kep Phak sai saa, Kep khaa sai muang." *Aseanie* 8:67-72.

Grabowsky, Volker, and Andrew Turton. 2003. *The Gold and Silver Road of Trade and Friendship: The McLeod and Richardson Diplomatic Missions to Tai States in 1837*. Chiang Mai: Silkworm Books.

Grabowsky, Volker, and Oliver Tappe. 2011. "'Important Kings of Laos': Translation and Analysis of a Lao Cartoon Pamphlet." *Journal of Lao Studies* 2 (1): 1-44.

Green, Gillian. 2012. "Verging on Modernity: A Late Nineteenth-Century Burmese Painting on Cloth Depicting the Vessantara Jataka." *Journal of Burma Studies* 16 (1): 79–122.
Griswold, A. B. 1953. "The Buddhas of Sukhodaya." *Archives of the Chinese Art Society of America* 7:5–41.
Griswold, A. B., and Prasert na Nagara. 1969. "The Pact Between Sukhodaya and Nân: Epigraphic and Historical Studies No. 3." *Journal of the Siam Society* 57 (1): 57–107.
———. 1973. "Epigraphic and Historical Studies No. 11, Part 1: The Epigraphy of Mahâdharmarâjâ I of Sukhodaya." *Journal of the Siam Society* 61 (1): 71–178.
Grow, Mary. 1991. "Laughter for Spirits, A Vow Fulfilled: The Comic Performance of Thailand's Lakhon Chatri Dance-Drama." PhD diss., University of Wisconsin–Madison.
———. 1996. "Tarnishing the Gold Era: Aesthetics, Humor and Politics in *Lakhon Chatri* Dance-Drama." In *State Power and Culture in Thailand*, edited by E. Paul Durrenberger, 47–67. Yale University Southeast Asia Monograph 44. New Haven, CT: Yale University Southeast Asia Studies.
Gunawardana, R. A. L. H. 1979. *Robe and Plough: Monasticism and Economic Interest in Early Medieval Sri Lanka*. Tucson, AZ: Association for Asian Studies.
Gunn, Geoffrey C. 1990. *Rebellion in Laos: Peasants and Politics in a Colonial Backwater*. Boulder, CO: Westview Press.
Haberkorn, Tyrell. 2011. *Revolution Interrupted: Farmers, Students, Law, and Violence in Northern Thailand*. Madison: University of Wisconsin Press.
Hadler, Jeffrey. 2008. *Muslims and Matriarchs: Cultural Resilience in Indonesia through Jihad and Colonialism*. Ithaca, NY: Cornell University Press.
Hallett, Holt. 1890. *A Thousand Miles on an Elephant in the Shan States (1890)*. Edinburgh: William Blackwood and Sons.
Hallisey, Charles. 1995. "Roads Taken and Not Taken in the Study of Theravada Buddhism." In *Curators of the Buddha: The Study of Buddhism under Colonialism*, edited by Donald S. Lopez Jr., 31–61. Chicago: University of Chicago Press.
———. 2005. "Buddhist Ethics: Trajectories." In *The Blackwell Companion to Religious Ethics*, edited by William Schweiker, 312–22. Malden, MA: Blackwell.
Hallisey, Charles, and Anne Hansen. 1996. "Narrative, Sub-ethics and the Moral Life: Some Evidence from Theravada Buddhism." *Journal of Religious Ethics* 24 (2): 305–27.
Halperin, Joel. 1973. "The Role of Religion in Government and Politics in Laos." In *Southeast Asia: The Politics of National Integration*, edited by John T. McAlister, 202–14. New York: Random House.
Handlin, Lilian. 2016. "A Man for All Seasons: Three *Vessantaras* in Pre Modern Myanmar." In *Readings of the "Vessantara Jātaka,"* edited by Steven Collins, 153–82. New York: Columbia University Press.
Hansen, Anne. 2007. *How to Behave: Buddhism and Modernity in Colonial Cambodia, 1860–1930*. Honolulu: University of Hawai'i Press.

Hardy, Rev. Robert Spence. (1853) 1967. *A Manual of Buddhism*. Varanasi, India: Chowkhamba Sanskrit Series Office.
Harris, Ian. 2005. *Cambodian Buddhism: History and Practice*. Honolulu: University of Hawai'i Press.
———. 2013. *Buddhism in a Dark Age: Cambodian Monks under Pol Pot*. Honolulu: University of Hawai'i Press.
Hart, Marjolein 't, and Dennis Bos. 2007. *Humour and Social Protest*. Cambridge: Press Syndicate of the University of Cambridge.
Hartmann, John. 2013. "Preserving the Past: Siang Miang as the Essence of Lao Humor and Poetic Genius." Paper presented at the Fourth International Lao Studies Conference, Madison, Wisconsin, April 19-21.
Haseman, John B. 1978. *The Thai Resistance Movement during the Second World War*. DeKalb: Center for Southeast Asian Studies, Northern Illinois University.
Hayashi, Yukio. 2003. *Practical Buddhism among the Thai-Lao: Religion in the Making of a Region*. Kyoto: Kyoto University Press.
Heinze, Ruth-Inge. 1977. *The Role of the Sangha in Modern Thailand*. Taipei: Chinese Association for Folklore.
Holt, John Clifford. 2009. *Spirits of the Place: Buddhism and Lao Religious Culture*. Honolulu: University of Hawai'i Press.
———. 2012. "Caring for the Dead Ritually in Cambodia." *Southeast Asian Studies* 1 (1): 3-75.
Horner, Isaline B., and Padmanabh S. Jaini, trans. 1985. *Apocryphal Birth-stories: (Pannasa Jataka)*. London: Pali Text Society.
Houtart, Francois. 1977. "Theravada Buddhism and Political Power: Construction and Destructuration of its Ideological Function." *Social Compass* 24 (2-3): 207-46.
Htin Aung, Maung. 1937. *Burmese Drama*. London: Oxford University Press.
———. 1962. *Folk Elements in Burmese Buddhism*. London: Oxford University Press.
———, ed. and trans. 1966. *Burmese Monk's Tales*. New York: Columbia University Press.
———. 1976. *Folk Tales of Burma*. New Delhi: Sterling.
Hundius, Harald. 1990. "The Colophons of Thirty Pali Manuscripts from Northern Thailand." *Journal of the Pali Text Society* 14:1-174.
———. 1995. "Notions of Equity in Lan Na: Insights from Literary Sources." In *Regions and National Integration in Thailand, 1892-1992*, edited by Volker Grabowsky, 46-67. Wiesbaden: Harrassowitz Verlag.
Hwang Soonil. 2012. "Dana of One's Own Body and Dana Perfection (Paramita) in the Vessantara Jataka." In *Buddhist Narrative in Asia and Beyond*, edited by Peter Skilling and Justin McDaniel, 67-81. Bangkok: Institute of Thai Studies, Chulalongkorn University.
Hyde, Lewis. 1998. *Trickster Makes This World: Mischief, Myth, and Art*. New York: North Point Press.
Hyers, M. Conrad, ed. 1969. *Holy Laughter: Essays on Religion in the Comic Perspective*. New York: Seabury Press.

Ingersoll, Jasper. 1966. "The Priest Role in Central Village Thailand." In *Anthropological Studies in Theravada Buddhism*, edited by M. Nash, 51-76. Cultural Studies 13. New Haven, CT: Yale University Southeast Asia Studies.

Irwin, Anthony. 2011. "'Imagining Boundaries': Sima Space, Lineage Trials and Transregional Theravada Orthodoxy." MA Thesis, University of Wisconsin-Madison.

Ishii, Yoneo. 1975. "A Note on Buddhistic Millenarian Revolts in Northeastern Siam." *Journal of Southeast Asian Studies* 6 (2): 121-26.

———. 1986. *Sangha, State, and Society: Thai Buddhism in History*. Translated by Peter Hawkes. Honolulu: University of Hawai'i Press.

Jackson, Peter A. 1988. *Buddhadasa: A Buddhist Thinker for the Modern World*. Bangkok: Siam Society.

———. 1989. *Buddhism, Legitimation, and Conflict: The Political Functions of Urban Thai Buddhism*. Singapore: Institute of Southeast Asian Studies.

———. 1993. "Reinterpreting the Traiphuum Phra Ruang: Political Functions of the Buddhist Symbolism in Contemporary Thailand." In *Buddhist Trends in Southeast Asia*, edited by Trevor Ling, 64-100. Singapore: Institute of Southeast Asian Studies.

Jacobsen, Trudy. 2008. *Lost Goddesses: Denial of Female Power in Cambodian History*. Copenhagen: Nordic Institute of Asian Studies.

Jaini, Padmanabh S. 1989. "Apocryphal Jatakas of Southeast Asian Buddhism." *Indian Journal of Buddhist Studies* 1 (1): 22-37.

Jaiswal, Suvira. 1993. "Historical Evolution of the Ram Legend." *Social Scientist* 21 (3-4): 89-97.

Janlekha, Kamol Odd. 1955. "A Study of the Economy of a Rice Growing Village in Central Thailand." PhD diss., Cornell University.

Jenkins, Ronald Scott. 1994. *Subversive Laughter: The Liberating Power of Comedy*. New York: Free Press.

Jetjaras na Ranong. 2009. "Spirited Masquerade." *Bangkok Post Horizons*, July 9, 2009, H1, H9.

Johnston, Tim. 2011. "Website Chief Faces Thai lèse majesté Case." *Financial Times*, September 14.

Jones, John Garrett. 1979. *Tales and Teachings of the Buddha: The Jataka Stories in Relation to the Pali Canon*. London: George Allen & Unwin.

Jordt, Ingrid. 2007. *Burma's Mass Lay Meditation Movement: Buddhism and the Cultural Construction of Power*. Athens: Ohio University Press.

Jory, Patrick. 1996. "A History of the *Thet Maha Chat* and its Contribution to a Thai Political Culture." PhD diss., Australian National University.

———. 2002a. "Thai and Western Buddhist Scholarship in the Age of Colonialism: King Chulalongkorn Redefines the Jatakas." *Journal of Asian Studies* 61 (3): 891-918.

———. 2002b. "The Vessantara Jataka, Barami and the Bodhisattva-Kings." *Crossroads* 16 (2): 36-78.

———. 2016. *Thailand's Theory of Monarchy: The Vessantara Jataka and the Idea of the Perfect Man*. Albany: State University of New York Press.

Judson, Ann H. 1823. *A Particular Relation of the American Baptist Mission to the Burma Empire, in a Series of Letters Addressed to Joseph Butterworth, Esq.* Washington City: John S. Meehan.

Kalab, Milada. 1994. "Cambodian Buddhist Monasteries in Paris: Continuing Tradition and Changing Patterns." In *Cambodian Culture since 1975: Homeland and Exile*, edited by May M. Ebihara, Carol A. Mortland, and Judy Ledgerwood, 57–71. Ithaca, NY: Cornell University Press.

Kamala Tiyavanich. 1997. *Forest Recollections: Wandering Monks in Twentieth-Century Thailand.* Honolulu: University of Hawai'i Press.

———. 2003. *The Buddha in the Jungle.* Chiang Mai: Silkworm Books.

———. 2009. *The Life and Works of Luang Ta Chi.* Washington, DC: Council of Thai Bhikkus.

Karpeles, S. 1931. "Voyage au Laos." *Bulletin de l'Ecole française d'Extrême-Orient* 31:331–34.

Kasian Tejapira. 2001. *Commodifying Marxism: The Formation of Modern Thai Radical Culture, 1927–1958.* Kyoto: Kyoto University Press.

Kaufman, Howard. 1960. *Bangkhuad: A Community Study in Thailand.* Locust Valley, NY: J. J. Augustin.

Keyes, Charles F. 1967. *Isan: Regionalism in Northeastern Thailand.* Data Paper 65. Ithaca, NY: Southeast Asia Program, Cornell University.

———. 1975. "Tug-of-War for Merit: Cremation of a Senior Monk." *Journal of the Siam Society* 63:44–62.

———. 1977. "Millennialism, Theravada Buddhism and Thai Society." *Journal of Asian Studies* 36 (2): 283–302.

———. 1987. *Buddhist Kingdom as Modern Nation-State.* Boulder, CO: Westview Press.

Khaimuk Uthayaawali. 1999. "Naphisiiphiisaanakhun, Phra." In *Saaraanukrom watthanatham Thai Phaak Nya*, 6:3037–39. Bangkok: Muunnithi Saaraanukrom Watthanatham Thai, Thanaakhaan Thai Phaanit.

Khin Thitsa. 1980. *Providence and Prostitution: Image and Reality for Women in Buddhist Thailand.* London: Change International Reports.

Kingkeo Attagara. 1967. "The Folk Religion of Ban Nai, a Hamlet in Central Thailand." PhD diss., Indiana University.

Kingshill, Konrad, ed. 1976. *Ku Daeng, the Red Tomb: A Village Study in Northern Thailand.* 3rd ed. Bangkok: Prachachon Co Ltd.

———. 2000. *Of Mechanical Swans and Rain-Producing Elephants: A Collection of Thai and Lanna Thai Tales and Sermons.* Tempe: Program for Southeast Asian Studies Monograph Series, Arizona State University.

Kirkland, Edwin Capers. 1966. *A Bibliography of South Asian Folklore.* Indiana University Folkore Series 21. Bloomington: Indiana University Research Center.

Kirsch, A. Thomas. 1967. "Phu Thai Religious Syncretism: A Case Study of Thai Religion." PhD diss., Harvard University.

———. 1973. "The Thai Buddhist Quest for Merit." In *Southeast Asia: The Politics of National Integration*, edited by John T. McAlister, 188–201. New York: Random House.

———. 1975. "Economy, Polity and Religion in Thailand." In *Change in Persistence in Thai Society: Essays in Honor of Lauriston Sharp*, edited by G.W. Skinner and A.T. Kirsch, 172-96. Ithaca, NU: Cornell University Press.

———. 1977. "Complexity in the Thai Religious System: An Interpretation." *Journal of Asian Studies* 36 (2): 241-66.

Kislenko, Arne. 2009. *Culture and Custom of Laos*. Westport, CT: Greenwood Press.

Klausner, William J. 1993. *Reflections on Thai Culture*. Bangkok: Siam Society.

Kobayashi, Satoru, 2005. "An Ethnographic Study on the Reconstruction of Buddhist Practice in Two Cambodian Temples: With the Special Reference to Buddhist Samay and Boran." *Kyoto Journal of Southeast Asian Studies* 42 (4): 489-518.

Koenig, William. 1990. *The Burmese Polity, 1752-1819: Politics, Administration, and Social Organization in the Early Kon-baung Period*. Center for South and Southeast Asian Studies. Ann Arbor: University of Michigan Press.

Koompong Noobanjong. 2013. *The Aesthetics of Power: Architecture, Modernity, and Identity from Siam to Thailand*. Bangkok: White Lotus Press.

Koret, Peter. 1998. "Past and Present Lao Perceptions of Traditional Literature." In *New Laos, New Challenges*, edited by Jacqueline Butler-Diaz, 109-24. Tempe: Program for Southeast Asian Studies, Arizona State University.

———. 2012. *The Man Who Accused the King of Killing a Fish: The Biography of Narin Phasit of Siam, 1874-1950*. Chiang Mai: Silkworm Books.

Kornvipa Boonsue. 1989. *Buddhism and Gender Bias: An Analysis of a Jataka Tale*. Toronto: York University Thai Studies Working Paper 3.

Kraisri Nimmanhaeminda 1965. "Put Vegetables into Baskets, People into Towns." In *Ethnographic Notes on Northern Thailand*, edited by L. M. Hanks, J. R. Hanks, and Lauriston Sharp, 6-10. Cornell Southeast Asia Data Paper 58. Ithaca, NY: Southeast Asia Program, Cornell University.

Kraus, Michael. 1998. "Die Weissen sind so komisch, so komisch . . ." Über den Spott der Indianer und den Ernst der Ethnologie." In *Wegmarken: Eine Bibliothek der Ethnologischen Imagination*, edited by Reinhard Kapfer, Marie-Jose van de Loo, Werner Petermann, and Margarete Reinhart, 238-69. Wuppertal: Peter Hammer Verlag.

Krikmann, Arvo, and Liisi Laineste. 2009. *Permitted Laughter: Socialist, Post-socialist and Never-socialist Humour*. Tartu: ELM Scholarly Press.

Kwanchewan Srisawat [Buadaeng]. 1988. "The Karen and the Khruba Khao Pi Movement: A Historical Study of the Response to the Transformation in Northern Thailand." MA Thesis, Ateneo de Manila University.

Ladurie, Emmanuel Le Roy. 1979. *Carnival in Romans*. George Braziller.

Ladwig, Patrice. 2009. "Narrative Ethics: The Excess of Giving and Moral Ambiguity in the Lao Vessantara-Jataka." In *The Anthropology of Moralities*, edited by Monica Heintz, 136-55. New York: Berghahn Books.

La Loubère, Simon de. (1693) 1969. *The Kingdom of Siam*. Introduction by David Wyatt. Singapore: Oxford University Press.

Landon, Kenneth Perry. 1939. *Siam in Transition: A Brief Survey of Cultural Trends in the Five Years since the Revolution of 1932*. London: Oxford University Press.

Leclère, Adhémard. 1895. *Cambodge, Contes et Legendes, le Satra du Roi Chealy*. Paris: Librairie Émile Bouillon.

———. 1899. *The Buddhism of Cambodia*. Translated from the French by Renata von Scheliha. Paris: Ernest Leroux.

———. 1902. *Le livre de Vesandar, le roi charitable*. Paris: E. Leroux.

———. 1916. *Cambodge: Fêtes Civiles et Religieuses*. Paris: Imprimerie Nationale.

Lefferts, H. Leedom, Jr. 2006/7. "The Bun Phra Wet Painted Scrolls of Northeastern Thailand in the Walters Art Museum." *Journal of the Walters Art Museum* 64/65:99–118.

Lefferts, Leedom, and Sandra Cate. 2012. "Theravada Buddhism and Political Engagement among the Thai-Lao of North East Thailand: The Bun Phra Wet Ceremony." *South East Asia Research* 20 (3): 329–41.

Lefferts, Leedom, and Sandra Cate, with Wajuppa Tossa. 2012. *Buddhist Storytelling in Thailand and Laos: The Vessantara Jataka Scroll at the Asian Civilisations Museum*. Singapore: Asian Civilisations Museum.

LeGoff, Jacques. 1980. *Time, Work, and Culture in the Middle Ages*. Translated by Arthur Goldhammer. Chicago: University of Chicago Press.

LeMay, Reginald. (1926) 1986. *An Asian Arcady: The Land and Peoples of Northern Siam*. Bangkok: White Lotus Press.

Lepowsky, Maria. 1993. *Fruits of the Motherland: Gender in an Egalitarian Society*. New York: Columbia University Press.

Lieberman, Victor B. 1984. *Burmese Administrative Cycles: Anarchy and Conquest, c. 1580–1760*. Princeton, NJ: Princeton University Press.

Linnekin, Jocelyn. 1990. *Sacred Queens and Women of Consequence: Rank, Gender and Colonialism in the Hawaiian Islands*. Ann Arbor: University of Michigan Press.

Lipman, Steve. 1993. *Laughter in Hell: The Use of Humor during the Holocaust*. Northvale, NJ: J. Aronson.

Long, Millard F. 1966. "Economic Development in Northeast Thailand: Problems and Prospects." *Asian Survey* 6:355–61.

Luce, G. H. 1956. "The 550 Jatakas in Old Burma." *Artibus Asiae* 19 (3/4): 291–307.

Lutgendorf, Philip. 2007. *Hanuman's Tale: The Messages of a Divine Monkey*. New York: Oxford University Press.

Lux, Thomas E. 1971. "From Dream to Folklore in Northeast Thailand." *Asian Folklore Studies* 30 (1): 85–96.

Lyman, Thomas. 1991. "The Thai Version of a Popular Buddhist Jataka." *Peninsule* 23:93–100.

Lyons, Elizabeth. 1960. "A Note on Thai Painting." In *The Arts of Thailand: A Handbook of the Architecture, Sculpture and Painting of Thailand (Siam)*, edited by Theodore Robert Bowie, 166–75. Bloomington: Indiana University Press.

Malalgoda, Kitsiri. 1976. *Buddhism in Sinhalese Society, 1750–1900*. Berkeley: University of California Press.

Manas Chitakasem, ed. 1995. *Thai Literary Traditions*. Bangkok: Chulalongkorn University Press.

Manee Phayomyong. 1976. "Kaanwikhroh lae priabthiab mahaachaat chabab phaak klang, phaak nya, phaak isaan lae phaak tai." Mahabandit thesis, Srinakarinwirot University.

Marshall, Sir John, and Alfred Foucher. 1982. *The Monuments of Sanchi*. Dehli: Swati Publications.

Matics, K. I. 1978. "Homage to the Abbot Prince Paramanuchit Chinorot." *Journal of the Siam Society* 66/1:126–28.

Mattani Mojdara Rutnin. 1988. *Modern Thai Literature*. Bangkok: Thammasat University Press.

McCarthy, James. 1900. *Surveying and Exploring in Siam*. London: John Murray.

McClintock, Sara L. 2011. "Compassionate Trickster: The Buddha as a Literary Character in the Narratives of Early Indian Buddhism." *Journal of the American Academy of Religion* 79 (1): 90–112.

McClung, Larry Gene. 1975. "The Vessantara Jātaka: Paradigm for a Buddhist Utopian Model." PhD diss., Princeton University.

McDaniel, Justin Thomas. 2000. "Creative Engagement: Sujavanna Wua Luang and Its Contribution to Buddhist Literature." *Journal of the Siam Society* 88 (1&2): 156–77.

———. 2002. "The Curricular Canon in Northern Thailand and Laos." *Manusya: Journal of Humanities*. Special Issue 4:20–59.

———. 2008. *Gathering Leaves and Lifting Words: Histories of Buddhist Monastic Education in Laos and Thailand*. Seattle: University of Washington Press.

———. 2009. "Questioning Orientalist Power: Buddhist Maonastic Education in Colonial Laos." In *Contemporary Lao Studies*, edited by Carol J. Compton, John F. Hartmann, and Vinya Sysamouth, 201–222. San Francisco: Center for Lao Studies; DeKalb: Center for Asian Studies, Northern Illinois University.

———. 2014. "The Material Turn: An Introduction to Thai Sources for the Study of Amulets." In *History and Material Culture in Asian Religions*, edited by Benjamin J. Fleming and Richard Mann, 135–48. New York: Routledge.

McFarland, George Bradley. (1928) 1999. *Historical Sketch of Protestant Missions in Siam 1828–1928*. Introduction, Commentary, and Bibliography by Herbert R. Swanson. Bangkok: White Lotus Press.

McGill, Forrest. 1993. "Jatakas, Universal Monarchs, and the Year 2000." *Artibus Asiae* 53:412–48.

———. 1997. "Painting the 'Great Life.'" In *Sacred Biography in the Buddhist Traditions of South and Southeast Asia*, edited by Juliane Schober, 195–217. Delhi: Motilal Banarsidass.

———, ed. 2009. *Emerald Cities: Arts of Siam and Burma, 1775–1950*. San Francisco: Asian Art Museum.

McGilvary, Daniel. 1912. *A Half Century among the Siamese and the Lao*. New York: Fleming H. Revel Co.

Mechai Thongthep, ed. 1991. *Tales of Sri Thanonchai: Thailand's Artful Trickster*. Bangkok: NAGA Books.

Mendelson, E. Michael. 1975. *Sangha and State in Burma: A Study of Monastic Sectarianism and Leadership*. Edited by John P. Ferguson. Ithaca, NY: Cornell University Press.

Mi Mi Khaing (1946) 1956. *Burmese Family.* Bombay: Orient Longmans.
Miller, Terry E. 1985. *Traditional Music of the Lao: Kaen Playing and Mawlam Singing in Northeast Thailand.* Westport, CT: Greenwood Press.
Mills, Mary Beth. 1995. "Attack of the Widow Ghosts: Gender, Death, and Modernity in Northeast Thailand." In *Bewitching Women, Pious Men: Gender and Body Politics in Southeast Asia,* edited by Aihwa Ong and Michael Peletz, 244–73. Berkeley: University of California Press.
———. 1999. *Thai Women in the Global Labor Force: Consuming Desires, Contested Selves.* New Brunswick, NJ: Rutgers University Press.
Milne, Lesley, ed. 2004. *Reflective Laughter: Aspects of Humour in Russian Culture.* London: Anthem Press.
Mizuno, Koichi. 1971. "Social System of Don Daeng Village: A Community Study in Northeast Thailand." Discussion Papers 12–22. Centre for Southeast Asian Studies, Kyoto University.
Moerman, Michael. 1968. *Agricultural Change and Peasant Choice in a Thai Village.* Berkeley: University of California Press.
Morell, David, and Chai-anan Samudavanija. 1981. *Political Conflict in Thailand: Reform, Reaction, Revolution.* Cambridge: Oelgeschlager, Gunn and Hain.
Mueller, F. Max. 1885. "Buddhist Charity." *North American Review* 140 (340): 221–36.
Murdoch, John B. 1974. "The 1901–2 'Holy Man's' Rebellion." *Journal of the Siam Society* 62 (1): 47–67.
Murray, Julia K. 1995. "Buddhism and Early Narrative Illustration in China." *Archives of Asian Art* 48:17–31.
Napat Sirisambhand and Alec Gordon. 1999. "Thai Women in Late Ayutthaya Style Paintings." *Journal of the Siam Society* 87 (1&2): 1–16.
Narayan, Kirin. 1989. *Storytellers, Saints, and Scoundrels: Folk Narrative in Hindu Religious Teaching.* Philadelphia: University of Pennsylvania Press.
Nash, Manning. 1965. *The Golden Road to Modernity: Village Life in Contemporary Burma.* Chicago: University of Chicago Press.
Nash, Manning, Gananath Obeyesekere, Michael M. Ames, Jasper Ingersoll, David E. Pfanner, June C. Nash, et al. 1966. *Anthropological Studies in Theravada Buddhism.* Cultural Report 13. New Haven, CT: Yale University Southeast Asia Studies.
Neale, Frederick Arthur. 1852. *Narrative of a Residence in Siam.* London: Office of the National Illustrated Library.
Ngaosrivathana, Mayoury, and Kennon Breazeale, eds. 2002. *Breaking New Ground in Lao History: Essays on the Seventh to Twentieth Centuries.* Chiang Mai: Silkworm Books.
Nguyen, Betty. 2011. "A *Sangha* without a King: A Buddhist Millenarian Response to the Collapse of Lanna Buddhist Kingdoms." Paper presented at the Informal Northern Thai Group, Chiang Mai, Thailand, March 8, 2011.
———. 2014. "Calamity Cosmologies: Buddhist Ethics and the Creation of a Moral Community." PhD diss., University of Wisconsin–Madison.
Nidhi Eoseewong. (1982) 2005. *Pen and Sail: Literature and History in Early Bangkok.* Edited by Chris Baker and Ben Anderson, with Craig J. Reynolds, Hong Lysa,

Pasuk Phongpaichit, Patrick Jory, and Ruth T. McVey. Chiang Mai: Silkworm Books.
Notton, Camille, trans. 1933. *The Chronicle of the Emerald Buddha*. Second impression.
Numrich, Paul David. 1996. *Old Wisdom in the New World: Americanization in Two Immigrant Theravada Buddhist Temples*. Knoxville: University of Tennessee Press.
Obeyesekere, Gananath. 1991. "Buddhism and Conscience." *Daedalus* 120:219-39.
Obeyesekere, Gananath, Frank Reynolds, and Bardwell L. Smith, eds. 1972. *The Two Wheels of Dhamma: Essays on the Theravada Tradition in India and Ceylon*. AAR Studies in Religion 3. Chambersburg, PA: American Academy of Religion.
Obeyesekere, Rajini, trans. 1991. *Jewels of the Doctrine: Stories of the Saddharma Ratnavaliya*. By Dharmasēna Thera. Albany: State University of New York Press.
O'Connor, Richard. 1978. "Urbanism and Religion: Community, Hierarchy and Sanctity in Urban Thai Buddhist Temples." PhD diss., Cornell University.
Ondam, Bantorn. 1971. "The Phrae Rebellion: A Structural Analysis." *Cornell Journal of Social Relations* 6 (Spring): 84-97.
Ohnuma, Reiko. 2012. *Ties That Bind: Maternal Imagery and Discourse in Indian Buddhism*. New York: Oxford University Press.
Ong, Aihwa, and Michael Peletz, eds. 1995. *Bewitching Women, Pious Men: Gender and Body Politics in Southeast Asia*. Berkeley: University of California Press.
Pailer, Gaby, ed. 2009. *Gender and Laughter: Comic Affirmation and Subversion in Traditional and Modern Media*. New York: Rodopi.
Pallegoix, Jean Baptiste. (1854) 2000. *Description of the Thai Kingdom or Siam: Thailand under King Mongkut*. Translated by Walter E. J. Tips. Bangkok: White Lotus Press.
Paritta Chalermpow-Koanantakool. 1980. "Popular Drama in its Social Context: Nang Talung, the Shadow Puppet Theatre of South Thailand." PhD diss., Cambridge University.
———. 1989. "Relevance of the Textual and Contextual Analyses in Understanding Folk Performance in Modern Society: A Case of Southern Thai Shadow Puppet Theatre." *Asian Folklore Studies* 48:31-57.
Pasuk Phongpaichit and Chris Baker. 2011. "Taming Women: Changes over Time in the Sexuality and Gender Roles of Women in *Khun Chang Khun Phaen*." Paper presented at the International Thai Studies Conference, Siam City Hotel, Bangkok, Thailand, July 26-28.
Patcharin Lapanun. 2013. "Logics of Desire and Transnational Marriage Practices in a Northeastern Thai Village." PhD diss., Vrije Universiteit Amsterdam.
Patcharin Peyasantiwong. 1992. "A Note on the 'Missing' Part in Mahaachaat Khamluang." In *Papers on Tai Languages, Linguistics and Literatures*, edited by Carol J. Compton and John F. Hartmann, 286-92. Occasional Paper 16. DeKalb: Northern Illinois University, Center for Southeast Asian Studies.
Pathom Hongsuwan. 2011. "Sacralization of the Mekong River through Folk Narratives." *Manusya: Journal of Humanities*. Special Issue 19:33-45.

———. 2013. "Hae Taa Chuchok." In *Naan maa laew: Mii ryang lao nithaan tamnaan chiwit*, 269–307. Bangkok: Chulalongkorn University Press.
Pattana Kitiarsa, 2012. *Mediums, Monks, and Amulets: Thai Popular Buddhism Today*. Chiang Mai: Silkworm Books.
Pattaratorn Chirapravati, M. L. 2008. "Illustrating the Lives of the Bodhisattva at Wat Si Chum." In *Past Lives of the Buddha: Wat Si Chum–Art, Architecture and Inscriptions*, edited by Peter Skilling, 13–40. Bangkok: River Books.
———. 2009. "Living the Siamese Life: Culture, Religion, and Art." In *Emerald Cities: Arts of Siam and Burma, 1775–1950*, edited by Forrest McGill, 27–45. San Francisco: Asian Art Museum.
———. 2012. "In Search of Maitreya: Early Images of Dvaravati Buddha at Si Thep." In *Buddhist Narrative in Asia and Beyond*, edited by Peter Skilling and Justin McDaniel, 97–107. Bangkok: Institute of Thai Studies, Chulalongkorn University.
Peacock, James. 1987. *Rites of Modernization: Symbols and Social Aspects of Indonesian Proletarian Drama*. Chicago: University of Chicago Press.
Peletz, Michael. 1996. *Reason and Passion: Representations of Gender in a Malay Society*. Berkeley: University of California Press.
Pfanner, David E., and Jasper Ingersoll. 1962. "Theravada Buddhism and Village Economic Behavior: A Burmese and Thai Comparison." *Journal of Asian Studies* 21:341–66.
Pierce, David C. 1969. "The Middle Way of the Jataka Tales." *Journal of American Folklore* 82 (325): 245–54.
Piker, Steven. 1964. "An Examination of Character and Socialization in a Thai Peasant Community." PhD diss., University of Washington.
———. 1968. "The Relationship of Belief Systems to Behavior in Rural Thai Society." *Asian Survey* 8:384–99.
Polson, Ivan. 2012. "The Art of Dissent: The Wall Paintings at Wat Thung Sri Muang in Ubon Ratchathani." *Journal of Lao Studies* 3 (1): 91–127.
Poree-Maspero, Eveline. 1962. *Etude sur les Rites Agraires des Combodgiens*. Paris: Mouton.
Potter, Jack M. 1976. *Thai Peasant Social Structure*. Chicago: University of Chicago Press.
Potter, Sulamith Heins. 1977. *Family Life in a Northern Thai Village: A Study in the Structural Significance of Women*. Berkeley: University of California Press.
Prakai Nontawasee, ed. 1988. *Changes in Northern Thailand and the Shan States, 1886–1940*. Pasir Panjang, Singapore: Southeast Asian Studies Program, Institute of Southeast Asian Studies.
Prakong Nimmanhaeminda. 1983. *Mahaachaat Laanaa: Kaansyksaa nai thaana thii ben waanakhadii thohngthin*. Bangkok: Munithi khrongkaan damraa sangkhomsaat lae manusayasaat.
Pranee Wongthet. 1989. "The Jataka Stories and Laopuan Worldview." *Asian Folklore Studies* 48 (1): 21–30.
Pranii Sirithorn na Pathalung. (1964) 1995. *Phet Laannaa*. 2 vols. Chiang Mai: Borisat Northern Printing.

Priyawat Kuanpoonpol. 1995. "Three Phra Malai Manuscripts at Harvard University's Sackler Museum: Should They Be Considered Classical or Regional?" In *Thai Literary Traditions*, edited by Manas Chitakasem, 186-97. Bangkok: Chulalongkorn University Press.

Pruess, James B. 1976. "Merit-Seeking in Public: Buddhist Pilgrimage in Northeastern Thailand." *Journal of the Siam Society* 64 (1): 169-206.

Radin, Paul. (1956) 1972. *The Trickster: A Study in American Indian Mythology*. New York: Schocken Books.

Raikes, D. 1988. "Esarn Patana." *Siam Society Newsletter* 4 (1): 21-23.

Rajavaramuni, Phra. 1990 "Foundations of Buddhist Social Ethics." In *Ethics, Wealth, and Salvation*, edited by R. F. Sizemore and D. K. Swearer, 1-11. Columbia: University of South Carolina Press.

Ramanujan, A. K. 1991. "Three Hundred Ramayanas: Five Examples and Three Thoughts on Translation." In *Many Ramayanas: The Diversity of a Narrative Tradition in South Asia*, edited by Paula Richman, 22-49. Berkeley: University of California Press.

Ramsay, James Ansil. 1971. "The Development of a Bureaucratic Polity: The Case of Northern Siam." PhD diss., Cornell University.

———. 1979. "Modernization and Reactionary Rebellions in Northern Siam." *Journal of Asian Studies* 38 (2): 283-97.

Ratana Boonmathya. 1997. "Contested Concepts of Development in Rural Northeastern Thailand." PhD diss., University of Washington.

Ratanaporn Sethakul. 1989. "Political, Social and Economic Changes in the Northern States of Thailand Resulting from the Chiang Mai Treaties of 1874 and 1883." PhD diss., Northern Illinois University.

Ratanaporn Sethakul. 2010. "Lan Na Buddhism and Bangkok Centralization in Late 19th-Early 20th Century: Changes and Reaction of the Sangha." Paper presented at conference on Theravada Buddhism under Colonialism: Adaptation and Response. Institute of Southeast Asian Studies, Singapore.

Raymond, Catherine. 2012. "Notes on a Burmese Version of the *Vessantara Jataka*, as Represented on three Shwe Chi Doe in the NIU Burma Art Collection." *Journal of Burma Studies* 16 (1): 123-48.

Reynolds, Craig J. 1972. "The Buddhist Monkhood in Nineteenth Century Thailand." PhD diss., Cornell University.

———, ed. and trans. 1979. *Autobiography: The Life of Prince-Patriarch Vajirañāṇa of Siam, 1860-1921*. Athens: Ohio University Press.

Reynolds, Frank E. 1972. "From Philology to Anthropology: A Bibliographical Essay on Works Related to Early, Theravada and Sinhalese Buddhism." In *The Two Wheels of Dhamma: Essays on the Theravada in India and Ceylon*, edited by G. Obeyesekere, F. Reynolds, and B. L. Smith, 107-121. AAR Studies in Religion 3. Chambersburg, PA: American Academy of Religion.

———. 1976. "The Many Lives of Buddha: A Study of Sacred Biography and Theravada Tradition." In *The Biographical Process*, edited by Frank E. Reynolds and Donald Capps, 37-61. The Hague: Mouton.

———. 1978. "The Holy Emerald Jewel: Some Aspects of Buddhist Symbolism and Political Legitimation in Thailand and Laos." In *Religion and Legitimation of Power in Thailand, Laos, and Burma*, edited by Bardwell L. Smith, 175-93. Chambersburg, PA: ANIMA Books.

———. 1990. "Ethics and Wealth in Theravada Buddhism: A Study in Comparative Religious Ethics." In *Ethics, Wealth and Salvation: A Study in Buddhist Social Ethics*, edited by R. Sizemore and D. Swearer, 59-76. Columbia: University of South Carolina Press.

———. 1997. "Rebirth Traditions and the Lineages of Gotama: A Study in Theravada Buddhism." In *Sacred Biography in the Buddhist Tradition of South and Southeast Asia*, edited by Juliane Schober, 19-39. Honolulu: University of Hawai'i Press.

Reynolds, Frank E., and Donald Capps, eds. 1976. *The Biographical Process*. The Hague: Mouton.

Reynolds, Frank E., and Mani B. Reynolds, trans. 1982. *Three Worlds According to King Ruang*. Berkeley: University of California Press.

Rhum, Michael. 1994. *The Ancestral Lords: Gender, Descent, and Spirits in a Northern Thai Village*. Special Report 29. DeKalb: Northern Illinois University, Center for Southeast Asian Studies.

Rhys Davids, T. W. (1880) 2000. *Buddhist Birth Stories or Jataka Tales*. London: Trubner.

Richman, Paula, ed. 1991. *Many Ramayanas: The Diversity of a Narrative Tradition in South Asia*. Berkeley: University of California Press.

Ricoeur, Paul. 1994. "History and Rhetoric." *Diogenes* 168:7-24.

Roveda, Vittorio, and Sothon Yem. 2010. *Preah Bot: Buddhist Painted Scrolls in Cambodia*. Bangkok: River Books.

Ruenruthai Sujjapun. 1995. "Female Characters in Thai Narrative Poetry." In *Thai Literary Traditions*, edited by Manas Chitakasem, 118-29. Bangkok: Chulalongkorn University Press.

Sahai, Sachchidanand. 1996. *The Rama Jataka in Laos: A Study in the Phra Lak Phra Lam*. 2 vols. Delhi: B. R. Publishing.

Sanders, Barry. 1995. *Sudden Glory: Laughter as Subversive History*. Boston: Beacon Press.

Sangaa Suphaaphaa. 1956. *Chiiwit læ ngaan khohng Khruubaa Sriiwichai*. Phra Nakhorn: Samnakphim Khlang Witthayaa.

Sarachchandra, E. R. 1966. *The Folk Drama of Ceylon*. Ceylon: Department of Cultural Affairs.

Sarassawadee Ongsakul. 2005. *History of Lanna*. Trans by Chitraporn Tanratanakul. Chiang Mai: Silkworm Books.

Sarkisyanz, E. 1965. *Buddhist Backgrounds of the Burmese Revolution*. The Hague: Martinus Nijhoff.

Sarkisyanz, Manuel. 1968. "Messianic Folk-Buddhism as Ideology of Peasant Revolts in Nineteenth and Early Twentieth Century Burma." *Review of Religious Research* 10 (1): 32–38.

Satow, Sir Ernest Mason. (1994) 2000. *A Diplomat in Siam: H.B.M. Minister-Resident, Bangkok 1885–1888*. Introduced and edited by Nigel Brailey. Bangkok: Orchid Press.

Sayadej Vongsopha, Ven. "The Role and Impact of *Vessantara Jātaka* in the Lao PDR." http://www.academia.edu/1407870/The_Role_and_Impact_of_Vessantara_Jataka_in_theLao_PDR. Accessed February 7, 2016.

Schlingloff, Dieter. 1988. *Studies in the Ajanta Paintings: Identifications and Interpretations*. Dehli, India: Ajanta Publications.

Schober, Juliane, ed. 1997. *Sacred Biography in the Buddhist Traditions of South and Southeast Asia*. Delhi: Motilal Banarsidass Publishers.

Schomburgk, Sir Robert H. 1863. "A Visit to Xiengmai, the Principal City of the Laos or Shan States." *Journal of the Asiatic Society of Bengal* 32:387–399.

Scott, James C. 1985. *Weapons of the Weak: Everyday Forms of Peasant Resistance*. New Haven, CT: Yale University Press.

———. 1990. *Domination and the Arts of Resistance: Hidden Transcripts*. New Haven, CT: Yale University Press.

Scott, James C., and Benedict J. Tria Kerkvliet, eds. 1986. "Everyday Forms of Peasant Resistance in Southeast Asia." Special Issue, *Journal of Peasant Studies* 13 (2): 1–149.

Scott, Rachelle M. 2009. *Nirvana for Sale? Buddhism, Wealth and the Dhammakaya Temple in Contemporary Thailand*. Albany: State University of New York Press.

Seeger, Martin. 2007. "Thai Buddhist Studies and the Authority of the Pali Canon." *Contemporary Buddhism* 8 (1): 1–18.

Seneviratne, H. L. 1978. *Rituals of the Kandyan State*. Cambridge: Cambridge University Press.

Sengpan Pannyawamsa, Ven. 2007. "The *Tham Vessantara Jataka*: A Critical Study of the *Vessantara Jataka* and Its influence on Kengtung Buddhism, Eastern Shan State, Burma." PhD thesis, University of Kelaniya.

Sharp, Lauriston. 1953. *Siamese Rice Village: A Preliminary Study of Bang Chan, 1948–1949*. Bangkok: Cornell Research Center.

Sharp, Lauriston, and Lucien M. Hanks. 1978. *Bang Chan: A Social History of a Rural Community in Thailand*. Ithaca, NY: Cornell University Press.

Shaw, Sarah, trans. 2006. *The Jatakas: Birth Stories of the Bodhisatta*. New York: Penguin Books.

———. 2012. "Crossing to the Farthest Shore: How Pali Jatakas Launch the Buddhist Image of the Boat onto the Open Seas." *Journal of the Oxford Centre for Buddhist Studies* 3:128–56.

Sheppard, Alice. 1986. "From Kate Sanborn to Feminist Psychology: The Social Context of Women's Humor 1885–1985." *Psychology of Women Quarterly* 10:155–70.

Shulman, David. 1985. *The King and the Clown in South Indian Myth and Poetry*. Princeton, NJ: Princeton University Press.

Shway Yoe. (1882) 1963. *The Burman: His Life and Notions*. New York: W. W. Norton.
Simms, Peter, and Sanda Simms. 1999. *The Kingdoms of Laos: Six Hundred Years of History*. Richmond, Surrey: Curzon Press.
Singkha Waanasai. 2010. *Saaraprawat Khruubaa Sriwichai Nakbun haeng Laanaa*. Printed on the occasion of the 11th cycle of Khruubaa Srivichai 11 June 2553/2010 or 132nd anniversary of Khruubaa Chao Sriwichai. By Saphaa Watthanatham Cangwat Lamphun together with Saphaa Watthanam Amphur Muang Lamphun. June 11.
Sinnott, Megan. 2014. "Baby Ghosts: Child Spirits and Contemporary Conceptions of Childhood in Thailand." *TRaNS: Trans-Regional and National Studies of Southeast Asia* 2 (2): 293–317.
Siraporn Nathalang, ed. 2000. *Thai Folklore: Insights into Thai Culture*. Bangkok: Chulalongkorn University Press.
Sivaraksa, Sulak. 1988. *A Socially Engaged Buddhism*. Bangkok: Thai Inter-Religious Commission for Development.
Sizemore, Russell F., and Donald K. Swearer, eds. 1990. *Ethics, Wealth and Salvation: A Study in Buddhist Social Ethics*. Columbia: University of South Carolina Press.
Skilling, Peter. 2006. "Jataka and Paññāsa-jātaka in South-East Asia." *Journal of the Pali Text Society* 28:113–73.
———, ed. 2008. *Past Lives of the Buddha: Wat Si Chum—Art, Architecture and Inscriptions*. Bangkok: River Books.
Skilling, Peter, and Justin McDaniel, eds. 2012. *Buddhist Narrative in Asia and Beyond*. Bangkok: Institute of Thai Studies, Chulalongkorn University.
Smith, Bardwell L., ed. 1978. *Religion and Legitimation of Power in Thailand, Laos, and Burma*. Chambersburg, PA: ANIMA Books.
Smith, John Sterling Forssen. 2013. *The Chiang Tung Wars: War and Politics in Mid-19th Century Siam and Burma*. Bangkok: Institute of Asian Studies, Chulalongkorn University.
Smith-Hefner, Nancy. 1999. *Khmer American: Identity and Moral Education in a Diasporic Community*. Berkeley: University of California Press.
Smyth, H. Warington. (1898) 1994. *Five Years in Siam: From 1891–1896*. Bangkok: White Lotus.
Sombat Chantornvong. 1981. "Religious Literature in Thai Political Perspective." In *Essays on Literature and Society in Southeast Asia*, edited by Tham Seong Chee, 187–205. Singapore: Singapore University Press.
Sommai Premchit. 2001. *Maha Wessandorn Chaadok: Wikhroh thang sangkhom lae wattanatham*. [The Mahavessantara Jataka: A Sociocultural Analysis]. Chiang Mai: Ming Muang Printing.
———. 2002. *Khruubaa Srivichai, nakbun haeng laannaa* [Khruubaa Sriwichai, the Holy Man of Lanna]. Chiang Mai: Rongphim Mingmyang.
Sommai Premchit and Amphay Dore. 1992. *The Lan Na Twelve-Month Traditions*. Chiang Mai: Faculty of Social Sciences, Chiang Mai University.

Sommai Premchit and Pierre Dore. 1991. *The Lan Na Twelve-Month Traditions: An Ethno-historic and Comparative Approach*. Chiang Mai: Faculty of Social Sciences, Chiang Mai University.

Sophaa Chanamuul. 1991. "Khruubaa Sriwichai 'tonbun' haeng laanaa (phoo soo 2421-2481)" [Khruubaa Sriwichai, Saint of Lanna, 1878-1938]. MA thesis, Thammasat University.

Sorasak Ngamcachonkulkid. 2005. "The Seri Thai Movement: The First Alliance against Military Authoritarianism in Modern Thai History." PhD diss., University of Wisconsin-Madison.

Sparkes, Stephen. 2005. *Spirits and Souls: Gender and Cosmology in an Isan Village in Northeast Thailand*. Bangkok: White Lotus Press.

Spiro, Melford E. 1970. *Buddhism and Society: A Great Tradition and Its Burmese Vicissitudes*. New York: Harper & Row.

Stamp Wench. 2015. "Vessantara Jatakaya on Stamps—Laos, Thailand and Sri Lanka." *The Stamp Wench* (blog), December 14. http://stampwench.com/2015/12/14/vessantara-jatakaya-stamps-laos-thailand-sri-lanka/.

Strate, Shane. 2015. *The Lost Territories: Thailand's History of National Humiliation*. Honolulu: University of Hawai'i Press.

Streckfuss, David. 1995. "Kings in the Age of Nations—The Paradox of Lèse-Majesté as Political Crime in Thailand." *Comparative Studies in Society and History* 37 (3): 445-75.

———. 2011. *Truth on Trial in Thailand: Defamation, Treason, and Lèse-Majesté*. New York: Routledge.

Strenski, Ivan. 1983. "On Generalized Exchange and the Domestication of the Sangha." *Man* (n.s.) 18:463-77.

Strong, John S. 1992. *The Legend and Cult of Upagupta: Sanskrit Buddhism in North India and Southeast Asia*. Princeton, NJ: Princeton University Press.

Stuart-Fox, Martin. 1996. *Buddhist Kingdom, Marxist State: The Making of Modern Laos*. Bangkok: White Lotus Press.

———. 1998. *The Lao Kingdom of Lan Xang: Rise and Decline*. Bangkok: White Lotus Press.

Suchit Bunbongkarn and Prudhisan Jumbala, eds. 2012. *Monarchy and Constitutional Rule in Democratizing Thailand*. Bangkok: Institute of Thai Studies, Chulalongkorn University.

Supaporn Vathanaprida. 1994. *Thai Tales: Folktales of Thailand*. Englewood, CO: Libraries Unlimited.

Suwanna Satha-anand. 1997. "Madsi: The Female Bodhisattva Denied?" In *Women, Gender Relations and Development in Thai Society*, edited by Virada Somswasdi and Sally Theobald, 243-56. Chiang Mai: Women's Studies Center, Chiang Mai University.

———. 2013. "Madsi and Mahapajapati as Great Women in the Buddhist Tradition." In *The Emergence and Heritage of Asian Women Intellectuals*, edited by Supakwadee Amatayakul, 27-42. Bangkok: Institute of Thai Studies, Chulalongkorn University.

Swearer, Donald K. 1978. "A New Look at Prince Vessantara." *Journal of the National Research Council of Thailand* 10 (1): 1-9.
———. 1981. *Buddhism and Society in Southeast Asia*. Chambersburg, PA: ANIMA Books.
———. (1995) 2009. *The Buddhist World of Southeast Asia*. 2nd ed. Chiang Mai: Silkworm Books.
———. 1995. "Hypostasizing the Buddha: Buddha Image Consecration in Northern Thailand." *History of Religions* 34 (3): 263-80.
———. 1996. "Bhikku Buddhadasa's Interpretation of the Buddha." *Journal of the American Academy of Religion* 62 (2): 313-36.
———. 2010. *The Buddhist World of Southeast Asia*. Albany: State University of New York Press.
Swearer, Donald, and Sommai Premchit. 1998. *The Legend of Queen Cama*. Albany: State University of New York Press.
Tachard, Guy. (1688) 1981. *A Relation of the Voyage to Siam: Performed by Six Jesuits Sent by the French King, to the Indies and China in the Year 1685*. Bangkok: White Orchid Press.
Tai, Hue-Tam Ho. 1983. *Millenarianism and Peasant Politics in Vietnam*. Cambridge, MA: Harvard University Press.
Tambiah, Stanley J. 1968. "The Ideology of Merit and the Social Correlates of Buddhism in a Thai Village." In *Dialectic in Practical Religion*, edited by E. R. Leach, 41-121. Cambridge Papers in Social Anthropology 5. Cambridge: Cambridge University Press.
———. 1970. *Buddhism and the Spirit Cults in North-east Thailand*. Cambridge: Cambridge University Press.
———. 1976. *World Conqueror and World Renouncer: A Study of Buddhism and Polity in Thailand against a Historical Background*. Cambridge: Cambridge University Press.
———. 1984. *The Buddhist Saints of the Forest and the Cult of Amulets*. Cambridge: Cambridge University Press.
Tanabe, Shigeharu. 1984. "Ideological Practice in Peasant Rebellions: Siam at the Turn of the Twentieth Century." In *History and Peasant Consciousness in South East Asia*, edited by Andrew Turton and Shigeharu Tanabe, 75-110. Osaka, Japan: National Museum of Ethnology.
Tannenbaum, Nicola. 1995. *Who Can Compete Against the World? Power Protection and Buddhism in Shan Worldview*. Monograph and Occasional Paper Series 51. Ann Arbor: Association for Asian Studies.
Taylor, J. L. 1993. *Forest Monks and the Nation-State: An Anthropological and Historical Study in Northeastern Thailand*. Singapore: Institute of Southeast Asian Studies.
Teiser, Stephen F., and Jacqueline I. Stone, eds. 2009. *Readings of the Lotus Sutra*. New York: Columbia University Press.
Tej Bunnag. 1967. "Kabot Phuumiibun Phaak Isaan" (The Holy Men Uprisings in the Northeast). *Sangkhomsaat Parithat* [Social Science Review] 5:78-86.

———. 1968. Kabot Ngiew Myang Phrae (The Shan Uprising in Muang Phrae). *Sangkhomsaat Parithat* [Social Science Review] 6:67–80.
———. 1977. *The Provincial Administration of Siam, 1892–1915*. Kuala Lumpur: Oxford University Press.
Terral, Ginette. 1956. "Samuddaghosa Jātaka: Conte Pali tirē du Paññāsa Jātaka." *Bulletin de l'Ecole française d'Extrême-Orient* 48:247–51.
Terweil, Barend Jan. (1975) 2012. *Monks and Magic: Revisiting a Classic Study of Religious Ceremonies in Thailand*. Copenhagen: Nordic Institute of Asian Studies Press.
———. 1989. *Through Travellers' Eyes: An Approach to Early Nineteenth Century Thai History*. Bangkok: Duang Kamol.
Terweil, B. J. 1972. "The Five Precepts and Ritual in Rural Thailand." *Journal of the Siam Society* 60 (1) (January): 333–44.
———. 1976. "A Model for the Study of Thai Buddhism." *Journal of Asian Studies* 35 (3) (May): 391–403.
Tesabaan Tambon Muang Klaeng. 2009. *100 Pii Baan Talaat Saamyaan, pho soh 2451–2551*. Muang Klaeng, Rayong: Tesabaan Tambon Muang Klaeng.
Textor, Robert B. 1961. *From Peasant to Pedicab Driver: A Social Study of Northeastern Thai Farmers Who Periodically Migrated to Bangkok and Became Pedicab Drivers*. Cultural Report Series 9. New Haven, CT: Yale University Southeast Asia Studies.
Thak Chaloemtiarana. 1979. *Thailand: the Politics of Despotic Paternalism*. Bangkok: Social Sciences Association of Thailand, and Thai Khadi Institute of Thammasat University.
Thiphakorawong, Chaophraya. 1978. *The Dynastic Chronicles, Bangkok Era: The First Reign*. Translated by Thadeus Flood and Chadin Flood. Tokyo: East Asian Cultural Studies.
Thompson, E. P. 1974. "Patrician Society, Plebian Culture." *Journal of Social History* 7 (4): 382–405.
Thompson, E. P. 1978. *The Poverty of Theory and Other Essays*. New York: Monthly Review Press.
Thompson, Virginia. (1941) 1967. *Thailand: The New Siam*. New York: Macmillan.
Thongchai Winichakul. 2012. "Hyper-royalism: Its Spell and Magic." Paper presented for Conference on Democracy and Crisis in Thailand, organized by McGill University and Thailand Democracy Watch, Faculty of Political Science, Chulalongkorn University, March 9. https://vimeo.com/76671391. Accessed February 7, 2016.
Thosaphol Cangphanichakul. 1994. *Chuchok bandaanchok*. Bangkok: Commabooks.
———. 2010. *Pathihaan chuchok bandaanchok*. Bangkok: Commabooks.
Tirrell, Lynne. 1990. "Storytelling and Moral Agency." *Journal of Aesthetics and Art Criticism* 48 (2): 115–126.
Townsend, Mary Lee. 1992. *Forbidden Laughter: Popular Humor and the Limits of Repression in Nineteenth-Century Prussia*. Ann Arbor: University of Michigan Press.
Turner, Victor. 1988. *The Anthropology of Performance*. New York: PAJ Publications.

Turpin, F. H. (1908) 1997. *A History of the Kingdom of Siam up to 1770.* Translation by B.O. Cartwright. Bangkok: White Lotus Press.

Turton, Andrew. 1978. "The Current Situation in the Thai Countryside." In *Thailand: Roots of Conflict*, edited by A. Turton, J. Fast, and M. Caldwell, 104-42. Nottingham: Russell Press.

———. 1980. "Thai Institutions of Slavery." In *Asian and African Systems of Slavery*, edited by James L. Watson, 251-92. Oxford: Blackwell.

Van Esterik, Penny, ed. 1982. *Women of Southeast Asia.* Occasional Paper 9. DeKalb: Northern Illinois University, Center for Southeast Asian Studies.

Van Esterik, Penny, and John van Esterik. 1980. "Royal Style in Village Context: Translation and Interpretation of a Thai Tonsure Text." *Asian Folklore Studies* 39 (1): 63-78.

Vatikiotis, Michael. 1984. "Ethnic Pluralism in the Northern Thai City of Chiang Mai." PhD diss., St. Catherine's College, Oxford University.

Veidlinger, Daniel M. 2006. *Spreading the Dharma: Writing, Orality, and Textual Transmission in Buddhist Northern Thailand.* Honolulu: University of Hawai'i Press.

Vella, Walter F. 1957. *Siam under Rama III: 1824-1851.* Locust Valley, New York: J. J. Augustin.

Verberckmoes, Johan. 1999. *Laughter, Jestbooks, and Society in the Spanish Netherlands.* New York: St. Martin's Press.

Vickery, Michael. 1970. "Thai Regional Elites and the Reforms of King Chulalongkorn." *Journal of Asian Studies* 29 (4): 863-81.

Vincent, Frank. (1873) 1988. *The Land of the White Elephant: Sights and Scenes in Burma, Siam, Cambodia, and Cochin-China (1871-2).* Bangkok: White Lotus Press.

Wajuppa Tossa, with Kongdeuane Nettavong. 2008. *Lao Folktales.* Edited by Margaret Read MacDonald. World Folklore Series. Westport, CT: Libraries Unlimited.

Wales, H. G. Quaritch. (1931) 1992. *Siamese State Ceremonies: Their History and Function.* Richmond, Surrey: Curzon Press.

———. 1934. *Ancient Siamese Government and Administration.* London: B. Quaritch.

Walters, Jonathan S. 1990. "The Buddha's Bad Karma: A Problem in the History of Theravada Buddhism." *Numen* 37 (1): 70-95.

Weiner, Annette. 1976. *Women of Value, Men of Renown.* Austin: University of Texas Press.

Wells, Kenneth. 1939. *Thai Buddhism, its Rites and Activities.* Bangkok: Bangkok Times Press.

Wenk, Klaus. 1968. *The Restoration of Thailand under Rama I, 1782-1809.* Translated by Greeley Stahl. Tucson: University of Arizona Press.

West, John O. 1990. *Cowboy Folk Humor: Life and Laughter in the American West.* Little Rock, AR: August House.

Wickberg, Daniel. 1998. *The Senses of Humor: Self and Laughter in Modern America.* Ithaca, NY: Cornell University Press.

Wijewardene, Gehan. 1967. "Some Aspects of Rural Life in Thailand." In *Thailand: Social and Economic Studies in Development*, edited by T. H. Silcock. Canberra: Australian National University Press.

Wilson, Constance M. 1970. "State and Society in the Reign of Mongkut, 1851-1868: Thailand on the Eve of Modernization." PhD diss., Cornell University.

———. 1997. "The Holy Man in the History of Thailand and Laos." *Journal of Southeast Asian Studies* 28 (2): 345-64.

———. 2009. "The Jataka in Laos II: The Phra Lak Phra Lam." In *The Middle Mekong River Basin: Studies in Tai History and Culture*, edited by Constance M. Wilson, 139-99. DeKalb: Southeast Asia Publications, Northern Illinois University.

Wilson, Constance M., and Lucien M. Hanks. 1985. *The Burma-Thailand Frontier over Sixteen Decades: Three Descriptive Documents*. Southeast Asia Series 70. Athens: Center for International Studies, Ohio University.

Wimon Wiriyawit, compiler. 1997. *Free Thai: Personal Recollections and Official Documents*. Bangkok: White Lotus Press.

Winaithorn Manop Paalaphan, Dr. Phrakhruu. 2010. *Syybsaan kaanthet mahaachaat*. Bangkok: Edisan Press.

Winternitz, M. 1928. "Jataka Gathas and Jataka Commentary." *Indian Historical Quarterly* (Calcutta) 4 (1): 1-14.

———. 1933. *A History of Indian Literature*. Translated by S. Ketkar and H. Kohn and revised by the author. New York: Russell and Russell.

Witayakorn Chiengkul. 1983. *The Effects of Capitalist Penetration on the Transformation of the Agrarian Structure in the Central Region of Thailand, 1960-1980*. Bangkok: Social Research Institute, Chulalongkorn University.

Wolf, Eric. 1982. *Europe and the People without History*. Berkeley: University of California Press.

Wong, Deborah. 2001. *Sounding the Center: History and Aesthetics in Thai Buddhist Performance*. Chicago: University of Chicago Press.

Woodhouse, Leslie. 2009. "A 'Foreign' Princess in the Siamese Court: Princess Dara Rasami, the Politics of Gender and Ethnic Difference in Nineteenth-Century Siam." PhD diss., University of California at Berkeley.

Woodthorpe, R. G. 1896. "The Country of the Shans." *Geographical Journal* 7/6:577-600.

Worrasit Tantinipankul. 2006. "Modernization and Urban Monastic Space in Rattanakosin City: Comparative Study of Three Royal Wats." PhD diss., Cornell University.

Wray, Elizabeth, Claire Rosenfield, and Dorothy Bailey. 1972. *Ten Lives of the Buddha: Siamese Temple Paintings and Jataka Tales*. New York: Weatherhill.

Wu Ch'Eng-En. 1958. *Monkey: Folk Novel of China*. Translated by Arthur Waley. New York: Grove Press.

Wyatt, David K. 1966. "The Buddhist Monkhood as an Avenue of Social Mobility in Traditional Thai Society." *Silapakorn* 10 (1): 41-52.

———. 1969. *The Politics of Reform in Thailand: Education in the Reign of King Chulalongkorn*. New Haven, CT: Yale University Press.

———. 1994. *Studies in Thai History*. Chiang Mai: Silkworm Books.
———. 1997. "History and Directionality in the Early Nineteenth-Century Tai World." In *The Last Stand of Asian Autonomies*, edited by A. Reid, 425-43. Basingstoke: MacMillan.
Wyatt, David K., and Aroonrut Wichienkeeo. 1995. *The Chiang Mai Chronicle*. Chiang Mai: Silkworm Books.
Yamada, Teri Shaffer. 2004. "The Spirit Cult of Khleang Moeung in Long Beach, California." In *History, Buddhism and New Religious Movements in Cambodia*, edited by John Marston and Elizabeth Guthrie, 213-25. Honolulu: University of Hawai'i Press.
Young, Ernest. (1898) 1982. *The Kingdom of the Yellow Robe*. Kuala Lumpur: Oxford University Press.
Younghusband, Lt. G. J. 1888. *Eighteen Hundred Miles on a Burmese Tat*. London: W. H. Allen.
Zago, Marcello. 1972. *Rites et Ceremonies en Milieu Bouddhiste Lao*. Rome: Universita Gregoriana.
Zimmerman, Carle C. 1931. *Siam Rural Economic Survey, 1930-1931*. Bangkok: Bangkok Times Press.

Index

Note: page numbers in italics refer to illustrations.

abuse of power stories, 187–89
Aggana Sutra, 102, 272
Ajarn Chop, 83
Ajarn Man Phurithatto, 224, 225, 234–35, 303n37
Ajarn Saiyan (Wat Welurachin, Thonburi), 73
Ajarn Son Suwannasuk (Suphanburi), 72
Ajarn Sui (Ubon), 222
Ajuta the hermit, 10, 71, 72, 131, 146, 148, 249
Akin Rabibhadana, 112, 286n29
almsgiving, 19, 78
Amarindra, Queen, 282n31
Amitataa: central region attitudes toward, 74–75, 283n54; in central Thai version, 293n39; in court version, 58–59; erasure of, in northeastern Hok Kasat, 116–17; husband-wife relations and, 157; Jujaka as trickster and, 173; northern development of, 143–46; in Pali version, 143, 293n39; portrayal of, 263–64, 307n38; village women and, 60, 61, *104*, 107, 116, 117, 144–45, 264, 287nn37–38
amulets, 111–12, 245–47, 251, 305n2
Anaukpetlun, King, 302n30
Anisong Vessantara ("blessings of Vessantara"), 127, 135, 291n24
Anuman Rajadhon, Phya, 48–49, 49–50, 63, 67, 69, 78–79, 284n61, 291n17, 296n4
Ariyawongsachan Yanawimon Ubon Sangkhapamok (Sui), Chao Khun Phra, 116
Ariyawongsakhatayana (Sa), Somdet Phra, 286n28
Arthid Sheravanichkul, 244–45
atyaa chao ("law by chao"), 188
Aung San Suu Kyi, 272
Ayutthaya, royal court temple of, 42

Baker, Chris, 30, 67, 276n7
Bakhtin, Mikhail, 29, 197
Bangkok: Grand Palace, 42–49; migration to, 87; northeasterners, attitudes toward, 99; Siriraj Hospital, *41*, 76, 254. *See also* central region and recitations; court and royal recitations; court control
bawdiness: Amitataa and, *104*, 116–17; Bunthong's concerns about, 204; in central region, 76; court concern over, 58, 165–66; in history of literature, 59–61, *60*; Jujaka wedding ceremony and, 140–42; "Jujaka with Large Testicles," 248; modern audiences and, 241; nineteenth-century trends, 30–31; phallic imagery (northeastern region), 111–15, 222; *phiitaakhon* ghosts, *113*, 113–14, 252; Rabelaisian humor and, 123; restrained, in northeastern region, 110–15; Rocket Festival and, 110, 111–12; tricksters and, 172; "wondrous scenes" (*bot atsachan*), 61. *See also* humor and comedy; *tujok* monks
Bayinnaung, King, 229, 302n30
beggars as sympathetic characters, 180–81
Bergson, Henri, 29, 171
Bhumiphol, King, 48, 100
binthabatr chiwit (monastic right to intervene in executions), 230, 302n31
birth year, lay sponsorship by, 135–36
boat symbolism, 52–57, *53*
Bock, Carl, 298n31
bodhisattva-king figure, 21
Bodin, Chaophraya, 302n18
Bowring, John, 190
Brahmin role in occasional ceremonies, 69–70, 283n44

Braudel, Fernand, 295n1
Brereton, Bonnie, 19, 102, 109, 117, 120, 192, 238, 286n26
British colonialism, 220-21
Buddhagosa's prophecy, 15
Buddhism: Gotama Buddha, 13-14, 194-95; Lent, Buddhist, 42-43, 61-63, 278n1, 278n2; Mahanikai order, 50, 214, 216, 217, 218, 224-25; philosophical approach of Rama I, 212-13; prophecy of lasting 5,000 years, 15-16, 20, 109, 196. *See also* monks; sangha control, centralized; Thammayut order
Bun Bangfai (Rocket Festival), 110, 111-12, 115, 222-23, 284n3, 287n34
Bunnag, Jane, 63, 77
Bun Pha Wet ("Merit-making for Vessantara"). *See* northeastern region and Bun Pha Wet
Burmese rule of Lanna kingdoms, 229

calamity cosmologies, 193-94
capitalism, global. *See* global capitalism and contemporary culture
capitation tax, 235-36
Cate, Sandra, 81, 84, 86-88, 94, 97, 98-102, 120, 121, 286n24, 288n43
central region and recitations: Amitataa, attitudes toward, 74-75; bawdy literature and, 59-61, *60*; during Buddhist Lent, 61-63; decline of *Vessantara Jataka* and, 76-80; favorite chapters, 70-72, 75-76; history of performances and style in, 39-40; influence on northeastern region, 98-109; Jujaka, attitudes toward, 72-74; Jujaka, depiction of, 12; language compared to northern region, 156-57; lay sponsorship, 66; millenarianism, 196-97; number of monks, 65-66; offerings, 66-70; over days or weeks, 63-65; processions in, 67; regional comparison, *166*; sangha, centralized state control over, 210-19. *See also* court and royal recitations
Chalii, *4*, 10, 11, 82, 203, 247, 262-63, 277n24, 304n52, 307n36
Chao Anuwong (Anu), 189, 220, 282n30, 302n18
Chao Dara, 234

Chao Mae Kuan Im, 266
Chao Muang (northeastern), 220-24
Chao Poh Kuan, 115
Chao Sri Suriyawongse, 44
chapters of *Vessantara Jataka*: birth years correlated with, 135-36; Chohkasat, 10, 57, 76, 101-2, 128; Chulaphon, 10, 51, 57-58, *170*; fund-raiser earning by chapter, 76; Himaphan, 10, 51, 57-58, 76, 85, 283n53; Mahaphon, 42, 51, 57-58, 66, 71-72, 156; Maharaat, 254; Munithi Hortrai recensions by chapter, 51; Nakornkan, 10-11, 58, 70, 71, 76, 85-87, 98, 128, 134-35, *268*; Sakabap, 10, 50, 51, 57-58, 76, 128; "Tearjerker," 6; Thanakan, 10, 45, 51, 57, 71, 135; Thotsaphon, 9-10, 51, 57-58, 135; voice types for, 66, 128; Wanaprawet, 10, 51, 58, 64, 135, 283n48. *See also* Jujaka chapter; Kumarn chapter; Maharaat chapter; Matsi chapter
charity. *See* generosity and gifts
Chiang Mai, Golden Age of Lanna literature in, 127
child-parent relations, 160-62
Chinaworn, Prince, 301n16
Chiu, Angela, 230
Chohkasat chapter, 10, 57, 76, 101-2, 128
Chulabhorn, Princess, 48, 280n15
Chulalongkorn, King: crown prince appointed by, 281n20; Maitreya worship, disapproval of, 282n40; as novice, 281n19; novice recitation of, 57; public education and, 226; references to 5,000 years suppressed by, 109, 196; sangha control and, 217; shock at local Jujaka sermons, 278n30; statue of, 112; Tu Ping vs. Sophaa and, 234; Wat Mani Cholakhan visit, 196-97
Chulaphon chapter, 10, 51, 57-58, *170*
Chulasakarat calendar, 45, 279n9
Ciñcamānavikā, 263
Coedes, George, 15, 108-9, 127
Collins, Steven, 6, 13, 18-19, 275n3, 277n23, 295n1, 305n14
colonialism, British and French, 220-21
Colquhoun, Archibald R., 229
comedy. *See* bawdiness; humor and comedy; *tujok* monks
communist guerillas, 99, 178, 198, 240

concubine stories, 183–86
Cone, Margaret, 12–13, 19, 261
confiscation stories, 182–83
contemporary culture. *See* global capitalism and contemporary culture
Cort, Mary, 29, 61, 279n11
Council of Elders. *See* National Ecclesiastical Council
Council of Seven, 229
coup of 1932, 40–42, 45, 78, 80, 238, 242, 269, 297n14, 299n36, 304n50
court and royal recitations: annual monastic recitations at Wat Phra Kaew, 43–45; authors of chapters, 50–51; boat symbolism and the Kumarn chapter, 52–57, *53*; comic recitations, suppression efforts against, 26–29; humor as inappropriate for, 59; Jory on *Vessantara Jataka* decline and political shifts in, 24–26; Jujaka chapter, 58–59; northeastern aesthetic and religious practices influenced by, 109–10; northeastern political ambiguity and, 98–109; novice recitations and crown princes, 48–51, 53–58; Sakabap, Chulaphon, and Mahaphon chapters, 57–58; special state occasions, recitations on, 45–48; support for formal recitations, 41, 50; triannual recitation during Buddhist Lent at Wat Phra Kaew, 42–43
court control: lèse majesté cases, 197, 299n35; Maitreya belief, millenarianism, and, 196–97; military dictatorships and insurgency campaigns, 197–98; trickster, hidden transcript, and, 197–207. *See also* sangha control, centralized
coyote dancing, 248, *249*
Crawfurd, John, 190, 191, 213
crown princes, novice recitations by, 49–50, 53–58
crows, 283n52
culture, contemporary. *See* global capitalism and contemporary culture

Damrong Rachanuphab, Prince, 123, 218, 225–26
Dansai Bun Pha Wet, 112–15
dasajati (final ten *jatakas*), 127, 275n3
Davis, Richard, 237, 291n17

Department of Religious Affairs (Krom Thammakan; now Krom Kaan Saasanaa), 43, 219, 279n3, 306n23
Devadatta, 11, 14, 74, 251, 305n14
De Young, John, 296n6
Dhawat Poonotoke, 288n40
Dii (Than Phanthulo), 222–23
Dodd, William, 192, 232
dogs of Jetabutr the hunter, *9*, 126, 131, 136–37, 146–48, *170*, 293n45
Doniger, Wendy, 13
Dore, Amphay, 91, 133, 238, 285n15, 303n45
Durkheim, Émile, 295n1
Dyan Yii Paeng (Full Moon Festival, aka Loi Krathong), 133–34, 166, 237, 287n39

education: Buddhist, under Rama III, 214; children sent to temples, 163–65; public, provincial, 225–28; secular, and impact on recitations, 239; Vajiranana's new religio-educational system, 218
Emerald Buddha, 20, 42–43. *See also* Wat Phra Kaew
Epstein, Steven Jay, 296n4

family reunification theme in northeastern region, 85–87, 97–98
famines, 179–80
Fausböll, Viggo, 14
feminist interpretations, 265
Ferguson, John P., 237–38, 276n15
five evils, 206, 300n49
flags and political subjectivity, 99
food shortages, 179–80, 296n8
Forbes, Charles, 11
Foucher, Alfred, 19
Fournereau, Lucien, 54–55, 56–57, 280n17
Freeman, John, 189
French colonialism, 220–21
Full Moon Festival. *See* Dyan Yii Paeng (Full Moon Festival, aka Loi Krathong)
fund-raisers: cultural heritage and, 258; Siriraj Hospital recitation, Bangkok, *41*, 76, 254; temple fair, northeastern region, 88
funeral of Jujaka, 26, 120–21, 149–55, *150*
funerary recitations, 7–8; central region and, 280n16, 291n21; Keyes first-person account,

funerary recitations (*continued*) 123–25; Matsi chapter and, 260; northeastern region and, 291n21; northern region and, 134

Gabaude, Louis, 22, 261
Garnier, Francis, 190
Gascoigne, Gwendolen Trench, 261
Gaston, Bruce, 276n6
generosity and gifts: beggars and, 180–81; Gift of the Seven Hundreds, 10, 43, 276n14; *krajaats* (offering baskets), 46–47; Lanna *tamnan* and, 230; merit-making and, 277n26; monastic interests in reinforcing, 19; moral economies and, 270–71; special state recitations and, 45–47; of Vessantara, as implicit critique of kings, 201–2; Vessantara giving away wife and children, 3, 4, 5–7, 22–23, 101, 261, 271
Gengenbach, Julia, 265
Gerini, Gerolamo Emilio, 25, 28, 39, 40, 45–49, 52, 55–57, 65, 278n29, 282n40, 284n57
Giant Swing Ceremony, 283n44
Gift of the Seven Hundreds, 10, 43, 276n14
gifts. *See* generosity and gifts
global capitalism and contemporary culture: cultural heritage promotion, state and local support for, 254–58; international performances, 258–59; Jujaka amulets, 244–47, 251; Jujaka House and coyote dancing, 247–48, *249*; motivational shifts, 259–60; statues of Jujaka, *244*, 249–51; tourism promotion, 251–53; wealth, promotion of, 244–51; women, portrayal of and appeal to, 260–66
Goldstein, Donna, 29
Gombrich, Richard, 6, 12–13, 19, 261, 276n15
Gordon, Alec, 282n35
Goss, L. Allan, 11
Gotama Buddha, 13–14, 194–95
Grandfather Jujaka (Taa Chuchok), 115, *257*, 304n52
"Grandfather Jujaka Who Increases Wealth" (*Poh Puu Chuchok Phyymphuun Sap*), 250
Grand Palace, Bangkok: 1807 state recitation in, 45–49; Wat Phra Kaew, 42–44, 47, 211

Griswold, A. B., 14, 15, 17, 23, 127, 277n22
Grow, Mary, 32

Hallett, Holt, 190, 195
Hallisey, Charles, 269, 272
Handlin, Lillian, 277n24
Hanks, Lucien, 19, 76, 78, 284n58
Hansen, Anne, 272, 278n29
Hardy, Robert Spence, 4
Hayashi, Yukio, 81, 285n9
head tax, 235–36
hells, 11, 16, 27, 31, 62, 95, 108, 121, 139, 154, 190, 206, 249, 288n42
hidden transcripts, 197–207
Himaphan chapter, 10, 51, 57–58, 76, 85, 283n53
historical agency in *jatakas*: monastic motivations, 18–19; peasant and villager motivations, 21–22; regional variation and, 17–18; royal motivations, 19–21
Hok Kasat ("The Six Royals"), 83, 85, 89, 97, 103, 116–17
Holt, John, 5
Holy Men's Revolts (1902), 99, 195–96
hong kwan ceremony, 141, 293n36
housewarmings, 134–35
humor and comedy: Amitataa and, 144–45; edginess of, 204–6; eschatological hope in scatological humor, 201–4; hidden transcript, covert anti-royalism, and, 197–207; as inappropriate for royal recitations, 59; Mahaphon chapter and, 72; in northern and northeastern elaborations, 121; in *Phra Malai Sutra* and *Traiphum*, 30–31; popular appeal and social role of, 29–30; Rabelaisian, 26–32, 123; royal suppression efforts and, 26–29; royalty mocked by, 30–32; scholarship on, 29; vaudevillian Jujaka (northeastern region), 102–7, *104*. *See also* bawdiness; Jujaka; tricksters; *tujok* monks
Hundius, Harald, 277n20, 290n11
husband-wife relations, 158–60, 265
Hyde, Lewis, 172

India, 3, 4, 6, 14–15, 243, 261, 269, 275n5
Insom, Poh Naan, 290n7
interest rates, 296n7

international performances, 258-59
irredentist movement, 229, 303n32

Jackson, Peter, 218
jatakas: about, 3, 275n4; *dasajati* (final ten), 275n3; historical agency in, 17-22; non-canonical, 277n20, 290nn11-12. *See also* historical agency in *jatakas*; *Vessantara Jataka*
Jesus, 270-71
Jetabutr the hunter, 10, 119, 131, 138-39, 146-48, *170*, 203-4, 288n41, 299n43
Jetjaras na Ranong, 113, 115
Johannsen, Christina B., 276n15
joi, 140, 241
Jory, Patrick, 13, 21, 24-27, 278n28, 288n43
Jujaka: abridged adventures of, in northeastern region compared to northern region, 118-22; amulets of, 244-47, 251; in Baan Nongkathao, Amphur Nakhonthai, 115; central region attitudes toward, 72-74; childhood, imagined, 139-40; comic and villainous depictions of, 11, 138; at court, *209*; in court version of chapter, 58-59; death and funeral scenes, 120-21, 149-55, *150*; description of, in Kumarn chapter, 138; eighteen characteristics of, 292n30; farewell scene, 145-46; food offerings to, 70, 283n45; funeral procession of, *26*; in hell, 139; home, description of, 143; northeastern vaudevillian version of, 102-7, *104*; northern region and, 128; regional comparison, *166*; regional differences in portrayal of, 11-12; role of, in *Vessantara Jataka*, 171-72; statues of, *244*, 249-51; tricking Jetabutr the hunter and Ajuta the hermit, 146-48, *170*, 203-4, 299n43; as trickster, 170-73, 178, 202; *tujok* monks dressed as, 130; *tujok* monks' invention of new episodes, 137-43; wedding ceremony, 140-42; worship of, 244-45. *See also* Amitataa
Jujaka chapter: bawdiness in, *60*, 116; Bunthong and, 134; central region and, 72-74, 75; court version of, 58-59; funerary readings of, 134; northeastern region and, 102-7, 118-19, 240; northern region and, 118-19, 128-31, 137-43, 240; sponsors, problems finding, 12, 66, 73; sponsors for, problems finding sponsors, 12, 66, 73, 103; unwillingness to perform, 12; variation of, regional, 123, 136-37; village life references, 156; voice for, 66. *See also* Amitataa; Jujaka; *tujok* monks

Jujaka House, 247-48, *249*
Jujaka Light and Sound Cave, Siam Cultural Park, Ratburi, 253

Kaiser, Thomas, 276n16
Kamala Tiyavanich, 71-72, 214-15, 218, 259, 278n32, 282n40
Kanhaa, *4*, 10, 11, 82, 247, 262-63, 277n24, 304n52, 307n36
Kanhaa-Chalii amulets, 247
Kaufman, Howard, 21-22, 63, 77
Kemika na Songkla, 247-48
Keyes, Charles, 5, 19, 21, 87, 123-25, 144, 165, 195, 198, 221, 302n26
Khaiwibaak Vessantara ("hardship of Vessantara"), 135, 291n24
kham khon ("to oppress or exploit people"), 188
Khathaphan, 83, 89, 97, 135
Khin Thitsa, 22, 260-61
"Khlong Chao Withuun Sorn Laan," 304n55
"Khlong Phra Lor Sorn Lok," 304n55
Khon Kaen, Preaching Institute in, 251-52
Khon Kaen village Bun Pha Wet, 92-93, 94-97, 103-7
Khruubaa Khao Pi, 195
Khruubaa Laa, 232
Khruubaa Sophaa, 232-34
Khruubaa Srivichai, 195, *228*, 236-37, 240, 303n32, 303n42, 303n44
Khun Chang Khun Phaen, 30, 67-70
Kingkeo Attagara, 77, 284n60
Kingshill, Konrad, 133-34, 180, 237, 291n17, 292n26, 296n6
kingship. *See* royalism, anti-royalism, monarchies, and kingship
Kin Khao Pun Bun Phawet (Rice Noodle Bun Phrawet), 252
Kirsch, Thomas, 81, 82
Klausner, William, 86, 89, 94, 110-12, 174, 285n12, 285n16

Korat Plateau, 220
Kornvipa Boonsue, 22, 260
Kraisri Nimmanhaeminda, 184, 189
krajaats (offering baskets), 46-47, 49, 53, 53-54, 61, 279n11; as Chinese junk, 52-55, 56
Kromsomdet Phra Bamrap Parapak, Prince, 51
Krom Thammakan (Department of Religious Affairs), 219
Kumarn chapter, 4; boat symbolism and royal reversion of, 40, 52-57; central region and, 71; court recensions of, 51; female audiences and, 264; fund-raiser earning, 76; funerary readings of, 134; hosting of, 68; as inappropriate, 58; Jujaka, description of, 138; northern region and, 128; voice for, 66, 128

labor commitment for recitations, 238-39
Ladwig, Patrice, 6, 100-101
lae Yannawa (boat chanting), 53
La Loubère, Simon de, 190
landlessness, 178, 296n6
Landon, Kenneth, 299n32
language in Lanna vs. central Thai version, 156-57
Lanna kingdoms and sangha, 229-30, 302n30
Lanna literature, Golden Age of, 127
Lanna versions. *See* northern region and recitations
Leclère, Adhémard, 5, 307n33
Lefferts, Leedom, 81, 84-88, 94, 97-102, 120, 121, 285nn12-13, 286n24, 288n43
LeMay, Reginald, 296n4, 298n31
Lent, Buddhist, 42-43, 61-63, 278n1, 278n2
lèse majesté cases, 197, 299n35
Lipman, Steve, 29
Lithai, King, 127
litters, lords carried by, 186-87
local council funds for cultural heritage, 256-58
Loei province, tourism in, 252-53
Loi Duangkaew, 257, 287n36
Loi Krathong. *See* Dyan Yii Paeng (Full Moon Festival, aka Loi Krathong)
lords, stories about: abuse of power, 187-89; concubine, 183-86; confiscation, 182-83; portering, 186-87; shooting oxen, 182; village

attitudes and, 181; water dipper, 181-82, 187
Luang Poh Bonsong (Lampang), 291n15
Luang Poh Bunthong: about, 125-26, 289n5; abuse power stories and, 188-89; childhood of Jujaka, 139-40, 163-65; on condemnation of humor, 239; on dialect changes, 304n47; edginess of humor and introductions of, 204-6; funeral performances, 134; hidden transcripts and, 198-206; on husband-wife relations, 158-60; Jetabutr's dogs, 147-48; Jujaka chapter and, 290n7; Jujaka in hell, 139; Jujaka's death and funeral, 151-54; Matsi, positive reading of, 265, 307n34; memorial shrine to, 9; on national sangha, 304n50; on parent-child relations, 160-62; on patience, 299n46; on peasant-court relations, 203-4; Phusadi's wishes and Vessantara's birth, 157-58, 202-3, 294n59; recordings, 8, 125, 126, 198; tree types, describing, 294n46; village life and, 156; wedding ceremony and bawdy song, 140-42
Luang Poh Daeng, (Uttaradit), 305n5
Luang Poh Klai (Nonthaburi), 247
Luang Poh Laan (Lampang), 291n15
Luang Poh Pankaew (Phrae), 307n32
Luang Poh Pii (Sukhothai), 257, 287n36
Luang Poh Somphong Thirathammo (Nakhon Pathom), 250-51
Luang Puu Khui (Petchabun), 305n5
Luang Puu Roht (Samut Sakorn), 245, 305n3
Luang Puu Thim Isariko (Rayong), 246, 305n4
Lutgendorf, Philip, 13
Lyons, Elizabeth, 13, 281n17

Maao (Than Thewathammii), 222-23
Mae Thoranii (earth goddess), 97, 298n31
Mahachat. *See Vessantara Jataka*
Mahachulalongkorn Buddhist University, 126, 217, 255
Maha Fai, 73, 283n51
Mahamakut Academy, 226, 227
Mahamakut Buddhist University, 217, 224
Mahanikai order, 50, 214-18, 224-25
Maha Nipata, 14
Mahaphon chapter, 42, 51, 57-58, 66, 71-72, 156

Maharaat chapter: central region and, 71; comic incidents in, 137; court recensions of, 51; fund-raising and, 76; as inappropriate, 58; modern audiences and, 254; northern region and, 128, 149; plot, 10; Princess Sirindhorn and, 47–48; regional differences, 120; voice for, 66

Maitreya: in *Anisong Vessantara*, 292n24; Chulalongkorn and, 282n40; Gotama as cheating Buddha vs., 194–95; historical association with *Vessantara Jataka*, 127–28; messianic readings of *Vessantara Jataka*, attempts to suppress, 288n43; millenarianism across regions and, 195–97; northeastern region and, 83, 108; in northern region millennialism and, 192–94; in post-canonical texts, 277n23; prophecy about *Vessantara Jataka* and return of, 16–17; story of Phra Malai and, 191–92; twenty-four-hour recitation and coming of, 16–17, 133, 191, 292n25. *See also* millenarianism and millennialism; millenarian revolts

Manee Phayomyong, 116, 118, 125–29, 239, 285n15, 286n31, 288n42, 289n7, 291n19, 292n25

Mara, 91–93, 285n14

Matsi: exile and return, political interpretation of, 100; as female Bodhisattva, 265; husband-wife relations and, 157–58; invitation to return (northeastern festival), 93–95, 252; portrayals of, 262, 307n34; story of saving Ajarn Chop's life, 83

Matsi chapter: central region and, 71; female audiences and, 264; fund-raiser earning, 76; for funerals, 260; funerary readings of, 134; as inappropriate, 58; northeastern region and, 85–86; northern region and, 128; plot, 10; Rama IV and, 50; voice for, 66

mazes (*wongkot*), 131–32, *132*, 291n17

McCarthy, James, 230–31

McClintock, Sara, 296n2

McClung, Larry, 18

McDaniel, Justin Thomas, 36, 278n36, 288n40

McGill, Forrest, 17, 20

McGilvary, Daniel, 229–30

McLeod, William C., 189

Mechai Thongthep, 176

Military Conscription Act (1905), 236

military dictatorships and insurgency campaigns, 197–98

millenarianism and millennialism: beliefs of, 298n28; calamity cosmologies, 193–94; Gotama as cheating Buddha, 194–95; northern history of, 192–93; Phra Malai story and messianic beliefs, 191–92; political subjectivity and, 99; regional comparison, 195–97. *See also* Maitreya

millenarian revolts: in central region, and court concerns, 196–97; court suppression of *jataka* recitations and, 25; Holy Men's Revolts (1902), 99, 195–96; Maitreyan timing and, 108; in northeastern region, 195–96; Rama I decree against, 196; "saints" or "holy men" and, 298n28

Mills, Mary Beth, 87, 111

Mizuno, Koichi, 82–83

modern culture. *See* global capitalism and contemporary culture

monarchies. *See* royalism, anti-royalism, monarchies, and kingship

monetary costs: of recitations, 23, 90, 238; of scroll, 285n16

money trees, 292n28

Mongkut, King (Rama IV): chapter editions composed by, 51; humor criticized by, 27–28; Mon refugees and, 301n10; nautical imagery and, 55; as novice, 281n19; novice recitation of, 49, 71; number of monks and, 279n3; succession to the throne, 216; support for recitations, 50, 278nn28–29; Thammayut order and, 25, 214–17, 222; Wat Prayoon and, 44

monies raised in recitations, 76, 77, 283n55

monks: annual monastic recitations at Wat Phra Kaew, 43–45; food shortages and, 296n8; historical agency and interests of, in jatakas, 18–19; magical self-protection by, 129; making fun of, 288n42; mass disrobings, in north, 240; novices, relations with, 162–65; number of, in north and northeast, 233, 235–36; number of, in recitations, 65–66, 89, *166*; specialization by, 128–29. *See also* sangha control, centralized; *tujok* monks

moral economies: charity and gift-giving in, 270–71; humor and morality in everyday village life, 155–56; Victorian morality, 30, 61, 165
morlam, 87, 107, 109, 112, 225
Mueller, Max, 270–71
Munithi Hortrai, 51

Nakornkan chapter, 10–11, 58, 70, 71, 76, 85–87, 98, 128, 134–35, *268*
Napat Sirisambhand, 282n35
Narayan, Kirin, 13
Naresuan, King, 302n31
National Buddhist Youth Society, 254
National Ecclesiastical Council (Mahatherasamakhom), 29, 48, 218, 239–40
nationalist symbolism, 99
New Year's (Songkran), 284n1, 284n4, 287n33
Nguyen, Betty, 193–94
Nidhi Eoseewong, 11, 13, 52, 55, 58, 61, 75, 281n25, 282n34
northeastern region and Bun Pha Wet: about Bun Pha Wet, 81; absences as signs of accommodation, 109–10; administration of, 220–21; Amitataa, erasure of, 116–17; bawdiness, restrained, 110–15; Hok Kasat version and, 83; the *jataka's* everyday and pervasive presence in villages, 81–83; Jujaka, depiction of, 12; Jujaka's adventures, abridgement of, 118–22; Laos and Bun Pha Wet, 43; Maitreyan timing, 108–9; monks in demand during, 83–84; Nakornkan chapter and family reunification theme, 85–87, 97–98; northern region compared to, 118–21; number of monks, 88; outmigration and return home, 87; political ambiguity, defiance, and accommodation, 98–109; processions, communal, 67; public, provincial education and, 225–28; regional comparison, *166*; Rocket Festival, 110, 111–12; scroll procession and invitation of Vessantara and Matsi to return, 82, 93–96, 98–102; Siang Miang tales, 174–76; socialism and communism, 99; sponsors and lottery, 88–89; strategic and defensive importance of, 219–20; Thammayut expansion into, 222–25; thousand balls of rice procession, 96–98; Upakut invitation procession, 91–93; vaudevillian Jujaka, 102–7; village unity theme, 87–88, 97–98
northern region and recitations: actions and language use, 156–58; beggars as sympathetic characters, 180–81; capitation tax, military conscription, and right to ordain, 235–37; chapter specializations and favorites, 128–29; demise of *Vessantara Jataka* recitation in, 237–42; dialect changes, 239, 304n47; geographical and cultural isolation from Bangkok, 231; historical importance, 127–28; Jujaka adventures, expansion of, 136–43, 146–48; Jujaka death scene and funeral, 149–55, *150*; Keyes account of funeral performance, 123–25; mazes, 131–32, *132*; millenarianism, 192–94; monks in region, number of, 235–36; northeastern region compared to, 118–21; number of Lanna versions of *Vessantara Jataka*, 123; political independence, 230–31; poverty and famine, 178–80; Rabelaisian humor, 123; regional comparison, *166*; Siang Miang tales, 174–76; sponsorship by birth year, 135–36; *syyb chataa* (life-lengthening ceremony) and temple decorations, *124*, 132–33, 135; Thammayut initiatives in, 231–36; timing, festivals, and special occasions, 133–35; *tujok* costumes and grand entrances, 130–31; village morality in everyday life, 155–66; women in temples, restrictions on, 7. *See also* peasant imaginaire; *tujok* monks
nostalgia, global, 258–60
novice-monk relations, 162–65
novice recitations, 48–51, 53–58, 280n16–281n18
nuns, 287n35

Obeyesekere, Gananath, 272
Obeyesekere, Rajini, 3, 277n24
offerings: in central region, 66–70; Jujaka, food offerings to, 70, 283n45; *krajaats* (offering baskets), 46–47, 49, *53*, 53–54, 61, 279n11; money trees, 292n28; in northeastern region, 90, 285n11; in northern region, 136. *See also* generosity and gifts
Ong Man, 195
ordination, 19, 236–37, 303n32, 304n46

Ordination Act (1913), 236
OTOP (One Tambon One Product) handicraft industry, 253, 306n19
oxen, stories of shooting, 182

Padipadana Jataka, 277n20
palat khik (penis-shaped amulets), 111-12, 245
Pali education, 214, 215
Pali imaginaire, 295n1
Pali texts: Amitataa in, 143, 293n39; Jujaka a villain in, 11; *Khathaphan*, 83, 89, 97, 135; read without translation or understanding, 79, 97; religious studies focus on, 12-13; sacrality of recitation and, 13-14
Pallegoix, Jean Baptiste, 76
Paramanuchit Chinorot, Prince, 16, 51, 213, 215, 281n24, 301n16
parent-child relations, 160-62
Paritta Chalermpow-Koanantakool, 278n33, 282n43
Pasuk Phongphaichit, 30, 67, 276n7
Pawaret, Prince, 214, 216, 301n12, 301n16
Peacock, James, 29
peasant imaginaire: beggars as sympathetic figure, 180-81; defined, 295n1; hidden transcripts and covert anti-royalism in *tujok* performances and, 197-207; landlessness and, 296n6; lords, northern stories about, 181-89; Maitreya, millenarianism, and, 191-97; political ambiguity in northeastern region and, 98; poverty and, 178-80; tricksters as moral distance and, 170-78; war captives, slavery, and, 189-91, *190*
peasants, historical agency and interests of, in jatakas, 21-22. *See also* northeastern region and Bun Pha Wet; northern region and recitations
Phichit Prichakorn, Prince, 223, 231-32, 302n23
phiitaakhon ghosts and festival, *113*, 113-14, 252
Phillips, Herbert, 76
Phra Ariyakawii (Orn), 223
Phrakhlang, Chaophraya (Hon), 50-51, 52, 55, 281n23
Phrakhruu Athong, 8-9, 291n22, 292n29, 293n37, 293n40, 293n44, 294n57, 304nn53-54, 307n32
Phrakhruu Danuphol (Lampang), 291n15

Phrakhruu Dr. Manop Winaithorn, Bangkok, 73-74, 280n15
Phrakhruu Khammuul (Bangkok), 307n32
Phrakhruu Sophon Withayaphorn (Chiang Mai), 307n32
Phrakhruu Wanna (Ratburi), 280n16
Phra Lak Phra Ram, 15
Phra Malai, 191-92. See also *Phra Malai Sutra*
Phra Malai Sutra, 16-17, 30-31, 77, 83, 95, 96, 108, 128, 135, 278n32, 284n59; story of Phra Malai and millenarianism, 191-92
Phra Phanarat, 46
Phra Phimonlatham, 279n10
Phra Rajathammawaathii (Bangkok), 44
Phra Thammaratmuni (Chun), 300n3
Phra Thepmuni (Duang), 51, 58
Phra Thepwethi (aka Prayut Payuttho, Ratchaworamuni), 31-32, 202
Phra Ubalii, 110, 223-25, 234, 302n25
Phra Vijit (Phra Racha Vijitphatiphaan) (Bangkok), 63-64, 282n39, 283n47
Phra Wannarat, 15-16
Phrayar Naga (the naga snake), 22, 77
Phusadi, 85, 157-58, 202-3, 261-62, 265, 294n59
Phu Thai, 82, 284n3, 285n5
Phutthamonthon, 41, 47, 73, 254, 280n15
pig's head offerings, 69
pointillism as methodology, 36
political ambiguity in northeastern region: ambiguity and accommodation, 98, 109; Maitreyan timing and, 108-9; royal procession and political subjectivity, 98-102; vaudevillian Jujaka and, 102-7
political legitimacy, 19-20, 45
portering stories, 186-87
poses of Buddhas, 194, 298n31
Potter, Jack, 296n6
power, stories of abuse of, 187-89
Prakong Nimmanhaeminda, 123, 126, 129, 134, 138, 144, 291n19, 294n58
Pranee Wongthet, 98
Prasat Thong, King, 45
Prasert na Nagara, 15, 17, 127, 277n22
Prayurawong, Somdet Chaophraya Borom Maha (Dit Bunnag, aka Somdet Ong Yai), 44
Preaching Institute, Khon Kaen, 251-52

processions: in central vs. northeastern region, 67; development of, 255–57; rerouting of, 112; scroll procession and invitation of Vessantara and Matsi to return (northeastern), 82, 93–96, 98–102; thousand balls of rice (northeastern), 96–98; tourism and, 252–53; Upakut invitation (northeastern), 91–93
prophecies: Buddhism's deterioration, 15–16, 20, 109, 196; Maitreya, 16–17
pulpits, raised, 129, 255, 290n14
Puu Sae Yaa Sae, 287n33

Rabiabrat Pongpanich, 276n12
Radin, Paul, 171–72
Rama I, King: death of, 213; decree against millenarian revolts, 196; Emerald Buddha and, 42–43; Jujaka chapter and, 58; philosophical Buddhism and, 212–13; Queen Amarindra and, 282n31; religious reforms and sangha laws, 27, 211–12, 300n5; succession to the throne and gifting by, 45
Rama II, King, 49, 213, 214, 220, 280n12
Rama III, King: coronation and gifting by, 47; death of, 216; Emerald Buddha robe ceremony and, 43; as Prince Isara Sunthon, 280n12; reign of, 213–14; rise of Thammayut order and, 214–15; Wat Prayoon and, 44
Rama IV. *See* Mongkut, King
Rama V, King: decrees on recitations, 109–10; Jory on political shifts and, 24; novice recitation of, 49, 51; sangha control and, 217; support for recitations, 50, 280n14
Rama VI, King, 281n20
Rama VII, King, 281n20
Ramayana, 13, 14, 15
Ramanujan, A. K., 13
Ramkhamhaeng, King, 189
Ramkhamhaeng inscription, 290n9
rationalism, 23, 216
Raymond, Catherine, 277n24
red shirt movement, 100
renunciation, 18–19
Reynolds, Craig, 215, 216, 219, 300n5, 301n7
Reynolds, Frank E., 3, 20

Rhys Davids, T. W., 24, 275n4
Rice Noodle Bun Phrawet (Kin Khao Pun Bun Phawet), 252
Richardson, Dr., 189, 229–30
Richman, Paula, 13
Ricoeur, Paul, 268
Rocket Festival (Bun Bangfai), 110, 111–12, 115, 222–23, 284n3, 287n34
Roi Et province, tourism in, 252, 253
royalism, anti-royalism, monarchies, and kingship: absolute vs. constitutional monarchy, 78; decline of *Vessantara Jataka* and, 24; historical agency and interests of, in jatakas, 19–21; mocked by comedy performances, 30–32; non-royalist egalitarian ethos, 156–58; northeastern region and, 99, 100; pro-royalist vs. anti-royalist interpretation, 32, 84, 166, 169; simultaneous pro-royalist, non-royalist, and anti-royalist agendas, 269; ten duties of rulers, 272; trickster, hidden transcript, and covert anti-royalism, 197–207; Vessantara as ideal king, 201–2. *See also* court and royal recitations; court control; specific monarchs
royal recitations. *See* court and royal recitations

Saeng, 224
Sakabap chapter, 10, 50, 51, 57, 76, 128
Sangat, 83, 89, 97, 108–9
Sangha Act (1902), 217–18, 227–28, 234, 303n43
sangha control, centralized: in central region, history of, 210–19; importance of, 208–9; in northeast region, 222–28; in northern region, efforts toward, 228–37
sangha laws (Rama I), 211–12
Sanphasitthiprasong, Luang, 302n23
Satra of King Chea-Ly, 307n36
Scott, James C., 29, 197
scroll procession, 93–96
scrolls, 94, 285n16
Senanurak, Prince, 280n12
Shalardchai Ramitanondh, 237–38
Sharp, Lauriston, 19, 76, 78, 284n58
Shaw, Sarah, 275n4, 276n17
shooting oxen stories, 182
Siam Cultural Park, Ratburi, 253

Siang Miang (Xieng Mieng), 174–76
Sirikit, Queen, 38, 47
Sirindhorn, Princess, 47–48, 254, 280n15, 281n28, 306n23
Siriraj Hospital recitation, Bangkok, *41*, 76, 254
slaves and war captives, 189–91, *190*
soh, 140, 241
soldiers, typology of, 117
Sombat Chantornvong, 20, 283n54
Somchai Kuakoon, 42, 279n3
Sommai Premchit, 91, 126, 133, 238, 285n15, 303n45
Somroay Yencheuy, 102, 109, 117, 120, 286n26
Songkran (New Year's), 284n1, 284n4, 287n33
Songtham, King, 42
southern region of Thailand, 35
Sparkes, Stephen, 21
Spiro, Melford, 4, 19, 277n25, 298n28
sponsorship: in central region, 66; Jujaka chapter, problems finding sponsors for, 12, 66, 73, 103; in northeastern region, 89–90; in northern region, 135–36; regional comparison, *166*
Sri Thanonchai, 176–78
stamps, 5, 276n8
state control. *See* court control
Strong, John, 287n39
Sukhothai, 127, 290n9
Sulak Sivaksa, 50, 57, 281n21
Supaporn Siripornlert, 253
Suttapitaka, 275n2
Suwanna Satha-anand, 265
Swearer, Donald, 13, 128, 144, 276n7, 291n17, 307n38
syyb chataa (life-lengthening ceremony), *124*, 132–33, 135

Taa Jujaka (Taa Chuchok) (Grandfather Jujaka), 115, *257*, 304n52
Tachard, Guy, 260
Ta Chi, Luang, 259
Taksin, King, 43, 210–11, 231, 282n31, 299n33
Tambiah, Stanley, 21, 81, 89, 92–93, 245, 285n16, 285nn12–14, 286nn20–21
Tang Tham Luang festival, 133, 135, 136, 237–38, 257, 291n23, 303n45
Taylor, Hugh, 179–80, 192–93, 194–95, 224–25

Tearjerker Chapter, 6
ten duties of rulers, 272
Terweil, Barend, 76–77, 190–91, 284n2, 284n59
Thailand, regions of. *See* central region and recitations; northeastern region and Bun Pha Wet; northern region and recitations
Thammayut order: boat imagery and, 55; centralized administrative control and, 217–19; northeastern region and, 93, 110, 222–25; northern region and, 231–36; rise of, 25, 213–17; temples and monasteries, number of, 224, 302n26
thamnong lae style, 59
thamnong luang style, 59
thamnong suat style, 42
Tham Pha Wet (Vessantara's Cave), 82
Thanakan chapter, 10, 45, 51, 57, 71, 135
Thep Singh, 192
Thet Thetsarangsii, 235
Thiphakorawong, Chaophraya, 216–17, 305n13
Thompson, Virginia, 78, 237
Thotsaphon chapter, 9–10, 51, 57–58, 135
thousand balls of rice procession (*hae khaophan kohn*), 96–98
Tilok, King, 189
timing and duration of recitations: Buddhist Lent and, 42–43, 61–63, 278n1, 278n2; in central region, 63–65; Maitreya's command for twenty-four-hour recitation, 16–17, 133, 191, 292n25; in northeastern region, 83, 108–9; in northern region, 133–35, 292n25; regional comparison, *166*
tourism, promotion of, 114, 251–53
Trailok, King, 20
Traiphum ("Three Worlds"), 31, 211
tricksters: as anti-monarchical folk heroes, 174; Jujaka and characteristics of, 170–73; kingship critiques and, 202; literature on, 29–30; Siang Miang in northern and northeastern regions, 174–76; Sri Thanonchai in central region, 176–78. *See also* Jujaka
Tripitaka, 212–13
tripods, *124*, 133
tujok monks: Amitataa development, 143–46; comic timing and funny sounds, 136–37; costumes of, 130; criticism of, 241; edginess

tujok monks (*continued*)
of humor and, 204-6; famous, 125, 291n15; grand entrances by, 130-31; initial formal chant in Pali, 138; Jujaka's death and funeral, 149-55, *150*; Jujaka tricking royal guardians, 146-48; Keyes first-person account of funeral performance, 123-25; Luang Poh Bunthong, 8, *9*; name, meaning of, 7-8; new Jujaka episodes, creation of, 137-43; Phrakhruu Athong, 8-9; younger generation and, 241-42. *See also* Luang Poh Bunthong

Tu Luang Som (Chiang Mai), 291n15

Tu Ping, 232, 234

Udom (Note) Taepanich, 273, 307n3

Upakut, 91-93, 285n13, 287n39

Uppalavanna (Ubonwanna), 263, 307n35

Vajiranana, Prince (Wachirayan), 28, 57, 217, 218, 226, 234, 280n14, 301n16

Vajirunhis, Crown Prince, 49, 57, 281nn19-20

Vallaya Piyarat, 11

Vessantara: birth of, 157-58; exile and return, political interpretation of, 100; in Hok Kasat version, 85; as husband, 265; as ideal king, 201-2; invitation to return (northeastern festival), 93-95, 252; name of, 275n2; wife and children given away by, 3, *4*, 5-7, 22-23, 101, 261, 271

Vessantara Jataka (*Mahachat*): about, 3; abridged version (Hok Kasat), 83, 85, 89, 97, 103, 116-17; appalled reactions to, 5-7; decline of performances, 5, 22-26, 76-80, 237-42; importance and popularity of, 3-5, 39-40; Lanna versions, variety of, 123; *Mahachat Khamluang* version, 42; Manee's abridged version, 289n7; modern controversies, 258; in range of media, 35; recordings, 125; royalist vs. political, anti-royalist reading of, 206-7; structure and plot of, 9-11; uncertain future of, 269-70; uniformity vs. variation in space and time, 12-17. *See also* chapters of *Vessantara Jataka*; *specific topics, characters, and regions*

Vessantara Jataka Park, 253

Vetarani hell, 31

Vickery, Michael, 221, 301n18

Victorian morality, 30, 61, 165

Vientiane, 42-43, 58, 189, 211, 220, 301n17

village unity theme in northeastern region, 87-88, 97-98

Vincent, Frank, 284n56

voice types for chapters, 66, 128

Waen, Chaochom, 58, 282n30, 302n20

Wales, H. G. Quaritch, 190

Wanaprawet chapter, 10, 51, 58, 64, 135, 283n48

Wan Sart festival, 62, 282n36, 306n15

Wan Thewo festival, 62, 282n37, 306n15

war captives, 189-91, *190*, 206

Wat Amphawan, Nonthaburi, 249

Wat Arun, Bangkok, 62

Wat Bangkhrai Nok, Nonthaburi, 247

Wat Bangphra, Nakhon Pathom, 249

Wat Ban Yang, Maha Sarakham, 110-11, 117

Wat Bowonniwet, Bangkok, 215, 216, 217, 222, 224, 226, 232, 234, 281n19, 302n25

Wat Bunyawat, Lampang, 255-56

Wat Chaichanasongkram, 62, 64, 283n48

Wat Chetuphon. *See* Wat Pho

Wat Dorn Taan, Chanthaburi, 63, 65-66, 77

water dipper stories, 181-82, 187

Wat Fai Hin, Chiang Mai, 73, 232

Wat Jaroen Muang, Chiang Rai, 150

Wat Jedi Luang, Chiang Mai, 232, 234

Wat Kalingkaraat, Uttaradit, 240

Wat Khon Kaen Nya, Roi Et, 111

Wat Klang, Chanthaburi, 63, 66

Wat Lahaanrai, Rayong, 246

Wat Laksi, Bangkok, 249, 254, 255, 302n24

Wat Lampang Luang, 143

Wat Mahachai, Udorn, 224

Wat Mahathat, Bangkok, 62, 64, 65, 77, 215, 217

Wat Mai Pinkriaw, Nakhon Pathom, 245, 250-51, 283n45

Wat Mani Cholakhan, Lopburi, 196-97

Wat Mongkol Kowithaaram, Ubon, 89

Wat Muang, Angthong, 249

Wat Niramit Vipassana, Loei, 170, 253

Wat Paa Noi, Ubon, 224-25

Wat Palelai, Suphanburi, 67, 72

Wat Pathumwanaram, Bangkok, 175, 296n5
Wat Phanomyong, Ayutthaya, 249
Wat Pho (Chetuphon), Bangkok, 46, 55, 62, 65, 73, 77, 211, 215, 234, 255, 281n24, 282n38, 306n23
Wat Phonchai, Loei, 113, 115, 252-53
Wat Phra Kaew (Emerald Buddha Temple), Bangkok, 42-44, 47, 50, 61-62, 70, 211
Wat Phrathat Duang Diaw, Lamphun, *190*
Wat Prayoon (Wat Prayurawongsawat), Bangkok, 44, 64, 65, 77, 281n24
Wat Raatbamrung, Bangkok, 281n22
Wat Saam Phrayaa, Bangkok, 255
Wat Saket, Bangkok, 116, 222, 301n9
Wat Samien Nari, Bangkok, 65, 255, 306n24
Wat Sangkrajai, Bangkok, 51, 58
Wat Sanuan Wari, Khon Kaen, 117
Wat Songtham, Samutprakarn, 245
Wat Sophanaram, Chiang Mai, 9, 125-26, 289n5
Wat Sri Sanphet, Ayutthaya, 42
Wat Supat, Ubon, 110, 222-23, 224-25
Wat Suthat, Bangkok, 62, 77, 211, 254, 301n9
Wat Suwannaram, Thonburi, 62, 64-66, 77, *209*

Wat Thung Sri Muang, Ubon, 116
Wat Yannawa, Bangkok, 53, *53*, 55, 281n27, 283n55
wealth, personal, promotion of, 244-47
Wells, Kenneth, 291n17
Wenk, Klaus, 279n10
wife-husband relations, 158-60, 265
Wilson, Constance, 219-20
Winternitz, M., 277n19
Winyu (John) Wongsurawat, 273, 307n3
women: listening audience, female, 6-7, 260, 264; portrayal of, 260-66, 307n33; temple restrictions on, 7; Vessantara gives away his wife and children, 3, *4*, 5-7, 22-23, 101, 261, 271
wongkot. *See* mazes
Wyatt, David, 226-28, 281n23

Xieng Mieng. *See* Siang Miang

Yasothon, 112
Young, Ernest, 30, 40, 48, 49, 57, 76

Zimmerman, Carle, 178

New Perspectives in Southeast Asian Studies

The Burma Delta: Economic Development and Social Change on an Asian Rice Frontier, 1852–1941
Michael Adas

Of Beggars and Buddhas: The Politics of Humor in the "Vessantara Jataka" in Thailand
Katherine A. Bowie

Voices from the Plain of Jars: Life under an Air War, second edition
Edited by Fred Branfman with essays and drawings by Laotian villagers

From Rebellion to Riots: Collective Violence on Indonesian Borneo
Jamie S. Davidson

Feeding Manila in Peace and War, 1850–1945
Daniel F. Doeppers

The Floracrats: State-Sponsored Science and the Failure of the Enlightenment in Indonesia
Andrew Goss

Revolution Interrupted: Farmers, Students, Law, and Violence in Northern Thailand
Tyrell Haberkorn

Amazons of the Huk Rebellion: Gender, Sex, and Revolution in the Philippines
Vina A. Lanzona

*Dreams of the Hmong Kingdom: The Quest for Legitimation
 in French Indochina, 1850–1960*
Mai Na M. Lee

*The Government of Mistrust: Illegibility and Bureaucratic Power
 in Socialist Vietnam*
Ken MacLean

*Policing America's Empire: The United States, the Philippines,
 and the Rise of the Surveillance State*
Alfred W. McCoy

An Anarchy of Families: State and Family in the Philippines
Edited by Alfred W. McCoy

*The Hispanization of the Philippines: Spanish Aims and
 Filipino Responses, 1565–1700*
John Leddy Phelan

*Pretext for Mass Murder: The September 30th Movement and
 Suharto's Coup d'État in Indonesia*
John Roosa

Hamka's Great Story: A Master Writer's Vision of Islam for Modern Indonesia
James R. Rush

*The Social World of Batavia: Europeans and Eurasians
 in Colonial Indonesia*, second edition
Jean Gelman Taylor

Việt Nam: Borderless Histories
Edited by Nhung Tuyet Tran and Anthony Reid

Thailand's Political Peasants: Power in the Modern Rural Economy
Andrew Walker

Modern Noise, Fluid Genres: Popular Music in Indonesia, 1997–2001
Jeremy Wallach

www.ingramcontent.com/pod-product-compliance
Lightning Source LLC
Chambersburg PA
CBHW050547160426
43199CB00015B/2565